COMMONWEALTH
TO PROTECTORATE

Austin Woolrych is Emeritus Professor of History,
University of Lancaster.

ALSO BY AUSTIN WOOLRYCH

Battles of the English Civil War (Phoenix Press)
Oliver Cromwell
Penruddock's Rising, 1655
Soldiers, Writers and Statesmen of the English Revolution
England Without a King 1649–1660
Complete Prose Works of John Milton (Ed.)

COMMONWEALTH TO PROTECTORATE

Austin Woolrych

PHOENIX
PRESS

5 UPPER SAINT MARTIN'S LANE
LONDON
WC2H 9EA

A PHOENIX PRESS PAPERBACK

First published in Great Britain
by The Clarendon Press in 1982
This paperback edition published in 2000
by Phoenix Press,
a division of The Orion Publishing Group Ltd,
Orion House, 5 Upper St Martin's Lane,
London WC2H 9EA

A CIP catalogue record for this book
is available from the British Library.

Printed and bound in Great Britain by
Clays Ltd, St Ives plc

ISBN 1 84212 201 0

For Muriel

Contents

viii   *Contents*

Preface

This book was first conceived, longer ago than I care to recall, as a study of Barebone's Parliament. The long delay in its completion is not wholly to be explained by other commitments and distractions or by sheer dilatoriness, though they have played their part. Besides these, however, there came an awareness that the subject needed to be enlarged if the events of 1653 were to be given their full significance in the unfolding of the Great Rebellion. Barebone's Parliament marked one phase in a larger crisis which proved to be a turning-point in the troubled history of the sixteen-fifties. Ten years ago, Professor David Underdown showed in *Pride's Purge* how the detailed study of one major episode could illumine the whole course of politics before and after. This book follows a long way after his distinguished example, but its purpose is similar. He charted England's transition from a monarchy to a republic; my theme is the demise of the republic and eventual emergence of the quasi-monarchy of Cromwell's Protectorate.

The story of Barebone's Parliament naturally bulks large in these pages, and a decision had to be taken whether to call it by its familiar traditional name or to refer to it, as contemporaries more often did, as the little parliament (or assembly), the nominated parliament, the assembly of saints, or some variant of these. It seemed pedantic, however, to avoid a nomenclature so long and widely current, though the much more recent form of 'the Barebones Parliament' is eschewed, for reasons that will be explained. That decision reached, it followed that poor Praise-God Barebone would have to go on suffering his name to be distorted, instead of having it restored to Barbone or Barbon.

I have incurred many debts of gratitude in the course of this work. For information and advice I particularly thank Gerald

Aylmer (whose place at the head of this roll-call is justified by
more than alphabetical accident), Thomas Barnes, B. G.
Blackwood, Robert Bliss, Bernard Capp, Norman Dore, Anthony
Fletcher, George D. Heath, William Kellaway, Valerie Pearl,
Arthur Searle, Paul Shuter, Peter Toon, Barbara Taft, and Blair
Worden. My special thanks go to David Underdown, who spared
some of his precious time in England in order to read the whole
typescript before it was delivered to the Press and made valuable
suggestions. I also gratefully acknowledge many kindnesses from
Professor Henning and his colleagues at the History of Parliament
Trust. To the University of Lancaster I am indebted for two
spells of sabbatical leave.

In quotations the spelling of the original has normally been
preserved, but italics have been reproduced only where they
appear to have been used, as in modern practice, for exceptional
emphasis. Punctuation has very occasionally been emended
where the sense seemed to demand it. In citations of contemporary
pamplets, the date in square brackets is that on which the
bookseller George Thomason acquired the item and inscribed it,
but precise dates which are not so enclosed are found in the
original. Thus a reference in the form '*Confusion Confounded* ([18
Jan.] 1654)' indicates that the tract itself bears only the year and
that Thomason wrote the day and the month on it, whereas
'John Lilburne, *The Afflicted Man's Out-Cry* (19 Aug. 1653)' was
precisely dated thus by Lilburne himself and published a few
days later. This method has the dual purpose of showing fairly
accurately when items were published, since Thomason normally
acquired them within a day or two, and of facilitating reference
to the *Catalogue of the Pamphlets* [etc.] *Collected by George Thomason*,
where fuller titles and bibliographical details are given.

Dates are given in the Old Style, except that the year is taken
to begin on 1 January.

Lancaster, August 1980   AUSTIN WOOLRYCH

Abbreviations

Abbott	W. C. Abbott, *Writings and Speeches of Oliver Cromwell* (Cambridge, Mass. 1937–47).
BIHR	*Bulletin of the Institute of Historical Research.*
BL	British Library.
Bodl.	Bodleian Library.
CJ	*Journals of the House of Commons.*
CSPD	*Calendar of State Papers, Domestic.*
CSP Ven	*Calendar of State Papers, Venetian.*
DNB	*Dictionary of National Biography.*
DWB	*Dictionary of Welsh Biography.*
EHR	*English Historical Review.*
Exact Relation	L.D. [Samuel Highland], *An Exact Relation of the Proceedings and Transactions of the late Parliament* (1654), as reprinted in *Somers Tracts*, ed. W. Scott (1809–15), VI, 266–84.
Firth and Rait	C. H. Firth and R. S. Rait (eds.), *Acts and Ordinances of the Interregnum* (1911).
Gardiner, *C & P*	S. R. Gardiner, *History of the Commonwealth and Protectorate*, 3 vols. (1894–1901).
Gardiner, *Documents*	S. R. Gardiner (ed.), *Constitutional Documents of the Puritan Revolution* (Oxford, 3rd ed., 1906).
HMC	Historical Manuscripts Commission.
Ludlow	C. H. Firth (ed.), *Memoirs of Edmund Ludlow*, 2 vols. (Oxford, 1894).
Nickolls	J. Nickolls (ed.), *Original Letters and Papers of State . . . among the Political Collections of Mr. John Milton* (1743).
NLW	National Library of Wales.

Old Parl. Hist.	*The Parliamentary or Constitutional History of England* (1751–66).
Pink MSS	John Rylands Library, University of Manchester, manuscripts of William Duncombe Pink.
PRO	Public Records Office.
Thomason Catalogue	G. K. Fortescue (ed.), *Catalogue of the Pamphlets, Books, Newspapers, and Manuscripts ... Collected by George Thomason, 1640–1661* (1908).
Thurloe	Thomas Birch (ed.), *Collection of the State Papers of John Thurloe* (1742).
VCH	*Victoria County History.*

Place of publication is London unless otherwise stated.

I

The Case of the
Commonwealth Stated

The history of the Great Rebellion in England is a story of
unforeseen consequences. The course of its twenty years of
upheaval hinged very much on four periods of intense crisis,
each between a year and two years long, and each having an
outcome that few had intended or expected when it began. The
train of events between each crisis-period, though sometimes
dramatic, can be seen mainly as a following-through of the course
set by the preceding one and a building-up of tension towards
the next, the two processes commonly overlapping.

The first of these four climacterics lasted from the meeting of
the Long Parliament to the outbreak of the Civil War. The
second exploded with the army's defiance of the parliament in
June 1647 and subsided after the execution of the king, the
establishment of the Commonwealth, and the suppression of the
Leveller mutinies. The third filled the year 1653 and is the
subject of this book. The last was initially fuelled by the rising
opposition against Richard Cromwell in 1659, and it ended in
the Restoration.

There is a superficial similarity of pattern in the way each of
these crisis-periods unfolded. In each, the initiators of change
gained enough of their objectives to cherish an illusion of success,
but their new structure or alignment proved unable to withstand
the internal and external stresses to which it was subjected. Thus
the Long Parliament largely achieved its aim of limited
monarchy through the legislation of 1641, but this proved
insufficient when the strains arising from the Irish rebellion

exposed the irreconcilable differences between the king and the more determined parliamentarians. Five years later, the army succeeded in averting the threat of counter-revolution and reached a degree of accord with both the king and the parliamentary Independents, but Charles's second appeal to arms and the ensuing conflicts at Westminster drove it finally to cut the knot with Pride's Purge. In 1653 Cromwell expelled the Rump and summoned an assembly which he hoped would launch a godly reformation at last, but Barebone's Parliament soon revealed the crippling incompatibilities between moderate puritan reformers and radical millenarian saints. The ensuing Protectorate was destroyed in 1659 by an alliance of army malcontents, commonwealthsmen, and saints, responding to emotional invocations of an ill-defined 'good old cause', but the restored Rump so disappointed their hopes that a fresh *coup* followed five months later and England drifted towards anarchy.

Each of these four critical phases had an outcome that was far from the desires or expectations of those who launched it: the Civil War in 1642, the execution of the king and the abolition of monarchy in 1649, the Protectorate at the end of 1653, and finally the Restoration. Moreover, each outcome achieved only a partial resolution, in which hindsight can see the germs of the next crisis. Civil war, of course, was not in itself a resolution but an appeal to force, but victory itself proved indecisive when the victors could not make the beaten king accept their terms. The Commonwealth, as established in 1649, could have no real stability while the political nation as a whole remained cold to both its principles and its personnel, and while the army remained in conflict with the Rump. The Protectorate never fully succeeded in transcending its military origins, and depended too much on the personality of Cromwell; when he was gone, neither its constitutional edifice nor its basis of social support was strong enough to withstand the resurgence of frustrated radicalism, both political and religious. The Restoration looks at first like a more decisive denouement, but the cry of 'forty-one is come again!' during the Exclusion Crisis and the continued rallying-power of the 'good old cause' are just two reminders that the old issues could not be buried so easily, and the Bill of Rights which sealed another revolution a generation later is eloquent testimony of what the Restoration settlement left unsettled.

The crisis of the year 1653 has already been illumined by several recent works of scholarship which have changed or enlarged our view of its whole context. Professor Underdown furnished in *Pride's Purge* an account of the origins of the Rump and an analysis of its membership which compelled a fundamental reappraisal of its subsequent aims and politics.[1] Dr Worden traced those politics in detail in *The Rump Parliament*, and brilliantly demonstrated that Gardiner and all other modern historians were wrong about Cromwell's motives for dissolving it. He has established beyond reasonable doubt that when it was interrupted the Rump was not perfecting a plan to hold elections only to the vacant seats, so that the sitting members could retain theirs indefinitely, but was on the point of legislating for a genuinely new parliament to meet in the following November.[2] The third work is Professor Aylmer's magisterial study of the administration of the Commonwealth and Protectorate, in which he demonstrates that 1653 was more than any other a seminal year for administrative development, but nevertheless stresses the continuity that ran through the whole decade.[3] Finally, Dr Capp has given us a full, sober, and accurate account of the Fifth Monarchy movement.[4] These are not the only contributions that have lightened the present writer's task, but between them they have enriched his whole conception of it. .

This book is about England's transition from a republic, dedicated to the proposition that all just power derives from the people and that their representatives must therefore be sovereign, to a mixed government based on the principle of a balance, not so much between the conventional elements of monarchy, aristocracy, and democracy as between the legislative, executive, and judicial powers in the state. It is not concerned simply with the detailed annals of a single year; it looks before and after, for its subject is a turning-point in a revolution, whether the word is used in its modern or its seventeenth-century sense. It has need of a retrospect in order to show why the roots of the

[1] David Underdown, *Pride's Purge: Politics in the Puritan Revolution* (Oxford, 1971).

[2] Blair Worden, *The Rump Parliament 1648–1653* (Cambridge, 1974; hereafter cited as *Rump*), and 'The Bill for a New Representative', *EHR*, lxxxvi (1971).

[3] G. E. Aylmer, *The State's Servants: The Civil Service of the English Republic 1649-1660* (1973).

[4] B. S. Capp, *The Fifth Monarchy Men: A Study in Seventeenth-Century English Millenarianism* (1972).

Commonwealth proved shallow and what winds were blowing upon it, and it looks forward from the interlude of Barebone's Parliament to see how far the Protectorate represented a response to the lessons of 1653. If it has a unifying theme, it is the continuing tension between radical millenarian Puritanism and moderate constitutionalism. That tension was at the heart of the army's quarrel with the Rump, but it was also present within the ranks of the officers and even of the parliament-men. In Barebone's Parliament it became so strong that it finally broke that assembly apart, and only a very superficial reading of the Protectorate could suggest that it was removed by Cromwell's assumption of power. Moreover it was not simply a tension between distinct and opposed bodies of men, for we must sense it at work within the minds of many of the actors in this story, not least in that of Cromwell himself.

Many difficult questions still hang over the year of crisis 1653. The first and perhaps the hardest is just why Cromwell dissolved the Rump, now that the answer which satisfied Gardiner and everybody else until a decade ago has been demolished. Despite all Worden's careful work, the precise intentions of the Rump are obscure, since its bill for a new representative does not survive and statements about it conflict. The army's politics are also in question, and it must be asked whether the aims of Cromwell and the majority of the Council of Officers had changed substantially by 1653 or whether they remained basically what they had been when Ireton had guided the New Model's political debates in the late forties. Then, when the Rump had been expelled, was the Nominated Assembly (alias Barebone's) conceived as a surrogate for elected parliaments until the real article could be safely restored, or as the first instalment of the millennial rule of the saints—or rather who conceived it as which? Did it fail because its members were collectively inadequate in respect of political experience, social standing, or intellectual calibre, or did it destroy itself by its own dissensions?

It is easier to pose such questions than to answer them, for the sources are meagre and often partisan; in particular the total absence of parliamentary diaries for either the Rump or Barebone's Parliament compels the historian sometimes to clutch at shreds of evidence which in better-documented phases of the revolution he would look upon doubtfully if at all. Occasionally, where reasonable certainty is unattainable, the reader is left with alternative hypotheses to choose between, though never without an indication of the author's preference. The book falls into four unequal parts. Its first three chapters deal with the Rump's failure to establish a viable republican regime, the grounds of the army's quarrel with it, and the causes of the final breach. The next four consider how Barebone's Parliament was conceived, summoned, inaugurated, and composed. Three more describe what it attempted and achieved, how and why it became increasingly divided, and what led to its final resignation. The last examines the establishment of the Protectorate in the light of the previous nine months' experience, and questions whether the conventional labels—'conservative reaction' and 'constitutional experiment' in particular—describe at all accurately what the new regime stood for.

The natural starting-point for our investigation is the autumn of 1651, after the victory at Worcester had crowned the long years of fighting and set Cromwell and his fellow-officers free to stir up the rather stagnant mill-pond at Westminster. Here we can take brief stock of the state of the Commonwealth as they found it on their return to active political life, nearly three years after Pride's Purge.

During that time the Rump had made very little progress towards either constitutional settlement or the practical reforms which the army (among others) had long desired. It is easy to understand why, in the light of what is now known about its membership. The Rumpers spanned a wide range of opinion, as the intricate story of their shifting factions demonstrates, but for the most part they were a far from revolutionary body of men. Although more than two hundred of them took their seats at some time between Pride's Purge and the end in 1653, only about sixty or seventy were at all regular in attendance, and the genuinely radical element was considerably smaller still. Forty-three had signed the king's death-warrant, and twenty-eight more had identified themselves positively with the Rump before the execution by promptly registering their formal dissent from the Commons' vote on 5 December to continue negotiating with Charles on the basis of the Treaty of Newport. Yet even this original core of seventy-one members included few whose temper could really be called radical.[5] Only a minority of them were republicans by conviction when they erected the Commonwealth. Most of them had been borne thus far by political convictions about parliament's superiority over prerogative which had hardened long ago, and very few felt any sympathy with the new social and religious currents that were coursing through the army, the City sects, and sundry other channels. Indeed a fair proportion clung to their seats because they wanted not so much to abolish the monarch's authority as to diminish the army's. That was still more the case with the eighty-three members who secured their seats during February and early March, when the dangerous business of killing the king was over and the formality of registering dissent from the vote of 5 December had been made somewhat smoother for scrupulous consciences. These 'February dissenters' included the powerful figures of Sir Arthur Hesilrige and Sir Henry Vane the younger, but the majority were distinctly more conservative then either of these or than the original seventy-one. The fifty or so who secured their membership at a later date carried less weight proportionately because so few of them attended the House at all frequently, but what influence they wielded tilted the balance still more against innovation or reform.

Inertia, faction, ingrained social conservatism, exaggerated respect for the laws as they were, prickliness to any hint of military pressure—varying combinations of these explain why the legislative achievement of the Rump was so meagre and why its occasional weak attempts to plan for the Commonwealth's future were so soon shelved. It had its genuine radicals, of course, but they were seldom of one mind, and the officer-members who might have strengthened them, such as Cromwell, Ireton, Harrison, Nathaniel Rich, and Charles Fleetwood, were absent for varying periods on active service. Occasional gusts of reforming zeal swept through the House, but they seldom blew as far as the statute book. The record was not entirely blank. In September 1650 parliament had, with many misgivings, repealed the penal laws which compelled attendance at Sunday worship in the parish church, but it had done nothing else towards replacing the exclusive and intolerant Presbyterian establish-

[5] Underdown, *Pride's Purge*, pp. 213–16 (and cf. pp. 185–7); Worden, *Rump*, pp. 26–7, 41–56, 387–91.

ment for which the unpurged parliament had legislated in 1646–8; indeed in August 1649 there had been a tied division on whether to confirm it, and only the Speaker's casting vote had settled it in the negative. The Rump had set up local commissions for the propagation of the gospel in Wales and in the north, but had done very little else towards meeting the ardent desire among puritans of many shades for much more positive measures to establish zealous preaching ministers in every corner of the land. It had left untouched the thorny problem of tithes. As for the reform of the law, for which the cry had been so long and loud, it sat for nearly two years before it managed to enact that all court proceedings should be conducted in English, and that was about the sum of its progress until it set up the Hale Commission after Worcester, when army pressure was really making itself felt again. With forty-four lawyer-MPs the House was pretty well proof against unwelcome legal innovations. Its record was still more barren in other fields where reform was being demanded, such as education, the relief of poverty (though the justices in many counties made brave efforts under the existing laws), copyhold tenures, rights of common, and the treatment of poor debtors. It was really not very interested in the hardships of the lower orders.

Its reasons for leaving so much undone were not all selfish, and not the least of them was its own unpopularity. It should not have been surprised that most of the political nation was outraged by the execution of the king and felt no commitment to the idea of a commonwealth—let alone to its present governors. But the leading Rumpers seem to have been shocked by the sheer chill weight of hostility which they encountered in the county communities. It depressed their morale as well as making government much more difficult.[6] So many complaints poured in from the counties, and so little support, that they were driven to practise a growing amount of centralization, which in turn aggravated their unpopularity. With the wartime county committees now increasingly unco-operative, purged and winnowed though most of them were, the Rump tended to work either through small juntos of lesser gentry and other men of the middling sort or through local bosses like Colonel Robert Bennett in Cornwall, Colonel John Pyne in Somerset, or Colonel Wroth

[6] Underdown, *Pride's Purge*, pp. 261–2 and ch. 10, *passim*.

Rogers in Herefordshire, to name just three who were (as it happens) to sit in Barebone's Parliament. The county families, who had increasingly withdrawn or been displaced over the years, were further alienated by a piecemeal but extensive purge of the commissions of the peace and by the government's strong reliance in matters of security upon the new and often socially inferior militia commissioners appointed under the act of July 1651. At the same time the urban oligarchies, from London downwards, had similar motives for resenting the Rump's frequent interventions in municipal affairs, especially its removal of their members who declined the Engagement to be faithful to the Commonwealth as now established.

Having been obliged to alienate so much opinion in the interests of security, it is no wonder that the conservative majority of Rumpers favoured conciliatory policies that would broaden the basis of support for them in the counties and boroughs. The revolution which the army had launched in Pride's Purge was not their revolution; indeed military dominance was a scarcely less repugnant prospect to them than royalist reaction. They shared the antipathy of the broad Country interest to 'mechanic' preachers and their dangerous doctrines, to rampant sectarian enthusiasm, to any blurring of the divides between master and servant or landlord and tenant, and to all overt or covert threats to redistribute power and wealth downward through the social order. Even those members with a genuinely radical streak in their temperament seemed to have formed a habit of regarding government as primarily a matter of survival.

The army came back from the wars with a very different spirit. Not all of it had been continuously fighting, of course, but for those who had the campaigns had been uncommonly long, comfortless, and hazardous. They had been waged in inhospitable countries where disease and exposure were often more deadly killers than swords and muskets. Their victories had strengthened their conviction that the Lord's presence was with them and that they were the humble instruments of some tremendous divine purpose for which England had been singled out. For many of them the vision of the New Jerusalem had brightened with the years. Moreover long absence in Ireland and Scotland had removed Cromwell and his fellow-commanders from direct contact with their gentry neighbours in their own counties, so that they lacked first-hand knowledge of the Country interest's animus against both parliament and army. But arduous marches, rough quarters, the tang of battle, and the comradeship bred by common danger must have immunized them to some extent against considerations of popularity, especially when a sense of divine mission sustained them. Certainly these experiences cast a different light on national issues from that which filtered through into the debating chamber and the committee room. We shall not fully grasp the nature of the coming quarrel between army and parliament if we dwell solely on specific issues and personalities, and fail to appreciate how the contrast had widened since 1648 between the spirit of the camp and the spirit of the Palace of Westminster.

For the politicians had not remained unchanged, any more than the soldiers. The active core of them had worked together more closely and continuously by 1651 than any body of members before them, and many had borne their part in the Council of State too. No previous House of Commons had been so utterly untrammelled by any power exterior to itself, at any rate so long as most of the army was engaged elsewhere. The habit of power, together with the Commonwealth's gradual attainment of security from external threats, had had its inevitable effect on the deportment of the leading Rumpers. They knew each others' tempers to a nicety; lobbying, blocking tactics, caucus-work, and all such minor arts of politics had become second nature to them. Cromwell was later to complain 'how hard and difficult a thing it was to get anything to be carried without making parties, without things indeed unworthy of a parliament! And when things must be carried so in a supreme authority, indeed I think it is not as it ought to be.'[7] But while their in-fighting could be rough, they could also stand together against any challenge to their authority from without. It is understandable that the army officers were inclined to draw sweeping comparisons between their own kind of service and that of the parliament-men, and to overgeneralize from those of the latter who had acquired handsome bargains in real estate out of the lands of the crown, the Church, or the beaten royalists.

It was also easy for the army to assume that most Rumpers

[7] W. C. Abbott, *Writings and Speeches of Oliver Cromwell*, 4 vols. (Cambridge, Mass., 1937–47), iii, 57.

were clinging to power for the sake of profit, but it was less than fair. The Commonwealth's whole claim to *de jure* as against *de facto* authority rested on the proposition that all just power derived from the people and was to be exercised by their chosen representatives. Yet a high proportion of constituencies were totally unrepresented, while many of those which still had members had had no chance to change them for over ten years. It was more than time, the army thought, for the people to elect 'a new representative', but if they were allowed to do so, what could stop them from returning men who would call in question the abolition of monarchy and the House of Lords, and utterly reject that liberty of conscience for the godly of all persuasions which to the army was the very marrow of the cause? Such fundamentals were all too likely to be challenged if the elections were conducted with the same bias in the gentry's favour as in the past, while the alternative of a Representative mainly of the middling sort had been sharply rejected by both the Rump and the army leaders when they had united against the Levellers in 1649.

The Rump had become increasingly aware of the dangers of holding general elections; the army evidently had not. In the act of 17 March 1649 which abolished the monarchy the House had undertaken to dissolve itself 'so soon as may possibly stand with the safety of the people',[8] but it waited until May before setting up a committee under Vane's special care to consider the matter further, and that committee did not report until January 1650. What it then recommended was not the election of a new parliament but the recruitment of the present one. The proposal, which had already been mooted in June 1649, was to expel finally all members who had not been readmitted since Pride's Purge and to hold elections only to the vacant seats. This was debated desultorily for months and then allowed to sleep until the army applied the spur again after its victory at Dunbar in September. That caused it to be briefly resuscitated in October, but then a further year passed without any real sign of a decision.[9] The recruitment scheme, by continuing the membership of a substantial body of men who were committed to the

    [8] S. R. Gardiner, *Constitutional Documents of the Puritan Revolution* (3rd ed., Oxford, 1906) p. 386.
    [9] Worden, *Rump*, pp 188–9, 194, 200, 219–21, 250–1.

Commonwealth, had the obvious advantage of safeguarding it against any attempt by the new members to dig up its foundations, but it had no appeal for the many who thought that the old ones had already sat for too long. And that is what most of the army officers thought.

Why they supposed that a new parliament would be likelier to promote a 'godly reformation' than the old is something of a puzzle, but they evidently did. Perhaps, being out of contact with a war-weary England, they imagined that joy and pride in their victories would dispose the people to share their ideals. Many of them no doubt held fast to a simple faith that the Lord who had so blessed their arms would continue to provide for his people. Some probably let the thought cross their minds that if malignants and neuters should gain too much success at the hustings, the army did not wield the sword in vain. At any rate the officers gave every appearance until well into 1653 of being virtually at one in desiring the early election of a new parliament.

In one way this is surprising, since by the time of Worcester Major-General Harrison was already the leader of an extreme millenarian party in the army. Standing as he did at the head of the Commission for the Propagation of the Gospel in Wales, he had come into close contact, and even closer community of spirit, with the Welsh apostles of the Fifth Monarchy, especially Vavasor Powell and Morgan Llwyd. During the emergency of the Worcester campaign he had recruited a very large local militia from the Welsh saints and given the command of troops to Powell and his fellow-ministers Walter Cradock and Jenkin Jones, while Morgan Llwyd had accompanied his own brigade as chaplain. But his Fifth Monarchist views probably dated from earlier than his passionate engagement in the evangelization of Wales. When in London he evidently worshipped at St. Anne's, Blackfriars, for three of his children were buried there between 1649 and 1653, and at St. Anne's Christopher Feake, one of the fieriest prophets of the millennium, had been lecturer since 1649.[10] Now the Fifth Monarchists believed not only that the reign of Christ on earth was imminent, but that it was their mission and duty to bring it about by fulfilling Daniel's prophecy

[10] Thomas Richards, *History of the Puritan Movement in Wales* (1920), pp. 100–1; C. H. Simpkinson, *Thomas Harrison: Regicide and Major-General* (1905), p. 273; Capp, *Fifth Monarchy Men*, pp. 248–9, 271.

that the saints shall take the kingdom and possess it. There was an inherent contradiction between their goal—government by the saints for the saints—and that of those believers in civil liberties (including Cromwell) who held that the promised kingdom was a spiritual one, that the spheres of nature and of grace should be distinguished, and that therefore mere natural men should not be debarred from their right in the choosing of their temporal legislators. The crisis of 1653 would bring this contradiction more into the open, but it was already perceived by one of the earliest groups of Fifth Monarchists, who addressed Cromwell and the Council of Officers from Norfolk in February 1649. 'How can the kingdom be saints' ', they asked, 'when the ungodly are electors and elected to govern?' Parliaments must be put down as well as kings, they declared, before the only true kingdom, that of Christ, could be established. What the people of God should do was to multiply their gathered congregations and choose representatives from them to sit in general assemblies or 'church parliaments'. God would then bestow authority on these to rule the nation, and eventually all the nations of the world.[11]

This was written very shortly after the long debates which the Council of Officers held at Whitehall before and during the king's trial. It had before it the new version of the Agreement of the People which a small committee of Levellers, army officers, MPs, and City Independents had hammered out and submitted as a constitutional blueprint for the new Commonwealth. Harrison was already very conscious of the apparent conflict between their efforts to settle the state in the light of human prudence and God's evident purpose to supersede all merely 'carnal' government. He wrestled with the problem in a longish speech. 'For the Agreement in the whole, I think it hath been acting upon the hearts of many of us, that it is not an agreement among men that must overcome the hearts of men; it shall not be by might, nor by strength, but by His Spirit. Now this Agreement doth seem to me to be a fruit of that Spirit.' Thereafter his syntax became tangled, but his sense was clear enough: since God had very evidently cast it upon the Council of Officers to hold forth a way of settlement to the nation, it was their duty so to order 'things of civil concernment, that we need not seek ourselves,

---

[11] *Certain Quæries Humbly presented . . . to the Lord General and Councel of War* (1649), printed in A. S. P. Woodhouse (ed.), *Puritanism and Liberty* (1938), pp. 244–6.

[but] that we will trust God and give them up in a common current again'. He had searched his conscience over the objection, which weighed (he said) with many, that by this Agreement 'we seem to put power into the hands of men of the world when God doth wrest it out of their hands'. The answer he found in his heart was that when the time foretold in the Scriptures should come for the powers of this world to be given into the hands of the Lord and his saints, God's spirit would so work upon his people as to enable them in wisdom and power 'to carry through things in a way extraordinary, that the works of men shall be answerable to His works'. But he did not find such a spirit in men yet, so he concluded by giving the Agreement his qualified support,

hoping there will appear [so] much of God in it, that by this we do very much hold forth a liberty to all the people of God—though yet it may so fall out that it may go hardly with the people of God. I judge it will do so, and that the Agreement will fall short. I think that God doth purposely design it shall fall short of that end we look for, because he would have us know our peace. Our Agreement shall be from God, and not from men; and yet I think the hand of God doth call for us to hold forth [something] to the Nation, and to all the world, to vindicate that profession that we have all along made to God, [and] that we should let them know that we seek not for ourselves but for [all] men.[12]

The Agreement passed into virtual oblivion after the Rump had shelved it and the Levellers had met their crucial defeat. But millenarian faith and hopes continued to grow in the army during the Irish and Scottish campaigns, and they were by no means confined to the minority who would emerge as militant Fifth Monarchists. They were memorably expressed in a declaration which Cromwell's army in Scotland put forth from Musselburgh on 1 August 1650, in reply to the Scottish clergy's charges of Covenant-breaking. It proclaimed as the objectives for which the army had first taken up arms, 'The destruction of Antichrist, the advancement of the kingdom of Jesus Christ, the deliverance and reformation of his Church, in the establishment of his ordinances amongst them in purity according to his word, and the just civil liberties of Englishmen.' It justified the execution

[12] Woodhouse, *Puritanism and Liberty*, pp. 177–8. I have however gone back at some points to C. H. Firth's more literal text in his edition of *The Clarke Papers*, Camden Society, 4 vols. (1891–1901), ii, 184–6.

of Charles I on the ground that his monarchy was one of the ten horns of the Beast in Revelation; and it continued

We are not soldiers of fortune; we are not merely the servants of men; we have not only proclaimed Jesus Christ, the King of Saints, to be our King by profession, but desire to submit to him upon his own terms, and to admit him to the exercise of his royal authority in our hearts, and to follow him whithersoever he goeth, he having of his own good will entered into a Covenant of Grace with his poor Saints. And be assured, it is he that leadeth us into Scotland, as he hath done in England and Ireland.[13]

This was written in the name of the 'under-officers and soldiers' by certain of their chaplains, but Cromwell himself commended it to the General Assembly of the Kirk as 'not a crafty politic [answer], but a plain simple spiritual one; such as it is God knoweth, and God also will in due time make manifest'.[14]

Cromwell looked forward to the kingdom of Christ as devoutly as any who fought with him, though he conceived it less literally than some, and he envisaged the role of 'the people of God' less in terms of their assumption of temporal power than of liberty of conscience and a sustained effort to redress civil and social wrongs. A month after endorsing the Musselburgh declaration he won his great victory at Dunbar, and his dispatch to the Speaker that evening included this justly famous passage:

Sir, it is in your hands, and by these eminent mercies God puts it more into your hands, to give glory to Him; to improve your power, and His Blessings, to His praise. We that serve you beg of you not to own us, but God alone; we pray you own His people more and more, for they are the chariots and horsemen of Israel. Disown yourselves, but own your authority, and improve it to curb the proud and insolent, such as could disturb the tranquillity of England, though under what specious pretences soever; relieve the oppressed, hear the groans of poor prisoners in England; be pleased to reform the abuses of all professions; and if there be any one that makes many poor to make a few rich, that suits not a Commonwealth.[15]

This was not the kind of message to endear Cromwell to the

---

[13] Woodhouse, *Puritanism and Liberty*, pp. 475–6, 478.

[14] Abbott, ii, 302.

[15] Abbott, ii, 325; cf. pp. 173–4 for a somewhat similar exhortation, written from Ireland on 25 Nov. 1649.

more cautious and conventional men in the House, anxious as they were not to antagonize their conservative gentry neighbours any further and worrying about their prospects when they would eventually have to face the necessity for fresh elections. The Rump's historian has indeed diagnosed in Cromwell 'a kind of ideological schizophrenia', which shut his eyes to the inevitable conflict between his own social conservatism and his championship of the army and the sects. After Worcester, Dr Worden considers, he practised a 'policy of radicalism on the public stage and conservatism behind the scenes'.[16] There is a touch of truth in both suggestions, but they invite two comments. One is that it is very rare, and in any case not always wise, for a public man with a multiple role such as Cromwell's to speak in quite the same language to all the different sorts of people with whom he has to deal. The other is that he was probably never unconscious of the gap between the legitimate aspirations of the saints, which he shared, and the common desires and prejudices of the Country gentry—between (as he put it) 'the interest of the people of God' and the 'concernments of men as Englishmen';[17] indeed he struggled constantly, especially as Protector, to bridge it. But he really did hope that men of goodwill would rise above their narrower interests and less worthy fears to share his faith that God had glorious dispensations in store for England and would not fail his people. This was the theme of that most self-revealing of all his letters, written to Robert Hammond on 25 November 1648, in which he deplored that 'this fear of Levellers ... that they would destroy nobility, had caused some to rake up corruption, to find it lawful to make this ruining hypocritical agreement', i.e. with Charles I at Newport.[18] Sometimes he seemed afraid that self-interest and inertia would triumph, as when he complained to Ludlow in 1650, between his Irish and Scottish campaigns, of how they were frustrating 'a thorow reformation of the Clergy and Law'. 'The sons of Zeruiah are yet too strong for us', he said.[19] But it was more typical of him to strive to win back the support of men who could usefully serve

[16] Worden, *Rump*, pp. 69, 278.
[17] Abbott, iv, 481–2; cf. p. 490: 'he sings sweetly that sings a song of reconciliation betwixt these two interests ...'
[18] Abbott, i, 698–9.
[19] Ludlow, i, 246.

the cause, as when he wrote to Lord Wharton from Ireland in January 1650:

It's easy to object to the glorious actings of God, if we look too much upon instruments. I have heard computations made of the members in Parliament: Good kept out, most bad remaining; it has been so this nine years, yet what has God wrought ... Be not offended at the manner; perhaps no other way was left ... What if the Lord have witnessed his approbation and acceptance to this also, not only by signal outward acts but to the heart also? What if I fear my friend should withdraw his shoulder from the Lord's work (Oh, it's grievous to do so) through scandals, through mistaken reasonings?[20]

Exactly a week before the battle of Worcester, between two long days' marches, he wrote again to Wharton:

In my very heart, your Lordship, Dick Norton, Tom Westrowe, Robert Hammond (though not intentionally) have helped one another to stumble at the dispensations of God, and to reason yourselves out of His service, etc. Now you have an opportunity to associate with His people, in His work; ... Would you be blessed out of Zion, and see the good of His people, and rejoice with His inheritance, I advise you all in the bowels of love, Let it appear you offer yourselves willingly to His work.[21]

This does not sound like a political manager selling away a radical cause behind the scenes, and it was surely in the same spirit that after Worcester he sought to renew old ties with some other former members of the middle group of the 'forties, including Oliver St. John, William Pierrepont, John Crewe, Samuel Browne, and Henry Lawrence.[22] By seeking to rally men of such experience and repute behind a programme of measured reform and a return to regular elections, he was hoping to bring these objectives nearer attainment, and to make them more acceptable to an apprehensive political nation by showing that they had broader support than that of the army and the sects. Perhaps this was ingenuous in the autumn of 1651, but it was neither hypocritical nor irrational.

Of course, these men were not the natural allies of such a zealot as Harrison. But Cromwell's millenarianism never

---

[20] Abbott, ii, 189–90.
[21] Abbott, ii, 453.
[22] Worden, *Rump*, pp. 277–8.

impelled him towards an exclusive rule of the saints, and at this stage it is very doubtful whether Harrison's did either. It had not done so at the time of the Whitehall debates, as has been seen, but after Worcester's crowning mercy it was inevitable that some of the wilder chiliasts would revive the idea of a supreme authority elected solely by and from the gathered churches. So they did; but what is interesting is that the most prominent preachers of the Fifth Monarchy in London, including Feake, promptly and publicly rejected the proposal.

It came up in its most thoroughgoing form in *A Model of a New Representative* in October 1651, soon after the Rump had started a new round of debates on how to provide for its successor. The anonymous author, assuming that God was 'hastening the government of the world into the hands of his saints', contended that He had spewed the Presbyterians out of His mouth as unfit to bear any part in it. He then put these queries (among others) to his readers:

X. Whether the case so standing as it doth, God doth not call upon those in power, to cast the honour of governing the nation upon the heads of his saints, and in particular upon the members of the churches of God in the nation (who are gathered according to the order of the Gospel) in conjunction with those that are friends to them.
XI. Whether it be not meet, in order to the more orderly carrying on the great work of modelling a new representative; that the churches of the saints (gathered as aforesaid) be the persons appointed for the choosing of parliament men, considering, that if these choose it will be done without distraction which by all other ways imaginable cannot be effected.[23]

About a week later another pamphleteer, without going so far as to limit the right of election to the gathered churches, nevertheless proposed that every member of the new representative should have to present a certificate of his soundness in the fundamentals of the faith, his godliness of life, and his membership of an

[23] *A Model of a New Representative* ([15 Oct.] 1651), pp. 2–3. There is a curious suggestion on pp. 5–6 that John Goodwin's church in Coleman Street should be expressly debarred from naming a representative, but the qualities ascribed to it as grounds for disfranchisement are so plainly those that the author prizes that his intention is clearly ironical. They suggest indeed that he may himself have been a member of Goodwin's church, though Goodwin himself had been in conflict with some leading Fifth Monarchists and with other gathered churches in London: see Tai Liu, *Discord in Zion* (The Hague, 1973), pp. 122–3.

approved congregation.[24] This was followed late in November
by another proposal, this time from Daniel Taylor, a member of
John Goodwin's congregation, for entrusting the choice of
members to the Congregational churches, and he named as
suitable examples those of which Sidrach and John Simpson,
Thomas and John Goodwin, Christopher Feake, Henry Jessey,
and William Kiffin were pastors. This is curious, considering
how widely the two Simpsons and the two Goodwins differed
from each other in their views, and it should certainly not be
assumed that all these men agreed with Taylor. He did not,
however, suggest restricting the franchise solely to his approved
churches, but would have left it to them to decide whom to admit
as voters besides their own members.[25]

Before his tract appeared, a striking reply to the earlier two
was published in *A Declaration of divers Elders and Brethren of
Congregationall Societies, in and about the City of London.* These
identified themselves as the same congregations which had
published an earlier declaration in 1647, dissociating themselves
from certain positions popularly attributed to the Levellers and
some of the ultra-radical sects. Then they had affirmed their
acceptance of the civil magistrate's authority, of property as an
institution, and of social subordination as necessary to good order
and consonant with the will of God. Now they roundly
condemned the 'unjust limitations' which would have restricted
the right either of voting or of standing for the new representative
to members of 'the Gathered-Congregationall-Churches'. This
new declaration, unlike that of 1647, bore eighteen signatures.
They included Christopher Feake and John Simpson, who would
soon make St. Anne's, Blackfriars, and Allhallows-the-Great the
very capitals of the Fifth Monarchy, as well as Baptists of a more
sober hue like Henry Jessey, Hansard Knollys, and William
Kiffin, and such respected Independent ministers as William
Greenhill and Thomas Brooks. In reply to the proponents of a
government based solely on the churches they affirmed three
principles. The first was that all people in all nations are bound
to honour and obey their rulers, even if they be infidels.

---

[24] *A Cry for a right Improvement of all our Mercies* ([22 Oct.] 1651), pp. 9–10.
[25] D[aniel] T[aylor], *Certain Queries or Considerations* ([29 Nov.] 1651), pp. 7–8. For
Taylor's authorship and identity, see Worden, *Rump*, p. 289, and Tai Liu, *Discord in Zion*,
p. 123.

(Somewhat inconsistently they commended the army for bringing about the change from a monarchy to a republic, though they expressly declared that England's present governors were 'now to be honoured'.) The second principle was that all who profess themselves to be God's people should seek to ensure that their rulers are men fearing God, 'so far as their place and power reacheth'—an important qualification. The third is worth quoting:

That in our dayes, wherein persons truely fearing God are of divers forms, dissenting in church-government, etc. Some that are termed Presbyterians, some Independents, some Anabaptists, and some that are not so resolved with any of these: the power of choosing rulers, or of being chosen, should not be limited to any of these formes or perswasions, to the excluding of others.[26]

The only people to be excluded on principle were those who denied magistracy or property, practised polygamy or libertinism, 'or such as have opposed, or doe not owne this present government'.

It is quite clear therefore that in the autumn of 1651 only a few extreme and untypical millenarians wanted to restrict political rights to the saints, and there is nothing to associate Harrison or anyone else in the army with them. One of his favourite preachers, Feake, had joined in condemning them; another, Vavasor Powell, had dedicated a sermon and other writings to the Rump in March 1651.[27] The declaration of the army in Scotland issued from Musselburgh in the previous August had rebuked the Scots for calling it 'a pretended parliament' and adjured them to speak more reverently of the sovereign authority in England.[28] The position had not significantly changed since then. There was a strong desire within the army for elections to a new parliament, but meanwhile it upheld the authority of the Rump; indeed in September 1651 Harrison himself wrote that God had 'owned and honoured the House in the eyes of all the world).[29]

[26] *A Declaration of divers Elders and Brethren* (10 Nov. 1651), pp. 3–5. The penultimate signatory, T. Harrison, was not the major-general but the Independent minister of St. Dunstan's-in-the-East of the same name. The earlier declaration referred to was *A Declaration by Severall Congregationall Societies* ([22 Nov.] 1647).

[27] Vavasor Powell, *Saving Faith Set Forth* ([March] 1651), dedicatory epistle.

[28] *A Declaration of the English Army now in Scotland* (12 Aug. 1650), p. 14.

[29] Worden, *Rump*, p. 265.

When Cromwell, at that very time, persuaded it to consider a date for its own dissolution and the election of its successor, he appeared to have the solid backing of his officers, and before long he would find he had to put a brake on their agitation for a new representative. Remarkably, the only member of the army who is known to have expressed misgivings about holding early elections is Harrison's close friend and co-religionary Colonel John Jones, who was in Ireland. In November he wrote to a friend of his fears that success at the hustings would go overwhelmingly to candidates who made dangerous promises to ease the people's burdens (which would presumably imply a drastic reduction of the army). He shrewdly perceived that it would be unsafe to rely on rules and qualifications to keep out disaffected members, because if a majority of such were returned there would be no means of excluding them except by force, and that would inevitably raise an outcry. He counselled patience, until with a gradual easing of burdens the people could 'enjoy some rest and opulency', and so come to appreciate the Commonwealth sufficiently for it no longer to need armies and garrisons for its internal security. Meanwhile, so that the regime might have time to take root in their allegiance, 'lett their be some trialls made by Elections to vacant places'[30]—in other words recruiter elections, the very expedient that would soon become so obnoxious to the army in general and to Harrison's party in particular. Nearly a month later he again expressed the misgivings of the Commonwealth's friends in Ireland in a letter to Thomas Scot, the close associate of Hesilrige, who would emerge as Cromwell's and Harrison's chief opponent over the whole business. Only some mortal disease at the heart of the Commonwealth, Jones and his friends advised, could justify changing the hands that guided it at this hazardous stage.[31] It is not possible to know, of course, whether Harrison was of the same mind as Jones, though the two men corresponded affectionately. But Jones should help to put us on our guard against assuming that the clash of policies which came into the open in the spring of 1653 arose from attitudes which had

---

[30] Joseph Mayer (ed.), 'Inedited letters of Cromwell, Colonel Jones [etc.]', *Transactions of the Historic Society of Lancashire and Cheshire*, N.S., i, (1860–1), 190–1; partly quoted in Worden, *Rump*, p. 288.

[31] NLW, Plas Yolyn MS 11, 440, p. 31.

hardened long before the dissolution. Jones thought that recruiter elections would be a useful interim expedient, but tacitly assumed that the Commonwealth would revert to general ones when it became safe. There was no sign yet of anyone in the army challenging the principle of parliaments elected by the people in favour of some kind of latter-day sanhedrin, representing only the self-styled saints.

Jones is also a useful corrective to any assumption that recruitment was a device favoured solely by the Rumpers, and for merely selfish reasons. He is not the only witness to the contrary. In the autumn of 1651 William Leach of the Middle Temple, who had published at least eight pamphlets proposing various reforms of the law, put out some curious proposals in *A New Parliament or Representative, for the perpetual Peace and quiet of this Nation.* In a passage which he claimed to have written in 1640, he maintained that in the times when parliaments had been held frequently, most members were elected with the intention that they should represent their constituents for life, or for as long as their health and memory lasted, so that the country could benefit from their long experience and mature judgement; 'of which desert', said Leach, 'it is hoped there be diverse now'.[32] He went on to deplore the increase of improper influence and corruption in elections, and to propound in some detail a form of secret ballot to counteract it. But elections were apparently to be held only if a member died or was judged by his constituents to have become unfit to represent them. Leach proposed that all future parliaments should automatically dissolve after one year, but that when each new parliament met, the old members and the new should sit together for a week (or some other agreed period). Where a constituency had elected a new representative to replace one who was still living, the latter must resign, 'unless the then present parliament shall be unwilling to depart with him'. Where no new member had been elected, the old one was to continue.[33] One can imagine that many Rumpers would have found much to like in this scheme.

They may have been even more pleased by a modification of

---

[32] William Leach, *A New Parliament or Representative* (1651), p. 1. This tract is not in Thomason, but is described as 'lately published' in Edmund Leach's *Short Supply* (see n. 34). Its BL pressmark is 523 c. 36(14).

[33] Ibid. 8, 14.

it which Edmund Leach promptly advocated in *A Short Supply or Amendment* in respect of the special problem of the next elections, which the Rump was then debating.[34] He thought it would be both unjust and dangerous if the present members were to lose their seats, so he proposed that they should all keep them in the next parliament except those whom the present one considered unfit to continue without submitting to a fresh election. As for those constituencies which currently lacked members, the Rump should send each returning officer four names, which might be chosen out of eight submitted by the chief commanders of the army, and from the four the electors should ballot for two. But Edmund Leach evidently envisaged a bigger turnover of members in the future than William did, for he advocated that a quarter or a fifth of those in each future parliament—or whatever proportion the Rump should now determine—should retain their membership in the next one. And looking ahead for a moment to February 1653, it was perhaps one of the Leaches who then published *A New Modell Humbly Proposed . . . Concerning a New Representative*.[35] Expressing an even stronger sense of the dangers to be expected from tumultuous general elections and a large influx of inexperienced members, the writer proposed for the future a system of annual rotation, under which one twelfth of the counties of England and Wales (reduced by amalgamation to forty-eight) should go to the polls on the first Tuesday of each month of the year. He also recommended, however, 'That the first elections be only for the supplying of those places that are wanting',[36] so that the first annual round of elections would merely have recruited the House.

On the whole, however, the presses did not put forth many 'models of a commonwealth' during this period of the Rump's debates on how the government should be determined for the future—far fewer than in 1659, when it was again faced with the problems of constitutional settlement. It is notable that no one tried to revive that heavily revised Agreement of the People

---

[34] Edmund Leach, *A Short Supply or Amendment* ([2 Nov.] 1651); what follows is a summary of pp. 3–8. The author describes himself as 'of New England, merchant', but does not say how he was related to William, if at all.

[35] Anon., dated 24 Feb. 1653 in Thomason Catalogue, but now missing (apparently stolen) from the Thomason collection. I quote the copy in Harvard College Library. It is printed by Francis Leach, who had printed some of William Leach's tracts.

[36] *A New Modell Humbly, Proposed* (1653), p. 5.

which had emerged from intense discussion in January 1649, only to be shelved by the Rump without further debate. One can understand why. For the Rump the whole concept of such an agreement was tainted by association with the Levellers, while for Cromwell and other senior officers it represented a compromise with certain interests with which they no longer needed to compromise. Nevertheless it embodied much that the army was consistent in advocating from the Heads of Proposals of 1647 through to the Instrument of Government more than six years later, and much that the Rump itself would eventually accept in principle, after unconscionable delays: parliaments of limited duration, elected at regular intervals; a rational reapportionment of seats, giving far more to the counties and leaving only the major towns separately represented; a uniform franchise based on modest property, which need not be freehold land; and a broad established church, with its clergy maintained by a more acceptable means than tithes, and with liberty of worship for Protestants (at least) who dissented from it. The Agreement attempted two things further. One was a very limited separation of the legislative and executive powers, with a Council of State enjoying somewhat longer tenure and greater responsibility than that of the Rump. The other was an affirmation of certain constitutional principles and rights of the subject which all future parliaments must hold inviolate, since the sovereign people expressly reserved them from their representatives.

The Agreement did not specify what authority was to enforce these 'fundamentals' if a future parliament infringed them, and there were various other particulars in it which would have required reconsideration and negotiation. But futile as it is to regret what might have been if men had been different, it may be that in burying the Agreement the Commonwealth's rulers passed over the most promising starting-point for a settlement that they would ever have. Apart from the obvious practical virtue of a programme to which the army officers had pledged their collective support—and with some self-sacrifice, for it excluded them (while serving) from standing for parliament— the Agreement at least glimpsed two needs to which the Rump remained blind, at least until after Cromwell expelled it. One was an executive power which, while ultimately accountable to the elected legislature, would not be so totally subordinate to it as the Rump's Council of State, and would be capable of maintaining some continuity of policy between one parliament and another. The other need was for some guarantee that the essential foundations and principles of the constitution would be safeguarded against the vagaries of future elected representatives, by some means less arbitrary than armed force. The Agreement perceived the need without providing the means; the Heads of Proposals had come nearer to doing this with its councillors of state enjoying a guaranteed term of office of up to seven years.[37] Cromwell was groping towards a solution in his soundings about a possible revival of monarchy in 1651 and 1652, and the Instrument of Government tackled the problem more purposefully in the light of the lessons of 1653. Its provisions won only limited acceptance, of course, and alternative solutions were propounded by Vane in the 'Standing Council' which he suggested in *A Healing Question* in 1656,[38] by the Council of Officers in the 'select Senate' which they urged in May 1659 after the overthrow of Richard Cromwell,[39] and by Edmund Ludlow in his rather desperate proposal for 'Conservators of Liberty' in the following December.[40] But the Rump ignored both needs altogether. It must now be shown how it was goaded reluctantly into providing for a successor to itself, and why in this and other matters it aroused the army's increasing distrust.

[37] Gardiner, *Documents*, p. 320.

[38] Reprinted in *Somers Tracts*, ed. Sir W. Scott, 13 vols. (London, 1809–15), vi; see p 311.

[39] *The Parliamentary or Constitutional History of England*, 24 vols. (London, 1751–66; hereafter cited as *Old Parl. Hist.*), xxi, 405.

[40] Ludlow, ii, 172–4.

II

A New Representative?

The quarrel which developed between the army and the Rump covered a wide range of issues and reflected some deep differences as to what the ultimate aims and values of the Commonwealth should be, but it came to focus more and more on the provision for a new parliament. In the end it was precisely to prevent the Rump's bill for a new representative from passing that Cromwell called in his famous file of musketeers and cleared the House. Since it is now established that the bill did not propose merely to recruit the present parliament by holding elections only to the vacant seats but provided for a new one to meet in the following November,[1] the traditional explanations of Cromwell's act of violence will clearly no longer serve. This chapter, therefore, re-examines the growing rift between army and parliament from the autumn of 1651 to the spring of 1653, with particular regard to the Rump's long delay in legislating for a successor to itself. The next will consider what may have been in the bill itself and why Cromwell should have been so concerned to stop it passing.

Some explanation is due to the reader for taking him again over ground that has lately been so thoroughly and accurately charted.[2] One is that it will be viewed, as far as the sources allow, from the standpoint of the army, and of Cromwell in particular—not to the exclusion of that of the Rumpers, but with rather more emphasis. Another is that more than one interpretation is possible of the final breach between army and parliament. This is not

---

[1] Worden, 'Bill for a new representative', and *Rump*, ch. 16.
[2] I refer again, of course, to Dr Worden's *The Rump Parliament*, which is so fully documented that in the following pages original sources are cited only where they are not readily apparent in his footnotes.

surprising, in view of the total absence of parliamentary diaries, the meagre and often suspect evidence that has come down about the politics of the army, and above all the non-survival of the bill for a new representative. No one knows what became of it after Cromwell stuffed it under his cloak as he angrily expelled the members on 20 April 1653. It is hard to say which is the more suspicious, his suppression of it or the Rumpers' virtual silence about it until he was dead and buried. No account can pretend to finality; this one will, at the crux, leave the reader with more than one hypothesis to choose from.

The pressure from the army for a new parliament went through three main phases. The first began immediately after Cromwell's return from Worcester, and ended in a sharp rebuff with the Rump's vote to extend its own life for up to three more years. The second culminated in the strong petition which the Council of Officers presented to the House in August 1652. The lack of any adequate response to this led in turn to the third upsurge, which began in the last days of 1652 and ended in the dissolution.

It is no coincidence that the House, on the very day that it welcomed Cromwell back from Worcester, voted to devote the morrow to a debate 'concerning an equal Representative in Parliament'. On 25 September 1651, after spending three days on this vaguely defined topic, it divided on the question whether to bring in a bill to set a terminal date to its own sitting and provide for the calling of a new parliament. The issue was critical, for an affirmative vote would imply a rejection of the alternative solution, which had been discussed at intervals since 1649, whereby the Rump would merely have recruited itself.[3] Cromwell was one teller for the proposed bill; the other was Thomas Scot, who in partnership with Sir Arthur Hesilrige would become one of his most obdurate opponents in future years. The lines of division had not yet been drawn where they would lie in 1653 and after. The Yeas mustered thirty-three votes against twenty-six, and accordingly a committee was immediately nominated to prepare the bill. St. John was named

---

[3] Dr Worden thinks that when Cromwell brought about the revival of the debate in mid-September the House at first merely resuscitated the Vane scheme for recruiter elections (*Rump*, p. 266), but I am not convinced that the sources he cites bear this meaning.

first on it, and though the conservative legal interest was heavily represented in the persons of Bulstrode Whitelocke and John Lisle (Commissioners of the Great Seal), Edmund Prideaux (Attorney-General), Nicholas Lechmere, Lislebone Long, William Say, and Roger Hill, it also contained those thorough-paced commonwealths men Henry Neville and Thomas Chaloner, as well as John Carew, an ardent reformist who would emerge in 1653 as one of the most militant Fifth Monarchists in Barebone's Parliament. The radical element in the committee was further strengthened next day when Cromwell, Vane, Henry Marten, and Richard Salwey were added to it.[4] 'Radical' is of course a very broad term, and these men would certainly not all pull the same way in the later debates on how the Rump should provide for its successor; but it is scarcely conceivable that the general shape of the bill, as it was first presented to the House on 8 October, can have been seriously unacceptable to Cromwell. This is important, for in the form in which it was revived in 1653 the bill clearly *was* unacceptable to him.

The House gave it its second reading two days after the first, and from 10 to 28 October devoted almost every sitting to debating it in grand committee. It spent seven more days on it in the first half of November before it could come to any kind of decision, for the thin chamber that had approved the bill in principle filled up as the more apathetic conservatives awoke to the danger that they might really have to face the electorate again. Cromwell, by dint of a long speech on 14 November, managed to secure a vote on whether it was now a convenient time to fix a date beyond which the present parliament would not sit. With St. John as his fellow-teller, he got it through by the narrow margin of forty-nine votes to forty-seven. It seemed like a victory, though a precarious one, but four days later, when the House came to determine what the date should be, it settled without a division on 3 November 1654.

This was naturally a severe disappointment to the army, but it was not the only one. Another was the act of general pardon and oblivion, which the Rump at length passed on 24 February 1652. Among the officers Cromwell, Lambert, Desborough, John Jones, and Nathaniel Rich are known to have favoured a policy of generosity towards the beaten royalists, and most of the army

---

[4] *CJ*, 16, 17, 24, 25 Sept. 1651.

probably shared their feelings. But this act was so clogged with exceptions as to belie its name, and it was the forerunner of two further acts for the sale of confiscated estates—the first had been passed in July 1651—which would not only frustrate any future efforts towards the healing of old sores within the county communities but would also offend the army's sense of honour by contravening the articles of surrender that commanders in the field had granted to some of the victims of these measures.[5]

At the same time the specific reforms about which the army cared most made feeble progress, despite the efforts of Cromwell and an active group of supporters. Prominent among these were his fellow-soldiers Harrison, Nathaniel Rich, and Charles Fleetwood, and four members-to-be of Barebone's Parliament, John Carew, Richard Salwey, Sir Gilbert Pickering, and Colonel Robert Bennett. During October they managed to revive debate on a bill for the propagation of the gospel on a national scale which had sunk twice before through apathy or hostility. In November it did so again. In the field of law reform they appeared to do rather better, for in the course of December and January they secured the establishment of the famous Hale Commission.[6] The House was persuaded to compose it entirely of non-members, and its final choice represented a broad range of backgrounds and opinions. It is striking that seven of the twenty-one commissioners were to sit in Barebone's Parliament.[7] The commission's subsequent proposals gave great promise of constructive and temperate reform; the trouble is that not one of them was enacted by the Rump.

The army was probably never more united than during the first few months after Worcester. It was still aglow from its almost unbroken run of victories, and in a troubled future it was to look back nostalgically upon the early fifties as the halcyon days of the Good Old Cause.[8] Cromwell's authority and prestige

[5] Worden, *Rump* pp. 267–70.

[6] See Mary Cotterell, 'Interregnum law reform: the Hale Commission of 1652', *EHR*, lxxxiii (1968).

[7] John Sadler, Samuel Moyer, Colonel Thomas Blount, Sir William Roberts, Sir Anthony Ashley Cooper, Colonel John Desborough, and Colonel Matthew Tomlinson. An eighth future member of Barebone's, Tobias Frere or Fryer, was proposed to the House by its nominating committee but was not appointed. A ninth, Robert Jermy, was also considered: *CJ*, 9, 14, 16, 17 Jan. 1652.

[8] A. H. Woolrych, 'The Good Old Cause and the fall of the Protectorate', *Cambridge Historical Journal*, xiii (1957), 133–61.

within it were at their zenith. Radical pamphleteers and news-writers vociferously proclaimed him as the champion of the saints and of the reforms that they desired, partly no doubt because they genuinely saw him as their friend and partly to put further pressure on him to act the role that they prescribed.[9] But there was a limit to what he could or would do for them. He saw the need to rally all he could of his old political allies of the centre, whose experience could be so valuable to the Common-wealth and whose adhesion could help it so much in the county communities. He did not want even to contemplate using force upon the Rump, so the only ways forward to the reforms that he desired were either by persuading a majority of the House to support them or by inducing it to make way for a new parliament that might be more disposed to them. But would it? He was probably slow to read the omens that a new parliament, if at all freely elected, would have even less enthusiasm for a godly reformation than the present one. Nevertheless, given that he was thinking of elections, it would have been folly to provoke gratuitously the men of substance who would most influence them. He had to steer a course between the procrastinating, propitiatory inertia of the Rump and the reckless radicalism of the military saints. He faced the first signs of serious dissatisfaction and dissension among his officers soon after his failure to persuade the Rump to promise a general election earlier than three years ahead. It was at about this point—late November or early December 1651—that he arranged a fairly large meeting of leading MPs and senior officers at the Speaker's house, and invited it to 'consider and advise what was fit to be done, and to be presented to the parliament'. Bulstrode Whitelocke, who provides our only record of it, places it under the date 10 December, but this has been questioned.[10] It seems plausible enough, however, for Cromwell is likeliest to have called such a meeting after the debates on the bill had ended in a way that was bound to widen the political differences between the army and the majority in the House. He was evidently feeling his way

[9] Worden, *Rump*, pp. 274–5.
[10] Bulstrode Whitelocke, *Memorials of the English Affairs* (1682), pp. 491–2. Worden, in *Rump*, p. 276, inclines to a date soon after Cromwell's return to London, on the grounds that Whitelocke's account begins 'Upon the defeat at Worcester . . . ' But 10 Dec. seems a plausible as well as a precise date, since the Rump's disappointing vote on 18 November may have furnished the chief occasion for calling this meeting.

towards some kind of understanding behind the scenes, in the hope of inducing a powerful group of members to press the House towards a settlement which had the backing of his chief officers; one thinks of those later meetings between officers and members which he arranged prior to the final breach in 1653. He probably hoped also to mitigate their mutual distrust, which showed through at the outset when Harrison suggested that their business was 'to advise as to a settlement both of our civil and spiritual liberties, and so that the mercies which the Lord hath given in to us may not be cast away'. But Whitelocke—was it by prior agreement?—soon raised the question which most interested Cromwell, which was whether the constitution should be settled in the form 'of an absolute republic, or with any mixture of monarchy'. Cromwell promptly concurred that this was 'the right point', and invited the meeting to consider, if it should favour 'any thing monarchical', in whom such power should be placed. One senses the tension in the exchanges that followed. St. John, Whitelocke, Sir Thomas Widdrington, Speaker Lenthall, and the lawyers generally favoured a mixed or limited monarchy and many spoke for vesting it in Charles I's youngest son, the twelve-year-old Duke of Gloucester. Fleetwood declared, with typical indecision, that the question would be a hard one to determine, but the rest of the officers came out firmly against monarchy in any form or person. Nevertheless Cromwell gave his own opinion at the end 'that a settlement with somewhat of monarchical power in it would be very effectual'.

He had taken his soundings, and failed to find a consensus on which he could act. What had been his purpose? He seems to have had a fairly close political understanding with St. John at this time, and St. John argued at this same meeting for 'something of monarchical power' on the grounds that without it 'the government of this nation . . . will be very difficult to be so settled as not to shake the foundation of our laws, and the liberties of the people'.[11] These words probably expressed the fears of both men, though their emphasis would doubtless have been different. The very statutes on which the Commonwealth had been founded in 1649 were precarious, since any sovereign parliament in the future could repeal them by a simple majority vote. As for the people's liberties, Cromwell was often to deplore the extent to

[11] Whitelocke, loc. cit.

which the Rump's committees and commissions had arbitrarily invaded the judicial sphere.[12] He also probably recalled how long it had taken the Rump to get round to enacting even a limited religious toleration, and considered how easily a more reactionary successor might limit it further. He may have envisaged his 'somewhat of monarchical power' as the guarantor of a body of defined 'fundamentals' and of the supremacy of the laws in general; he spoke for it only 'if it may be done with safety and preservation of our rights, both as Englishmen and Christians'. It was clearly to be a limited power, but it could have restored a healthier balance between executive and legislature. The fascinating question is whether he was thinking yet of assuming it himself. He threw out such a suggestion privately to Whitelocke (if the latter can be believed) about a year later, but much was to happen between the two encounters, and at this stage he may conceivably have been pondering the possible advantages of a royal princeling as a figure-head. The words 'something' and 'somewhat of monarchical power' also perhaps hint that the function need not necessarily have been performed by an individual. We should not read into Cromwell's mind at this time political doctrines which he may have acquired only from later experiences or later advice, but he could well have perceived already that some form of monarchy could best set limits to the vagaries of future parliaments—and to their duration. Still, with Cromwell it is always worth asking who is likely to have influenced his political thinking at a given period, considering how often it seemed to take its cue from men with a keener flair and a quicker grasp than his own: Pym in the early forties, Ireton in the later, and Lambert by the end of 1653, to name three. After Worcester the likeliest influence was St. John, as he had been to some extent earlier, in the Committee of Both Kingdoms, and as he may well have been again at times later, under the Protectorate.

Two predictable developments ensued upon the Rump's apparent determination to cling to power. One was an increase in the mutual antagonism between army and parliament; the other was something of a breakaway movement among the more extreme radicals, both within the army and outside it. Some of the Fifth Monarchists were the first to react, and also to become

[12] Abbott, ii, 589; iii, 453; iv, 487–8.

frankly disatisfied with Cromwell when they found him not
prepared to go at their pace. In December, after two unsatisfactory meetings with him, Christopher Feake, John Simpson, and
others began to hold inflammatory gatherings at Allhallows the
Great, where they prayed 'That all corrupt, wicked and ungodly
magistrates might be removed, and put out of place and power;
and that a righteous generation of rulers might be set up in their
stead.'[13] Shortly afterwards Walter Cradock and Vavasor Powell,
the Welsh itinerant preachers, left London in similar disillusion-
ment. This was doubtless intensified by allegations, which were
current from the end of October onwards, of corrupt and
oppressive dealings by the Commission for the Propagation of
the Gospel in Wales. These touched Harrison as leading lay
commissioner no less than the preachers; he lost his seat on the
Council of State in the elections of December 1651, and there
was talk of a design to get him expelled from the House. That did
not happen, but the conservative Rumpers were only too glad to
listen to tales of tithes misappropriated and revenues from
sequestered estates embezzled. There is nothing to suggest that
Cromwell gave any credence to them, but from now on the gap
did widen between Harrison's Fifth Monarchist associates on the
one hand and Cromwell and the moderate Independents closest
to him, such as John Owen, Thomas Goodwin, and Philip Nye,
on the other. The excesses and pretensions of the extreme
sectaries were to shock orthodox Puritan opinion more and more
as the year 1652 proceeded, for many of them were already
aiming beyond liberty of conscience and at the total abolition of
a national parochial ministry.

There was a political as well as a religious element in the
growing discontent of the radical men in the army. It was
brought into the open by the Rump's harsh treatment of John
Lilburne in his quarrel with Hesilrige, culminating in the act for
his banishment passed on 30 January 1652. This aroused a wave
of protest in which many officers and soldiers, thousands of
London citizens, and most of the City's gathered churches took
part, though Cromwell would lend it no support.[14]

---

[13] Christopher Feake, *A Beam of Light* ([2 May] 1659), p. 41; and for what follows see
also Worden, *Rump*, pp. 281–2, 291–4, and Capp, *Fifth Monarchy Men*, pp. 58–9.
    [14] Worden, *Rump*, p. 283. For the latest review of this case see Aylmer, *The State's
Servants*, pp. 149–50, 294–5. Aylmer throws considerable doubt upon the truth of

While the reactions of the army and of the sects provided one kind of commentary on the course of politics after Worcester, the weekly press provided another. In all the journalism of the Great Rebellion there is nothing to compare in interest with editorials which Marchamont Nedham wrote during 1651–2 for *Mercurius Politicus*, the livelier of the two government-sponsored newpapers. Nedham's career had already been spectacular. During the Civil War he had risen to become editor in all but name of the parliamentarian *Mercurius Britanicus*, and in May 1646 the House of Lords had gaoled him briefly for attacking the king with a virulence that was still thought improper. Just over a year later, however, he signalled his conversion to royalism in a typically ambivalent way by publishing, within three weeks of each other, one tract defending the monarchy and another vindicating the New Model Army in its defiance of the Long Parliament.[15] Then from September 1647 to December 1648 came the great run of his witty royalist weekly, *Mercurius Pragmaticus*; but Nedham was not one to languish for a lost cause, and in November 1649 he secured his delivery from another spell in prison, allegedly with the help of Speaker William Lenthall and John Bradshaw, by undertaking to serve the Commonwealth. He established his new republican credentials in May 1650 with *The Case of the Commonwealth of England Stated*, and the Council of State promptly made him editor of *Mercurius Politicus* under the very general oversight of John Milton.[16]

From September 1650 to September 1651 he drew directly upon *The Case of the Commonwealth* for the substance of most of his weekly editorials. But he had milked it dry by the time the Rump took up the debate on a new representative, and thereafter his editorials, though they still avoid direct allusion to contemporary events, take on a much more topical air.[17] They are interesting

Lilburne's charges against Hesilrige, but still considers that the House proceeded against Lilburne with 'ferocious zeal' and inflicted a 'savage sentence'.

[15] The monarchy in *The Case of the Kingdom Stated* ([12 June] 1647), the army in *The Lawyer of Lincolnes-Inne reformed* ([1 July] 1647).

[16] For his career see *DNB*; Joseph Frank, *The Beginnings of the English Newspaper 1620–1660* (Cambridge, Mass., 1961); and Philip A. Knachel's introduction to his edition of *The Case of the Commonwealth of England Stated* (Charlottesville, Virginia, 1969).

[17] Much of the matter in the editorials between Sept. 1651 and Aug. 1652 was refurbished by Nedham in *The Excellence of a Free State* (1656). H. Sylvia Anthony in 'Mercurius Politicus under Milton', *Journal of the History of Ideas*, xxvii (1966), 593–609,

(*continued*)

as the reactions of a clever journalist who was anxious to keep his political commentary in step with the thinking of his employers, and if possible one step ahead if there should seem to be a prospect of a change of regime. Miltonists used to look for the poet's influence in them, but though the two men became friends as well as colleagues, there is little real affinity, beyond a broad republicanism, between Milton's political thought and Nedham's. Nor is there any sign that Nedham worked to a close brief from any particular person or faction in the Commonwealth; within the limits set by a strong desire to keep his job, his ideas seem to have been his own. At any rate, while at the the end of September 1651 he was still turning out good conventional stuff about the enslaving effects of monarchy and the liberating virtues of a republic, his piece in the issue for 2–9 October touched for the first time on the need for checks and balances. It probably reached the bookstalls on the day the Rump gave a second reading to the bill for a new representative. Casting a sweeping glance over the histories of Rome and Venice, Nedham drew the lesson that government was best where the legislative power lay in a popular assembly, but where it was moderated and stabilized by a senate constituted as a standing council: 'so that it seemes the people gave rules whereby to govern, and the secrets of government were intrusted in the hands of the Senate. The people without the Senatick Councell were like sulphur and mercury, ever in motion or combustion, . . . but the Senate were as salt to season, fix and fasten the body of the people.'[18]

Nedham seems to have been adumbrating the idea of a select senate, co-ordinate with the people's representatives and preferably with membership for life, for which both Vane and the Council of Officers would contend in 1659.[19] But he quickly

---

advances a theory that this pamphlet was actually written before the editorials. I find her evidence unconvincing, and equally so her attempt to revive the old notion that Milton strongly influenced the editorials.

[18] *Mercurius Politicus*, no. 70, 2–9 Oct. 1651, pp. 1109–11. A passage in praise of the Roman Senate in *The Case of the Commonwealth*, ed. Knachel, pp. 105–6, is worth comparing. But whereas Nedham in the 1650 pamphlet was primarily contending against the annual and democratically elected representatives advocated by the Levellers in their final *Agreement of the People* of May 1649, in the editorial quoted above he was tentatively proposing some kind of senate as a complement to the very different kind of successive parliaments for which the Rump was expected to provide.

[19] Woolrych, 'Good Old Cause', pp. 153–5, and *Complete Prose Works of John Milton*, vii, 70–2, 104–6, 126–7, 130.

hauled in his line when he found that his kite would not fly, for two weeks later he described how the Roman senate had degenerated through the abuses and intrigues of the grandees until the people rose in arms. Only when they had restored supreme power to their own large assemblies, and opened every office in government to themselves, could they truly be said to have attained to a free state or commonwealth.[20] He may even have heard a report, or made an inspired guess, that Cromwell was having thoughts about the monarchy, for his editorial for 13–20 November printed a passage from Cato's funeral oration on Pompey, as composed by Lucan and translated by Thomas May, the jaundiced historian of the Long Parliament. The leader who had taken up the sword 'but knew the time to lay it down' could hardly be mistaken, nor the message in the tribute to

> one powerful grown
> Not wronging liberty; the people prone
> To serve, he onely private still remain'd;
> He sway'd the Senate, but the Senate raign'd.[21]

Nedham's main message during late November and early December was that the Commonwealth needed no other safeguards against tyranny, corruption, or a return to kingship than successive parliaments, elected by the people at regular intervals. He was now arguing that *any* kind of 'standing authority' laid the republic open to ambitious seekers after monarchical power or to 'Surprise by a Grandee-Cabinet or Juncta', such as the Decemviri.[22] Yet by the following March he was qualifying these views again. He granted that there was force in the objection that frequent new parliaments—especially if some limitation on re-election, which he sometimes appeared to favour, ensured a large turnover of membership—would lack sufficient judgement and experience in affairs of state. He

---

[20] *Mercurius Politicus*, no. 72, 16–23 Oct. 1651, pp. 1141–3.

[21] Ibid., no. 76, 13–20 Nov. 1651, p. 1205. Nedham does not mention that it is a translation, but it is from Book 9 of Lucan's *Pharsalia* (p. 215 in 1650 ed.). On Lucan's popularity among English intellectual radicals see Christopher Hill, *Intellectual Origins of the English Revolution* (Oxford, 1965), p. 150.

[22] Ibid., no. 77, 20–27 Nov. 1651, pp. 1221–3, and no. 78, 27 Nov.–4 Dec. 1651, p. 1237. For other condemnations of 'any standing power whatsoever' see (e.g.) no. 85, 15–22 Jan. 1652, pp. 1349–52; no. 87, 29 Jan.–5 Feb. 1652; pp. 1381–5 (esp. p. 1382, which expressly condemns the vesting of such a power in 'a set number of great ones, as in a Senat'); no. 91, 26 Feb.–4 March 1652, p. 1442; no. 101, 6–13 May 1652, pp. 1585–6.

answered by distinguishing between *acta imperii*, which belonged to the legislative power, and *arcana imperii*, which belonged to the executive. The latter did require wisdom and experience; 'much in reason may be said, and must be granted, for the continuation of such trusts in the same hands as relate to matters of council, or administration of justice, more or less, according to their good or ill behaviour'. The executive body should govern in the intervals between one people's assembly and the next, and be accountable to the incoming one. The popular assemblies themselves should deal with 'easy, necessary things, such as common sense, and reason instructs the common sort of men in', and each one should 'continue of right no longer then meer necessity requires, for their own redress and safety'.[23]

This was bold talk from the Council of State's salaried publicist, especially since the Rump was under no particular pressure to shorten its life at the time. He took an equally independent line on the question of early elections and on whether to hold general or recruiter ones—though not always a consistent line. Before Worcester he had been all for successive parliaments at regular and brief intervals, but when in November 1651 the Rump really came under pressure to dissolve he had doubts. He found the timing difficult; there were ruptures that had first to be mended, wounds that needed to be cured; 'the old physicians' who had attended all the body politic's 'fits and distempers' had better carry on for a while longer.[24] By December, however, he was harping once more on the virtues of a frequent succession of parliaments.

The matter became highly topical again when on 21 April 1652 the Rump voted that on 7 May it would 'take into consideration how, and in what manner, the House may be supplied with members, as may be most for the advantage of the Commonwealth'.[25] This signalled a revival of the recruitment scheme, and Nedham did not wait for the actual debate before writing an outspokenly hostile comment. One error to which republics are prone, he wrote early in May, is to allow tyranny

[23] Ibid., no. 94, 18–25 March 1652, pp. 1473–4. Nedham here shows that dislike of parliaments in perpetual session which he was to express strongly in *A True State of the Case of the Commonwealth*, pp. 9–11, 36–8.

[24] See the quotation from *Mercurius Politicus*, no. 75, 6–13 Nov. 1651, pp. 1189–90, in Worden, *Rump*, p. 289.

[25] *CJ*, 21 Apr. 1652.

to pass from one form to another, for 'the interest of monarchy may reside in the hands of many, as well as of a single person'. It dwells indeed in any unlimited and unaccountable power, and even a commonwealth may succumb to it, as history has shown:

for the people not keeping a strict watch over themselves according to the rules of a free state, but being won by specious pretences, and deluded by created necessities, to entrust the management of their affairs in some particular hands, such an occasion was given thereby to those men to frame parties of their own, that by this means they in a short time became able to stand upon their own legs, and do what they list without the peoples consent; and in the end not only discontinued but utterly extirpated their successive assemblies.[26]

This sounds almost like one of the army's apologies written a year later, after the dissolution, but Nedham was certainly not pressing the interests of Cromwell and his fellow-officers. His next three editorials urged that neither military commands nor civil offices should remain long in the hands of the same persons, or be allowed to raise one family unduly high. He opposed professional armies in principle and harped on the example of Cincinnatus, who returned so readily to the plough when he had brought victory home.[27]

The promised debate on 7 May did not bring a new parliament any nearer. True, the House did not pursue the recruitment scheme any further, nor another that was mooted for restoring the members secluded in Pride's Purge. It voted instead to revive consideration of the bill for a new representative that had been allowed to sleep since last November.[28] But after spending three days debating it in grand committee without reaching any

[26] *Mercurius Politicus*, no. 100, 29 Apr.–6 May 1652, pp. 1569–70.

[27] *Mercurius Politicus*, no. 101, 6–13 May 1652, pp. 1587–9; no. 102, 13–20 May 1652, pp. 1593–7; no. 103, 20–27 May 1652, pp. 1609–13. In no. 99 Nedham had attacked the whole principle of a national church and of the civil magistrate's authority over matters ecclesiastical. This was strongly against the views of most of the Rump, and of Cromwell too, but it accorded very much with Milton's. Yet *Politicus* can hardly have been criticizing Cromwell at Milton's instance, since it was at just this time (May 1652) that Milton addressed Sonnet XVI to Cromwell 'our chief of men'.

[28] *CJ*, 7 May 1652; S. R. Gardiner, *History of the Commonwealth and Protectorate*, 3 cols. (1894–1901; hereafter *C & P*), ii, 112–13; Underdown, *Pride's Purge*, p. 192; Worden, *Rump*, pp. 297–8. Although the vote of 7 May was quite specific about what was to be debated on the 12th, *The Weekly Intelligencer*, no. 73 (11–18 May 1652) gave the topic as 'the qualifications of more Members to be received into the House'. *A Perfect Diurnall*, no. 127 (11–17 May 1652) reported similarly (p. 1879).

decisions, the House dropped it again for another period as long
as the last. The Dutch war had begun, and it imposed financial
and other demands which crowded the bill out, along with the
other reforms on which the army had set its heart. That was
understandable, but it was unwise of the Rump to give the army
gratuitous offence on some other counts. During May, for
example, it proceeded with a bill for confirming to those royalists
who had capitulated under articles of war the conditions which
they had been granted. This was a point of honour to the officers
and should have pleased them, but the House spoilt it all by
rejecting Colonel Pride as a commissioner after he had been
named in the bill. In the same month it antagonized Lambert
more seriously by abolishing the office of Lord Deputy of Ireland
(along with Cromwell's lord lieutenancy), nearly four months
after it had nominated him to it. Harrison on his side made more
enemies in the House by taking the lead in getting Gregory
Clement expelled from it for adultery.

On the religious front the Rump on 29 April alienated the
sectaries and most of the army by ordering that tithes should
continue to be paid as formerly until some other form of
maintenance for the ministry was devised, of which there was no
sign.[29] This strengthened the disquiet that the gathered congregations had felt increasingly since February, on account of a
scheme which John Owen and a group of orthodox Independents
had put to the Rump for regulating the parochial clergy through
commissioners similar in principle to the later Triers and Ejectors
of the Protectorate. Owen and his brethren had further tried to
set the bounds of toleration by attempting to define fifteen
doctrinal 'fundamentals'.[30] The trend towards a state-imposed
orthodoxy moved Milton in May and June to compose his twin
sonnets to Cromwell and Vane, calling on the first to save free
consciences from a hireling clergy and praising the second for
knowing where to draw the frontiers between the civil power
and the spiritual.

Not all the army reacted alike to these various provocations;
Cromwell and the hotter sectaries, for example, held very

[29] Carried by 27 votes to 17, with Sir Gilbert Pickering and Henry Marten tellers for
the Noes.

[30] Worden, *Rump*, pp. 284–5, 294–7; Peter Toon, *God's Statesman: the Life and Work of
John Owen* (Exeter, 1971), pp. 83–6.

different views about a parochial ministry and tithes,[31] as Milton would discover to his disappointment. Nor were the discontents of the military grandees necessarily the same as those of the rank and file. The stirs of the spring of 1653 were to reveal, as will be seen, currents of a more basic popular radicalism among the soldiery and the junior officers, which had not been repressed along with the Leveller movement. From time to time during 1652 *The Faithful Scout*, a weekly paper edited by Daniel Border, appealed to this democratic strain among the soldiery and to their sympathy for Lilburne's ideas and sufferings.[32] During February its editorials twice incorporated, without acknowledgment, large excerpts from Gerrard Winstanley's *Law of Freedom in a Platform*, the first one appearing shortly before that work was published. The first passage demanded that all public officers should be elected annually by the people, since 'Great offices in a land and army have changed the disposition of many sweet-spirited men.'[33] The second declared that if any army was raised to overthrow kingly oppression and its officers maintained some part of the kingly power to advance their own particular interest, they were worse thieves and tyrants than the kings they cast out. These words of Winstanley's had a prophetic force in the context: 'A monarchical army lifts up mountains, and makes vallies, *viz.* advances tyrants, and treads the oppressed in the barren lanes of poverty. But a common-wealths army is like John Baptist, who levels the mountains to the valleys, pulls down the tyrant, and lifts up the oppressed.'[34]

Whatever the potential differences within the army, however,

---

[31] 'For my part I should think I were very treacherous if I should take away tithes, till I see the legislative power to settle maintenance to [ministers] another way': Cromwell, speech on 17 Sept. 1656, Abbott, iv, 272.

[32] The paper's career is described in Frank, *Beginnings of the English Newspaper*, chs. XI–XIII.

[33] *Faithful Scout*, no. 56, 6–13 Feb. 1652, pp. 438–9. For other samples of the *Scout's* radicalism, see no. 54, 23–30 Jan. 1652, pp. 419–20; no. 57, 13–20 Feb. 1652, p. 444; no. 61, 19–26 March 1652, pp. 486–7; no. 79, 16–23 July 1652, p. 622; no. 93, 22–29 Oct. 1652, pp. 727–9. Annual election of all public officers was also proposed by Samuel Dunkon (whose kinsman Robert was to sit in Barebone's Parliament) in *Several Propositions of Publick Concernment* ([18 March] 1652), p. 4.

[34] *Faithful Scout*, no. 38, 20–27 Feb. 1653, pp. 454–5. Whether Border got this material from Winstanley himself, or copied it from three short contemporary tracts, all printed for George Horton, which incorporated the same and other passages from *The Law of Freedom*, is unknown. I hope to publish a note on this extensive pirating of *The Law of Freedom*, which Thomason acquired on 20 Feb. 1652.

it was at one in its dissatisfaction with the Rump. This eventually
found expression in a petition which was worked out in some
lengthy meetings of the Council of Officers early in August and
presented to the House on the 13th.[35] This is a key document,
since eight months later Cromwell and the officers were to justify
their dissolution of the Rump largely because so little action had
been taken on it.

Its first request, predictably, was for speedy and effectual
measures for the propagation of the gospel, so as to rid the
churches of ignorant and scandalous ministers and encourage
godly and gifted ones. Equally predictably, the officers asked
that tithes should be replaced by a more acceptable form of
maintenance. But it was as easy to be for godly ministers as it was
to be against sin, and they cannot have foreseen that the means
of establishing and maintaining them would be so controversial
that Barebone's Parliament would finally shipwreck on this very
issue. Nor were they yet aware of the hidden reefs in their next
request, which was for the reform of the law and the speedy
implementation of the Hale Commission's recommendations.
Perhaps it also seemed straightforward to them when they called
for swift action by statute or otherwise to remove all profane,
scandalous, or disaffected persons from public office, and to
ensure that the Commonwealth should be governed solely by
'men of truth, fearing God, and hating covetousness'. Variants of
this last formula would echo through the promises and petitions
and declarations of the next twelve months, but it did not specify
by what criteria truth and godliness were to be judged, or who
should judge them. If this was a bow in the direction of a rule of
the saints, it was as yet a very distant one. But doubts about the
probity of England's present governors came through in several
further requests: for a commission *excluding* MPs to investigate
monopolies, redundant offices, excessive salaries, and official
pluralism; for a cessation of grants to individuals from the public
revenues until loans on the public faith had been repaid; for all
receipts and disbursements of public revenue to be published
yearly or twice yearly; and for a committee in every county to
redress abuses in the excise. The petition also asked that all the
various revenues should be brought into a single treasury with a

[35] *To the Supreame Authority the Parliament: . . . The humble Petition of the Officers of the Army*
(12 Aug. 1652).

competent professional staff, instead of the assortment of *ad hoc* committees and commissions that the Rump had inherited from the Civil War period. There was a genuine concern here for much needed administrative reform, as there was for the problem of poverty in an article which called on the parliament to put an end to begging and vagabondage by providing work for the unemployed and relief for the aged and infirm. Further articles dealt with the particular needs of the soldiery and their dependants—their arrears of pay, their right when disbanded to practise crafts for which they had not served a full apprenticeship (which some gilds and corporations were resisting), and better provision for their crippled comrades and for the widows and children of the fallen. Another asked once more that articles of war granted to the royalists on surrender should be honoured.

The officers left till last the matter about which they were coming to care most, the provision for a new representative. Since this was to be their chief bone of contention from now on, article 12 is worth quoting in full: 'That for publique satisfaction of the good people of this nation, speedy consideration may be had of such quallifications for future and successive parliaments, as tend to the election only of such as are pious and faithfull to the interest of the Commonwealth, to sit and serve as members in the said parliament.' This was more moderate than might have been feared, or than most of the officers had probably intended. Gardiner thought that Cromwell had caused them to modify an original demand 'that a new representative be forthwith elected'; but the pamphlet he quoted was not, as he thought, a draft of the petition but an unofficial report which named five topics which the officers had met to discuss—probably an ill-informed report at that, since the other four were equally vaguely related to the actual content of the petition.[36] Yet Gardiner was probably right all the same in sensing Cromwell's restraining influence. On 10 August the regular newswriter to

[36] Gardiner, *C & P*, ii, 167–8; the pamphlet he cites is *A Declaration of the Armie to his Excellency* ([10 Aug.] 1652). Gardiner also states strangely, on the authority of a dispatch by Paulucci dated three months earlier, that Cromwell did not sign the petition. The original does not survive, so it is not known who signed it, nor is it particularly relevant. As published, it concludes with the words 'At the Council of War at Whitehall', which would have sufficiently conveyed his assent to it, even if he had not subsequently expressed his support for it in his declaration of 22 April 1653 and his speech of 4 July 1653.

army headquarters in Scotland—almost certainly Gilbert Mabbott—reported a large meeting of officers that day, with
Cromwell present, at which the contents of the petition were in
large part agreed. He accurately recorded most of them, in some
cases almost verbatim, but concerning a new representative he
gave it as their request that 'this Consideration of putting a
period to this parliment be resumed and a speedier time ordered
then was formerly voted (if it be convenent) and that they passe
when this parlment be disolved and when another be chosen'.[37]
It would be entirely in character with Cromwell's position for
him to dissuade the Council of Officers from exerting overt
pressure on the Rump to name an earlier date for its dissolution,
and to divert their emphasis to the difficult problem of securing
the return of men who would be faithful to the true interests of
the Commonwealth. He did not at all mind the officers telling
the parliament what in general terms they expected of it—
indeed he brushed aside an attempt by Whitelocke to advise him
to stop them petitioning, as he put it, with the sword in their
hands[38]—but he still wanted them to leave such an essentially
political decision as the date for calling a new parliament to the
supreme authority in the Commonwealth, which the petition
acknowledged the Rump to be. Nevertheless what it did say on
the subject assumed that the present House would be followed by
a succession of elected parliaments; there was no hint yet of any
alternative in the shape of a nominated assembly or a sanhedrin
picked solely by the saints.

It was on the whole a moderate and responsible petition, and
it asked little that the Rump had not at one time or another
pledged itself to do something about. It certainly reflected on the
way the members had executed their trust, and some of them
naturally objected that it was not for a paid army to teach its
masters their political duty. But this was not a mere professional
army, nor was this parliament's claim to represent the people a
strong one. Some of the Rumpers who now most resented
military pressure had once welcomed it; and some would do so
again, when finding themselves in a minority in Richard
Cromwell's parliament they proceeded to harness the army's

[37] Worcester College, Oxford, Clarke MS XXIV, fo. 5.
[38] The edition quoted by Gardiner in *C & P*, ii, 168 n.3 makes it clear that the advice
was Whitelocke's own, which the first edition does not.

discontents to their own designs.[39] They were hardly the most convincing body to try to impose ideal constitutional norms in a post-revolutionary situation. And comparing like with like, this petition was less menacing, and far less of an encroachment on sovereign authority, than either the army's remonstrance of 16 November 1648 or its subsequent petitions in April, September, and October 1659.

The House at any rate had the sense to show a friendly face to the petition when it was presented. It set up a committee to report which of the officers' requests were already under consideration, what progress had been made in them, and what further measures were needed to expedite them. The committee was given a thoroughly radical chairman in John Carew and ordered to meet daily. On 9 September, however, it had to be prodded into making its report, which it eventually did on the 14th. The main matter was the election of a new representative. Carew recounted the desultory manner in which the Rump had so far proceeded with its bill, and recommended that to secure its speedier passage it should be transferred from the dormant grand committee to a select one. To this the House agreed without a division and it entrusted the bill to the same committee from which Carew had reported. Since the latter was to have charge of it for the next five critical months, its membership is of some importance. It numbered thirty-four, and of these Richard Salwey, Walter Strickland, Sir Gilbert Pickering, Robert Bennett, and Richard Norton were to sit in Barebone's Parliament, as well as Carew. Cromwell, Harrison, and the latter's friend Colonel Rich were there to voice the army's views, but so were such opponents as Marten, Scot, and John Weaver, as well as the conservative lawers Whitelocke and John Lisle. Notable by their absence were Hesilrige, Vane, and St. John, but the list of names was followed by the formula, commonly added when a committee's business was of very general interest, 'and all that come to have voices'. It was a body from which almost anything might have emerged, if the variety of opinion within it did not result in deadlock. The House did however instruct it to leave the date of dissolution blank, thereby reserving all debate on this to the full membership but at the same time indicating

[39] Woolrych, 'Good Old Cause', pp. 144–9.

that it was prepared to consider something earlier than 3 November 1654.[40]

So far this was hopeful, as were several other signs of activity in matters of concern to the army such as the propagation of the gospel, articles of war, exclusion of disaffected persons from office, relief of poor prisoners for debt, and poor relief more generally.[41] But once again this trickle of reforming zeal soon ran out into the sands. It was in vain that Cromwell arranged a series of meetings—ten or twelve, he claimed, between October 1652 and April 1653—between groups of officers and MPs.[42] The House's committee for the propagation of the gospel settled nothing before it sank into inactivity again before the end of the year. Carew's committee sat daily at first, but nothing was heard from it for months, though on 8 December the House did order it to consider how many members should represent Scotland and Ireland. The latter months of 1652 are indeed among the most barren in the Rump's annals. It could not plead the pressures of the Dutch war as an excuse, for during October and November it spent day after day considering each one of the names of 678 royalists who were the victims of its third act for the sale of forfeited estates. And its time-scale was certainly on the leisurely side. Its critics reasonably complained—the more reasonably because it was so unwilling to delegate responsibility—that it sat on only four mornings a week, and usually for a mere two or three hours.[43] Yet when a motion was put on 11 November to suspend the order against sitting on Mondays and Saturdays until the end of the year it was narrowly lost.[44]

It was about then, or soon after, that Cromwell had a famous private talk with Whitelocke in the course of which he threw out the momentous question 'What if a man should take upon him to

---

[40] *CJ*, 13 Aug. and 14 Sept. 1652. Hesilrige did not attend the Council of State between 27 July and 26 Oct., nor did Vane between 29 June and 9 Sept.; St. John made only two appearances in July and three in August. Vane's absence is discussed inconclusively by Violet A. Rowe, *Sir Henry Vane the Younger* (1970), pp. 147–8.

[41] Worden, *Rump*, pp. 309–10.

[42] Abbott, iii, 55–6; cf. Worden, *Rump*, pp. 310–11.

[43] Samuel Chidley, *A Remonstrance to the Valiant Souldier* ([23 Apr.] 1653), p. 14; [John Hall], *A Letter written to a Gentleman in the Country* (3 May 1653), p. 5, copied in *Mercurius Britannicus*, 23–30 May 1653, and in *Moderate Occurrences*, 24–31 May 1653. For other accusations of dilatoriness see Worden, *Rump*, p. 89 n.2.

[44] *CJ*, 11 Nov. 1652. Hesilrige was one of the tellers against the motion, Vane one of those for it.

be king?'[45] Whitelocke dates it no more precisely than November, but it is tempting to place it after the House's annual elections to the Council of State on the 24th and 25th. Cromwell as usual headed the poll, gaining the votes of all but two of the 116 members present. Next came Whitelocke with 102 votes, and then the two chief justices, St. John and Rolle, with 101 and 100. All three had a bias towards monarchy, and they came out ahead of the most successful republicans, Vane with 98 votes, and Hesilrige and Scot, paired here as in so much else, with 93 apiece. Marten and Neville lost their seats, while Harrison and Pickering scraped in only after lots had been drawn for the last two places. It was not a result to rejoice either the army or the radical interest in general.

It was Cromwell who sought the conversation with Whitelocke, because he feared that the fruits of victory would be lost through the army's and the politicians' 'jarrings and animosities one against another'. He granted Whitelocke's point that his officers were prone to faction and resentful at being (as they felt) underrewarded, especially in respect of their small share of the places of power and profit in the Commonwealth. But he wished there was not so much cause for their 'strange distaste' against the Rumpers, whom he charged with pride, ambition, factiousness, and greed for office. He also accused them of meddling in private suits, delaying public business, and designing to perpetuate themselves, and he deplored the scandalous lives of some of the chief of them. He blamed it on there being no authority to keep them within the bounds of justice, law, or reason, since they were accountable to no one. He feared that the Commonwealth faced ruin unless there could be devised 'some authority and power so full and so high as to restrain and keep things in better order, and that may be a check to these exorbitancies'. Whitelocke objected with a lawyer's logic that since he and Cromwell and countless others had taken their commissions from the Rump and acknowledged its supreme authority, it would be hard to bridle it now. Then Cromwell sprang his dramatic question. Whitelocke promptly replied that he thought the remedy of a King Oliver would be worse than the disease. The ensuing arguments, as he records them, sound

---

[45] Whitelocke, pp. 523–6; reprinted in Abbott, ii, 587–92, and *Old Parl. Hist.*, xx, 104–12.

curiously anticipatory of those between Cromwell and those later parliament-men (including Whitelocke) who pressed the crown on him in 1657—with the difference that Cromwell in 1652 was propounding the advantages of monarchy and Whitelocke the objections to it. But when Whitelocke was pressed for his own solution to their present dangers, with an intransigent army challenging a parliament that would brook no curb on its sovereignty, the best advice he could offer Cromwell was to do a private deal with Charles II. Or so he tells us; all these *ipsissima verba*, revealed only after the Restoration, are best received with caution.

Yet the dilemma which Cromwell is described as putting to Whitelocke was a very real one and his tentative suggestion about the crown is entirely credible. One would dearly like to know whether he put it to anyone else, but to whom could he turn? Ireton was dead, Vane dogmatically opposed to monarchy and perhaps already becoming estranged, while St. John seems by his increasingly rare attendances at the Council of State to have been steadily withdrawing from the political scene. He wrote after the Restoration that he had given his voice for a new and free parliament as the best way of healing the nation's distractions,[46] so if his influence with Cromwell counted for anything at this time it was probably on the side of persevering with his attempts to induce the Rump to provide for its own successor. There is just a possibility that Lambert was already entertaining the idea of a crown for Cromwell, since his Instrument of Government contained the title of king when it was first presented, only about a year later; but Lambert's support would have been balanced by strong opposition from Harrison and many other officers. As for the politicians, if the influential lawyers and old middle-group men could not yet see the royal title as a possible solution, Cromwell would have been almost isolated against the inevitably bitter hostility of such diverse opponents as Hesilrige, Vane, Marten, Neville, and Chaloner.

He had to decide his stance fairly quickly, because the army was becoming restive again in face of the Rump's relapse into inertia. In the hope of promoting a better understanding and of gaining some compliance with the army's wishes, he initiated

[46] *The Case of Oliver St. John, Esq.* ([30 July] 1660), p. 7.

that series of meetings between selected officers and MPs that has already been mentioned.[47] During November, however, there was also renewed agitation among the millenarian congregations in London. Harrison was much involved in it, and helped to link the Welsh saints with Feake and the other Fifth Monarchists of the City. Messengers from various outlying churches had gathered there, and on 7 November Harrison wrote on their behalf to Colonel John Jones in Dublin, urging him to get his congregation to send him and one or two others over to consult with them about 'the propagating of our Lord's Gospell and Kingdome'. 'Though here bee a very greate ebb to carnall sense', he wrote, 'yett Manie pretious Ones think itts a time of much Mercie; and that our blessed Lord will shortly worke with eminence.'[48] On the 30th he told Jones how they had spent four or five hours in prayer the day before, and how the elders of the churches then agreed to spend one day more in solemnly seeking the Lord at Allhallows the Great, so that they might be sure of their duty 'in this great thing'. 'There are thoughts', he added, 'of having up my whole Regiment and consequently your troop up to the guards here. Itt may bee you may see a cleere call to come with them, and give the Churches here a visitt.'[49] But what great thing the churches were collectively contemplating he did not specify, nor whose thoughts were bent on bringing up his whole regiment, nor what business he had to call home a commissioner for the government of Ireland. Jones stayed at his post.

The final phase of agitation in the army at large, as distinct from its Fifth Monarchist faction, began quite abruptly at the very end of the year. Shortly before, on 15 December, the French ambassador Bordeaux heard from the son-in-law of a leading MP (unnamed) that there was a plan afoot in the Rump to remove Cromwell from his command, and that Cromwell had ordered some outlying forces closer to London in order to secure the army against the Presbyterians in the House, who were becoming too powerful.[50] Such reports are of course to be treated

[47] Abbott, iii, 55–6.
[48] Mayer, 'Inedited letters', p. 214.
[49] Ibid. 218.
[50] PRO transcripts: Bordeaux to Brienne, 16/26 Dec. 1652, PRO 31/3/90, fo. 531. The word Bordeaux uses for what the Rump meant to do to Cromwell is 'désoctoriser', which

(continued)

cautiously, though Bordeaux, young as he was and new to England, was the most judicious and generally the best informed of the foreign residents then in London. What is certain is that by the end of the month officers were gathering in the capital, and that during the last day or two of December 1652 and the first week of January 1653 they met almost daily, and in growing numbers, to seek the Lord in prayer and fasting. It was no secret that some of them meant to press for an early dissolution of the parliament.[51] A formal Council of Officers was held on 8 January, with Cromwell present, to consider what stand the army should take on the great questions before the Commonwealth. After long debates, it set up a committee 'to draw uppe the sense of the Councell concerning the consistency of the Civil authority by successive parliaments', as well as about matters of religion and the better dispensation of justice throughout the nation.[52]

The Rump, true to form, reacted promptly to this new wave of pressure. As early as 31 December it took up two matters on which action had long been demanded, the repayment of debts on the public faith and the better provision for probate of wills.[53] Then on 6 January it turned to what was exercising the officers most, the bill for a new representative. Without changing the committee that had had charge of it since October, the Rump placed the bill under Harrison's care instead of Carew's, and

---

I take to be his spelling of *désautoriser*. It is not clear whether he got the report of troop movements from the same source, and I have not been able to verify it; both on 3 and 6 Jan. he again reported (fos. 555, 559ᵛ) that not only the officers but also their troops were continuing to approach London.

[51] C. H. Firth, 'Cromwell and the expulsion of the Long Parliament in 1653', *EHR*, viii (1893), p. 527, though Worden correctly reads the date of the second letter there quoted as 1 Jan. instead of Firth's 7[?] Jan. (*Rump*, p. 317 n.1); PRO 31.3/90, fos. 555 and 555ᵛ, 559ᵛ, where Bordeaux reports on 6/16 Jan. that the officers had spent the last eight days in continuing prayer and fasting. *Severall Proceedings*, no. 186, under the date 21 Apr. 1653 (p. 2944), said that the army had been exercising its persuasions upon the parliament for the past sixteen weeks, i.e. since 30 Dec., and Whitelocke noted its renewed agitation in his last entry for December (*Memorials*, p. 526).

[52] Firth, 'Cromwell and the expulsion', p. 527. Firth reads the date of the relevant Clarke newsletter as 8 Jan., Worden (*Rump*, p. 317) as 5 Jan.; *A Perfect Diurnall*, no. 161, 3–10 Jan. 1653, p. 2424, reports the meeting under the joint dates 7 and 8 Jan., without specifying which. Bordeaux wrote on 10/20 Jan. that the army's debates had begun, which suggests that they had taken on a new formality since he reported their eight days of prayer meetings on 6/16 Jan. (PRO 31.3/90, fos. 559ᵛ, 562).

[53] Worden, *Rump*, pp. 318–19.

ordered that it be brought in with all speed.[54] In retrospect this is remarkable, since in little more than two years' time Harrison and Carew would together be arraigned before Cromwell -and the Council, and would defend their attempts to subvert the Protectorate on the ground that 'It had a parliament in it, whereby power is derived from the people, whereas all power belongs to Christ.'[55] But whether either man was yet firmly opposed to elected parliaments is doubtful, and even if Harrison was, the Rump is unlikely to have been aware of it. During the past month the Council of State had been trying to associate him more closely with its activities by appointing him to a number of important committees, in spite of his sporadic attendance,[56] and in giving him special responsibility for this most important of bills the House must have simply hoped that it was binding him to a parliamentary way of resolving the current crisis.

There was an obvious interconnection between the mounting agitation in the army and the heady preachings at Allhallows-the-Great and St. Anne's, Blackfriars. But the Council of Officers was not prepared to let the clamorous millenarians set its pace, and its coolness towards them surely reflected Cromwell's own. William Erbery, who was closely involved with the London sectaries at the time, recorded early in January that 'some army preaching men joyned in a body at Allhallows, to pray for a new representative, and to preach somewhat against the old'; but 'they received no countenance, but rather a check from the state, and some of the highest in the army'.[57] Later in the month several of the London congregations tried to present a paper of advice to the assembled Council of Officers, but the latter would

[54] Worden (*Rump*, p. 319 n.1) notes that the Journal here calls it 'the bill touching equal representatives', a description associated earlier with the recruitment scheme. But the report of the vote in the official *Severall Proceedings* (no. 172, 6–13 Jan. 1653, p. 2698) confirms that the committee's brief had not changed: 'The House ordered a report to be made from the committee touching future representatives, and ordering their elections.'

[55] *Clarke Papers*, ii, 244.

[56] 8 Dec., new Committee for Examinations (*CSPD 1652–3*, p. 16); 15 Dec. Admiralty Committee (p. 18); 17 Dec. Ordnance Committee and Committee for Foreign Affairs (p. 37); and on 21 Dec. another less important committee (p. 45). Harrison attended only 10 out of 33 meetings of the Council of State during December (only one before the 14th) and only 5 all through January (none before the 13th).

[57] William Erbery, *The Bishop of London* ([8 Jan.] 1653), p.1. Christopher Feake, who presided over similar preaching bouts at St. Anne's Blackfriars, said that 'the spirit which prevail'd at the headquarters was wonderfully displeased with us' for attacking the self-seeking practices of both army and parliament: *A Beam of Light*, p. 46.

not receive it.[58] Ludlow was probably referring particularly to these much reported preaching sessions at Allhallows and Blackfriars when he wrote of certain ministers who began to prophesy the destruction of the parliament from their pulpits, 'and to propose it openly as a thing desirable'. From there he went straight on to recount how Cromwell complained to Quartermaster-General Vernon—hypocritically, he thought, though in all likelihood Cromwell was quite sincere—'that he was pushed on by two parties to do that, the consideration of the issue whereof made his hair stand on end'. One was headed by Lambert, the other by Harrison; both were ready to threaten force against the Rump, though from different motives. Cromwell may or may not have attributed Lambert's animosity to his disappointment over the lord deputyship, as Ludlow tells us, but his words about Harrison, as here reported, have an authentic ring. Harrison, said Cromwell, 'is an honest man, and aims at good things, yet from the impatience of his spirit will not wait the Lord's leisure, but hurries me on to that which he and all honest men will have cause to repent'.[59] This seems exactly to express Cromwell's admiration of Harrison's courage and integrity, his shared belief in the ultimate ends that they both sought, and his strong reservations about his major-general's political judgement. Anyone who would explain Cromwell's dissolution of the Rump on the hypothesis that Harrison slid into the role of intimate counsellor that had once been Ireton's must take account of this and other evidence that the two men viewed each other with a cautious and critical eye, both before and after the dissolution.[60]

The Council of Officers met again on Thursday, 13 January, to consider the draft of a programme or declaration prepared for it by the committee that it had appointed on the 8th. On the following Thursday, if not earlier, it decided to seek a broader basis of support by sending a circular letter to all the military units in England, Scotland, and Ireland, and it devoted much of that day's meeting to discussing what it should say. There was evidently some disagreement, but the last amendments to the letter were approved on the 28th and it was sent out soon

[58] Firth, 'Cromwell and the expulsion', p. 527 (newsletter dated 21 Jan.).

[59] Ludlow, i, 346.

[60] See also pp. 74–7.

afterwards.[61] Its preamble was well larded with the rhetoric of the saints, which may indicate that the 'preaching party' was making itself felt more, though it really differed from earlier army pronouncements such as the Musselburgh declaration not in its scriptural imagery but in its loss of confidence. They were not reaping the fruits of their victories, it complained, because they were not doing what God expected of a people whom he had so blessed. It lamented that 'the work of the Lord hath seemed to stand still, and all the instruments thereof have been men of no might, or like a woman in travail ready to faint for want of strength to bring forth'. Satan had thereby been encouraged to stir up his agents to pervert the Lord's interest, and make those whom God had used and blessed turn into offenders against it. The officers felt impelled to confess, after seeking the Lord together for several days, 'That our hearts have been looking after the things of this world, and our own private affairs, more than the things of Jesus Christ and his People.'

This was ominous, considering what actions such beatings of the breast had led to in 1647–8 and would do again in 1659, but there was nothing new or extreme in the four specific objectives to which the letter invited the whole army's concurrence. The second, third, and fourth dealt in carefully moderate terms with the regulation of the laws (in such a way 'that what is good in them is maintained'), liberty of worship (though without tolerating popery or licentious practices), and the propagation of the gospel (with all due encouragement to those who laboured faithfully in the work). The first ran thus: 'For the preventing the many inconveniences apparently arising from the long continuance of the same persons in supreme authority, That there may be successive parliaments consisting of men faithful to the interest of the Commonwealth; men of truth, fearing God, and hating covetousnesse.' This was very much in the same spirit as the petition of the previous August. The letter did not demand an immediate dissolution, or attempt to dictate a date for it; it left the means of ensuring that future parliaments should consist of well-affected and God-fearing men to the present one to determine. Above all it contained no hint that the successive parliaments that it desired should be anything but normally

---

[61] Firth, 'Cromwell and the expulsion', p. 527. The letter was promptly published as *A Letter from the General meeting of the Officers of the Army* (28 Jan. 1653).

elected ones. In demanding that future members should be faithful and godly it probably meant no more than that the Rump should write such qualifications into the bill for a new representative, as in fact it proceeded to do, and as the Instrument of Government would do in turn. Confirmation that the officers consistently pressed for a new parliament, to be followed by a regular succession of parliaments, comes in the issue of the official *Severall Proceedings* which came out eight days after the dissolution. It describes how the officers, after sending out this letter, tried to persuade the better-disposed MPs to take such steps that the army would not be driven to intervene. 'And the officers of the army made it their sole desires to have a new parliament, and lay aside all other considerations, clearly perceiving an impossibility for the honest men of the House, to carry on the good things that were so much longed for.' It was only when they saw that the bill actually before the House 'would not answer the thing desired' that they arranged further meetings with some leading members and urged a different course.[62] Bordeaux, although he reported divisions among the officers during January, believed that they were nevertheless united in desiring a new representative, and had the impression that after the terms of their circular letter had been agreed their differences were allayed.[63]

The letter certainly dissatisfied the more extreme Fifth Monarchy men, one of whom called Benjamin Nicolson, a prisoner in York Castle, attacked it specifically for failing to demand the disqualification of the ungodly from either voting or standing for the new representative; 'for those only are fit to rule for the Lord, that are ruled by the Lord in all things, which power is ordained of God'. He also objected strongly to the implication in its request concerning the propagation of the

---

[62] *Severall Proceedings*, no. 187, 21–8 April 1653, pp. 2958–9. This narrative, headed 'A further account of the grounds and reasons of the dissolving of the parliament', was reprinted in at least two other newspapers and again, almost verbatim, in *Another Declaration, Wherein is Rendered, a further Account . . . by the Lord Generall and his Council* ([3 May] 1653). In 'The calling of Barebone's Parliament', *EHR*, lxxx (1965), 495 n.4, I suggested that this declaration was spurious. I noticed subsequently, as Dr Worden also did (*Rump*, p. 353), that it was plagiarized from *Severall Proceedings*. It has no independent value and is not what its title suggests, but the original account in *Severall Proceedings* has the kind of authority attaching to a press release and was probably inspired or approved by the officers or an agent of theirs.

[63] PRO 31.3/90, fos. 573, 575, 598, 600, 606.

gospel that ministers should receive a settled maintenance.[64] But if Harrison, Rich, Chillenden, or any other millenarians in the Council of Officers objected to its terms, no record of it has survived.

Meanwhile the Rump had been jolted into a semblance of activity over other reforms about which the army had petitioned. On 20 January it had the whole report of the Hale Commission read to it, and after debating it that day and the next it voted for the immediate introduction of a bill to establish county registers for recording land transactions.[65] It had discussed this useful measure desultorily in the previous summer and earlier, but on 2 February the conservative lawyers blocked it once more by getting it referred back to the committee dominated by themselves. Another reforming bill, which would have provided for county courts to give probate of wills, was shelved in favour of a temporary measure entrusting the function to the Hale Commissioners themselves.[66] Perhaps the House felt a sense of false security because of the temporary lull in the army's agitation during February, while the Council of Officers waited for the responses of the outlying regiments and garrisons to its circular letter.

At about the same time the House began to deal seriously with another matter of deep concern to the army when on 11 February Thomas Scot reported at last from the committee for the propagation of the gospel, which had been considering those proposals which John Owen and his associates had presented a year before.[67] The committee recommended only eleven of the fourteen proposals to the House, probably judging that at least two of the three others would offend the champions of liberty of conscience in the army and elsewhere. One of these would have required dissenters who wished to worship elsewhere than in their parish churches to do so in places publicly known and duly certified to a magistrate. Another would have banned from preaching or promulgating their opinions all who denied any tenets that the Scriptures affirm to be necessary to salvation—a

[64] Benjamin Nicholson, *Some Returns to a Letter* (1653: dated 12 March by Thomason but 8 Feb. by the author), pp. 4–5.
[65] *CJ*, 20 and 21 Jan. 1653.
[66] Worden, *Rump*, pp. 306, 320.
[67] See p. 38.

restraint which could have been oppressive if those tenets were defined anything like as strictly as they had been by Owen and his brethren in their proposed fundamentals. It was wise to hold these particular proposals back, and it is characteristic of the Rump that having entrusted the consideration of Owen's scheme for so long to its committee, it now overrode it and decided to hear and consider all fourteen proposals. This was only one of several signs of its hostility towards the sects at about this time.[68]

But though the army cared strongly about the reform of the law and the propagation of the gospel, its chief touchstone of the honesty of the Rump's intentions was the bill for a new representative. Yet for nearly seven weeks after it was given into Harrison's special care nothing was heard of it. Very probably the committee of thirty-four that was supposed to be working on it found it difficult to agree, but another explanation of its silence may be that Harrison virtually withdrew from it. He attended only five of the Council of State's meetings during January, and in February none at all after the 11th. Perhaps he had finally ceased to trust the Rump to provide for the Commonwealth's future government; perhaps he had come now to believe that the kingdom of Christ was too imminent for the saints to trust any longer to elected parliaments. At any rate, when the committee at last presented its proposed amendments to the bill for a new representative on 23 February, its spokesman was not Harrison but Hesilrige. This is remarkable, for not only had Hesilrige become Cromwell's most determined opponent in the House, but if the *Commons' Journal* is to be trusted—and admittedly its record is far short of perfect in 1652–3—he had not even been formally appointed to the committee.

Alas, there is scarcely any evidence as to what the proposed amendments were, or how far they altered the character of the bill from its original form in October 1651, or how much Hesilrige had had to do with framing them. But the bill in the form in which the House now proceeded to debate it seems to have been quite unacceptable to the army officers, for instead of suspending their agitation during the period of debate they very

---

[68] *CJ*, 11 Feb. 1653; cf. Worden, *Rump*, pp. 321–7. The proposals originally numbered fifteen, but in Scot's report nos. 6 and 7 were run together as a single proposal.

soon intensified it. During the remainder of its existence the Rump spent every Wednesday except one upon the bill and its amendments, sitting in grand committee. The *Journal* gives no clue to any provisions which might have offended the army. It records apparently innocuous votes on the numbers of members who should represent Scotland and Ireland, and on the apportionment of seats among the English counties and boroughs. On 30 March the House decided after a division, in which Hesilrige and Vane were tellers on opposite sides, that the franchise should be given to owners or possessors of real or personal estate to the value of £200. A fortnight later it voted that members must be 'persons of known integrity, fearing God, and not scandalous in their conversation'. But none of these particulars can have been obnoxious to the army's commanders, for the Instrument of Government was to repeat them almost to the letter.

What is not known, however, is whether Hesilrige in his report on 23 February recommended further amendments of a more controversial kind. It would have been natural to draft the bill so that its sections fell into a kind of ascending order or contentiousness: apportionment of constituencies, franchise, qualifications of members—we know that it ran thus, as far as it was debated. If, however, there were to be special provisions to apply to the next elections only, so as to safeguard the hazardous transition from the Rump's authority to that of its unknown successor—and what is more likely?— the logical place for them would have been at the end of the bill. But what the bill may have contained and how far it provoked the dissolution will be discussed further in the next chapter. All that remains for this one to do is to trace the build-up of dissension and distrust between army and parliament during the last two months of the latter's life.

One disturbing feature of the Rump's debates on the bill, considering how important they were, was the thin attendance at them. The recorded divisions show that only forty-two members in all were present on 23 March and only forty-four on the 30th. And Cromwell was not among them. He ceased to attend the Council of State after 8 March and the House very soon afterwards, and the only further debate on the bill at which he appeared was the last one of all, which he so dramatically interrupted.[69] Whatever one may think of his withdrawal, it surely indicates that he had no confidence that the Rump's bill would provide in any acceptable manner for what the army had been consistently demanding.

Early in March the Council of Officers resumed its meetings, after allowing due time for replies to come in to its circular letter. On the 7th Cromwell attended a session enlarged to include all the officers about London and summoned expressly to consider what the army should do with regard to a new representative—further evidence that he and they thought that what the Rump was doing about it was profoundly unsatisfactory. After a full debate the meeting appointed a committee to advise with him further on the matter. Only four days later, however, against a background of violent preaching against the Rump in the millenarian storm-centres, the Council of Officers came to the point of resolving to expel it forthwith, and was only dissuaded by the urgent intercessions of Cromwell and Desborough. Cromwell asked them what sort of government they would offer if they destroyed the Rump. They would call a new parliament, they replied. 'Then', retorted Cromwell unanswerably, 'the parliament is not the supreme power, but this is the supreme power that calls it.'[70] He further urged that the Rump was now working towards a treaty with Holland, whose masters would not enter into negotiation if the army drove it out. This was probably a very real consideration with him, for he had a strong sense of what the Commonwealth could gain in security against its enemies by a good understanding with the Dutch Republic.[71]

It must have been this same intervention by Cromwell and Desborough that Ludlow describes, and he links it (like the newswriter last quoted) with a new petition to parliament which the officers were hatching. According to Ludlow, who got much of his information about this period from Harrison, the officers

---

[69] A newsletter dated 15 April (Bodl. Clarendon MS 45, fo. 293) states that he went to the House 'yesterday' after absenting himself almost a month. He attended on 10 March for the debate on transactions with the Dutch, and was a teller with Vane for continuing it next day, so his withdrawal presumably dates from after the 11th. He did not attend the Council between 8 March and 7 April, except for one emergency meeting on Sunday, 27 March (*CSPD 1652-3*, pp. xxxi–xxxii).

[70] Firth, 'Cromwell and the expulsion', pp. 527–8.

[71] Ibid.; cf. Michael Roberts, 'Cromwell and the Baltic', *EHR*, lxxvi (1961), 402–46, reprinted in *Essays in Swedish History* (1967).

intended to request the House to embody its vote to dissolve not later than 3 November 1654 in a statute.[72] If this is true, it is intelligible only if they feared that in spite of the bill for a new representative, or perhaps by its very means, the Rumpers would still find some way of clinging longer to their seats. That of course is what they said they had feared, after the dissolution.[73] Ludlow typically alleged that Cromwell himself secretly inspired the petition, but it is likelier that he and Desborough meant what they said when they urged the assembled officers to trust the parliament's promise and not to undermine its authority, which was so necessary to the army. Meanwhile other officers were getting up in the pulpit at Blackfriars and bewailing the great divisions among them, and some preachers there were reviling the Rump so offensively that Cromwell was expected to take action against them.[74] Even though he ceased for a month to attend the House, he was still striving to prevent an open breach, and he was getting no thanks for it. A newswriter thus describes the situation on 1 April:

Our souldiers resolve to have speedily a new Representative, and the Parliament resolve the contrary; the General sticks close to the House; which causeth him to be daily railed on by the preaching party, who say they must have both a new Parliament and General before the worke be don; and that these are not the people that are appointed for perfecting that great Worke of God which they have begun.[75]

When a cavalry regiment arrived in London 'fullmouth'd against the Parliament', apparently without orders, Cromwell knew how to act. He ordered it promptly to Scotland, along with three others that were getting out of hand, and for a short while this pressure from below was relieved.[76]

Just at this time, however, the Rump dealt a damaging blow

[72] Ludlow, i, 348–9. Firth in his annotation most implausibly identifies this petition with that of August 1652, and Gardiner follows him (*C & P*, ii, 168 n.3). Whereas the August petition had been comprehensive, the one described by Ludlow apparently contained only one demand, and one that seems more relevant to the context of March 1653. Ludlow places the episode immediately before the events of April, and although he describes the framing of the petition as preceding Cromwell's and Desborough's intervention, whereas the newsletter of 18 March (cited above) places it immediately after, I have very little doubt that both sources refer to the same incident.

[73] See pp. 80–4.

[74] Firth, 'Cromwell and the expulsion', p. 528.

[75] Ibid.

[76] Ibid. 528–9.

to his efforts to contain the excesses of the fanatics and to persuade his responsible colleagues to go on seeking a parliamentary solution. At the end of March the original three-year term of the Commission for the Propagation of the Gospel in Wales, which Harrison and the Welsh apostles had used so effectively to propagate their millenarian ideals, was due to expire. On 1 April the House, after raising hopes that it would be renewed, terminated the commission without even a division. It was a disastrously ill-timed decision, and its background and implications need to be explained.

One result of the mounting stridency and pugnacity of the sects during 1651-2—not only of the Fifth Monarchists but also of the Ranters and the Quakers too, in their different ways—was a drawing together of moderate, orthodox puritans, both ministers and laymen. Whether conservative Independents or moderate Presbyterians or 'meer Catholicks', as Richard Baxter called his own ecumenical kind,[77] they had a common interest in opposing the various extremists who were now attacking the very existence of a parochial clergy, demanding that tithes be abolished and no other form of public maintenance substituted for them, and denying to the civil magistrate any authority whatever over matters of religion. One manifestation of this *rapprochement* was an abortive initiative in 1652 by Baxter and John Dury, who explored the possibility of getting the leaders of the various denominations round a conference table.[78] A more fruitful outcome was the formation from 1653 onwards of voluntary associations of the parochial clergy in many a county, starting with the one which Baxter himself organized in Worcestershire.

The proposals which Owen and his associates had put to the Rump in February 1652 were themselves a reaction to the threat of the sects to any kind of established ecclesiastical order, though their sponsorship was more specifically Independent than the Baxter–Dury initiative. It so happened that on 1 April, the day on which it extinguished the Commission for the Propagation of the Gospel in Wales, the House approved the third of the Owen

[77] *Reliquiae Baxterianae*, ed. M. Sylvester (1696), Part I, p. 97.
[78] G. F. Nuttall, 'Presbyterians and Independents: some movements for unity 300 years ago', *Journal of the Presbyterian Historical Society of England*, x (1952), 4–15; Tai Liu, *Discord in Zion*, pp. 146–7.

proposals, having already passed the first two. The result would have been, if the Rump had survived to give them legislative effect, to establish a commission of ministers and laymen in each county to approve all candidates for benefices, who would have had to furnish testimonials from six godly Christians, two at least of them ministers.[79] This would not in itself have been objectionable to the more moderate officers, for the Triers established by Cromwell and his council a year later were to have the same function. Besides, Owen's fellow-signatories to the proposals had included not only moderates like himself but also Independents of a more radical hue such as John Goodwin and John Dury, and a number of army officers, not all tame conformists, including John Okey, Edward Whalley, William Goffe, and Francis White.[80] But in the context of other developments in the early months of 1653 the Rump's votes looked to the sectaries like one more move to shackle them.

One such development was a wave of mass petitions from various counties, themselves symptomatic of a defensive reaction by conservative puritans. The first was drafted and promoted by Baxter in Worcestershire in December 1652, and it was followed by others from Hampshire, Wiltshire, Somerset, and Sussex. It prayed the Rump to go on maintaining a godly and learned ministry, protested against the way the sectaries were assailing the very principle of an established clergy, and called for a new assembly of divines to consider ways of healing the present sad divisions in religion. The House returned its hearty thanks to the petitioners. It happened that the broadly similar petition from Wiltshire was presented on 29 March and the Hampshire one on 8 April, each with its great roll of signatures. These too received the House's hearty thanks, just before and just after it gave its dusty answer to the Commission for the Propagation of the Gospel in Wales.[81]

That commission had been the subject of contention for a long time, and this is not the place to stir the murky waters of

---

[79] *CJ*, 4, 17 March, 1 April 1653.

[80] W. A. Shaw, *A History of the English Church during the Civil Wars and under the Commonwealth 1640–1660*, 2 vols. (London, 1900), ii, pp. 82–3. I take it that the T. Harrison who signed them was the City minister of that name and not the major-general; so does Dr Toon in *God's Statesman*, p. 84 n.

[81] *Severall Proceedings*, no. 170, 23–30 Dec. 1652, pp. 2664–70; no. 183, 34–31 March 1653, pp. 2890–3; no. 185, 7–14 April 1653, pp. 2918–21; Worden, *Rump*, pp. 322–5.

controversy that surrounded it. But it was suspect to the more
conservative Rumpers for three main reasons. One was the
dominance that militant Fifth Monarchists like Vavasor Powell
and Morgan Llwyd had won over its organization, and their
strong links through Harrison with the fire-eating saints of the
army. In the second place the commissioners had been accused
of ruthlessly mulcting those who were not of their party and of
misusing the funds that came into their hands. The third main
charge was that they domineered oppressively over those who
differed from them in doctrine and unjustly ejected many honest
ministers.[82] More recently, during March, there were uglier
rumours that Harrison had enlisted four thousand Welshmen
'for his own purposes'; Cromwell was reported to have questioned
him privately about this and to have received an absolute denial
of its truth.[83] The other complaints, at least in so far as they
affected the six counties of South Wales, had been under
investigation by the Rump's Committee for Plundered Ministers
for over a year when Colonel Robert Bennett at length reported
its findings on 25 March. These were basically favourable to the
commissioners and highly critical of their accusers' tactics. After
some debate the House voted to recommit the matter to the same
committee, at the same time enlarging its powers. It also ordered
that the act of 1650 which had first set up the Welsh Propagators
should be read as the first business on 1 April, 'in order to the
reviving thereof, if the House shall see cause'.[84] But on that day
it must simply have declined to proceed with the act, which
thereby lapsed; for there is not a further word about it in the
Commons' Journal or in any of the newspapers.[85]

This was as foolish as it was unjust, for the commissioners seem
to have been in the process of vindicating themselves against
largely captious attacks, and whatever else might have been said
about them they were undoubtedly propagating the gospel.
They included a considerable number of highly reputable as

---

[82] For the charges against the Welsh Propagators see *Mercurius Cambro-Britannicus* ([4
Sept.] 1652); also William Erbery, *The Sword Doubled*, 2nd ed. ([Feb.14] 1653) and *A
Call to the Churches* (19 Feb. 1653). For a full, sympathetic, but not uncritical account of
their activities see Thomas Richards, *History of the Puritan Movement in Wales* (1920).

[83] Newletters, 18 and 25 March 1653, in Clarendon MS 45, fos. 204, 206.

[84] *CJ*, 25 March 1653.

[85] Gardiner, *C & P*, ii, 196–7; Richards, *Puritan Movement in Wales*, pp. 270–1; Worden,
Rump, p. 328.

well as zealous men; thirteen of them were to sit in Barebone's Parliament, besides Harrison, and by no means all of these would side with its radical faction. Under their encouragement Wales had benefited from the inspiring piety and tireless evangelism of Walter Cradock and other true pastors, as well as the more lurid ministrations of Powell and Llwyd. Tactically the jettisoning of them at this point was stupid, because it immediately brought Cromwell and Harrison closer together, whereas if the Rump had had any sense it would have been playing on the differences between them. Cromwell said afterwards to Barebone's Parliament that this business 'was as plain a trial of their spirits as anything—it being known to many of us that God did kindle a seed there hardly to be paralleled since the primitive times'.[86] It may even have been decisive in swinging Harrison over to the militant wing of the Fifth Monarchy movement which wanted to jettison parliaments as well as princes, for it is far from certain that that was his aim at the start of 1653.[87] The folly, however, was certainly not all on one side, for if Cromwell and Harrison did not want to see their favourite measures defeated it was their business to attend the House and speak for them.

The final stage of the army's quarrel with the Rump filled the first three weeks of April, and it is not without its puzzles. One is whether the officers presented a further petition or remonstrance to the House. Bordeaux is quite positive that they did, on or about 7 April, and that besides reiterating their desires for a new representative ('leurs mesmes propositions') it set forth the qualities or qualifications which they considered that its members should have.[88] There is some support for this from the first, somewhat incoherent, account of the crisis which appeared in *Severall Proceedings* the day after the dissolution. This said that the officers had taken pains to 'propose the particulars' of what the parliament should do for the common good, and after vainly doing all they could through personal contacts they had 'sent a letter'—shortly, it appears from the context, before the final series of meetings between officers and MPs in mid-April.[89] Yet

[86] Abbott, iii, 57. For a most perceptive appraisal of Cradock, Powell, and Llwyd see G. F. Nuttall, *The Welsh Saints, 1640–1660* (Cardiff, 1957).

[87] Gardiner, *C & P*, ii 181; Richards, *Puritan Movement in Wales*, p. 184.

[88] Bordeaux to Brienne, 21 Apr./1 May 1653, PRO 31.3/90, fo. 653; Gardiner accepted his evidence: *C & P*, ii, 198–9.

[89] *Severall Proceedings*, no. 186, 14–21 Apr. 1653, p. 2944.

on 8 April a newswriter to the exiled court wrote, 'We heare no talke now of our new Representative, the heate of the souldiers being somewhat abated by the Generall's sticking close to the House, and sending some of the maddest of them into Scotland.'[90] He was almost certainly mistaken. Another newsletter on the same day reported that, 'Our Parliament ... are resolved to wave for the present a new Representative; but there is a zealous party in the Army (and it's thought instigated by some of the Parliament) that resolve, and in my hearing preached it openly, to have a new Representative, nay, and threaten it within a few weekes.'[91] These threatening preachings were probably uttered at Blackfriars, and the reports that the new representative was in abeyance probably arose from the fact that 6 April was the one Wednesday in eight weeks that the House did not spend in grand committee upon the bill. Whether the House suspended the debate because it knew that the officers were about to present a new petition, or whether the officers submitted a petition or letter because they thought the House was going to shelve the bill again, can only be guessed at. But Whitelocke, conversing with Cromwell on the 6th, found him 'still in distast with the Parliament, and hastening their dissolution';[92] and when the weekly debate was resumed on the 13th, it concentrated on the qualifications of future members, about which the petition was (according to Bordeaux) especially concerned.

A day or two later Cromwell took his seat in the House for the first time in about a month.[93] After a long period of rumination, and of restraining his subordinates from a deed of violence whose consequences they had insufficiently considered, he had decided how to act. One newswriter reported on 25 April that the army was hotter than ever for pulling the parliament down and had 'drawne the General to them'. On the 19th a letter to the army headquarters in Scotland, probably written by Gilbert Mabbott, announced that Cromwell and the Council of Officers had met that day 'and partly concluded of dissolving this government, and also of constituting another (by consent of parliament if

[90] Firth, 'Cromwell and the expulsion', p. 529.
[91] Ibid.
[92] Whitelocke, *Memorials*, p. 528; *CJ*, 13 Apr. 1653.
[93] On Friday, 15 April, according to the Clarke newsletter in *EHR*, viii, 524, but 14 April according to Clarendon MS 45, fo. 293.

possible) till another representative shall bee chosen'.[94] This is the first intimation in a contemporary source of a proposal from him for an interim government to take over the reins between the dissolution of the Rump and the election of a parliament to succeed it. That same evening he opened up his scheme to a meeting of officers and MPs which he had summoned for the purpose to his lodgings at Whitehall, the last of the ten or twelve such conferences that he had arranged since October. It was probably the first time he had broached it outside the Council of Officers. About twenty Rumpers came to hear him, and the debate went on far into the night. What he proposed was that the Rump should dissolve itself very shortly and commission a select body of about forty men, chosen both from its own number and from the army officers, to exercise the supreme authority over the Commonwealth until it was judged to be in a fit state to elect a new representative.[95]

His reasons for making this proposal, and the functions that he expected these forty godly trustees to perform, will be considered in the next chapter. What is striking is not only that he appears to have carried his fellow-officers with him without overt dissension, but also that many even of the Rumpers present agreed that no good could come of the House as it was then constituted and that it would be better for it to dissolve on the terms he proposed.[96] Whitelocke, who was there, is witness to this, and though he and Widdrington, his fellow commissioner for the great seal, opposed the scheme, he stated that St. John supported it. After the Restoration, however, St. John himself declared that he had 'endeavoured the bringing in of a free parliament' and that Cromwell and the army had frustrated it.[97] Yet despite a few dissentient voices, Cromwell and his army

[94] Firth, 'Cromwell and the expulsion', pp. 528–9.

[95] Whitelocke, *Memorials*, p. 529, and manuscript annals in BL, Add. MS 37,354, fo. 270; Ludlow, i, 350; Gardiner, *Documents*, p. 402; Abbott, iii, 59. Whitelocke is the only authority for the figure of forty, but he was present at the meetings on both 19 and 20 April and he gives it both in the published *Memorials* and in the MS original on which they are based. He seems an altogether better source than John Streater's recollections six years later in *Secret Reasons of State* ([23 May] 1659), p. 3, where he reports Cromwell as talking of handing over to 'five or six men, or a few more'. James Heath's account in *Flagellum* (1663) clearly derives from Streater.

[96] Gardiner, *C & P*, ii, 203 n.2.

[97] *The Case of Oliver St. John*, p. 7, quoted in Worden, 'Bill for a new representative', p. 489.

colleagues believed that they parted that evening with a firm undertaking by some of the most influential members to persuade the House to put off the next day's debate on the bill so that they and the officers could have a further meeting on the new proposals in the afternoon or evening.[98] But there is some discrepancy here. In the printed declaration of 22 April, Cromwell asserted that the members present had given their general consent to this, whereas in his speech on 4 July he claimed only that 'two or three of the chief ones, the very chiefest of them' promised to try to suspend further proceedings upon the bill until they had had a further conference, and that most of those present had undertaken only to sleep on his proposals and consult their friends.[99]

Nevertheless he seems to have been strangely confident that these few members would succeed in persuading the House to give up its appointed business the next morning, which, since it was a Wednesday, was to proceed with the bill in grand committee. He himself correctly reckoned that the attendance at that time scarcely ever exceeded fifty-three, but in fact that final day's debate, according to Ludlow, drew in between eighty and a hundred.[1] He evidently had no thought of attending it himself. Instead he put on plain black clothes and homely worsted stockings, and held an informal early morning meeting with a small gathering of members and officers at his lodgings. There he resumed with them the discussion of the interim nominated government which he had outlined the evening before, 'considering how to order that which we had farther to offer them in the evening' when the fuller conference of the evening before was to

----

[98] *Severall Proceedings*, no. 186, p. 2944; Gardiner, *Documents*, pp. 402–3.

[99] Gardiner, *Documents*, pp. 402–3; *The Lord General Cromwel's Speech* (1654), p. 16. I quote the earliest printed version, because Abbott, without any authority that I know, changes 'the very chiefest' to 'and very chiefest'. Another early text of the speech in J. Nickolls (ed.). *Original Letters and Papers of State . . . Found Among the Political Collection of . . . John Milton* (London, 1743), p. 110, has 'two or three of the chief of them, one of the chief, and two or three more did tell us . . .' The version in Bodl. Lib., MS Tanner 52, has 'one of the cheifest of them promised us . . .' (fo. 21ᵛ). On the sources for this speech see Appendix A. Carlyle shrewdly assumed Cromwell to be singling out Vane.

[1] 'I think there was scarce any day, that there sat above 50 or 52 or 53': *The Lord General Cromwel's Speech*, p. 16; Ludlow, i, 354. The text in the pamphlet makes clear, as Abbott's version does not, that Cromwell was referring to normal attendances and not to the number present on 20 April.

reassemble.[2] It came as a complete surprise to him to hear that the House was not only going ahead with the bill but was also intent on passing it through all its remaining stages that very morning. Indeed he did not credit it at first, but when a second messenger and then a third confirmed it—indeed warned him that the bill was very near the point of passing—he broke up the meeting and made for the House with all speed. What he did there has often been recounted, and the details of that scene need not concern us here.[3] It is just worth remarking how much it rankled with him that the members whom he had thought 'honest' had made no attempt to get the proceedings on the bill suspended, and perhaps the reason why he singled Vane out for such bitter reproaches was that Vane was that 'very chiefest of them' on whose pledges he had counted.[4]

If it was odd of Cromwell, even rather grossly egotistic, to be so confident that the House would meet his wishes without his so much as going there to explain them in person, he had rather more reason to be surprised at the 'preposterous haste' with which it now pressed on with the bill. This was in sharp contrast with the sluggish pace and thin attendances that had marked its progress so far. Yet one can understand why the majority of members were persuaded to try and rush it through that morning. They well understood the threat implicit in the intensified meetings of the Council of Officers, and the crescendo of denuciations from the pulpits at Blackfriars and Allhallows appalled them. They probably interpreted Cromwell's proposal on 19 April as even more of an ultimatum that he intended it to be, especially if it is true that he had just summoned all the cavalry within reach to a rendezvous near London.[5] They would see it as at worst a cloak for military dictatorship and at best a device for taking the control over the elections to the next parliament out of their hands. But the army officers had their own grounds for fear, which will be explored in the next chapter. The crisis was one of mutual suspicion, not unlike the later ones that led to the breaking of Richard Cromwell's parliament in

[2] Abbott, iii, 60; Whitelocke, *Memorials*, p. 529.

[3] For the fullest accounts see C. H. Firth, 'The expulsion of the Long Parliament', *History*, N.S., ii (1917–18), 129–43, 193–206; Abbott, ii, 637–46; Worden, *Rump*, pp. 335–9.

[4] Gardiner, *Documents*, p. 403; Abbott, iii, 59–60.

[5] Newsletter, 19 Apr. 1653, Clarke MSS XXV, fo. 10.

April 1659 and to the second interruption of the Rump in the following October.

It is likely that the same man played a key role in all three crises. Sir Arthur Hesilrige had already become Cromwell's chief opponent in the Rump, over a number of issues.[6] It was Hesilrige who would lead the onslaught on the Instrument of Government in the first parliament of the Protectorate, and on the Humble Petition and Advice in the second and third parliaments; Hesilrige who would employ every tactic to make Richard Cromwell's parliament unmanageable, while covertly fomenting disaffection in the army; Hesilrige who would lead the Rump in picking new quarrels with the army almost as soon as it was restored in May 1659; Hesilrige who would urge it to send Lambert to the Tower in September, and press its suicidal votes in October; Hesilrige who in February 1660 would lead the defiance of Monck which spelt its final doom. The apparent fact that at some point early in 1653 he quietly took over the management of the committee entrusted with the bill for a new representative, and reported its proposed amendments on 23 February, is almost enough to create a presumption that the bill, thus amended, contained matter that the army could not stomach or omitted provisions that it considered essential.

During March and April Hesilrige was in the habit of commuting between the country and London in order to be present for the weekly debates on the bill, and for not much else. He was seventy miles away when he got wind of Cromwell's proposals for a temporary nominated government. By his own account years later, he rode up in time to appear at the meeting of officers and members on the evening of 19 April, and to tell them that 'the work they went about was accursed'.[7] He would probably have been travelling up for the debate on the 20th anyway, and if Ludlow is right that the attendance that day was almost double what it had been three and four weeks ago, it sounds as though the army's opponents were being rallied. Did

---

[6] I believe that Ludlow, where he describes the efforts to 'countermine' Cromwell 'by those who had the direction and management of the war with Holland' (i, 347), was referring primarily to Hesilrige and his ally Scot; see H. R. Trevor-Roper, *Religion, the Reformation and Social Change* (London, 1967), pp. 358–60, but cf. Worden, *Rump*, p. 301.

[7] Worden, *Rump*, p. 338. The only meetings of the Council of State during April which Hesilrige attended were those on the 13th, 14th, 15th, and 20th (*CPSD 1653*, p. xxxii; Ludlow, i, 357).

Hesilrige or anyone else cause some new twist to be given to the bill—some substantial fresh amendment—in this final session? It is not necessary to assume so, for never since it had emerged from committee had the army acknowedged the bill as an acceptable answer to its repeated calls for a new parliament. The crucial question is why Cromwell thought it so vital to prevent it from passing.

III

The Bill

It is much easier to tell the story of Cromwell's breaking of the Rump than to explain it. It used to be simple when the House was assumed to have been rushing through a bill to keep its present members in their seats indefinitely, but the now irrefragable evidence that it was on the point of legislating for its own dissolution makes it necessary to look afresh for reasons why he felt such a desperate urgency to stop the bill from passing.

At least four possible lines of explanation need to be explored. One is that there was a design afoot, or that the army thought there was, to remove him from the generalship, weed out the other senior commanders whose political and religious attitudes offended the House, and perhaps exclude all serving officers from future parliaments. Another possible explanation is that he dissolved the Rump in order to counter a dangerous threat to his leadership from Harrison and re-establish himself as the hero of the radicals. A third is that he had come under the powerful influence of Harrison and the millenarians, and that they had genuinely convinced him that the cause of the people of God required not an elected representative but a nominated assembly of saints; in other words that he destroyed the Rump and its bill because he no longer wanted a new parliament at all. But a fourth possibility is that what finally pushed him into expelling the House was some defect in the bill itself, even though it did not provide for a mere recruitment in lieu of a new parliament, and even though he had not turned against parliaments in principle. Only the last two of these possible explanations need be mutually exclusive.

It is easiest to start with the stray signs and rumours that the

Rump planned to relieve Cromwell of the generalship and to reconstruct the command of the army. The evidence is rather slight and inconclusive, but one could hardly expect it to be otherwise. Politicians who aim to depose a powerful and popular general are not apt to write about it in advance, or to talk about it afterwards if their plans come unstuck. Bordeaux heard of such a plan among some of the members in mid-December 1652,[1] but he did not mention it again. A newswriter employed by Sir Edward Nicholas reported on 18 March that parliament had sent 'under hand' for Fairfax and Lambert; some believed, he wrote cautiously, that it would restore Fairfax to generalship if it could, since he could be relied on to obey orders, instead of giving them as Cromwell did. A week later he transmitted some gossip that Fairfax had called on Cromwell, and Cromwell had refused to see him.[2] Rather less tenuous is a circumstantial story from the Venetian resident Paulucci of high words in the House a few days before the dissolution, in the course of which one of the leading members told Cromwell to his face that rather than have a change of parliament there was no time like the present for a change of general.[3]

Taken by themselves such reports would not bear much weight, but there is also some interesting testimony from the republican side. That uncompromising commonwealthsman Major John Streater, who was engineer and quartermaster-general of the foot in Ireland, came over to England on leave in March or early April and watched the events leading to the dissolution from close quarters, with growing dismay. His account dates from six years later, but his contacts with both camps, the army's at the time and the republicans' subsequently, lend it some interest. He was assured that the House was on the point of providing for its own dissolution and for future successive parliaments when it was turned out. Cromwell, in his view, foresaw that he would 'be reduced to a private capacity . . . for

[1] See p. 47.

[2] Clarendon MS 45, fos. 204–5. The contacts with Fairfax may have been in fact over the defence and government of the Isle of Man, about which the Council of State had corresponded with him in Jan. and Feb. On 13 Apr. Hesilrige and Brereton were sent from the Council to confer with him about it in person (*CSPD 1652–3*, pp. 82, 126, 141, 167, 276). This could conceivably have been a cloak for more secret proposals, but if so Fairfax is most unlikely to have been interested.

[3] Paulucci's dispatch of 17/27 April, quoted extensively in Gardiner, *C & P*, ii, 202, n.1, is virtually identical with that of 19/29 April in *CSP Ven 1653–4*, p. 60.

it were not to be imagined, that they would dissolve, and leave the sole command of the arms of the Common-wealth in his hands: this J.S did apprehend was the principall reason why he interrupted their sitting'.[4] Ludlow too attributed Cromwell's action largely to his apprehension 'of the consequences of suffering the army to be new-moulded, and put under another conduct'.[5] Ludlow and Streater are hostile witnesses and neither sat in the Rump at the time, but a general 'new-moulding' of the army's command must have seemed highly probable and it is significant that they so readily admitted it.

Both assumed with hindsight that Cromwell already had his sights set on the supreme power, but the charge breaks down at several points. The weight of the contemporary evidence is that the pressure to dissolve the Rump came spontaneously from his officers, and that until the last moment he worked hard to curb it. It does not appear, moreover, that they were planning to make him head of state, and some of them, especially Harrison and his faction, would have opposed any such idea. Furthermore when he did have some sort of dictatorship in his grasp, after the dissolution, he showed a strong and genuine aversion to it. But if there were rumours abroad of a remodelling of the army's leadership, as there evidently were, they probably disturbed his senior subordinates at least as much as himself, for the commands of all the military grandees would be in danger, Harrison's perhaps most of all.

How much substance may these rumours have had? The hot words reported by Paulucci could easily have been spoken, but it is unlikely that the Rump as a body would have tried to remove Cromwell so soon after putting him top of the poll in the council elections. Yet this could well have been the long-term aim of Hesilrige's faction, and they may have been planning some immediate measure to get rid of the officers whom they most distrusted and to keep the army out of politics, especially during the coming elections and the change-over of parliaments.

[4] John Streater, *Secret Reasons of State* ([23 May] 1659), pp. 3–4. He himself dates his arrival in England at about the beginning of April (p. 2), but I suspect that he was already in London when his *Glympse of That Jewel . . . Libertie* ([31 March] 1653) went through the press. For information about Streater and his contacts I an indebted to conversations with Dr Barbara Taft and to her as yet unpublished work on the English republicans.

[5] Ludlow, i, 347.

One recalls how suicidally they were to react to military pressure during their second incarnation, cashiering nine senior officers at a stroke in October 1659 and twice putting the army's command into commission. If they nursed any such intentions in 1653 they were playing with fire, but if they once got their bill for a new representative through, any resistance by the army would have appeared in a very bad light. It would have been seen as blatant self-interest, and an attempt to frustrate the long-desired general elections; furthermore it would have made the army's prospects of erecting an acceptable alternative government pretty bleak.

If there was any such plan, one can understand why both parties kept quiet about it afterwards. Cromwell and the officers, besides having in all probability no hard evidence to publish, would never have opened themselves to the damaging charge that they broke a parliament to keep their places; they found it embarrassing enough as it was to explain why they had thought it so urgent to prevent the bill from passing. As for the Rumpers, once expelled their best prospects of a come-back lay in winning back the army's support, as they tried to do at intervals under the Protectorate and as they finally succeeded in doing in 1659. But since the evidence is so thin, one cannot weigh how much such fears as these contributed to end the Rump; all that can be said is that since the officers quite evidently believed all along that the bill for a new representative as it was debated between February and April was not an honest bill, they must have been sensitive to the rumours that were current of a design against their leadership.

The next possibility to consider is that Cromwell switched from defending the Rump to destroying it because the pressure from his radical subordinates became too much for him, and he could see no other way of revivifying his own leadership and the army's unity in face of a dangerous challenge from Harrison. Did he even fear that if he did not break the Rump Harrison would, with consequences for the future of the Commonwealth and the army that did not bear contemplating? This really seems improbable, for it requires us to construe what he did on 20 April as a premeditated act, instead of the impromptu one that it seemed and that he claimed it to be. He so evidently went to bed on the 19th trusting that he would *not* have to end the session violently, and next morning it took three warnings of increasing urgency to bring him to the House at all. Moreover if the dissolution was a calculated move one would expect him to have had some plans laid for the next one ahead, and he had none.

But both the hypothesis that he acted to forestall Harrison out of fear of his strength, and the alternative one that he frustrated the bill for a new parliament because he had been genuinely converted to the Fifth Monarchist ideal of a rule of the saints, call for a closer look at the divisions within the army and at Cromwell's relations with his fellow-commanders. Here again most of our sources of information—the guesses and gossip of newswriters and diplomats, pieced out with the recollections of memorialists with axes to grind—are treacherous guides, casting an uncertain light on a few quicksands amidst ill-charted currents. But there is tolerably firm ground in Ludlow's well-known analysis, which he attibutes to Cromwell himself, and which describes two main parties in the army, led respectively by Lambert and Harrison. Both were strongly hostile to the Rump, though their motives and their goals were very different.[6] Historians have tended to picture Cromwell as partly estranged from Lambert during March and April, and strongly drawn towards Harrison. Both suppositions may be doubted.

Lambert's animosity towards the Rump probably rested on broader foundations than his personal disappointment over the lord deputyship of Ireland, which the House had offered him and then snatched away. He typified the perennial distrust which brisk young generals feel towards temporizing politicians. Being very able himself, he could not see what special right to seemingly interminable power could be claimed by the generally mediocre oligarchy which certain twists of fate and the army's suffrance had left sitting at Westminster, and he was ready to believe the worst of its motives. He would regard the leading Rumpers differently when, having lost his commission, he temporarily allied with them in 1659, but what he was to say in retrospect then is not good evidence of how he stood towards Cromwell in

---

[6] Ludlow, i, 346, 358. Dr Worden has demonstrated that Ludlow's text was heavily tampered with by his 1698 editor (probably Toland); see his masterly introduction to Ludlow's *A Voyce from the Watch Tower*, Camden 4th ser., xxi (1978). Here, however, Ludlow's account is vivid, circumstantial, and in all probability authentic, even though he was in Ireland in 1653 and derived it from Harrison and others. Toland could hardly have invented it.

1653. There is a well-known story that about a month before the dissolution Cromwell refused to see him and referred to him as 'bottomless Lambert'. It comes from a lively newswriter to the exiled court, who linked it with a report that the Rump had sent for Lambert at the same time as it summoned Fairfax.[7] This gossip of a passing coolness between the two men is not altogether implausible. Probably it was the Council of State that sent for Lambert, if anyone did, because it was planning to make him commander-in-chief in Scotland. It discussed this on 30 March, and again on 7 April, when Cromwell attended at its special request for only the second time in nearly a month. On the 14th it instructed him to commission Lambert to command the forces in Scotland for six months.[8] One can imagine Cromwell reacting at first with strong suspicion, especially if the Council made its first approaches to Lambert without his knowledge. He would scent a stratagem to drive a wedge between his popular subordinate and himself, and to propitiate the former for his setback over the lord deputyship. But if he wanted to know the Council's intentions he should have attended its meetings, and no doubt all was explained when finally he did. In any case the command did not appeal to Lambert; the talk in the army was that he would resign his commission sooner than accept it.[9] If the episode did arouse ill-feeling between the two men, it was no more than a passing cloud, and it probably left them more firmly linked than before. Lucy Hutchinson depicts the pair of them as close allies, who 'finding themselves not strong enough alone ... took to them Major-General Harrison, who had a great interest both in the army and the churches'.[10] Years later, when Cromwell was safely dead and buried, Lambert professed to believe that his chief had hypocritically enlisted him in a premeditated design to break the parliament.[11] But this merely confirms that the two men had been close at the time, for what

[7] Newsletters, 18/28 March and 25 March/4 April 1653, Clarendon MS 45, fos. 204–6. According to a newsletter of 22 Feb. in Clarke MS XXIV, fo. 119, the Council had already sent for Lambert by that date.

[8] *CPSD 1652–3*, pp. 242, 260, 279.

[9] Clarke MS XXV, fo. 9. The slightly ambiguous wording is 'Major-generall [name omitted?] itt's conceived will not accept the command, and then itt's thought hee must lay downe, and M. G. Disbrow come downe.' Lambert is obviously referred to.

[10] Lucy Hutchinson, *Memoirs of the Life of Colonel Hutchinson*, ed. J. Hutchinson and C. H. Firth (1906), p. 292.

[11] Thurloe, vii, 660.

else had Lambert to explain? Certainly, when on that momentous 20 April Cromwell moved on from clearing the Parliament-House to dismiss the Council of State, it was Lambert and Harrison whom he took with him,[12] and when nine days later a provisional new Council of State was set up, Lambert was made its president.

Cromwell's relations with Harrison are not altogether easy to interpret, for whereas most contemporary reports suggest that they headed factions in the army that were to some extent opposed, Cromwell's eventual conversion to the idea of a nominated assembly has been seen—and was seen by some at the time—as a triumph for Harrison's millenarian ideals. It is important to keep hindsight in check here. We have noted how during January 'some of the highest in the army' looked coldly upon the inflammatory preachings at Allhallows, with which Harrison was closely associated; how the Council of Officers refused to accept a paper of advice from a group of the gathered churches, and how by the end of March 'the preaching party', evidently within the army as well as outside it, were saying that they would need a new general as well as a new parliament.[13] The royalist agent Daniel O'Neill wrote an analysis of the situation in March which was wrong in many things but probably right in stating that the most obvious rift within the army was between Harrison's supporters and Cromwell's, while the credulous Paulucci believed shortly before the dissolution that Harrison was striving to oust Cromwell from the general-ship.[14] Ludlow and Lucy Hutchinson agree that Cromwell had to woo Harrison and his party in order to gain their support.[15] That may be their jaundiced way—or Harrison's own, since he may be the ultimate source of Ludlow's information, if not Mrs Hutchinson's—of interpreting Cromwell's championship of the Commission for the Propagation of the Gospel in Wales, which must have brought the two closer together, though Cromwell had not been prepared to break his boycott of the House to go and speak for the commission when its fate was decided. And differences did remain, notably over the Dutch war, which

---

[12] Ludlow, i, 357.

[13] See pp. 49, 57; cf. Capp, *Fifth Monarchy Men*, pp. 60–2.

[14] Firth, 'Cromwell and the expulsion', p. 529; *CSP Ven 1653–4*, p. 60.

[15] Ludlow, i, 345; Lucy Hutchinson, *Memoirs*, p. 292.

Cromwell was striving to end, whereas Harrison was convinced that the Dutch were the Lord's enemies, and that it ought not to be the saints' work to seek peace with them.[16] Nor did the dissolution itself wholly resolve them, if we can credit a newswriter's report on 6 May that Harrison had recently written to an intimate friend that the Lord had at last made Cromwell instrumental in putting power into the saints' hands, contrary to his intentions, but 'that it was the Lord's worke and no thankes to his Excellency'.[17] Even on 7 May an observer in London could write that Harrison and the army sectaries were 'irreconcileably bent against Cromwell', who was nevertheless courting them assiduously.[18]

On the other hand Hyde's impression from his various intelligencers, which he transmitted to the Earl of Rochester on 6 May, was that 'all the seeming divisions in the army between Cromwell and Harrison appeared to be merely counterfeits, and there is I thinke little doubt to be made that the Army is intirely at Cromwell's disposall'.[19] So it was, in the sense that his military authority was unshaken; but the army's political decisions had to be carried in the Council of Officers, and there the divisions were not 'merely counterfeits'. They were probably not as deep as hostile newswriters reported, and even if they had been the members of the Council of Officers who were at all likely to support Harrison against Cromwell, judging by the few lists of names that have survived,[20] must have been a smallish minority. There is indeed really little to support a hypothesis that Cromwell, after holding back his officers for as long as he could, finally turned against the Rump in order to steal Harrison's thunder and save his own leadership from a serious threat.

Nevertheless the differences of opinion between the two men, and their reservations about each other's judgement, are so well attested both before and after 20 April that it seems highly questionable to attribute Cromwell's action that day to 'his

[16] Harrison to John Jones, 8 March and 30 Apr. 1653, in Mayer, 'Inedited letters', pp. 200, 226. Mayer misdates the first of these letters 8 Jan. 1652, through misinterpreting Harrison's '8th daie 1st m. 52'.
[17] Firth, 'Cromwell and the expulsion', p. 529; Capp, *Fifth Monarchy Men*, pp. 65–6.
[18] Langley to Leveson, 7 May 1653, in D. A. Johnson and D. G. Vaisey (eds.), *Staffordshire and the Great Rebellion* (Stafford, 1964), p. 73.
[19] Hyde to Rochester, 6/16 May 1652, printed by Firth, 'The expulsion of the Long Parliament', p. 134.
[20] See pp. 111–2.

infection by millenarian élitism' and to present it as 'the triumph of Harrison and the prophets of the imminent millennium'.[21] The thesis that Cromwell underwent a dramatic conversion to their views shortly before the dissolution has generally rested on some or all of four suppositions: that his proposal of an interim nominated government on 19 April signified that he had turned against elected parliaments in principle; that Barebone's Parliament as he conceived it approximated closely to the Fifth Monarchist ideal of a rule of the saints; that it was chosen mainly from lists of candidates which the Council of Officers solicited from the gathered churches; and that Cromwell's opening address to it proclaimed him a convert to Fifth Monarchist principles. But the first three of these suppositions are largely erroneous, and it will be argued later that the millenarium expectations which he expressed on 4 July were of a kind shared by many besides the Fifth Monarchists.

Furthermore it is not clear how far Harrison himself was committed _before_ the dissolution to substituting a hand-picked assembly of saints for an elected parliament. He was evidently pondering some such goal when he posed the question in a letter to Colonel John Jones on 8 March, 'Whether is most the Saints worke, to run after Christ to Sea [i.e. prosecute the Dutch war] whereon hee hath begun to sett his right foote, or to [cause?] men fearing the Lord to bee putt into all places of power att home.'[22] There is also the rather dubious story in Heath's _Flagellum_ that Harrison told Streater, shortly before the dissolution, that 'the Lord General sought not himself, but that King Jesus might take the sceptre'.[23] But Harrison seems still to have had his doubts on 20 April, when he warned Cromwell, as the latter rose to dissolve the Rump, 'Sir, the work is very great and dangerous, therefore I desire you seriously to consider of it before you engage in it.'[24] If he had contended for a nominated assembly before the dissolution, one would have expected some word of it to come

[21] Worden, _Rump_, pp. 361, 374; cf. pp. 357–8, 380. I do not of course attribute to Dr Worden all the suppositions mentioned in my next sentence.

[22] Mayer, 'Inedited letters', p. 200.

[23] Quoted in Firth, 'The expulsion of the Long Parliament', pp. 197–8. Although words quoted as second hand so long after the event must be received cautiously the story is worth preserving for Streater's alleged reply 'that Christ must come before Christmas, or else He would come too late'.

[24] Ludlow, i, 352. Harrison himself told Ludlow of the remark.

through in contemporary reports of the Council of Officers' deliberations, whereas all the accounts (including the officers' own) agree that they pressed continually and consistently for a new representative and successive parliaments until Cromwell mooted his alternative scheme just after the middle of April. For further evidence that the saints had no settled scheme yet to oppose to elected parliaments, there is the fact that after dissolution they offered very diverse proposals as to how a new government should be constituted.[25] They were to move towards agreement only gradually, as they came to terms with a situation which they had never very clearly envisaged.

This is not to deny that there was a strong religious impulse behind the army's quarrel with the Rump, or that Cromwell and many other officers nursed ardent millenarian hopes. They believed that their victories were testimonies of a great purpose which God had in store for his people in England, even the beginning of the fulfilment of the Scriptures' promises concerning the last times. They thought that the parliament was wantonly throwing away the opportunities opened by this tremendous dispensation. Instead of attending to the works of reformation which they had urged upon it in their petition of last August, so they declared on 22 April 1653, they had found 'more and more ... an aversion to things themselves, with much bitterness and opposition to the people of God, and His spirit acting in them'. They therefore concluded 'that this parliament, through the corruption of some, the jealousy of others, the non-attendance and negligence of many, would never answer those ends which God, His people, and the whole nation expected from them'.[26]

But granting all sincerity to these opinions, they do not explain why Cromwell drove the Rump out at the very moment when it was passing a bill for a new parliament to succeed it in six months' time. Had he suddenly turned against elected parliaments? There is not a word in this declaration to suggest more than that general elections would not be safe 'for a time'. Indeed it states that the interim nominated government which Cromwell had proposed was to rule only until the people came to 'understand their true interest in the election of successive

---

[25] Capp, *Fifth Monarchy Men*, pp. 63–4; below, pp. 112–5.
[26] Gardiner, *Documents*, p. 401. For comparable passages condemning the Rumpers in Cromwell's subsequent speeches, see Abbott, iii, 55–8, 452–4; iv, 485–8.

parliaments', and this tallies with the fervent hope he expressed in his opening speech to Barebone's Parliament that God would fit the people for such a thing soon.[27]

It is surely more plausible to suppose that he cut the proceedings short not because he was fundamentally against a new parliament but because he could not possibly accept the way in which the Rump was providing for one. The reason in other words lay in the bill itself, whether in what it contained, or in what he supposed it to contain, or in something vital that it omitted. As has been demonstrated, the army had never trusted the bill since it had reappeared on 23 February. The official *Severall Proceedings* confirmed this eight days after the dissolution. Maintaining that all through January and February the officers had made the calling of a free parliament their sole desire, it recounted how under their pressure the House at last

set about the bill for a new parliament, and went on with that; but (as clearly appeared) not so much to answer their desires, as to effect their own ends in the thing, by passing several things in that act of dangerous consequence. The officers beholding, that the bill would not answer the thing desired, and being unwilling (if possible, to prevent it) to use any other way then entreaties: they used means to procure several meetings with divers of the House.[28]

It is therefore necessary to consider what those 'things of dangerous consequence' may have been, even though this is bound to involve an uncomfortable amount of conjecture. The bill vanished after Cromwell confiscated it, and his own subsequent accounts of it shifted their ground suspiciously. But none of the Rumpers published any denial of his allegations while he lived, and what they said or wrote subsequently was always suspiciously brief and generalized. It is very evident, as Dr Worden has remarked, that 'both sides had something to hide', and we can best begin by recapitulating what his re-examination of the evidence has put beyond reasonable doubt.[29]

The bill certainly provided for a new parliament to meet on 3 November 1653 and for future parliaments to succeed each other at regular, probably biennial, intervals. But the Rump was to remain the supreme authority in the Commonwealth until the

[27] Gardiner, *Documents*, p. 402; Abbott, iii, 64.
[28] *Severall Proceedings*, no. 187, 21–28 April 1653, p. 2959.
[29] Worden, 'Bill for a new representative', p. 495; *Rump*, ch. 16, *passim*.

day its successors took over, though it would have adjourned for part of the intervening period. It reapportioned the seats in the House and determined the franchise exactly as the Instrument of Government was to do, and as has been shown there is nothing in the meagre record of the debates to account for the army's dissatisfaction with it.[30]

So much is now certain, but it was common ground that the elections to the *next* parliament presented a particular problem and danger. The Commonwealth was still young, unsettled, and at war, the common enemy was only recently defeated and still threatening it from overseas, the divisions among the victors as acute as ever they had been, and most of the traditional leaders of the county communities hostile. We do not know whether the bill made special arrangements for these elections, but its critics suggest that it did. That is one point at which they attacked it, though the charges are suspect because of their inconsistency. Another is the related matter of the qualifications to be required of members, in order to keep disaffected men out—and the more difficult question of who was to enforce those qualifications if the next parliament was to be as sovereign as the present one. These were the main areas of uncertainty, the matters still to be dealt with in mid-April; though the House had embarked on the qualifications on 13 April, and it is plausible to suppose that proposals on the other points had been put forward by Hesilrige on 23 February when he presented the committee's recommended amendments to the bill.

One of the earliest clues to what had provoked the final breach, too early to derive from any of the printed accounts of the dissolution, comes in a dispatch written on 21 April by Bordeaux, who by this time had contacts with several MPs. He reported that the Rump, instead of trying to give any satisfaction to the army officers in respect of their last petition of about 7 April, had taken to courting the favour of the London citizens—an ominous echo of the Presbyterians' abortive counter-revolution in 1647, and an anticipation of the tactics of Hesilrige and his allies early in 1658 and again in February 1659.[31]

---

[30] See p. 55.
[31] See Valerie Pearl, 'London's Counter-Revolution', in *The Interregnum*, ed. G. E. Aylmer (1972), pp. 29–56; C. H. Firth, *The Last Years of the Protectorate*, 2 vols. (London, 1909), ii, 30–4; *Complete Prose Works of John Milton*, vii, 20–1.

According to Bordeaux, the members thought only about the means of continuing their own authority, 'ordonnans une nouvelle convocation avec telles conditions qu'ils pourraient se faire confirmer, et que les Officiers d'armée n'y auroient aucune part'.[32] This conduct, he says, caused the officers to meet on the evening of Monday, 18 April, and to resolve on dissolving the parliament. That sounds plausible, for Cromwell presumably held a meeting of the Council of Officers very shortly before the evening of the 19th in order to get its consent to the proposals that he then put to the conference of officers and members. It was perhaps the same meeting that a Clarke newsletter places earlier in the day on the 19th, at which Cromwell and the officers 'partly concluded of dissolving this government'[33]— meaning presumably that they agreed on a dissolution if Cromwell's proposals were rejected. But the real interest of Bordeaux's dispatch lies in the allegation that the Rump was framing such conditions for the new representative that army officers would have no place in it. No other source says just this, but one would not expect the officers to publicize something that would make it seem they had acted out of self-interest, while the Rumpers became careful about antagonizing the army when they were out of power.

Although we now know that the bill in its final form did not propose to substitute recruiter elections for general ones, it is difficult to escape the conclusion that as late as 20 April Cromwell and the officers believed that it did. The earliest apologia for the dissolution, in the official *Severall Proceedings* for 14–21 April, said so unequivocally.[34] It was clearly a rushed job, for the paper was due out on the day after the event, but though Henry Walker was not the most zealous of editors he would hardly have concocted a whole page in vindication of the army's action without getting some sort of briefing, or at least clearance, from his new masters. More surprisingly Gilbert Mabbott, who as official licenser of military news should have known better, was still writing on the 23rd that 'the bill resolved to be carried on by Parliament was not for dissolving this Parliament but recruiting

---

[32] Bordeaux to Brienne, 21 Apr./1 May 1653, PRO 31. 3/90, fo. 653.

[33] Firth, 'Cromwell and the expulsion', p. 528.

[34] *Severall Proceedings*, no. 186, 14–21 April, p. 2944. On the paper and its editor see Frank, *Beginnings of the English Newspaper*, p. 222.

itt with such as probably would bee disaffected'.[35] Perhaps he was lazy in keeping up to date with his information, for although what he wrote was probably what the officers at first believed, the official declaration framed by Cromwell and the Council of Officers on the 22nd said something significantly different. Its version was that when the Rumpers found themselves forced to take the bill into consideration, 'they resolved to make use of it to recruit the House with persons of the same spirit and temper, thereby to perpetuate their own sitting'.[36] This was ambiguous, no doubt deliberately so, and *The Weekly Intelligencer* glossed the last clause rather interestingly by expanding it to read 'and by these proxyes to perpetuate their own sitting'.[37]

The awkward and obscure wording of the declaration, which retreats from the outright charge of recruitment without totally abandoning it, gives the impression that Cromwell and his fellow-officers were having to cover up a mistake. It is not easy to believe that they first put out a deliberate lie about the bill, only to have to back down from it almost immediately. Yet it is even harder to credit that they simply did not know what the bill's essential provisions were intended to be, all through the debates since 23 February. Even though Cromwell had personally ceased to attend them after the first two or three Wednesdays, there were still more than half a dozen other officers with seats in the House and plenty more friends to tell him how this most vital measure was shaping. But it is still possible that he was mistaken about what was in it *at the moment when the House was about to pass it on 20 April.*

Here there may be a clue to glean from the only document

---

[35] *Clarke Papers*, iii, 1. The Clarke MSS do not show who wrote this letter, but Dr Worden established that it was Mabbott from an almost identical letter which Mabbott wrote on the same day to the corporation of Hull (*Rump*, p. 351). I am greatly indebted to Dr Worden for lending me his photocopies of Mabbott's newsletters to the Hull city fathers. On Mabbott and his appointment see Frank, *Beginnings of the English Newspaper*, *passim*, esp. p. 229.

[36] Gardiner, *Documents*, p. 401. Bordeaux's words 'avec telles conditions qu'ils pourroient se faire confirmer' similarly suggest that the bill was so framed that the Rumpers could make use of its provisions to keep their seats, even though it did not in plain terms ordain a mere recruitment.

[37] *The Weekly Intelligencer*, no. 115, 12–19 Apr. 1653, p. 816. Despite its ostensible dates this issue appeared after the declaration of 22 April, which it reported. Whether it had any authority for the words 'by these proxyes' is unknown; it was not an official newspaper, though its editor Richard Collings generally played very safe with domestic news: Frank, *Beginnings of the English Newspaper*, pp. 219, 238.

which positively denies that the bill included any provision for recruitment. This is the important paper, purporting to be a letter to Cromwell, which Professor C. M. Williams discovered among the papers of Henry Marten in the Brotherton Library in Leeds.[38] Tempting though it is to attribute it to Marten, its author claims to have received a writ of summons to Barebone's Parliament, and it strains credulity to imagine Cromwell issuing one to a man whom he had publicly denounced as a whoremaster when he expelled the Rump.[39] Nor was it like Marten, one of the bitterest opponents of the Presbyterian politicians and most committed of regicides, to lament that Pride's Purge had deprived the Commonwealth of the counsels of 'many wise and honourable patriots'.[40] Yet Marten may have written it. He was possibly assuming a character—that of a sort of generalized Rumper—calculated to throw the government off the scent of his identity and to appeal to the widest possible range of anti-Cromwellians; for this piece looks much less like a personal address to Cromwell than one of those open letters which were a popular genre among pamphleteers. If this is the case, its credibility is a little tarnished, especially since, so far as is known, it was not published. Did Marten (or whoever wrote it) get cold feet, or did his political associates persuade him that his disclosures were unwise—that they would open up questions better left sleeping? We cannot know; and making all due reservations we still have to take very seriously a document, ostensibly written by a member, which unequivocally denies that the Rump 'ment to recreut and so perpetuate themselves'. Moreover it has this to say to Cromwell: 'Whereas if you please to view the Bill you took from the Clerke (if it bee not burnt) you will be convinced of the contrary, if you are not so already by having bene present at the debate of dissolving upon the 3rd of November next at the very instant of putting which question you did interrupt the Parliament.'[41]

There is a strong hint here that Cromwell had some cause to be surprised at what he found in the bill when he read it, unless he had already been enlightened by what he heard in the House on 20 April. Now since it is scarcely credible that he did not

[38] C. M. Williams, 'The political career of Henry Marten' (Oxford D. Phil. thesis, 1954), Appendix C, no. 3.
[39] Whitelocke, *Memorials*, p. 529.
[40] Williams, 'Political career of Henry Marten', pp. 540–1.
[41] Ibid. 549; printed with the preceding passage in Worden, *Rump*, p. 365.

know what it had been about for the past eight weeks, the question is whether some important change was introduced on the 20th, for there had been no formal debate on it since the 13th. Can there have been a last-minute attempt to substitute recruiter elections for general ones, which brought him rushing to the House? It is scarcely conceivable, after the House had spent several Wednesdays in grand committee arranging a radical reapportionment of seats. And if such a reversal *was* proposed, it must have been rejected before Cromwell rose to end the sitting, for the bill which he took away did not provide for recruiter elections. His own subsequent abandonment of the charge is even more eloquent testimony of this than the 'Marten' letter's denial.

But we are probably on the wrong trail if we look for surprise clauses which may have been brought *into* the bill at the last moment. It is altogether more plausible to consider what may have been dropped *from* the bill in order to hustle it through in one day on the 20th. There is little doubt that most of the Rumpers would have opted for recruitment rather than general elections if they could have got away with it. It is a fact that virtually all the newswriters, foreign diplomats, and other observers whose letters have survived believed at the time of the dissolution that the bill would have kept the Rumpers in their seats; indeed Cromwell seems to have believed it too. Is it not possible that there had been some such provision in the proposed amendments which Hesilrige reported on 23 February? This is not to suggest that he put forward a straight substitution of recruiter for general elections, for that would have been inconsistent with the bill's radical redistribution of constituencies.[42] But he may still have proposed that, in order to mitigate the special hazards of the next elections, a select number of the more active and trusted of the present members should continue to sit in the forthcoming new representative, whether as supernumeraries or by transferring them where necessary to county seats, of which the number was greatly increased. This would have given it a backbone of committed commonwealthsmen who would have the strongest reasons for opposing any

---

[42] This really disposes of Firth's suggestion in 'The expulsion of the Long Parliament', p. 142, that the Rumpers could have retained their own seats without any express clause in the bill, simply by suspending the issues of writs for their constituencies.

threat to the fundamental acts on which the republic was established. It could still be called a new parliament, for elections would still be held in every constituency. If this was an intended ingredient of the bill from February onwards, Cromwell would have thought that it was still part of it when he was called to the House in a hurry on the 20th. But (so our hypothesis goes) the House was persuaded before he arrived to drop the whole provision in order to get the bill passed before the army could stop it, and Cromwell did not know it had been dropped until he examined the bill later. To Hesilrige and his allies the imminence of the army's threat warranted the sacrifice, while those members who had promised Cromwell to try to get the proceedings on the bill suspended felt the ground cut away from them because the main objection to it, the exemption of the leading Rumpers from having to seek re-election, was removed. But Cromwell's anger and sense of betrayal become intelligible. So do those confident charges of self-perpetuation, followed by the army's embarrassed and equivocal retreat from them, though not without a lingering suspicion that the Rumpers would still have found some way of clinging to their seats.

There is an alternative hypothesis which might seem extravagant if it were not based on what the Rump actually tried to do after it had returned to power in 1659. This is that the bill, as reported by Hesilrige on 23 February 1653, proposed that elections should immediately be held to the vacant seats, as a prelude to the election of a full new parliament in the autumn, and that the Long Parliament, thus enlarged to its proper strength, should dissolve at the moment when it transmitted the supreme authority to its successor on 3 November next. This may sound bizarre until one compares the Rump's actual manoeuvres six or seven years later. On 6 June 1659, a month after its reinstatement, it voted that it would not sit beyond 7 May 1660; yet in the course of January and February 1660, under the tacit threat of Monck's advancing army, it arranged to hold immediate recruiter elections to bring its strength up to four hundred, with the seats apportioned 'as they were agreed in the Year 1653'.[43] It did not rescind its vote to dissolve no later than next May; indeed it publicly declared anew that its present

---

[43] *CJ*, vii, 673, 803, 834; *Complete Prose Works of John Milton*, vii, 101, 162–3, 169–71, 174.

members did *not* intend to perpetuate themselves in authority.[44] It professed its purpose to be to make up the present House 'so as to be a foundation for future parliaments, and the settlement of the nation'.[45] Until a late stage Monck appeared to encourage these proceedings, and there is no knowing what their outcome would have been if he had not cut them short by readmitting the members secluded in Pride's Purge. But strange though they may seem, they may be an echo of a scheme first hatched in the period under consideration, for they would have made a certain sense in the context of 1653 as well as of 1660. A short-term recruitment of this kind would have taken much of the sting out of objections that the Rump was too unrepresentative to determine the future government of the Commonwealth. It would greatly have strengthened the outgoing parliament's claim, otherwise so disputable, to adjudge the qualifications of the members of the incoming one. It would have made a military *coup* more difficult and unpopular, for the relatively favourable public reaction which attended Cromwell's actual breaking of the Rump would have been very different if the country had already been assured of widespread by-elections immediately and general elections within six months. Furthermore, if the Rumpers had any success in influencing the by-elections they would have had a flying start in the general ones.

These were all reasons why the army would have found such a scheme intolerable, especially if at any time it feared drastic changes in its own high command and perhaps the permanent exclusion of serving officers from parliament. But it would have felt another obvious fear. Would the newly elected members, who would have constituted a working majority, willingly have accepted so short a tenure of their seats? What was to prevent them from promptly introducing a new bill, extending the recruited House's life for as long as they dared?

This hypothesis of a short-term recruitment is necessarily tentative because of the lack of positive evidence, but it does reconcile much of the apparently conflicting evidence rather nicely. If, however, such a device had been recommended as part of the bill by Hesilrige on 23 February, it may not have been in it when Cromwell seized it on 20 April. Being a provision which

[44] *Old Parl. Hist.*, xxii, 61.
[45] *CJ*, vii, 807.

affected only the transition from the present parliament to the next one, its natural place was near the end of the bill, and the House had evidently not reached it on 13 April. As in the case of our first hypothesis, Cromwell probably thought it had been rushed through before he arrived on the 20th, and may have been surprised to discover that it had been dropped in order to secure the bill's swifter passage. If this *is* what happened, it would explain both why contemporaries so readily believed that the bill provided for recruiter elections and why those Rumpers who found their tongues when Cromwell was dead and buried declared so confidently that it provided for a new parliament in November, that being the part of it that they cared to recall.[46] Both versions were right. Whether or not the clauses for a short-term recruitment were passed on the 20th, the 'Marten' letter could still deny that the Rumpers 'ment to recreut and so perpetuate themselves', because the term was to be so short; while Cromwell's suspicion that once effected it would not be short at all would explain what he meant in this comment on the bill for a new representative, in his speech to Barebone's Parliament: 'And had it been done with integrity, there could nothing have happened more wellcome to our judgements then that; but plainly the intention was not to give the people right of choice, it would have been but a seeming right; the giving them a choice was [intended] only to recruit the House, the better to perpetuate themselves.'[47] Going on to recount how he had proposed his expedient of a temporary nominated government, to be established by themselves, he said their reply had been 'that nothing would save this nation but the continuance of that

[46] Worden, *Rump*, pp. 366–8.

[47] Nickolls, p. 108; 'intended' supplied from *The Lord General Cromwel's Speech*, p. 9. The pamphlet version becomes garbled at a critical point, but is worth quoting: ' . . . the which, had it been done, or would it have been done, with that integrity, with that caution, that would have saved, this Cause and the Interest, we have been so long ingaged in; there could nothing have happened to our judgments, more welcome then that would have bin; but finding plainly, that the intendment of it was not to give the people the Right of Choice, although it had been, but aseding [*sic*] right either the seeming, to give the people that Choice intended and designed, to recrute the House, the better to perpetuate themselves'. Cromwell's meaning appears in both texts to be that behind a 'seeming' right of election was still an intention to recruit the House, so as to 'perpetuate' the sitting members. It is likely enough that he conveyed this rather dark hint in equally opaque and confused syntax. Earlier, I guess that he interjected not 'or would it have been done', but 'oh would it had been done!' On the various texts of this speech see Appendix A.

parliament, though they would not say the *perpetuating* of it, at that time; yet [we found] their endeavours did directly tend to it'.[48] There is the same implication in his speech of 12 September 1654 to the first parliament of the Protectorate: 'And that there was a just cause of their dissolving is most evident, not only in regard there was a just fear of the parliament's perpetuating themselves, but because it was their design.'[49]

What if neither hypothesis is correct, and the allegations about self-perpetuation were either clumsy falsehoods or the result of a strange ignorance about the bill's contents? Cromwell may still have stopped it from passing because of the way it arranged, or failed to arrange, for the election of the next parliament. He and other sources close to the army subsequently complained much about two related things: the inadequate barriers against the return of men who were disaffected to the Commonwealth, and the unsatisfactory arrangements (or non-arrangements) for enforcing such qualifications as the bill imposed. It is unlikely that he objected to the qualifications already agreed by the House, which excluded papists, participants in the Irish rebellion, and all who had fought for the late king, while the formula requiring members to be 'persons of known integrity, fearing God, and not scandalous in their conversation' accorded closely with the army's own requests. The problem was how to keep out men with sound parliamentarian records who felt no commitment to a republic and no sympathy with what the army understood by a godly reformation, but would voice all the Country interest's strong dislike for swordsmen, sequestrators, sectaries, and jumped-up local bosses. True, the engagement of 1649 to be faithful to the Commonwealth as now established had still to be taken, but so much casuistry had grown up around it that its effectiveness as a political test was very limited.

The earliest apologia for the dissolution, in *Severall Proceedings*

[48] Nickolls, p. 110. The 1654 pamphlet text conveys exactly the same meaning, but obscures it with perverse punctuation.

[49] Abbott, iii, 453. The same suspicion that self-perpetuation was the Rumpers' aim to the end appears in a letter to all the officers in Scotland which twenty-seven members of the Council of Officers signed on 3 May 1653. It states that they came to the conclusion that 'the onely way left us was to endeavour a speedy change in the supreme Authority if the perpetuate sitting of the Parliament might be prevented and the government laid upon the shoulders of such men as might hopefully give us the fruit of all our labour and blood . . . And it was in our hearts to seeke this thing in such a way that the Parliament might have the honour of it': Clarke MS XXV, fos. 48–9.

for 14–21 April, condemned the bill because it gave 'so much liberty that many disaffected persons might be chosen'. Mabbott wrote a day or two later that it would have let in 'such as probably would be disaffected, neuters, lawyers, or the like'. Cromwell said that he himself asked the members who came to his conference on 19 April 'Whether the next Parliament were not like to consist of all Presbyters? Whether those Qualifications would hinder them? or Newters?'[50] The Rump did not totally ignore the danger; its last recorded vote on the bill was to nullify 'every vote and votes, election and elections, given or made for any person or persons, contrary, or not according, to the qualifications before expressed'.[51] But it is most unlikely to have been willing to impose tests which would have excluded 'Presbyterians' and 'neuters' as stringently as the army desired, though just how Cromwell himself would have kept them out he did not say. One hopes not by the methods of 1654 and 1656. Nevertheless it does seem to have backed away from the problem of how to enforce the qualifications which it *had* imposed, and with the popularity of the regime as low as it was in 1653 the manner of enforcement was even more important than the qualifications themselves. The elections to the Convention in 1660 would show how worthless qualifications laid down by an outgoing parliament could be if the incoming one did not care to endorse them. Cromwell made two significant statements in his speech to Barebone's Parliament on 4 July. 'We could not tell', he said, 'how it would bee brought to passe, to send out an Act of Parliament into the Country, to have qualifications in an Act to be the Rules of Electors, and Elected, and not to know who should execute this.'[52] A little later he stated that on 20 April the Rump had been rushing the bill through 'with that haste as was never before exercised, leaving out all things relating to the due exercise of the qualifications which had appeared all along, and as we heard, to pass it only in paper'.[53] No one ever contradicted

[50] *Severall Proceedings*, no. 186, 14–21 Aprl 1653, p. 2944; *Clarke Papers*, iii, 1; *The Lord General Cromwel's Speech*, p. 15.

[51] *CJ*, 13 Apr. 1653.

[52] *The Lord General Cromwel's Speech*, p. 15. The Nickolls text is similar but briefer, and has 'elect' instead of 'execute'—probably a slip.

[53] Nickolls, p. 110; though Nickolls has 'height' instead of 'haste', which is from *The Lord General Cromwel's Speech*, p. 17. The latter goes on: 'leaving out the things that did necessarily relate to due qualifications'. I suspect that Cromwell actually said 'the due execution of the qualifications'.

these charges. If the House, for the sake of dishing the army, really had been trying to hustle the bill into law without prescribing how its most vulnerable provisions should be enforced, there may be no need to look further for Cromwell's chief reason for so suddenly dissolving it.

Everything seemed to have come down to a question of power by mid-April: from the Rump's viewpoint the army's physical power to stop it sitting, from the army's the power to govern until the new parliament met, and still more the power to supervise the elections and determine who was duly elected to the new representative. Indeed by the time Cromwell arranged that final conference between officers and members on 19 April, the central issue was whether the Rump could be brought to dissolve itself very shortly, before elections were held to a new parliament, or whether it would insist on retaining the supreme authority until its successor took over. How much this weighed with him he showed in his opening speech to Barebone's Parliament, for he reiterated three times that the Rumpers' only answer to his proposals had been that nothing would save the nation but the continuance of the present parliament.

Here we come upon another uncertainty regarding the Rump's intentions. Did 'continuance' mean continued sitting, or did the House mean to adjourn shortly after passing the bill and reassemble only at the beginning of November? It has been stated as certain that it intended an early adjournment,[54] but it is by no means so. In support of this assumption there is a royalist correspondent's statement that 'on Wednesday morninge the House meant a delusory adjournment, and a new Representative on the 3d of November next',[55] though what 'delusory' meant here is unclear. There is also a remark in the account of the Rump's last hours in the issue of *Severall Proceedings* covering 21–28 April: 'and if themselves having passed it had that day adjourned, as probable, had they not been dissolved, the nation would have been in a sad condition'.[56] Here, in a paper that had

[54] Worden, *Rump*, p. 346.

[55] Firth, 'Cromwell and the expulsion', p. 532. John Langley wrote to Sir Richard Leveson on 30 Apr. that the Rump's bill 'was to perpetuate themselves and to recruit the house with newe supplies according to the old number, and then would they have adjourned for 6 monthes' (Johnson and Vaisey, p. 73). But this was mere common report.

[56] *Severall Proceedings*, no. 187, 21–28 Apr. 1653, p. 2959; repeated with only minor verbal variations in at least two other newspapers and in *Another Declaration wherein is*
(continued)

official status, and more than a week after the bill came into Cromwell's hands, an immediate adjournment is described merely as probable, which is surely evidence enough that it was not laid down in the bill itself. That is no proof, of course, that the Rump did not intend it.

The officers or their editor may have thought a snap adjournment probable because it would have put the Rump out of reach of the army's physical violence, but surely it was *not* probable. Eventually the House would have adjourned—certainly in time for the members to campaign in their constituencies for the autumn elections—but meanwhile there was a lot of unfinished business that it would not willingly have left to the Council of State or to its successor. 'We stayed to end the Dutch war', said Scot in 1659, deploring that Cromwell had not let them sit a little longer; 'this we might have done in four or five months.'[57] The House as a whole cared too intensely about the outcome of the war and the terms on which peace might be negotiated to let such decisions be taken during its adjournment. It would surely have stayed also to complete the long-delayed bill for uniting Scotland with the Commonwealth. And further, after so many debates, it must have wanted to give legislative effect to its decisions on the Owen proposals for the approbation of ministers and other matters of ecclesiastical policy, if only to shut the door on the pressure for more radical solutions. There were also all the Hale Commission's recommendations still awaiting bills to embody them, though the conservative majority would probably have been glad to let those sleep a while longer. Whitelocke is another witness against any plan for an immediate or very early adjournment, for he states that the bill for a new representative, as debated on 20 April, 'would occasion other meetings of them again, and prolong their sitting'.[58]

It can therefore be taken as certain that the Rump proposed

---

rendered a further account of the Reasons for Dissolving the Parliament ([3 May] 1653). Dr Worden states (*Rump*, p. 348) that as early as Nov. 1651 the bill had provided for the Rump to adjourn and then reassemble just before the inauguration of its successor. But there is nothing about adjourning in the source that he cites, namely *Faithful Scout*, 14–21 Nov. 1651, p. 339. It merely announced that on 18 Nov. 'a certain day shall be declared for the limiting of this parliament, and a day immediately to follow for the calling of a new representative'.

[57] *Diary of Thomas Burton*, ed. J. T. Rutt, 4 vols. (1828), iii, 111–12.
[58] Whitelocke, *Memorials*, p. 529.

2 or 3 November next as the day of its dissolution—on that there is no dispute—and probable that it intended to spend an appreciable part of the intervening time in continued session. This in itself was enough to arouse serious apprehensions in Cromwell and his fellow-officers, even if there were no provisions in the bill for an interim recruitment of the House or for the continuance of its leading members. The Rump naturally reasoned that if it abdicated authority before the elections, the army would control them and adjudge their results. But Cromwell and the army had their own reasons for being loth to leave that control absolutely to the Rump or its Council of State—reasons which did not at all necessarily include a sudden disenchantment with parliaments as such.

They must have had three main fears. The first, which has been discussed already, was that the Rump might make some drastic changes in the army's command or otherwise deprive it of political influence, once it had made itself relatively immune to military violence by an act which promised the country a general election to a lawful parliament in the autumn. The second lay in the very fact that the elections would be supervised either by the Rump or its Council of State, and that the House intended to reassemble in order to determine formally which elections were valid and which new members duly qualified. Why this should have dismayed the army so, recent studies of the Rump have made much clearer. Most of the House was hostile to the kind of godly reformation that the army desired. Critical occasions, such as the concluding sessions in November would certainly be, brought a larger attendance than usual, and a full House generally meant a bigger conservative majority. So far from excluding those Presbyterians and neuters whose preponderance Cromwell with so much reason feared, and whom the bill itself did not disqualify, the general inclination in the case of disputed elections would have been to discriminate against political and religious radicals. Judging by scattered hints in his speeches, he may also have thought that the bill armed the present House with more positive powers to manipulate the elections or tamper with their results, but even without these the prospect of a new parliament fashioned in the Rump's image was bad enough.

But there was worse to fear. For an outgoing parliament to

continue in being during the election of its successor was of course unprecedented, and the incoming one was all too likely to claim that it alone should exercise the historic right to determine whether its members were duly elected. If the Rump's act for a new representative ruled otherwise, the new parliament had only to pass a brief bill declaring the power to reside in itself, on the ground of fundamental law. It could then have admitted men whom the Rump had sought to disqualify, and if it contained as many Presbyterians, crypto-royalists, and alienated Country conservatives as Cromwell quite reasonably apprehended, the result can be imagined. Nothing could have reversed it but another Pride's Purge, and he did not want that.

Since such were the prospects, the expedient that he proposed to his conference on 19 April was not without merit. A caretaker government of compact size, nominated and authorized by the Rump but adequately representing the army (which the Council of State did not) as well as its own membership, could have been a competent body to hold the reins between one parliament and the next and to umpire the elections. It would have been more acceptable if its period of office could have been strictly defined and if the elections could have been assigned a precise and not too distant date. But the conference on the 19th was the tenth or twelfth in a series, according to Cromwell, and we do not know what he may have suggested at earlier meetings. It is a fair inference that he had been seeking for some time, both in such meetings and in private discussions with fellow-members, for agreement on a manner of electing a new parliament which would be safe for the Commonwealth as a whole and fair to the interests of the army. Pedantic constitutionalists, of whom the Rump had plenty, no doubt objected that it was none of the army's business to concern itself with how the people chose their representatives. They might have reflected that if the army had not played a very large political role in December 1648, Charles I would probably be still on his throne, with a new House of Commons already sitting and a House of Lords reinforcing the inevitable reaction, and that most of themselves would be in the political wilderness. Both Rump and army represented minority interests in the fragmented post-revolutionary Britain of 1653, and if they could not agree on how to manage the risky business of general elections it would not be safe to hold them at all.

Cromwell was prepared to risk elections until a very late stage; certainly until the end of January, when the circular letter went out from the Council of Officers, almost certainly until early March, when that body appointed a committee to advise with him about a new representative,[59] and quite probably until he finally concluded that the Rump was determined not to call a new parliament under conditions that he considered safe and equitable. By mid-April, however, the rift between army and parliament had opened too wide for the hazard of early elections to be any longer acceptable. And as their quarrel split the thin ranks of the Commonwealth's true adherents, there were royalists active in the Scottish Highlands, while stability at home was further disturbed by the strident preachings at Allhallows and Blackfriars and by other manifestations of sectarian fanaticism.[60] So when Cromwell made his last proposal for an agreed solution on the 19th, he stipulated a longer term and a larger role for his interim nominated government than he might have done earlier. He presented it

as the most hopeful way to encourage and countenance all God's people, reform the law, and administer justice impartially; hoping thereby the people might forget monarchy, and understanding their true interest in the election of successive parliaments, may have the government settled upon a true basis; without hazard to this glorious cause, or necessitating to keep up armies for the defence of the same.[61]

Hereby he plainly envisaged that 'the election of successive parliaments' would be put off for an indefinite period, even though the army had been pressing for it for so long. But his apparent change of policy did not necessarily signify his conversion to a millenarian rule of the saints. It can be more simply explained. Only the Rump could legally ordain elections in the near future; it would not do so in a manner that he thought honest or safe; the resultant divisions between officers and parliament-men had ended by making elections altogether too dangerous for the present, so they would have to be postponed. But successive parliaments remained the ultimate goal, and he thought that the best way to educate the country for them was to give it a taste of truly disinterested and reforming

[59] See pp. 51–2, 56.
[60] Gardiner, *C & P*, ii, 390–1; Worden, *Rump*, p. 321.
[61] Gardiner, *Documents*, p. 402.

administration. It has been suggested that the role he proposed for his forty godly men 'sounds a pretty long-term programme for an interim government'.[62] But some allowance must be made for the wording of a document hastily put together with the object of putting the best light on a *coup* which Cromwell had not even intended. He cannot have expected these forty to exercise the legislative power indefinitely, and if he had not envisaged the calling of a true parliament reasonably soon his proposals would not have commended themselves to St. John and a fair number of other MPs, as Whitelocke says they did. He probably had in mind the sort of modest but significant programme of reform that he and his council were to carry out by ordinance in less than nine months, between the establishment of the Protectorate and the meeting of its first parliament.

It has been argued that Cromwell's apologias for the dissolution, along with the others emanating from sources close to him, are vitiated by their self-contradictions and shifts of ground.[63] There is some force in this, and the apparent inconsistencies need to be faced. But two things should be remembered. The first is that none of these statements vindicated his action on one ground alone. Whatever they said about the bill for a new representative, they presented the Rump's attempt to rush it through on that final morning as no more than the precipitating cause of the dissolution, which was warranted essentially by the House's settled aversion to those works of reformation which the cause of God and his people required of it. The other is that when Cromwell in his speeches worked laboriously over past actions he was not just seeking to justify his own deeds; he was searching the pattern of events for providences, indications of divine blessing or rebuke, dispensations that would light the way to present decisions and future goals. It is admittedly clear that of all his public acts the breaking of the Rump was the one that seemed to him most to need justifying—far more, for example, than his share in bringing Charles I to the scaffold. But the lessons that he drew from it naturally changed somewhat as the problems with

[62] Christopher Hill, *God's Englishman: Oliver Cromwell and the English Revolution* (1970), p. 136.
[63] Worden, *Rump*, ch. 16, *passim*.

which he was currently wrestling changed, and he would not have been human if he had not read back into his motives in April 1653 some considerations that had only come into clear focus for him through subsequent experiences.

Those earliest accounts—not Cromwell's own—which accused the bill of providing for a mere recruitment are best explained, as has been suggested above, as arising from a sheer mistake as to what the bill *in its final form* contained. But the accusation is made so laconically in them—in a mere parenthesis, in Mabbott's newsletters[64]—that their writers seem to have assumed that their readers would share an expectation that the bill was a recruiter bill. It has been shown how this mistake led to some tortured and evasive phrases in Cromwell's and the Council of Officers' declaration of 22 April, but also how both there and in Cromwell's speech to Barebone's Parliament the suspicion evidently lingered that the Rumpers would have found a way to cheat the people of the 'seeming right' to choose their representatives. In both the declaration and the speech the charge is maintained, though with a damaging lack of precision, that the bill was a deceitful bill and that the attempt to hurry it through on 20 April had been a final and dangerous act of bad faith.

Once Cromwell had beaten his awkward retreat from charging the Rump with open self-perpetuation, his apologias revealed changes of emphasis rather than blatant inconsistencies. Before he spoke again he had to digest the bitter lesson of Barebone's Parliament. It taught him not only that godliness is no guarantee of political competence but also that no one assembly, however well motivated, should be entrusted with an unlimited and undifferentiated authority. Henceforth the necessity of separating the legislative and executive powers bulked large in his speeches, though there is no knowing how far he came to this conviction on his own and how far two other men helped him to formulate it. One was John Lambert, whose Instrument of Government furnished the Protectorate with a constitution of checks and balances; the other was the versatile Marchamont Nedham, who published anonymously the classic vindication of the Protectorate and the Instrument in *A True State of the Case of*

---

[64] *Clarke Papers*, iii, 1; Hull Corporation MSS, L565.

the Commonwealth.[65] Cromwell drew largely on Nedham's pamphlet in his subsequent speeches, especially those of 12 September 1654 and 22 January 1655, in the second of which he expressly commended it.[66] On the subject of the bill, Nedham repeated the oft-made accusation that the Rump had proceeded with it only because of the army's pressure, 'and', he added with fine effrontery, 'this meerly out of designe too, that they might have had some shadow of pretext to thwart or scandalize that most necessary work of dissolution by the army'. He said nothing about recruitment, but he did give a new twist to the self-perpetuation theme. 'An opportunity was given in that bill', he said, 'to the next, or any succeeding parliament (no manner of balance or check being reserved upon them) by claiming an absolute authority to be in themselves, for ever to have continued the power (if they pleased) in their own hands, upon pretentions of safety.'[67] But another parliament had fallen since the Rump, and Nedham was less concerned to analyse last year's crisis dispassionately than to point the dangers of having the legislature perpetually in session, with no limitations upon its powers. It is rather intriguing that in his argument for a separation of powers he lifted a short passage from an editorial that he had published in *Mercurius Politicus* in July 1652.[68] The over-all tendency of the two writings, eighteen months or so apart, was however quite different. The earlier was part of a series which had upheld the sovereignty of successive parliaments and condemned any kind of 'standing powers' whether monarchs, juntas, professional armies, or even the long continuance of particular individuals in high office or command.[69] It advocated a distinct executive

---

[65] Acquired by Thomason on 8 Feb. 1654. Its attribution to Nedham by Firth (*Last Years of the Protectorate*, i, 156) and Abbott (iii, 193), which was convincing both on stylistic grounds and because Nedham was employed by Cromwell's government in more than one capacity, is virtually clinched by its inclusion of matter drawn from one of the *Mercurius Politicus* editorials (cf. n.68).

[66] Abbott, iii, 587.

[67] *A True State of the Case of the Commonwealth*, pp. 9–10.

[68] *Mercurius Politicus*, no. 109, 1–8 July 1652, pp. 1705–6; compare *A True State*, p. 10. The borrowing was remarked by Worden, *Rump*, p. 362.

[69] Ibid., e.g. no. 87, 29 Jan.–5 Feb. 1652, pp. 1381–2; no. 91, 26 Feb.–4 March 1652, p. 1442; no. 101, 6–13 May 1652, pp. 1587–8; no. 103, 20–27 May 1652, pp. 1610–11; no. 110, 8–15 July 1652, pp. 1721 ff. But Nedham was doing a balancing act even then, for besides advocating that the legislature should delegate the executive power, he granted the need for experience and continuity in transacting matters of state and administering justice: see no. 94, 18–25 March 1652, pp. 1473–4.

power, certainly, but one which derived its authority from the sovereign legislature and was accountable to it. But what he borrowed from it early in 1654 was neatly fitted into an enthusiastic exposition of a constitution which repudiated the conception of sovereignty and tilted the balance in favour of the executive rather than the legislature.

Cromwell delivered the next of his own ritual retrospects on 12 September 1654. The first parliament of the Protectorate had been sitting for just over a week, and Hesilrige and other ex-Rumpers had been challenging the whole legality of the new constitution in the name of the inalienable rights of the people's representatives. It was natural in the context that in looking back on the Rump's bill for a new representative Cromwell dwelt mainly on Nedham's major criticisms of it: that it provided no safeguard against *future* parliaments perpetuating themselves, and that a legislature in perpetual session was bound to encroach upon the lives, liberties, and estates of the people.[70] But he still maintained that there had been 'high cause' for dissolving the Rump, 'not only in regard there was a just fear of the parliament's perpetuating themselves, but because it was their design'.[71] This suggests that he still thought it had been their design to the last, for otherwise why should it have been a cause for dissolving them?

He went over the ground once more, four years and a day after that violent dissolution, in one of his speeches to the parliamentary committee that was then negotiating with him over the offer of the crown. He still accused the rumpers of striving for as long as they could to recruit themselves instead of calling a new parliament, but no longer of designing to make use of their actual bill to that end. Their aim, he said, 'seeing a parliament might not be perpetual', was 'that parliaments might be always sitting; and so to that end was there a bill framed . . . that as soon as one parliament went out of their place, another might leap in. And when we saw this, truly we thought we did but make a change in pretence and did not remedy the thing.'[72] This was certainly different from what he had objected at the

[70] Abbott, iii, 454.

[71] Ibid. 453. Abbott and his pamphlet source, following seventeenth-century typographical usage, omit the apostrophe in 'parliaments', but the context makes it clear that 'parliament' is singular and refers to the Rump.

[72] Abbott, iv, 487.

time, though the warmth and vividness with which he arraigned the Rump's encroachments on the judicial sphere suggest that it was not a merely retrospective grievance. He had evidently come to terms with the fact that the bill did not in the end contain what he thought it did, but it was still bad enough. What mattered now, however, was the great decision before him, and the lessons to be drawn for those who listened to him. Now that a parliament, even though a purged one, had presented him with a genuinely balanced constitution, it was natural for him to criticize the Rump mainly for 'assuming to itself the authority of the three estates that went before', and for 'their hasty throwing of the liberties of the people of God and the nation into a bare representative of the people'.[73] He had not had so clear an idea in 1653 of the danger of committing boundless power to a single-chamber legislature, but he had almost certainly begun to sense it even earlier.

Having prefaced this rather lengthy discussion of the bill with a warning that it would lead down dark paths of conjecture, it may be helpful to conclude it by summarizing the possibilities and suggesting where the balance of probability may rest.

One is constantly driven back to the bill because all other explanations of the dissolution seem in themselves insufficient. Cromwell may have been influenced to some extent by apprehensions that once it got the bill passed the Rump would remodel the army's command, but it is not possible to tell how much this weighed with him, if at all. As for pressures and dissensions within the army, there is no good evidence that they were ever great enough to make Cromwell change his policy against his better judgement. The dissolution had the effect of restoring his prestige among the hotter radicals and saints, or most of them, but it would be unjustifiable to suppose that he staged it for that purpose. Rather more plausible is the hypothesis that his attitude to the Rump dramatically changed because Harrison and the militant millenarians won him over to their ideals. It is weakened, however, by the evidence that he and Harrison continued throughout to regard each other with mutually critical eyes, by uncertainty whether Harrison was

[73] Ibid. 487–8.

clearly aiming yet at any form of government other than elected parliaments, and by the fact that the Fifth Monarchists came out with such diverse proposals as to what should be settled in place of the Rump.

The problem remains that the Council of Officers, Cromwell evidently included, went on pressing the Rump to make way for successive parliaments almost until the end, yet never showed any sign of regarding the bill for a new representative, as reintroduced on 23 February, as an admissible means to that end. Cromwell's abstention from the House and the Council of State for a crucial month surely expressed his total distrust of it, misguided though he probably was to withdraw from the debate. The likeliest reason why he finally advanced the expedient of a temporary nominated government was that the Rump would have nothing but the bill, and the army would not have it at any price. But what was so obnoxious about it, given that it provided for a new parliament to meet in little more than six months' time? The answer probably lies in the unknown history of what happened to it in committee, when first Carew and then Harrison gave up the care of it and Hesilrige apparently took over.

Three hypotheses have been offered here. The first is that one proposed amendment was for a select but substantial number of the present members to be given places in the next parliament without having to seek re-election, in order to ensure a stiffening of committed commonwealthsmen. This had not yet been reached when the House met for its weekly debate on the bill on 20 April, and Hesilrige and his fellow-managers (it is suggested) dropped it in order to beat the army's threat and get the bill through all its remaining stages that day. Cromwell, however, thought that it *was* in the bill when he expelled the parliament.

The second hypothesis is that the amended bill would have provided for an immediate filling of the House by recruiter elections, to be followed by general elections in the autumn and the handing over of power to a new parliament on 3 November. If this was so, the strong contemporary reports that it would have caused elections to be held to the vacant seats and the Rumpers' belated claims that it promised a genuine new parliament were alike true. It is unlikely that such complex provisions were passed without leaving a trace in the *Journal*, or were pushed through on 20 April before Cromwell got to the House, but this scenario (unlike the first) does not absolutely require that this part of the bill was deliberately dropped that morning.

The third possibility is that the bill, without ever including proposals for either the continuance of present members in the new parliament or for a short-term recruitment, nevertheless disquieted the officers so much over the way in which the new representative was to be called that they were prepared in the last resort to expel the House rather than let it pass. This may have been because they thought it gave the Rumpers improper power to manipulate the elections in their favour, or because its qualifications for future members were too lax, or because it failed to provide adequately for their enforcement, so that if the new parliament fully reflected the political nation's dislike of the present regime even the qualifications already agreed might be overridden or ignored.

These hypotheses do not exhaust the possibilities, and there is simply not enough evidence to justify any very firm preference for one of them over the other two. The first has in its favour that from the Rump's point of view such a course would have made political sense, and it would explain why the army officers and so many other contemporaries believed right up to the dissolution and beyond that some Rumpers at least were bent on holding on to their seats. The second accommodates the conflicting statements about the bill even better and prefigures what the Rump actually attempted in 1660, and though it is admittedly an elaborate structure for its slender evidential foundations to bear it is a possibility that appeals (for what that is worth) to the present writer. The third takes us least far beyond the actual surviving evidence, but while it may be sufficient it does not account for the confidence and persistence of those charges of self-perpetuation. These *may* have rested only on nothing more than the fact that some members tried to make the bill into a recruiter bill and failed, but if so it remains a puzzle why no Rumper ran the risk even of an anonymous pamphlet to say so, and why the sharper-eared foreign diplomats and royalist agents were so deceived.

It will be seen that the reading of the evidence presented here does not support the view that by April Cromwell and the Rump had changed places as to the desirability of calling a new parliament, or 'that the Rump attempted to pass a bill for fresh elections for the simple reason that it wanted to hold them'.[74] It would doubtless have held them eventually, but on its own terms, and not until the army had been rendered politically harmless. As things were, it had taken the bill up again only under army pressure. It had spared it one morning a week—not even every week at that—and had sometimes mustered barely forty members for the business, though Hesilrige always took care to be present for it. No wonder Cromwell was taken by surprise when it suddenly tried to finish it off in one day. When these same men returned to power in 1659 they proved as costive as ever when pressed once more to provide for successive parliaments, and they goaded two more armies, Fleetwood's and Monck's, into defying them in turn. Their subsequent behaviour makes it seem all the more questionable whether their bill, as it was framed early in 1653, was a straight answer to the army's and the country's desire for a new representative.

The mutual distrust between parliament and army is entirely understandable. To speculate on what might have been is an exercise of limited value, but to one who feels a pang at the gulf between Milton's vision of the Commonwealth's future and the reality, it seems tragic that the Rump's leaders were so eager to plunge into the hazards of a general election while setting at defiance the army which had been its partner in so many victories, and to which it owed its own continued being. The breach was not of course the fault of one side only, and the fear of military dictatorship was a wholesome fear. Cromwell's behaviour in withdrawing for weeks from the formal debates on the bill, and then expelling the parliament without knowing, it seems, just what it was trying to pass, is not easy to understand, let alone to justify. But so far from aiming at military dictatorship, he kept a strong curb on those who threatened it, and his forces still had as much right as ever to claim that they were 'not a mere mercenary army'. If the Rump could have had the magnanimity, at an earlier stage than April, to devolve the power of executive government for a strictly limited period on a body of nominees

---

[74] Worden, *Rump*, p. 375 f. Dr Worden grants however that 'it is unlikely that the Rump would have debated the bill in the spring of 1653 but for army pressure' (p. 377), and that from Worcester onwards it probably 'intended to delay elections until the army had been disbanded or at least reduced to impotence' (p. 376). I fully agree with both statements.

acceptable both to itself and to the army, charging it thereafter to conduct general elections in accordance with a well-framed act for a new representative and to lay down its power when the new parliament met, then the transmission of authority from the Long Parliament to its successor might have been effected with as much safety and harmony as could be had in the circumstances. The trouble with the Rump's leaders was that most of them persisted, until their world collapsed upon them in 1660, in closing their minds to the fact that the house of Stuart was a greater enemy to the good old cause than the house of Cromwell.

IV

Interregnum

There was no easy way forward from the position in which Cromwell put himself on 20 April 1653. The expedient that he had proposed the evening before was no longer available to him. A limited period of rule by forty worthies might just have been feasible if they had been invested with statutory authority by the Rump and charged to hold general elections to a lawful parliament as soon as the state of the nation made it safe to do so. But if Cromwell or the army alone had set them up, they would have been seen as too oligarchic, too unrepresentative, and too dubious in their credentials to command the obedience of the country at large, and the fittest men would probably have declined to serve. They would not have resembled Barebone's Parliament as it actually emerged so much as the Committee of Safety which the army established in October 1659 after interrupting the Rump a second time, and they would probably have foundered as dismally.

There was even less possibility now of summoning a new parliament, as the officers had been urging the Rump to do until so recently. If general elections had become too hazardous for Cromwell to contemplate by mid-April, the very fact of the dissolution put them out of the question for a considerable time to come. Not only had the army no shred of legal right to issue writs for elections, but the range of enemies that it would have had to face in the resultant House of Commons would have been overwhelming—more so than under the Protectorate, which at least offered stability after the convulsions of 1653. Even if overt royalists could have been kept out, only arbitrary force or quite unacceptably restrictive political tests could have excluded two formidably prevalent political types: the Presbyterians who had been the army's enemies since the Civil War, and the large uncommitted Country interest that hated swordsmen, high taxes, centralization, and political and religious radicalism in every shape. These were the sorts of men who would make Cromwell's subsequent parliaments so hard to manage. And besides these, some at least of the leading Rumpers would have got back to Westminster, in a mood no less hostile to the military usurpers than they were to display in all the Protectorate's parliaments. Unpopular though they had been when in the saddle, they would soon have shown what trouble they could make when they deployed all their oratorical and tactical skill in appeals to the privileges of parliament and the sacred rights of the people's representatives. Although most of them dispersed quietly into the country after the *coup*,[1] John Bradshaw, the former president of the court that had tried Charles I, spoke for the bolder of them when Cromwell went to the council chamber with Lambert and Harrison on the afternoon of the 20th to tell the Rump's Council of State that its authority was terminated.

'Sir [he said], we have heard what you did at the House in the morning, and before many hours all England will hear it: but, sir, you are mistaken to think that the parliament is dissolved: for no power under heaven can dissolve them but themselves; therefore take you notice of that.'[2]

A week or so later he was still declaring indomitably, in open court, that the parliament was not dissolved but only disturbed.[3] Fortunately for Cromwell, few but the members themselves were of the same mind. London and the country took the whole affair very calmly, and seemed on the whole more glad about the Rump's departure than apprehensive of what might succeed it.

The first pronouncement from Cromwell and the Council of Officers came in their declaration dated 22 April and published next day. It made no secret of their lack of any preconcerted plan

---

[1] Worden, *Rump*, pp. 339–40.

[2] Ludlow, i, 357. His fellow-members did not adhere consistently to this position. Hesilrige, for instance, would uphold in 1659 the unlimited right of Richard Cromwell's parliament to enact whatever was in the people's interests, and would recall that the Rump had an unextinguished and exclusive right to sovereign authority only when the malcontents in the army had been worked up to the pitch of reinstating it: see *Diary of Thomas Burton*, iii, 101–2, iv, 196.

[3] Johnson and Vaisey, p. 72; Clarendon MS 45, fo. 356.

for the country's future government; indeed it made a virtue of it. It could only say 'that as we have been led by necessity and Providence to act as we have done, even beyond and above our own thoughts and desires, so we shall ... put ourselves wholly upon the Lord for a blessing'. It promised—what else could it?— 'to call to the government persons of approved fidelity and honesty', though it significantly refrained from any pledge to constitute it from the self-styled saints. Beyond that it could only adjure the public to 'wait for such issue as [the Lord] should bring forth'.[4] When Nedham came to write his vindication of the Protectorate about nine months later, he thought that Cromwell and the officers needed no other exoneration from the charge that they broke the Rump in order to seize power for themselves than 'the irresolution and unpreparedness of the army at that time, as to any particular settlement'.[5]

They were not only unprepared, but as soon as they began to discuss the question of settlement their latent differences came to the surface. Almost immediately they took into consultation those Rumpers on whose goodwill they still hoped to rely: Richard Salwey, Colonel Robert Bennett, and Walter Strickland by 23 April, reinforced within the next three days by Sir Gilbert Pickering, John Carew, Anthony Stapley, and others.[6] According to Ludlow, Cromwell sent privately for Salwey and Carew even before he invited these former members to sit round the table with his officers and himself, and asked them to try to persuade St. John, Selden, and some others 'to draw up some instrument of government that might put the power out of his hands'.[7] The story is credible, especially as Ludlow was to be very closely associated with Salwey in later years, and St. John was known to be so incensed by the violent dissolution that Cromwell may have felt unable to approach him directly.[8] If true, it is highly significant that Cromwell's first reaction to his predicament was to appeal to these great experts in public law to draft some kind of written constitution. It would confirm not only what he always declared, namely that he was anxious to shed his virtual

[4] Gardiner, *Documents*, pp. 403–4.

[5] *A True State*, p. 12.

[6] *Clarke Papers*, iii, 2. The six named would all be summoned to Barebone's Parliament, though Salwey ceased to collaborate with the officers early in May.

[7] Ludlow, i, 357–8.

[8] *Clarke Papers*, iii, 3; *The Case of Oliver St. John, Esq.* (1660), pp. 6–7.

dictatorship as soon as possible, but also that he already consciously felt the need for a firmly defined scheme of government, within which parliaments would take their due but not unbounded place. It came to nothing, however, for Salwey would not carry his message. He told him that the best way to free himself from the temptation of personal power was 'to rest persuaded that the power of the nation is in the good people of England, as formerly it was'.[9] It was the sort of smugly unhelpful advice that Cromwell would have to put up with from more than one republican in the coming years.

He said in retrospect that the dissolution had left him with unlimited authority in his hands because he was commander-in-chief of all the forces by act of parliament.[10] Constitutionally this was of course a very dubious assumption, though many of the saints were ready to acclaim him as a second Moses by divine dispensation. It was a fact, however, that power lay in the hands of the army, which meant that the government would be settled in whatever manner Cromwell could persuade the Council of Officers to agree. But it soon became apparent that they would not agree easily, or at least that the settlement was going to take some time, so on 29 April he set up a provisional administration in the shape of a small Council of State. At this stage, or slightly earlier, he seems to have decided to separate the functions of the civilian advisers whom he had called in from those of the Council of Officers, for it was the latter who from now on shared with him the decisions on what form the new government should take and who should be summoned to it. The Council of State on the other hand took over relations with foreign powers and the ordinary administration of the realm, to much the same extent as its predecessors under the Rump had done.

It was a mixed body, and probably as eclectic a one as could be found ready to serve in the peculiar circumstances. Only three of its original ten members besides Cromwell were officers, and during its first five weeks Cromwell managed to attend only about half its meetings. Lambert and Harrison were inevitable choices, and Desborough, the fourth officer, was the only other one then in England with the rank of major-general. Of the civilians, Strickland, Pickering, and Sydenham were proven

---

[9] Ludlow, i, 358.
[10] Abbott, iii, 454.

administrators and members of county families. The first two had already been councillors under the Rump, while Sydenham, after a hard-fighting career in the Civil War, had shown his solid dependability on many Rump committees and as governor of the Isle of Wight. John Carew and Anthony Stapley had also been councillors under the Rump; both were substantial landowners and both had shown themselves to be reformists, though Carew a considerably more active one. Stapley and Robert Bennett were both garrison colonels, and Bennett had been so busy and powerful as the Commonwealth's chief agent in Cornwall that he has been aptly described as 'Intendant' of the county.[11] To these original ten three more were added shortly after the middle of May. Colonel Matthew Tomlinson was a serving officer; he had sat on the Hale Commission, and would later receive a knighthood from Henry Cromwell in Ireland and (along with Strickland, Pickering, and Sydenham) a seat in the Cromwellian upper house. Colonel Philip Jones would also sit there, as well as on the Protectoral council. An administrator rather than a soldier, he was already on the way to becoming the most powerful man in Wales and to building up that imposing landed estate that would raise him from the fringes of the minor gentry to a wealth that lesser peers could envy. Samuel Moyer, a rich East India merchant and a radical Independent, had wide experience in administering several branches of the Commonwealth's revenues.

The thirteen names do not suggest that Cromwell was committed to any one party or interest, although the situation was one in which radical men were likelier than moderates to be ready to serve as councillors. But Harrison was balanced by Lambert, and while Carew, Bennett, Stapley, and Moyer would part company with Cromwell when Barebone's Parliament split apart, Strickland, Pickering, Sydenham, and Jones were to become central pillars of the Protectoral Council of State. Only Harrison and Carew were Fifth Monarchists, though Moyer, Bennett, and Stapley would also side with the religious radicals. The rest, with the possible exception of Tomlinson, were relatively moderate and would support the Protectoral ecclesiastical establishment. Only Cromwell, Harrison, Carew, and Stapley were regicides. All these men would be nominated to

[11] Underdown, *Pride's Purge*, pp. 261, 308.

Barebone's Parliament except the serving officers, and they would be co-opted by the House itself.

Cromwell announced the appointment of the Council of State in a declaration dated 30 April.[12] It was to manage the affairs of the Commonwealth until a new 'supreme authority' was constituted, but all he said about the latter was that 'persons of approved fidelity and honesty' were 'to be called from the several parts of this Commonwealth', and that the assembling of them would take some time. This is enough, however, to show that the Council of Officers had settled the first major question which divided it, namely 'whether the power should be reserved in the hands of a few, or of a greater number of persons'.[13] That had come up very early, while Salwey was present by special invitation. Lambert spoke for entrusting the supreme power to a compact body of not more than ten or twelve men, but Harrison favoured a larger one, preferably numbering seventy after the precedent of the Jewish sanhedrin.[14] Presumably Lambert thought of his small council as the executive element in a scheme of government which would in good time include also an elected legislature, as his own Instrument of Government would do a few months later. Such ideas were in the air, for at the beginning of May a pamphleteer proposed that power should be entrusted to a body of ten 'Conservators' until 1 June 1654, when the first of successive biennial parliaments should be summoned to meet.[15]

The Council of Officers made an intelligible choice between comprehensible alternatives. On Lambert's side it could be argued that reforms on a scale that required legislation had better wait until a properly elected parliament could enact them, and that meantime a compact and unified council would administer the country more safely and vigorously than a larger body. Of all the senior officers, he was probably the least inclined

[12] Abbott, iii, 16–17. Gardiner in *C & P*, ii, 221, was mistaken in supposing that Cromwell held up this declaration until 6 May, and in the mean time published another on the 3rd. With regard to the latter, he mistook the nature of a pamphlet misleadingly entitled *Another Declaration . . . by the Lord Generall and his Council* (see ch. II, n. 63), and he overlooked the fact that Thomason acquired the 30 April declaration on 3 May.

[13] *A True State*, p. 12.

[14] Ludlow, i, 358.

[15] 'J.W.', *A Mite to the Treasury* ([5 May] 1653). John Spittlehouse broadly hinted in *A Warning-Piece Discharged*, pp. 20–21, that J.W. was John Wildman, but he was almost certainly mistaken.

to millennial visions and aspirations. Those who argued for an assembly of seventy or more probably did not all do so for the same reasons, though the difference is likely to have been more one of emphasis than of conscious principle. Harrison believed that their one duty now was to put power into the hands of the saints in order to hasten the kingdom of Christ, though he was not indifferent to the practical reforms, temporal as well as spiritual, that all the officers expected of the new government. Cromwell stood somewhere between the poles represented by Lambert and Harrison, though at this time closer to Harrison. He wanted to embark on the work of reformation without the delay that Lambert would presumably have tolerated, and he shared Harrison's desire to commit that work to men worthy of the Lord's cause and people. But his undoubted sense that God had mighty providences in store for England did not lead him to think that parliaments had been superseded, and he and the majority of the officers reckoned that the reforms they desired would gain more acceptance from the public and recognition by the courts if they were promulgated by a body with some claim to be representative. They were desirous, as Nedham put it, 'to promote a succession of supreme assemblies, in that form of a free-state or commonwealth which had been declared by parliament'.[16]

Since elections of the traditional kind were out of the question, the next supreme assembly would have to be nominated, but at least its members could be chosen so as to represent all the English counties, as well as the nations of Scotland, Ireland, and Wales. Once this was decided, seventy must soon have been seen to be an unpractical and inadequate number. It was probably first proposed in print by the Fifth Monarchist John Rogers on 25 April,[17] and it was widely canvassed by the saints and tipped by the newswriters for a while. But its brief vogue, which seems to have started only after the fall of the Rump, died away again before Barebone's Parliament met, though it was to crop up again during periods of Fifth Monarchist agitation in 1657 and

---

[16] *A True State*, p. 12.

[17] John Rogers, *A few Proposals, relating to Civil Government* (25 Apr. 1653). Rogers, however, thought that there would be equally good Old Testament parallels for choosing one member from each county, or, if the situation demanded an immediate settlement, committing the government to twelve worthies.

1659.[18] The Council of Officers evidently rejected it quite soon in favour of a considerably larger number, which suggests that they cared more about securing a rational spread of representatives than taking the Scriptures as their only guide. Cromwell later said that he himself had proposed 140,[19] the number finally agreed upon, but there may be no significance in the fact that this is just twice seventy, since there is some evidence that until a late stage the intention was to summon only 130.

One pamphleteer wrote an interesting defence of the decision to call a nominated assembly instead of an elected one. He was John Hall, a journalist whom Cromwell had employed on more than one occasion and whose *Letter Written to a Gentleman in the Country*, which he dated 3 May, may well have been commissioned. He argued that the qualifications laid down in the Rump's bill for a new representative would never have sufficed to keep out Presbyterians and crypto-royalists, and that no amount of zeal in scrutinizing the returns would have solved the problem; firstly because the scrutineers could not see into men's hearts, and secondly because they would have been accused of robbing the people of their right of election. Indeed, he said, 'I see not how it could be salved otherwise than by choosing such *idoneous* persons, and that in such a number as might carry on the work.' But in the situation that the country had faced before the dissolution who was to choose them: the Rump, the people, or the army? 'The first like cunning brokers would not do it; the second like troublesome ideots cannot do it, and the third as wise guardians must do it.' 'And', he asseverated to objectors, 'if you will say that the liberty of the people by this meanes is stifled, I must tell you again, it is only suspended, 'tis a sword taken out of a mad mans hand, till he recover his senses.'[20]

[18] *Clarke Papers*, iii, 4; Thurloe, i, 240; Clarendon MS 45, fos. 380, 398; Johnson and Vaisey, p. 72; *Moderate Occurrences*, no. 8, 17–24 May, p. 64; Bordeaux to Brienne, 9/19 May (with 72 instead of 70); Capp, *Fifth Monarchy Men*, pp. 63, 117, 123, 138–9. The more general idea of 'church-parliaments' elected exclusively by the saints had of course a longer history, but Fifth Monarchists had always been divided over it.

[19] Abbott, iv, 418.

[20] [John Hall], *A Letter written to a Gentleman in the Country*, pp. 11–12, 15–16. Although dated 3 May by Hall, Thomason did not acquire it until 26 May, and the reproduction of parts of it in the issues of *Mercurius Britannicus* for 23–30 May and of *Moderate Occurrences* for 24–31 May confirm that it was probably first printed after the 20th. Did Hall antedate it in order to suggest that some decisions of principle had been taken earlier than was the case?

Once the Council of Officers had decided on a fairly large assembly, the most pressing questions were how its members should be selected and who should summon them. Harrison described the debate in a letter to John Jones on 30 April: 'Being resolved to have in power, men of truith, fearing and loving our Lord, his people and Interest; the difficultie is to gett such: whether my Lord [i.e. Cromwell] onelie shall call them, or the Saints should choose them; very much sweetly said both waies.'[21] Harrison's authentic words are obviously more authoritative than an allegation by a newswriter on 6 May that he had recently written to an intimate friend 'that the Lord had now at last made the General instrumentall to put the power into the hands of his people (meaning the phanatique gathered churches) contrary to his intentions; that it was the Lord's worke and no thankes to his Excellency'.[22] The sharpness of Harrison's reflections probably got exaggerated in the telling, but it need not be doubted that the officers did discuss a proposal that the new supreme authority should be elected by the gathered congregations, or at least chosen from nominations submitted by them. It is certain that Harrison was in favour of it, and all but certain that Cromwell, while prepared to listen to recommendations from anyone he respected, preferred to retain a larger initiative and a greater freedom of choice for himself and his fellow-officers. At any rate, the procedure finally agreed was that the members of the assembly should be chosen by the Council of Officers, all of whose members were free to make nominations, and that the writs of summons should be issued in the name of Cromwell as commander-in-chief. But before describing further how it went about its business, it is worth considering just who composed the Council of Officers and what kind of advice was addressed to it in pamphlets, sermons, and addresses.

There seems to be practically nothing in contemporary sources to indicate who was entitled to attend it, or indeed whether it was constituted simply at the Lord General's discretion. It did not normally consist of all the commissioned officers about London, for occasionally we hear of such an omnium gatherum as though it were exceptional, and called for a particular purpose, as on 7 March, when it met to consider what the army should do

[21] Mayer, 'Inedited letters', p. 226.
[22] Firth, 'Cromwell and the expulsion', p. 529.

with regard to a new representative.[23] A letter from the Council of Officers written on 3 May to the commander-in-chief in Scotland, to explain the change of government to all the officers in that country, bore twenty-seven signatures;[24] a similar letter to Fleetwood in Ireland, dated 11 May and reprinted in a pamphlet of 1659, bore forty-one,[25] including all those found on the earlier letter. Most were of men who made some mark in the history of the army. A newsletter of 1 July said that the Council of Officers then numbered thirty-six,[26] which was probably about its average size. Perhaps Cromwell gave a clue to its membership when he said later that he had nominated fewer candidates than any other officers present, even captains; captain may have been the lowest rank entitled to attend.[27]

From outside its circle the most vociferous reactions came as was to be expected from the saints. We get a vivid little picture of the mood among the London congregations just after the dissolution in a letter written to Morgan Llwyd on 23 April by an elder of his flock in Denbighshire who had only just come up to the big city—'this Sodom', as he called it.

I Cannot give you any perfect account of thinges here onely this that men (eminent proffessors and for ought I know really godly too) doe differ in their mindes and Judgments of present transactions more then their faces differ one from another, but this I observed amonge some

23 Ibid. 527–8.

24 Clarke MS XXV, fos. 48–51.

25 *The Fifth Monarchy, or Kingdom of Christ ... asserted* ([23 Aug.] 1659), p. 24. The signatories are: John Lambert, John Desborough*, Edward Whalley, Thomas Harrison, William Constable, Adrian Scrope, Nathaniel Rich*, Matthew Tomlinson*, Philip Twistleton, Thomas Pride*, Thomas Cooper*, William Goffe, Ralph Cobbett*, Francis Hacker, Charles Worsley, Francis White*, Thomas Kelsey, Thomas Biscoe, Robert Swallow, Roger Alsop, Arthur Husbands*, Griffith Lloyd*, John Mason, Thomas Saunders, John Hodgson*, Geoffrey Elatson, Edward Orpin, Samuel Lark*, John Caitness*, John Wigan, Edward Walley (whose name, so spelt, appears as well as Colonel Edward Whalley's both on this letter and on that of 3 May to Scotland), Richard Merest, John Robinson*, Edmund Chillenden, George Smithson, William Packer, William Style, Francis Allen, William Farley*, William Malyn, Richard Hatt (or Hatter). I have not reproduced the pamphlet's spelling of the names. The asterisks denote those who did not sign the letter of 3 May to Scotland.

26 Clarendon MS 46, fo. 32.

27 Abbott, iv, 418. A few subaltern officers attended the Whitehall Debates in Dec. 1648, but these were larger gatherings, with over fifty present on all but one recorded occasion. Out of 94 named officers, 9 including a quartermaster ranked below captain; see Barbara Taft, 'Voting Lists of the Council of Officers, December 1648', *BIHR*, lii (1979), 138–52.

that the question is not so much now who is Independent Anabaptist seeker etc as who is for C[hris]t and who is for Crom[well] but the day of god will put an end to these things.[28]

Most of the gathered churches, however, welcomed the end of the Rump with enthusiasm, and it was by no means general yet for the Fifth Monarchists to think of Christ and Cromwell as opposed. John Rogers, writing on 25 April, could think of more than one good scriptural way of constituting a government safe for the saints, but he was positive that its members should be chosen by Cromwell, whom he regarded as a second Moses or Joshua.[29] John Spittlehouse, another Fifth Monarchy man, who had fought with the Ironsides from Gainsborough to Worcester, hailed his old general joyously on the 23rd. Affirming that the 'real members' of the Commonwealth consisted of the congregational churches and the army, he posed the question whether they should join together in electing a new representative or whether either should rule the Commonwealth alone. Although he believed that the time had come when God would deliver the kingdoms of the world into the hands of the saints, he concluded nevertheless that it would be 'altogether improper' for the churches to assume a magisterial authority and that the Lord of Hosts had designated the army as the inheritor of political power. He therefore hoped to see it vested in a 'representative of officers of the army', consisting of two from each regiment and one from each garrison, elected by their fellow-officers, together with some representatives of the fleet.[30] By mid-May, however, Spittlehouse had become convinced that God had ordained Cromwell himself to rule England as clearly as he had ordained Moses to rule Israel, and when Barebone's Parliament first met he adjured him to make no further use of it than to destroy Antichrist and advance the kingdom of Christ, which done—no long task, apparently—he should resume the power of Moses himself.[31]

[28] Philip Rogers to Morgan Llwyd, 23 Apr. 1653, NLW, Plas Yolyn MS 11, 439, no. 12. This anticipates by nearly eight months the notorious sermon in which Vavasor Powell, two days after the establishment of the Protectorate, urged his congregation to go home and pray, 'Lord, wilt thou have Oliver Cromwell or Jesus Christ to reign over us?' See p. 363.

[29] Rogers, *A few Proposals*.

[30] J. Spittlehouse, *The Army Vindicated* (23 Apr. 1653).

[31] J. Spittlehouse, *A Warning-Piece Discharged* ([19 May] 1653) and *The First Addresses to the Lord General* ([5 July] 1653).

Most of the gathered congregations, however, welcomed the prospect of being governed by an assembly named by Cromwell, with or without the concurrence of the Council of Officers. An unnamed 'church of Christ', which like Rogers and Spittlehouse acclaimed him as 'our Moses', begged him 'that you will not leave the choice of those that shall govern to the liberty of the counties, but that your Excellency will be pleased yourself to provide Conservators for us out of all the people'.[32] The brethren of Herefordshire, Chester, and Colchester, in various addresses, all rejoiced that God had made Cromwell instrumental in transferring power from the hands of corrupt men to the saints, and contented themselves with advising him as to the general qualities he should seek when choosing them.[33] Much the same came from the saints of Norwich and Norfolk, who urged Cromwell alone to select them, and those of Newcastle, who rejoiced that he and the officers were going to do so together.[34] The Fifth Monarchist preacher John Canne also expressed satisfaction that God had appointed Cromwell to be a happy instrument in transferring authority to fitter hands, but urged him specially to call such men as were best qualified to interpret the scriptural prophecies of the later times.[35] William Aspinwall, another minister of the same persuasion, wanted all subordinate officers and magistrates to be appointed upon recommendation by the churches, but he upheld the right of 'the Lamb's military officers' to dispose of the supreme authority in the present circumstances. On the other hand a strongly millenarian congregation 'at the Chequer without Aldgate', which was notable for its military membership, recommended that at least treble the number of men needed to make up the supreme assembly to its agreed size should be nominated, and that from these the actual members should be chosen by lot, after solemn prayer. The signatories included Lieutenant Colonel John Mason and Captain Chillenden, who sat in the Council of Officers, and

[32] *Severall Proceedings*, no. 187, 21–28 Apr. 1653, p. 2954; reprinted in *Old Parl. Hist.*, xx, 144–5 with 'Church' unwarrantably altered to 'Churches', as though it spoke for the gathered congregations collectively.

[33] Nickolls, pp. 92–3; *The Remonstrance of divers well-affected inhabitants of the town of Colchester* ([30 May] 1653).

[34] Capp, *Fifth Monarchy Men*, p. 64. Further addresses of support, dated slightly later, came from the churches of Radnorshire (printed in *Severall Proceedings*, 26 May–2 June, and other papers) and from Cumberland (printed in *Perfect Diurnall*, 6–13 June).

[35] John Canne, *A Voice from the Temple* ([13 June] 1653), epistle dedicatory.

also a former army chaplain called Samuel Oates, who had a little son called Titus.[36]

A few churches did, as will be shown shortly, recommend particular names to Cromwell, but only one address survives which requested him, as a general method, to 'suffer and encourage the saints of God in his spirit, to recommend unto you such as God shall choose for that worke';[37] in other words to solicit nominations from the congregations. Significantly, this came from Denbighshire, the centre of Morgan Llwyd's ministry. Llwyd and Vavasor Powell were the two fieriest preachers of the Fifth Monarchy in Wales and Harrison's closest associates in the Commission for the Propagation of the Gospel there. The address bore 153 signatures, and it pointedly exhorted Cromwell and the Council of Officers to 'rejoyce that yee are made a morning star, though yee should not be the rising sunne'. Christopher Feake, preaching at Christ Church in Newgate on 8 May, is reported to have put it more bluntly, declaring 'that although the General had fought their Battles with successe, yet he was not the Man, that the Lord had chosen to sitt at the Helme'.[38] According to the same source, Harrison at about the same time announced that the Spirit had told him 'that there would speedily be a king again, but not one of the former race, nor such carnal persons as some eminent in present power'.[39] But the writer was probably mistaken in thinking that Harrison was hinting at a crown for himself, and may have misreported his subsequent words slightly. Such an ambition would have gone clean against the Fifth Monarchist war-cry of 'no king but Jesus', and the probability is that Harrison was alluding to the imminent reign of Christ.

It is worth noting that the only sections of the Fifth Monarchist movement which displayed open distrust of the way Cromwell might wield the power in his hands, or urged him to commit the choice of England's new rulers to the saints, were those with whom Harrison was in close touch, though who influenced whom among them is a matter for conjecture. It used to be thought that

[36] William Aspinwall, *A Brief Description of the Fifth Monarchy* ([1 Aug.] 1653), pp. 4–7, written, on internal evidence, before Barebone's Parliament met; Nickolls, pp. 121–2; Capp, *Fifth Monarchy Men*, pp. 64–5, 245, 271.

[37] Nickolls, pp. 120–1; discussed by G. F. Nuttall, *The Welsh Saints 1640–1665* (Cardiff, 1957), pp. 37–9.

[38] Newsletter, 13 May, Clarendon MS 45, fo. 380.

[39] Ibid., quoted by Gardiner, *C & P*, ii, 225; cf. Capp, *Fifth Monarchy Men*, p. 66.

Cromwell bowed to them. 'Letters were despatched', wrote Gardiner, taking an unwonted plunge into sheer conjecture, 'in the name of the General and the Council of the Army to the Congregational Churches in each county, asking them to send in the names of a definite number of persons whom they considered fit to be members of the new representative.'[40] But no such letters were sent out.[41] Gardiner—and he was not the first—based his supposition on the fact that addresses survive from certain churches in six counties and two individual towns which recommend varying numbers of their brethren as fit to be nominated.[42] Not only, however, is no copy of a circular letter extant, but none of the 'replies' make any mention of one. The only two which suggest that they were responding to any invitation at all, those from Kent and Gloucestershire, cite Cromwell's public declarations, clearly meaning those of 22 and 30 April.[43] They would certainly have adduced a better authority, had they had one, for presuming to advise him whom to summon to the supreme power. Some of these churches may have been prompted to write by individual members of the Council of Officers, who may well have personally consulted ministers whom they trusted about possible candidates for their own counties. Others seem to have sent in names simply out of their own sense that the time had come for the saints to take over the seats of power.

Chronology also tells against the hypothesis that the Council of Officers consulted the gathered churches on a nation-wide scale and selected most of the members from their nominees. Those of the known addresses which submitted names and are also dated—unfortunately only four out of the eight—were written between 13 and 25 May. Yet on 3 May Gilbert Mabbott could already report that 'there [are] 100 names (and upward) presented to the Officers to bee made Choice of for the next

[40] Gardiner, *C & P*, ii, 224.

[41] What follows is documented slightly more fully in my article on 'The calling of Barebone's Parliament', *EHR*, lxxx (1965), 492–513. Tai Liu, in 'The calling of Barebones Parliament reconsidered', *Journal of Ecclesiastical History*, xxii (1971), 223–36, corrects me in one or two minor particulars and adds some interesting detail, but does not persuade me to depart in any way from my essential argument, which he appears to have misunderstood (see n. 65).

[42] Seven of the eight surviving addresses which proposed names are in Nickolls; for the eighth see n. 51.

[43] Nickolls, pp. 96, 125–6.

Government but not one is yet confirmed'.[44] By that date they could not have been presented by anyone more than a short ride from London, especially if Harrison's letter to Jones of 30 April, quoted earlier,[45] can be taken as showing that it was then still an open question whether to seek nominations from the saints or to leave the choice to Cromwell. Moreover on 7 May Mabbott could report that the Council of Officers was already nominating members for a number of counties, and the three whom he correctly named[46] came from much too far north for anyone in their locality to have been consulted. It is clear that the officers were free to propose whom they pleased, and that when recommendations came to them from outside, including those which some of the gathered churches sent in on their own initiative, these received the same consideration as the names put forward within the Council. Years later Cromwell, in an angry speech to a meeting of officers, many of whom must have shared in the selecting of the members, reminded them forcefully of their collective responsibility: 'those were nominated by themselves', he said; 'not an officer of the degree of a captain but named more than he himself did'.[47] His writ of summons to the members stated that 'divers persons fearing God ... are by myself, with the advice of my Council of Officers, nominated'.[48] Nedham in his commissioned account of the year's proceedings describes the procedure with some precision:

It was agreed likewise, that such persons should be called together out of the several counties, as were reputed men fearing God, and of approved fidelity; in the choice of which persons such indifferencie was used, and so equal liberty allowed to all then present with the Generall, that every officer enjoyed the same freedom of nomination, and the majority of suffrage carried it for the election of each single member.[49]

That the surviving recommendations from particular counties

[44] Clarke MS XXV, fo. 39ᵛ; virtually the same letter is in Hull Corporation MS L568.
[45] See p. 111.
[46] Walter Strickland, Charles Howard, Colonel Robert Fenwick: *Clarke Papers*, iii, 5. A similar letter in Hull Corporation MS L569, signed by Mabbott, establishes his authorship.
[47] Abbott, iv, 418.
[48] Abbott, iii, 34. John Spittlehouse addressed Barebone's Parliament on the day it met as 'the assembly of elders elected by him [Cromwell] and his council': *The First Addresses*, title page.
[49] *A True State of the Case of the Commonwealth*, pp. 12–13.

or churches do not represent a response to any formal invitation is further evidenced by their diversity of form and address and their varying degree of knowledge of how many seats were to be filled. Norfolk and Suffolk, being nurseries of radical Puritanism, predictably came out well. Suffolk's address, signed by fifty-two delegates from 'several churches', named six candidates, five of whom were actually chosen, the county's full complement. The church at Bury St. Edmunds, however, sent in three names of its own, though it knew that recommendations had already been made in the name of the county.[50] Norfolk sent an address signed by two delegates from each of seven churches, who probably knew that five was the county's quota of seats, though only three of the five men whom they named were successful. Bedfordshire also got the number right at two, but only one of those whom it put forward was summoned. Kent's address spoke for by far the largest number of churches— nineteen, represented by two commissioners each—and also submitted the right number of names, which was five. But only two of these were to sit for Kent, though two more were chosen to represent other counties. The churches in Gloucestershire, by contrast, named no fewer than twenty candidates, though they specially recommended three, of whom two got in. The congregation at Henley which unsuccessfully proposed a single candidate probably did not know that representation was to be by counties, but the address from Abingdon and Reading begged leave to name the members for Berkshire—with what success is unknown, since the names have been deleted from the only surviving text.[51]

Of the forty-one men whose names appear as the churches' choice in these addresses, fifteen were actually summoned to Barebone's Parliament; though the success rate is perhaps more fairly stated as fifteen out of twenty-four if Gloucestershire's twenty candidates are reduced to the three specially commended ones. Clearly the officers listened to the churches' advice with respect, but did not feel at all strictly bound by it. There may of

[50] Nickolls, p. 126. The explanation is that the county address emanated from Ipswich, chief town of the county division known as the Gildable. Bury was capital of the other division, called the Franchise, and wanted to ensure that it was adequately represented. But of Bury's three nominees only John Clarke was chosen, and he had already been recommended in the county address.

[51] In *Severall Proceedings*, no. 195, 16–23 June; the point at which the original put forward the names is obvious, and their removal suggests that they were not all accepted.

course have been other addresses and nominations that have been lost, but there is no reason to suppose that there were many. Of the fifteen known 'church-nominees', most were moderate Congregational men rather than sectarian extremists. Two exceptions came from Suffolk: Jacob Caley, reputedly a Fifth Monarchy man, and Edward Plumstead, who later became a Quaker. The only others were the four successfully proposed by the churches of Kent, all of whom showed mildly radical leanings in both their religion and their politics.[52]

Recently a rather tentative attempt has been made to revive the thesis that 'the members of the Barebones Parliament, or, at least, the bulk of them, were chosen either from the names sent up by the Congregational churches or through consultation with the Congregational leaders'.[53] The evidence adduced for it will not bear much weight. Too much trust is placed in a dispatch from the Dutch deputies, who had arrived in England well after the writs had gone out, and who wrote that the members had been selected 'after a foregoing communication with the ministers of the Independent party, which are spread through all England under the name of the gathered churches'.[54] It is argued that they must have been well informed because Hugh Peter had been associating with them; but there is nothing to indicate that he discussed the process of selection with them, and if he did, who is likelier to have exaggerated the influence of the Independent ministers than the voluble and self-important Peter! Since they were quite wrong about the number of members in Barebone's Parliament, four weeks after it met, they do not command much credence. As for Richard Baxter's allegation, written long afterwards, that Cromwell and the officers chose the members 'upon the advice of their sectarian friends in the country',[55] it is too general, bearing in mind his anti-sectarian prejudices, to mean more than Cromwell himself meant when he told Barebone's Parliament that 'the saints . . . have been somewhat instrumental to your call'.[56] Both statements were true to the

[52] Thomas Blount, William Kenrick, Samuel Highland, and Thomas St. Nicholas. The last two actually sat for Surrey and Yorkshire respectively.

[53] By Dr Tai Liu, in the article cited in n. 41, and hereafter cited as 'Calling . . . reconsidered', pp. 225–6.

[54] Thurloe, i, 395, quoted by me in *EHR*, lxxx, 502.

[55] *Reliquiae Baxterianae*, Part I, 70.

[56] Abbott, iii, 61.

limited extent that some officers *had* personally consulted
ministers and others whose advice they valued,[57] and some
churches *had* had their nominees accepted. Nor did Samuel
Highland's *Exact Relation* imply any more when it said that, 'It
was great satisfaction and encouragement to some that their
names had been presented as to that service, by the churches and
other godly men.'[58] To some of the members, yes; but if the bulk
of them had been so presented this author, a lay preacher who
had been recommended by the Kentish churches and actually
sat for Surrey, would have made the most of it. As for the
anonymous pamphleteer who two years later described Barebone's Parliament 'not as a representative of the people of three
nations; but, as may be conceived, a representative of certain
churches congregated',[59] his gibe does not even pretend to be
more than a travesty; his salvo 'as may be conceived' admits as
much.

Compare these vague or partisan allegations with the much
more exact intelligence sent to Secretary Nicholas on 3 June that
the forthcoming assembly was to number 130 or 140, 'most of
them named by the General without consulting the respective
Countys; but some officious Countrys (or rather particular
factions in those Countrys) as Kent, and some few others have
returned the names of 5 or 6 quallifyed persons out of which his
Excellency hath chosen 2 or 3'.[60] This probably requires no
other essential correction than that the actual choice was made
collectively by the Council of Officers. John Lilburne charged
them with imposing 'a parliament picked and called by
yourselves, that have not with all the officers of the army (the
honest people of England's paid and hired servants ...) any
other pretence to set up such a parliament but the right of
conquest'.[61] And besides these positive statements, to which
Nedham's and Cromwell's (already quoted[62]) should be added,
there is all the negative evidence of those Fifth Monarchist and
other sectarian pamphleteers who later lamented the demise of

---

[57] For examples see *EHR*, lxxx, 500–2, 506–7.
[58] 'L.D.' [Samuel Highland], *An Exact Relation* (1654), reprinted in *Somers Tracts*, ed.
W. Scott (London, 1809–15), vi, 269.
[59] *A Representation concerning the late Parliament* ([9 Apr.] 1655), pp. 2–3.
[60] Clarendon MS 45, fo. 482.
[61] J. Lilburne, *The Upright Mans Vindication* (1 Aug. 1653), p. 11.
[62] See p. 117.

Barebone's Parliament. If they could have claimed for it the nation-wide suffrages of the gathered churches they would surely have done so, but they did not.[63]

One of them did however accuse Cromwell of making deliberately deceitful promises to the saints, and his testimony, though written over six years later and with a very obvious bias, may cast a little light on the kind of consultations that accompanied the selection of members, outside the formal sessions of the Council of Officers. This Fifth Monarchist pamphleteer describes a private conference on the subject between Cromwell, Lambert, Harrison, Pickering, the ministers Walter Cradock and Nicholas Lockyer, and others unnamed. Cromwell allegedly declared, 'That if there were one man more faithful to the saints, and more suited to the work then another, and that had not been left behinde in former dispensations, by the blessing of God he should be chosen.' Yet for some time *before* Barebone's Parliament met, this writer tells us, Cromwell, Lambert, Desborough, Whalley, Goffe, Pickering, John Owen, and others nursed a secret enmity towards those members who were to strive hardest in it to advance the kingdom of Christ, and thanks to them other men 'of a contrary spirit and principle [were] purposely chosen and packt together, (viz. Coll. Montague, Coll. Barton, Coll. Matthews, Sir William Roberts, Alderman Tichborn, and others) and those the greater number'.[64] Obviously such allegations, from such a source, must be treated with great caution, for it is the perennial habit of disappointed ideologues to attribute their defeat to a conspiracy. Yet the words attributed to Cromwell are perfectly credible, and taken in the context of what he went on to say they signify no more than a pledge to put commitment to the cause of the people of God and

---

[63] See *EHR*, lxxx, 503 n. 4.

[64] *A Faithfull Searching Home Word* ([13 Dec.] 1659), pp. 14 16. Dr Tai Liu ('Calling . . . reconsidered', p. 229) accuses me of misinterpreting this pamphlet in my article, alleging that it dates the banding together of Cromwell, Lambert, and the rest only from after the meeting of Barebone's Parliament. He is wrong, for it states that this happened 'some time before these words [i.e. Cromwell's speech of 4 July] were spoken' (p. 16). The only point at which he finds me in error (*EHR*, lxxx, 500) concerns the secret correspondence between the army leaders in England and Henry Lawrence and others in Ireland, which the pamphlet places in 1659, not in 1653 as I misread it. This does not, however, materially affect the pamphlet's charge, for what it is worth, of a concerted hostility towards the extreme saints and an attempt to balance them with fellow-moderates.

fitness for the tasks ahead before kinship or any other personal considerations. 'Faithful to the saints' did not have such narrow connotations for him as for the Fifth Monarchists, and 'suited to the work' meant to him not only sanctity but also general soundness of judgement and political competence. Furthermore, considering how strenuously Harrison and his friends were caballing to get all they could of their own kind nominated, it would not have been unnatural or sinister if Cromwell and his fellow-moderates had taken counsel together to secure a counterpoise of less extreme and more experienced members.

To argue thus is not of course to interpret the whole process of nomination as a competition in packing the assembly between Cromwell and Harrison.[65] Their aims and aspirations had far too much in common, and they were not yet aware of the extent of their latent differences. Both wanted to commit authority into the hands of godly and faithful men. Both believed, as did the majority of Puritans with any streak of enthusiasm in them, that the providences that had brought them thus far were linked with the promised overthrow of Antichrist and the prophecies of the last times, though they differed as to what precise role the present conjuncture cast upon the saints, and how far it had rendered obsolete the familiar laws and civil liberties of England. Moreover the Council of Officers contained men who did not regard themselves as tied to either commander's faction, and many names must have been proposed that did not cause it to divide on factional lines at all. Nevertheless there was a certain polarization among both choosers and chosen: between those whose eyes were fixed on inaugurating the millennial kingdom of the saints and those who thought of the forthcoming assembly primarily as a temporary surrogate for a parliament elected by the people; between those who conceived a rule of the saints in terms of immediate power and those who looked first for the realization of Christ's kingdom in the hearts of men; and between those who assumed that distinctions of worldly rank would soon

---

[65] Dr Tai Liu unwarrantably attributes this interpretation to me in 'Calling ... reconsidered' (p. 225 and *passim*) and then proceeds elaborately to 'refute' it. My only mention of packing was in the course of my summary of *A Faithful Searching Home Word*, which I described as biased evidence, coloured by hindsight (*EHR*, lxxx, 500). In saying that Cromwell and his fellow-officers 'generally named whom they pleased' I naturally did not intend to deny that they chose in accordance with their conscience and convictions.

become irrelevant in the New Jerusalem and those who considered that the work of winning over the political nation to the benefits of a Commonwealth would best be done by men whose social standing did not invite its contempt. Those of the one persuasion thought first and foremost of bringing in their fellow-zealots. Harrison gives us a glimpse of how they did it in a letter he wrote to John Jones on 17 May, asking his advice as to whether the three Fifth Monarchists that he and Vavasor Powell and their circle had picked to represent North Wales were the right men.[66] Apparently they were, for they were all summoned. Cromwell and his fellow-officers of more moderate views, however, were more disposed to value experience and reputation in the world of men. The nineteen former Rumpers whom they summoned were probably as many as they could find both fit and willing to sit; they would have liked to call Fairfax, Vane, Luke Robinson, and Gervase Piggot too, but none of these men would serve.[67] Cromwell and his kindred spirits were far from indifferent to godliness, but one can be sure that it was through them that representatives of such houses as Howard, Montagu, Sidney, Eure, Wolseley, and Ashley Cooper were called.

One thesis that has been advanced is that the key both to the genesis and to the ultimate collapse of Barebone's Parliament lies in the politics of the City of London.[68] Whether or not this was the case, Cromwell's relations with the City government were obviously important to him and to the army. Fortunately for him they were on the whole good, especially with the Lord Mayor, John Fowke. He had the sense and tact to send for Fowke immediately after the dissolution and to come to terms with him about the maintenance of law and order in the capital.[69] Shortly afterwards he obtained Fowke's collaboration in suppressing a coarse anti-Rump ballad with the refrain 'Twelve parliament-men for a penny'.[70] When a witty citizen hung a portrait of Cromwell at the Exchange, subscribed with verses inviting him

[66] Mayer, 'Inedited letters', p. 227. There is no hint whatever that the congregations in Wales were consulted about the choice of members.

[67] See *EHR*, lxxx, 500, 507–8.

[68] J. E. Farnell, 'The usurpation of honest London householders: Barebone's Parliament', *EHR*, lxxxii (1967), 24–46.

[69] *Faithful Post*, no. 92, 15–22 Apr., p. 716.

[70] *Clarke Papers*, iii, 3.

to assume the crown, it was the worried Lord Mayor who brought it to him and awaited his orders.[71] It is true that the only overt condemnation of the dissolution and request for the restoration of the Rump came in a petition signed by six aldermen and thirty-one common councilmen of London, which was presented to him exactly a month after the parliament had been ejected. His reply was to obtain an order from the Council of State, dismissing all the petitioners who held offices of profit under the Commonwealth. This was harsh, but only three of them suffered more than temporarily by it, and it was probably a necessary act of firmness, especially since Hesilrige and other Rumpers were reported to be behind the petition.[72]

But thirty-seven was a small minority among London's city fathers, and the episode does not seem to have seriously disturbed Cromwell's relations with the majority of them. Within a week of it, and when the selection of members of the new supreme authority was largely complete, Cromwell arranged two conferences, a private one on 23 May and a more public one at the Guildhall two days later, between a committee of army officers and a group of prominent citizens headed by Alderman John Ireton (one of London's representatives in Barebone's Parliament). Their purpose was to discuss the future government of the City.[73] A newswriter described Lord Mayor Fowke on 3 June as one of Cromwell's 'privados'.[74] And when John Lilburne returned to England in mid-June in defiance of the Rump's act of banishment against him, it was certainly helpful to Cromwell that he could persuade Fowke, despite a revival of vociferous demonstrations by the Levellers, to commit their old leader to Newgate.[75] The co-operation which the City government (or most of it) gave him in 1653 is in striking contrast with its independent, indeed hostile, attitude towards the army after the latter's second interruption of the Rump in 1659.[76]

There is however no specific evidence that either the City government or any other identifiable group of Londoners made

[71] Ibid. 6; Gardiner, *C & P*, ii, 228.

[72] Gardiner, *C & P*, ii, 229–30; *CSPD 1652–3*, p. 342; Clarendon MS 45, fo. 435.

[73] Clarendon MS 45, fo. 436.

[74] Ibid, fo. 484.

[75] *CSPD 1652–3*, pp. 410, 415, 420, 436; see pp. 304, 429, 434 for further evidence of good relations between Cromwell and Fowke.

[76] *Complete Prose Works of John Milton*, vii, 143–6, 151–3.

any concerted attempt to influence the officers' decisions on what kind of government to establish or who should compose it. London was given seven representatives in the new supreme authority, and it is worth inquiring whether either they or the members who represented the adjacent counties into which the suburbs spilt over reflected the overriding influence of any particular political or religious interests. To take politics first, Dr Farnell has suggested that the origins of Barebone's Parliament can be found in the politics of the City, and more specifically in the contrast between the leaders of the Common Council during the first year or two of the Commonwealth and the new leaders who emerged in 1650 and 1651 and who espoused more radical schemes of reform.[77] But in the absence of any positive indication that either group helped to bring down the Rump or influenced the choice of its successor, this thesis seems difficult to sustain. Of those whom Farnell names as leaders of the Common Council in 1649, Robert Tichborne and Samuel Moyer sat in Barebone's Parliament but generally took opposite sides, while of his new leaders of 1650–1 John Ireton and Praise-God Barebone were the only two to be called. Moyer and Barebone, different though their fortunes and backgrounds were, stood closer to each other in their radical political and religious affiliations than to the moderate Tichborne. He does not explain why no others of his 1650–1 leaders found seats, nor why the officers chose men as obscure as John Langley and Henry Barton and the as yet little-known John Stone to make up the tally of the City's representatives. It seems evident that the breach between the army and the Rump had thoroughly divided the aldermen and common councilmen, and while only a minority were prepared to run the risk of petitioning for the Rump, with whose policies their fortunes had been closely tied,[78] fewer still were prepared to participate actively in a government whose future was so doubtful.

Dr Farnell particularly associates the new leaders of 1650–1 with the congregation of the radical Independent John Goodwin, yet not one of Goodwin's flock seems to have sat in Barebone's

[77] Farnell, pp. 24–6, 30.

[78] Robert Brenner, 'The Civil War politics of London's merchant community', *Past and Present*, no. 58 (1973), pp. 97–106. This interesting article ends tantalizingly just before the calling of Barebone's Parliament.

Parliament. Elsewhere he stresses the social dimension of City radicalism and associates it particularly with the Baptists.[79] The Baptist preachers, he tells us, were strengthening their organization and proselytizing in the army during 1652. He does not cite his evidence, but he presumably refers to the extreme millenarians who forgathered at Blackfriars and Allhallows and were closely linked with Harrison's faction. Their outpourings did indeed exhibit a strong vein of social discontent, but they were certainly not all Baptists, and they represented a different vein of radicalism, socially and doctrinally, from that of most of the newer City leaders. The latter were predominantly Independents of a more moderate hue.[80] No Baptists were called to represent London in 1653, and such prominent and able Baptist citizens as John Fenton, William Kiffin, and Josias Berners were passed over. Kiffin, however, like the great Baptist preacher Hanserd Knollys, was out of sympathy with the Fifth Monarchist firebrands at Blackfriars, and a few months later he and other Particular Baptists came out in strong condemnation of them.[81] In the end Farnell admits that his radical citizens failed in their 'bid for national power', largely, he thinks, because they 'gave over the decision for the structure and election of the new representative to their fellow Saints on the Army council'.[82] The decision was never theirs to give, and in so far as there was a bid for national power by the saints it rested on a much wider geographical basis than London. One can only conclude that 'honest London householders', however identified, had very little to do with either the conception or the calling of Barebone's Parliament.

There is really little need to invoke outside pressures in order to explain why the officers chose most of London's seven representatives as they did. Tichborne and Ireton were obvious nominations, both being aldermen of substance who had been friends of the army since Civil War days and had later served as sheriffs of the City. Fairfax had installed Tichborne as Lieutenant of the Tower when he marched into London in 1647 to thwart

[79] Farnell: compare p. 34 with pp. 36, 39–43.

[80] Brenner, pp. 99–101.

[81] Nickolls, pp. 159–60; Capp, *Fifth Monarchy Men*, pp. 93, 101. For evidence that neither Moyer nor Barebone were Baptists see Murray Tolmie, *The Triumph of the Saints: the Separate Churches of London 1616–1649* (Cambridge, 1977), p. 236 and *passim*.

[82] Farnell, 'Usurpation', p. 42.

the Presbyterian counter-revolution, while Ireton had a special link with Cromwell and the officers through his deceased brother Henry. Both men worshipped in the same Independent congregation, whose pastor was George Cokayne. Barebone was not of the same standing, and he probably owed his place to the religious radicals among the nominating officers. They probably favoured Samuel Moyer too, but as an alderman, as a really wealthy merchant who had already served a four-year term on the Court of Assistants of the Levant Company and was currently Master of the Mercers' Company, above all as a commissioner with years of experience in handling several branches of the Commonwealth's revenues, Moyer really needed no further recommendation than his willingness to serve. There is nothing to suggest religious radicalism in John Stone, though he was certainly a religious man. He was a member of the Corporation for the Propagation of the Gospel in New England, and he was probably the John Stone who had signed John Owen's proposals for ecclesiastical settlement in 1651, but he also had in his favour his experience as Receiver-General for London's monthly assessment.[83] John Langley was an alderman who had served both on the Levant Company's Court of Assistants and on the East India Company's Committee, and had been elected Prime Warden of the Fishmongers' Company in 1652. Since that year he had been one of the Rump's Admiralty and Navy Commissioners, in company with Vane, Salwey, and Carew, but his reappointment as such is the only appearance he makes in the *Journal* of Barebone's Parliament. He had been co-owner of a privateer with Moyer. The one really obscure London member was Henry Barton, listed in 1654 like Langley among the religious radicals, though on what evidence is not known. If he was the Captain Henry Barton who had commanded a troop in Colonel Rich's regiment, his nomination would be explicable.[84]

In elected parliaments it was common for Londoners to find

---

[83] Shaw, *English Church*, ii, 84; C. H. Firth and R. S. Rait, *Acts and Ordinances of the Interregnum*, 3 vols. (1911), ii, 198; Aylmer, *State's Servants*, p. 241. For Tichborne and Ireton see *DNB*; A. B. Beaven, *The Aldermen of the City of London*, 2 vols. (1908–13), ii, 72, 78; Nuttall, *Visible Saints*, p. 151.

[84] On Langley I follow Beaven, *Aldermen*, ii, 73, rather than John Rylands Library, Pink MS 306, fo. 43; see also *CSPD 1625–49, Addenda*, p. 667; *CSPD 1650*, p. 280; PRO, PROB 11/411 (PCC 155 Fane). On Barton (if this identification is correct) see C. H. Firth and G. Davies, *Regimental History of Cromwell's Army*, 2 vols. (Oxford, 1940), i, 149.

seats in the adjacent counties, but few did so in 1653. One such was the Fifth Monarchist Arthur Squibb, but his fellow-members for Middlesex were the wealthy and moderate Sir William Roberts, who had been much engaged in the Commonwealth's sale of crown, church and royalists' lands, and the barrister Augustine Wingfield, who was later to declare himself an ardent Cromwellian. Samuel Highland, the lay preacher of Southwark, was recommended by the churches of Kent but chosen to represent Surrey; he and the only other Surrey member, Lawrence Marsh of Dorking, seem to have been struck off the Commission of the Peace during the Rump's last months and reinstated after its expulsion.[85] Kent is the only home county where the churches are known to have recommended candidates; they were all religious radicals, but only Highland came from near London, and the officers balanced those whom they accepted with Viscount Lisle and William Cullen, the moderate Mayor of Dover. Essex displays as mixed a bag as Middlesex; none of its five members were Londoners but two of them, Joachim Matthews and John Brewster (both moderate men), belonged to the same gathered church.[86]

Throughout England, most counties give the impression that the nominations came from no single source and that the officers voted on them according to what they thought to be their merits. Kinship, neighbourhood, and former comradeship in arms must often have borne upon their choice, as well as judgements of political fitness and shared religious convictions. The latter were important, of course; the great majority of the Council of Officers were Congregationalists of one shade or another, and so were most of the men they chose. They were pledged in all sincerity to call godly men to the work of government, and whether or not they were directly prompted by the gathered churches they turned naturally to their co-religionaries. Not many others, after all, were eligible. Anglicans were out of the question, and most Presbyterians had for years been so estranged from the army that they were as unlikely to accept as they were to be invited. Nevertheless Francis Rous, the Speaker and father of the House,

[85] PRO, C.193/13/4.
[86] An acre of Waltham Forest on which its meeting-house had been built was assigned to them by name in the act for the sale of royal forests which was passed on 22 Nov. 1653: Firth and Rait, ii, 812.

was a Presbyterian; so probably was John Pyne, the Rump's virtual ruler of Somerset,[87] and Monck was as near a Presbyterian as his sceptical erastianism permitted. 'Independency' is itself a comprehensive term, and the religious spectrum of an assembly which ranged from Rous through orthodox Congregational men to left-wing Baptists and Fifth Monarchists was not narrow, even if most of the political nation lay outside it. The divisions within it would be deep enough in the end to break Barebone's Parliament.

If the main difference within the Council of Officers was as to whether the new supreme authority should be conceived more as an assembly of Puritan notables temporarily deputizing for an elected parliament or as a government by the saints for the saints, a much wider range of possibilities was being canvassed by the presses. The Levellers, for example, although broken as an organized political movement, were far from being silenced. Before the dissolution they had seemed divided as to whether the Rump or Cromwell was the greater enemy. If the democratic commonwealthsman who wrote *Vox plebis* on 1 April can be accounted a Leveller, his wrath was directed almost wholly against the parliament, with only a side-swipe at its 'red-coated slaves'. 'We looked for liberty, and behold slavery! . . . Cast your eyes back into the rock out of which you were hewn; were you not our fellow-commoners?'[88] Yet late in March John Lilburne was publishing fresh vituperations against 'that grand tyrant Cromwell and his lawles blood-thirstie crue', and promising to 'instruct the people of England, in the best way, method or form that I can, to set themselves in, to obtain the reall exercise of their declared rightfull supreme power'.[89] The dissolution, however, made him temporarily change his tune. Might not those who had turned the Rump out reverse the act of banishment that it had passed against him? In a sanguine mood he returned to England, and on 14 June published an emotional broadsheet in

[87] David Underdown, *Somerset in the Civil War and Interregnum* (Newton Abbot, 1973), pp. 122, 143.

[88] *Vox plebis* (1 Apr. 1653; acquired by Thomason on 18 Apr.), p. 3.

[89] *L. Colonel John Lilburne revived* ([27 March] 1653), pp. 3, 9. Lilburne himself dated this piece 4 Feb. 1653. It opens with a bitter personal attack on Edmund Chillenden, formerly an army agitator but now a captain, Fifth Monarchist, and member of the Council of Officers (Clarke MS XXV, fo. 51).

which he cast his life and all that was his upon Cromwell, excusing his recent provocations as best he could and promising to live as quietly and submissively as any man in the land.[90] His fellow-Levellers held their fire until his case was heard, and Samuel Highland, our member-designate for Surrey, prayed publicly for him at Blackfriars, despite Cromwell's temporary ban on the preaching sessions there.[91] Yet Lilburne remained inconsistent, for he later published a long address which he claimed to have sent to the Council of State on 4 June, just ten days before his pathetic appeal to Cromwell, telling it among other things that the Rump could not be legally dissolved except by its own act, and that a new parliament could 'by no power or persons whatsoever in England be summoned, called or chosen ... but by a new and rational contract and agreement of the people of England'.[92] The Levellers of London and Westminster published early in July a new set of twenty-eight fundamental laws and liberties, including: 'That yearly parliaments (to be chosen of course by the people) is the onely supreme lawful government of England.'[93]

Occasionally the stark contradiction between the Leveller and the Fifth Monarchist positions was fully perceived. William Aspinwall, for instance, insisted that Christ alone must be acknowledged as lawgiver, and that for anyone else to pretend to a legislative authority would be an encroachment on his regality. Parliaments could claim no such authority from the people, for the people had none to confer.[94] And John Spittlehouse warned Cromwell against accepting any commission, military or civil, from what he called the new 'assembly of elders', since by doing so he would deny Jesus Christ to be the king of the nation.[95]

The solutions held forth by the pamphleteers and preachers were not of course confined to the Leveller and Fifth Monarchist ones. Nothing was heard publicly from the parliamentary republicans apart from Bradshaw's protests in court, though

[90] J. Lilburne, *The Banished mans suit for Protection* (14 June 1653); Pauline Gregg, *Freeborn John* (1961), pp. 319–23.

[91] Clarendon MS 46, fo. 32.

[92] J. Lilburne, *The Upright Mans Vindication* (1 Aug. 1653), p. 12.

[93] *The Fundamental Lawes and Liberties of England* (9 July 1653), p. 3.

[94] W. Aspinwall, *A Brief Description of the Fifth Monarchy*, p. 8.

[95] J. Spittlehouse, *The First Addresses*, dedicatory epistle.

Hesilrige was reported to 'bluster much'.[96] Apart from the London aldermen and common councilmen who petitioned for their restoration, their only other known champion was John Streater, who circulated ten queries attacking the dissolution among his fellow-officers and was court-martialled and cashiered for his pains.[97] At the other end of the spectrum there were said to be petitions afoot in Essex, Kent, and Wiltshire, asking Cromwell to take on the headship of the state as Protector or by whatever title he liked best, and here comes to mind again that London citizen who hung up his portrait at the Exchange, with verses appended which ended with 'God save the King!' in golden capitals. Cromwell reacted to that incident with amused tolerance; 'it was some odd fellow to make sport', he is alleged to have told the Lord Mayor, 'but such trifles as these were not to be considered these serious times'.[98]

A few other voices declared that supreme authority had devolved by right upon the army as a whole. *The Army no Usurpers* argued that parliament, after wresting the sovereign power from the king, remained as subject to popular consent as he by right should have been. So far from being entitled to any 'uncontrollable power' the Rumpers had been mere tenants at will, and the people had always retained the right to lay them aside if they became dissatisfied with them. But who could rightfully exercise it in the people's name? The answer was the army.

The armies are intrusted for the people (or trained bands) to do in their absence whatsoever being present they might have done, and therefore are a national power, such as the parliaments heretofore, which have authority to remove evil rulers if they see cause . . . The chief end of the militia is to act as if they were the nation; and therefore if the army had not done that which the nation in arms might undoubtedly have done, they had overthrown the end of their own being.[99]

---

[96] Worden, *Rump*, p. 340.

[97] J. Streater, *Secret Reasons of State* (1659), p. 6. A contemporary MS copy of the queries is in BL, E693(5). Streater was not (as has been said) imprisoned at this stage; that occurred after Barebone's Parliament met, for publishing further matter which its Council of State considered seditious (ibid., pp. 6–7).

[98] Clarendon MS 45, fos. 398–9; Gardiner, *C & P*, ii, 227–8. There is a most unlikely story in the same newsletter that Alderman Tichborne summoned a private meeting of prominent citizens to consider means of restoring parliamentary government, preferably by recalling the Rump, but that Captain Fenton proposed instead that Cromwell should assume the crown.

[99] *The Army no Usurpers* ([20 May] 1653), p. 10 and *passim*.

Another pamphleteer argued even more crudely that parliament, being the king's great council and summoned to parley with him, had become extinct when the monarchy was abolished, and that thereafter the government of the nation inhered naturally in the Lord General and his Council of Officers. Where the power of protection lay, he contended, there should authority lie too; for God is the Lord of hosts as well as the God of peace, and the first is the more honourable title.[1] Such blatant vindications of military power were not new, nor would these be the last of them,[2] but there is not the slightest suggestion that they were inspired by the Council of Officers. When Cromwell persuaded that body to refrain from nominating serving officers (other than garrison commanders) to the new assembly, he demonstrated that he was as anxious to avoid a collective military dictatorship as a personal one.

If warnings were needed, they were not lacking. A particularly thoughtful one was published by Isaac Penington the younger, son of the famous wartime Lord Mayor of London. His basic theme was that power corrupts. All who assume it disappoint the hopes placed in them; just as the Rump had done, so might the army. 'So soon as a man is exalted, he forgets the Lord, and returns into himself, and in that very day all his good thoughts die and perish.' His pessimistic advice to the people was to: 'Expect not that fruit from your governours, the root whereof is not in them. Did man ever bring forth righteousness or peace? Have ye not had enough of looking for reformation and amendment of things from this or that party?... If ye yourselves were governours, ye would act like those that had gone before you.' As for that great truth foretold of the rule of the saints, it would come when the spirit of Christ was poured out upon them, but if men tried to bring it about without this divine effusion they would effect the very opposite.[3] Another writer, who was more confident that England was to become the citadel from

---

[1] *Reasons why the Supreme Authority of the Three Nations, for the time, is not in the Parliament* (17 May 1653), pp. 3–5.

[2] For earlier affirmations of the army's right to act for the people against parliaments and other powers see Woodhouse, *Puritanism and Liberty*, pp. 212–20, 330–4, 395–6, 404, and 443; and for a more extravagant assertion in 1659, *Complete Prose Works of John Milton*, vii, 124–6.

[3] Isaac Penington, Jr., *A Considerable Question about Government* ([9 May] 1653), pp. 6–8. It is not surprising that Penington became a Quaker convert a few years later.

which the Lord would establish the reign of his saints, nevertheless adjured the army not to follow the Rumpers in 'a building their own nests with the feathers of the poor', and warned them that if they would 'grow lordly, lofty, worldly and humoursome, fierce, self-confident, by-ended, and touchy, that a man cannot speak to them; down they also tumble with their swords, pikes and cannons, and a better generation shall take their place'.[4]

Yet widely as the views varied as to who ideally should inherit the Rump's authority, there was no serious challenge to Cromwell's and the officers' assumption of the right to dispose of it. Very little discontent appeared, at least on the surface, and it seems that the wide popularity of the dissolution outweighed forebodings about the new government that they had undertaken to erect. 'Nothing could be more pleasing to all degrees of men than the dissolution of these parliament men', wrote Viscount Conway on 26 April, and the Bishop of Exeter echoed him three weeks later.[5] The record of May, whether from newspapers, newsletters, foreign diplomats, or royalist correspondence, gives the impression of Cromwell very much in command, in spite of the undeniable divisions of opinion within the Council of Officers. The outbreaks of sectarian fanaticism that had disgusted moderate observers before the dissolution seem to have given way to a more quietly expectant mood among the gathered churches, thanks partly to his prompt order forbidding officers and soldiers to disturb the public worship of God on pain of court martial.[6] He probably did much to reanimate the saints' faith in him when on 25 April he wrote to the Commissioners for the Propagation of the Gospel in Wales advising them 'to go on cheerfully in the work as formerly' despite the lapse of their statutory authority.[7]

One rather interesting little disturbance, shortly before mid-May, demonstrated that the army's sense of a right to participate in political decisions was not confined to the Council of Officers. A party of about thirty officers, presumably junior ones, appeared

[4] *A Warning Seriously offered to the Officers of the Army* (1653), pp. 6–7; dated 18 May by Thomason but 3 May by the anonymous author.

[5] *CSPD 1652–3*, p. 298; Bodl. Tanner MS 52, fo. 12. For further evidence of the popularity of the dissolution, see (e.g.) *Weekly Intelligencer*, 12–19 Apr., and *CSP Ven 1653–4*, pp. 65, 68, 72, 74.

[6] Printed in several newspapers late in April, including *Perfect Diurnall*, 18–25 Apr.

[7] Abbott, iii, 13.

unbidden at the door of the council chamber in Whitehall and demanded the right to participate in the Council of State's proceedings, 'saieing they were souldiers and had acted as well as any, and therfore ought to share with the best'. Harrison began to reprimand them, but Cromwell found the right tactful words to send them away pacified.[8]

Meanwhile Cromwell and the Council of Officers busied themselves with the selection of the members of Barebone's Parliament throughout most of May. By the 3rd they are said to have had over a hundred names before them, and ten days later Nicholas's newswriter, reporting that Cromwell had sent privately to his friends in most parts of the country for advice on whom to summon, claimed that he himself had seen 'a private List of them which were returned'.[9] If he did see such a very confidential list, the names were probably yet to be passed by the Council of Officers, with whom Cromwell was still reported to be sitting 'very close' towards the end of the month.[10] The task of selection cannot have been proving easy, and it would be very interesting to know whether more time was spent in seeking for suitable names or in arguing over rival candidates. Unfortunately nothing is known of their deliberations until Gilbert Mabbott, still the licenser of army news, opens a gap in the mists with a newsletter which he wrote to the corporation of Hull on 24 May:

The Large Remonstrance of the Armie past the last night and the select Councell of Officers appointed to draw it up attended the Councell of State to comunicate the same to them and afterward to have it read before a generall Councell of Officers mett for the purpose, but the Council of State sitting long, prevented the passing thereof, whereby its

---

[8] Johnson and Vaisey, p. 74. The writer of this letter of news is specific about the council chamber, which was the meeting-place of the temporary Council of State; and that it was the latter and not the Council of Officers that was threatened with invasion is confirmed by a newsletter of 13 May in Clarendon MS 45, fo. 181, which reports the junior officers' 'Many bold addresses, or assaults rather, to our new Council of State, with turbulent demands . . .'

[9] *Clarke Papers*, iii, 8; Clarendon MS 45, fo. 381, quoted at greater length in *EHR*, lxxx, 500–1.

[10] *The Perfect Diurnall*, no. 181, 23–30 May, p. 2747. On 27 May a newswriter reported that Cromwell seldom came to council, and when he came did not stay long, 'the dispatch being only in his Cabinet' (Clarendon MS 45, fo. 437). This probably means that the Council of Officers was taking up more of his time than the Council of State, but his attendance at the latter was irregular only until 21 May.

conceived it will [bee put*] off till Thursday next. In this Declaration there are chosen 8 for the County of Yorke [etc.][11]

Mabbott was right about the number of representatives for Yorkshire, and though he gave slightly too low a figure for the other counties that he went on to name, his information was clearly of a different order of accuracy from that of any other reports on the officers' proceedings until well into June.

There are several points of interest here. Firstly, the Council of Officers had a list of agreed nominations ready to put before the Council of State by 23 May, two weeks before Cromwell signed any writs summoning members to Barebone's Parliament.[12] Secondly, they evidently intended to announce this list publicly in a remonstrance or declaration, but no such document was ever published. Thirdly, Mabbott mentions a select Council of Officers and a general one. The latter was probably to have been one of those occasional gatherings of all commissioned officers within reach, summoned for a special purpose, in this case to hear the declaration read, with perhaps some exhortation by Cromwell to give loyalty and support to the new supreme authority. There is no record, however, of any such meeting being held. The select Council may have been the normal body of about thirty or forty, but in this context it sounds more like a smaller drafting committee.

It is clear from Mabbott's letter that the declaration listed all the members whom the Council of Officers had approved, and that the roll was thought to be complete. On 'Thursday next', i.e. 26 May, the date on which he expected the Council of State to consider it, that body's order book records only one small item of business instead of the usual score or more,[13] so it probably did devote the day to discussing it. But it evidently did not get through it, for on the 28th Mabbott wrote that Cromwell and the officers had during that week 'sat cloce in chooseing the persons to sit in the next Representative; it will bee a busines of more time then was at first conceived'.[14] This sounds very much as

* MS torn; probable reading.

[11] Hull Corporation MS, L571.
[12] For the dates of the surviving writs see Abbott, iii, 34 n. 109.
[13] *CSPD 1652–3*, p. 352.
[14] *Clarke Papers*, iii, 8.

though the Council of State had not fully approved the names submitted to it, or perhaps, in view of the rather low numbers of members per county that Mabbott reported on 23 May, had recommended that the representation of some counties should be increased. His next news was that the Council of State had risen early on the 30th in order to meet Cromwell and the officers 'for completing the names of the next Representative'. They were not finally agreed even then, however, for not until 4 June could he report that, 'The Declaration for calling a new parliament was yesterday perfected, and likewise all the members' names to · be inserted therein, but secrecy is enjoined both as to the names and substance of the Declaration for some time.'[15] Cromwell did in fact sign most of the writs summoning the members on the 6th, but of the declaration no more was heard. The obvious inference is that the civilian members had demanded a greater say in the whole business than Cromwell had anticipated. They may also have queried the contents of the intended declaration, apart from the names. Certainly their ordinary business was brief again on 30 May, and when it swelled to sixty-two items on 4 June they were probably clearing a backlog caused by days of concentration on the new assembly.

There is some doubt as to how many members Cromwell summoned at this stage. Mabbott on 4 June gave 120 as the total, which he repeated on the 7th when he stated that, 'The General and officers have now agreed upon 120 names to sit as a parliament.' In view of the fact that he had reported their agreement more than two weeks earlier, this suggests again that they had had to think afresh about some nominations which the Council of State had questioned. He added that Cromwell had had to send the writs out in his own name, since the Commissioners of the Great Seal had refused to seal them on his authority. On the 11th he reported that all the writs had been sent out.[16] The number 120 was widely reported in the newspapers from 9 June onwards, and it recurred in the pungent query of a satirist, 'Whether our Saviour's riding into Jerusalem upon an ass's foal, were any more than a type of our deliverer Cromwell's riding into his throne upon the backs of 120 asses.'[17] Then, just before

[15] Clarke MS XXV, fos. 61, 63ᵛ.

[16] Ibid., fos. 64, 68, 69.

[17] *Bibliotheca Parliamenti* ([23 June] 1653), p. 7. John Langley reported this suspicion of Cromwell's purpose on 18 June as common gossip: Johnson and Vaisey, p. 76.

the middle of June, an unknown printer put out a broadsheet *Catalogue of the Names of the New Representatives*; Thomason got hold of it on the 15th, perhaps just after he had acquired a manuscript list which resembles it closely, though it contains two names fewer.[18] The broadsheet names 109 members for the English counties, only one for Wales, and states that Scotland and Ireland were to have five members each, without naming them.

That adds up to 120, but the broadsheet is unlikely to have been the source of the widespread reports that 120 was to be the new assembly's size, firstly because such reports were current well before it is known to have appeared, and secondly because it is so patently incomplete. Besides giving only one name for the whole of Wales, it also names only one member apiece for Berkshire, Herefordshire, and Huntingdonshire, and it leaves Buckinghamshire out altogether. A careful reader would have deduced from it a total membership of nearer 130. Its source is unknown; it was clearly unauthorized, for it garbled many of the names, some almost beyond recognition, and it was printed anonymously.[19] But it is probably a faulty transcription of an authentic list, for the official *Severall Proceedings* announced in its issue for 2–9 June that there were to be 130 members, including five each for Scotland and Ireland, and printed the text of Cromwell's writ of summons.[20]

It may be that 120 was the number of names first submitted by the Council of Officers to the Council of State, and 130 the number approved on 3 June after their joint deliberations. Admittedly Mabbott still thought it was 120 on 4 and 7 June, but he may just have added up the names on the list from which the broadsheet *Catalogue* was copied without spotting the gaps in it.

[18] BL, 669 f. 17 (14) and (15), and E698 (19). On the possible relationship of these documents see *EHR*, lxxx, 507–8.

[19] The two printed copies in the Thomason Collection are not identical, but though taken from different type-settings they reproduce exactly the same errors in the names. This may mean that the errors represent misreadings of a MS list in circulation among the Council of Officers; but they are puzzling, for some suggest the mishearing of a name (e.g. Moyle for Moyer, Oddorsall for Odingsells) and others the misreading of an unclear hand (e.g. Baxton for Barton, Briglile for Bright). Perhaps the printer obtained a list already containing mistakes attributable to dictation and then committed further blunders in trying to read it.

[20] *Severall Proceedings*, no. 193, 2–9 June, p. 3056. Other papers which gave 130 as the number, all in issues subsequent to 9 June, were *Faithful Scout*, *Moderate Publisher*, *Moderate Intelligencer*, and *Faithful Post*.

That is conjectural, but cumulatively the evidence is strong that the names approved early in June were not identical with those of the members who actually constituted Barebone's Parliament, and that they were slightly fewer. The pirated *Catalogue* has recently been described as 'highly misleading',[21] but the arguments adduced against its essential authenticity are unconvincing, and several pointers tend to vindicate it. It contains only seven, or at most eight, authentic names of men who did not appear in the later, official lists of members, and two of these are known to have been invited. One was Fairfax and the other Gervase Piggot, whose writ of summons survives, inscribed by him, 'I rather chose to be made a sacrifice then to yeild obedience to these comands.'[22] Whether the other five actually received writs is not known. Readers of the newspapers must have been expecting a membership of 130 almost (if not quite) until Barebone's Parliament actually assembled, for there seem to survive only two earlier predictions of a larger number, both in private correspondence, one of them imprecise, and neither from a source close to the Council of Officers.[23]

[21] Tai Liu, 'Calling . . . reconsidered', pp. 230–1. Dr Liu states most misleadingly that I cited this *Catalogue* in *EHR*, lxxx, 507–9 'as collateral evidence of the hypothesis of "packing"'. That is not how I presented it. He says that it names a dozen non-members of Barebone's Parliament, but in fact it names only seven or eight (seven if 'Daniel Pisick' is a wild misreading of Samuel Dunch). He makes much of its omission of John James; but James is there, disguised as John Sands, a misreading easier in the case of a seventeenth-century hand than a modern one. He cites a letter of Edward Harley's as proof that John Herring was nominated early; perhaps he was, for the *Catalogue* has only one name for Herefordshire and is plainly incomplete, but Harley's letter does not name him. Dr Liu makes the unwarrantable assumption that when the Council of State ordered lodgings for members at Whitehall, those members had necessarily arrived already in London. The number of names given in the *Catalogue* for English counties is not 110, as he states, but 109, as I stated, though it is slightly reduced by the facts that Luke Robinson and Col. 'Briglile' (=Bright) are given as alternatives, and that 'C. W. Darsheire' is nobody's name but the misreading of a rubric indicating that the succeeding names represented Cumberland, Westmorland, and Co. Durham. He overlooks my acknowledgement that the list was 'clearly incomplete' and that what I took (and still take) to be mainly late nominations provided only 'a slender basis for speculation'.

[22] Gardiner, *C & P*, ii, 222, 231; Abbott, iii, 34 n. 109. The others named in the *Catalogue* but not in the final list of members are Durant Hotham, Luke Robinson, and Col. John Bright (Yorks); William Palmer (Lincs.); John Goring (Staffs); and possibly 'Daniel Pisick' (Berks).

[23] Viscount Conway wrote on 19 May that he had heard that the officers, instead of imitating the Jewish sanhedrin of seventy, now proposed to call twice that number (*CSPD 1652–3*, p. 339). A newswriter on 3 June gave it as 130 *or* 140 (Clarendon MS 45, fo. 482).

Turning now to the members who received writs but were not named in the *Catalogue*, there were, if those for Wales, Scotland, Ireland, and Buckinghamshire (whose omission was probably a slip) are ignored, nineteen of them. Were they nominated later than the rest? Most of them probably were. In the later and officially printed lists, almost all appear either after those named in the *Catalogue*, or—in the cases of Monck and Tichborne and John Sadler, who had obvious claims to precedence—inserted at the head of them. Those particular three seem unlikely to have been afterthoughts, but perhaps they hesitated for some time before signifying their willingness to sit. One can understand Cromwell's desire to avoid any more damaging rebuffs like Fairfax's. The writ sent to one of the nineteen, Edward Cludd of Nottinghamshire, was still extant in the eighteenth century; it was allegedly dated 29 June.[24] Two contemporary reports support the hypothesis that there were some late changes. Nicholas's newswriter wrote on 24 June that some who had earlier received writs had since been sent letters 'to unbid them again', and Paulucci reported a week later that Cromwell and the Council of Officers had revised the list of members and sent out some fresh invitations, because some earlier nominees were suspected to be undependable and others had refused the summons.[25] It is true that Samuel Highland wrote subsequently that 'there were but two that refused the call and work',[26] but he was probably referring to the official membership as it was published after Barebone's Parliament met. If some earlier nominees had proved unwilling and had been quietly replaced during June, there is no reason why he should have known of it.

If most of these nineteen were indeed late nominees, what strikes one most about them as a group—Monck, Tichborne, and Sadler obviously excepted—is their obscurity.[27] Only nine of the remaining sixteen appear to have been JPs for more than a few

[24] Abbott, iii, 34 n. 109. Cludd obviously replaced Piggot, who had first been summoned for Nottinghamshire, which he had represented in the Long Parliament.

[25] Clarendon MS 46, fo. 9; *CSP Ven 1653–4*, p. 96.

[26] Highland, *An Exact Relation*, in *Somers Tracts*, vi, 269.

[27] They were Vincent Goddard and Thomas Wood (Berks.), Samuel Warner (Cambs.), John Brewster (Essex), John Herring (Herefordshire), Stephen Pheasant (Hunts.), William West (Lancs.), John Pratt (Leics.), William Thompson (Lincs.), Thomas Brooke (Northants.), Edward Cludd (Notts.), John Chetwood (Staffs.), Henry Henley (Somerset), Thomas Dickenson, Roger Coates, and Edward Gill (Yorks.).

months, if at all,[28] which is far below the over-all proportion in the House, and they include half a dozen of that small minority of members about whom it is hard to find any but the barest biographical information. This makes it difficult to particularize about their religious affiliations, but only five[29] seem to have shown radical sectarian tendencies and none can be positively identified as Fifth Monarchy men. Seven were to sit in one or more parliaments under the Protectorate, and twelve would be named on their local commissions of 'Ejectors' under Cromwell's ordinance of August 1654. Two or three were men of tolerably large estates, particularly Henry Henley of Leigh and Colway, but as a group their social level was somewhat below the modest average of the assembly as a whole. If any generalizations can be risked on the basis of their evidence, they are that the officers were finding it rather difficult by June to fill up the new governing body with men of substance, and that their later choices do not indicate any swing in favour of the militant millenarian faction.

Even slight evidence for or against such a swing is worth remarking, because a reader of the public prints could well have formed the impression that the radical saints were uppermost in the temporary government and could therefore be expected to dominate the forthcoming assembly. That sort of impression was indeed transmitted to the exiled royal court and is reflected in the correspondence of royalists and others who were ready to believe the worst (as they saw it). One can see how it arose. The newspapers printed addresses of congratulation and support from the brethren in various counties, rejoicing (for example) over 'the various and wonderful appearances of God for you, in carrying you on (as it were) through a sea of blood, to act for the liberties (especially) of the saints in these nations';[30] and from garrisons, such as those in the north of England which hoped

[28] The others are either omitted from, or interlineated in, the crown office entry book which commences in May 1652: PRO, C.193/13/4.

[29] Vincent Goddard, Chetwood, Brooke, West, and Herring. Coates, identified in *A Catalogue of the names* . . . (1654; repr. in Gardiner, *C & P*, ii, 259–61) as being opposed to the godly learned ministry and the universities, seems in fact to have been a conforming Cromwellian; see A. Gooder, *Parliamentary Representation of Yorkshire*, 2 vols. (Wakefield, 1935–8), i, 535; *CSPD 1654*, p. 449, and *1655–6*, p. 342.

[30] *Perfect Diurnall*, no. 183, 6–13 June, p. 2768; cf. *Severall Proceedings*, no. 192, 26 May–2 June, pp. 3025–8, 3037–8; *Severall Proceedings*, no. 194, 9–16 June, pp. 3068–70, etc.

they could say, 'This is the day of God's power, who will overturn until the government be established in his hands whose right it is.'[31] Cromwell and the Council of State themselves talked in the same language when they declared a day of thanksgiving for the naval victory over the Dutch off the Gabbard on 2–4 June, which they hailed in apocalyptic terms, resonant with echoes of Isaiah, as heralding 'the day of [the Lord's] righteousness and faithfulness . . . of his beginning to heal the Creation; the day of gathering his people'. 'A mercy at such a time as this', they went on, 'what mercies it hath in the bowels of it, time will declare: who knows?'[32] When this was followed a month later by Cromwell's famous speech to Barebone's Parliament, hailing in strikingly similar language 'a day of the power of Christ', sober observers had plenty of excuse for thinking that the chiliasts had got the bit between their teeth and that the Lord General had become one of them.

His millenarian hopes were not new, nor were they of the same violent colour as (say) Powell's or Feake's, but they were certainly becoming more intense. He was going through the phase of optimism and energy which for him commonly followed upon a decision of unusual difficulty and accompanied his embarkation upon a new and hopeful political course. But there may also have been more immediate and practical motives for these appeals to all the people of God to rise to the great opportunities that the latest divine dispensations had opened up. That effervescent army of his was not easily held in check, and around the middle of June it gave signs of unrest at two levels. One symptom reflected a momentary upsurge of the kind of democratic aspirations that had once given the Levellers their hold over the soldiery, and it was probably not unconnected with Lilburne's sudden return to England. On 18 June a remonstrance was presented to Cromwell and the Council of Officers, one report said 'by the agitators of the army', claiming that every single soldier should have an equal voice in electing the members of the forthcoming new representative, and that no

[31] *Severall Proceedings*, no. 193, 2–9 June, pp. 3041–2; cf. ibid., pp. 3044–5 (mispaged); *Perfect Diurnall*, no. 179, 9–16 May, pp. 2709–10; and *More Hearts and Hands Appearing for the Work* ([7 June] 1653; from Col. Overton and the Hull garrison).
[32] *A Declaration from the General and Council of State* (2 June 1653).

one should be admitted to it who had handled any public money since the civil wars.[33]

The other centre of army unrest was Harrison. He seems to have become increasingly disgruntled at the decision, which Cromwell is said to have carried before the end of April,[34] whereby he and all other serving officers were debarred from nomination to the new assembly unless they resigned their commissions. According to a well-informed newswriter, some of his fellow-councillors tried in about mid-June to persuade him to leave the army, telling him 'how fit and necessary he was for the Administration of the Civil part, and such a pretious pillar was not to be hazarded in the continuall rage of warre; but he answered, if the State thought much to pay him his wages, he would serve them gratis'.[35] This same writer reported a week later that the great Monday prayer-meetings of what he called 'Harrison's gathered churches at Blackfriars' had been suspended by Cromwell's orders, and Feake forbidden to preach within the lines of communication, but that the brethren had nevertheless congregated there defiantly last Monday, and that Highland, member-designate for Surrey, had been the first to rise and lead them in prayer.[36] No such ban by Cromwell or the Council of State is on record in any other source, but it would have been understandable at a time when Lilburne's trial was imminent as well as the opening of Barebone's Parliament. It is perhaps significant that Harrison's attendance at the Council of State, which had been assiduous ever since its inception on 29 April, became much more irregular after 22 June, and ceased altogether

[33] Thurloe, i, 306; Clarendon MS 46, fo. 8. The latter newsletter also mentions a threat by the soldiers to pull the judges out of Westminster Hall, but no one else records it.

[34] *Clarke Papers*, iii, 4; Firth, 'Cromwell and the expulsion', p. 534.

[35] Newsletter, 24 June, Clarendon MS 46, fo. 9 (though this same writer had reported on 20 May that Harrison had appeared to be very much Cromwell's creature of late: MS 45, fo. 399); Johnson and Vaisey, p. 76; Thurloe, i, 306; Capp, *Fifth Monarchy Men*, pp. 65–6.

[36] Clarendon MS 46, fos. 32–4. Here we may dispose of a sermon, allegedly preached to the assembled members on 30 June by the Independent William Strong, which has received some misplaced attention (Tai Liu, *Discord in Zion*, pp. 120–1; Nuttall, *Visible Saints*, pp. 151–2). The error arises because in Strong's *XXXI Select Sermons* (1656) one entitled 'State Prosperitie' is described on p. 617 as having been preached 'At a Fast in the Parliament house, June 31, 1653'. 'June' is obviously a mistake for 'Jan.', for Strong had preached before the Rump at its fast-day on 31 Jan. 1653 (*CJ*, vii, 251–2). There was no meeting of Barebone's Parliament before 4 July and no sermon before Cromwell's opening address.

at the end of July. Perhaps those famous visionary flights in Cromwell's opening speech to Barebone's Parliament reflect not so much his conversion to the ideals of Harrison's co-religionaries as his sense of a need to emphasize all that he and they still had in common.

V

The Inauguration of the
New Government

The members gathered in London in increasing numbers as the opening date approached. Almost since the first writs of summons went out, many of them had been securing lodgings for themselves at Whitehall, where there was a corresponding exodus of Rumpers. What the new assembly would be called and where it would sit were still open questions. Cromwell and the council were carefully avoiding the word parliament; they usually referred to it simply as 'the supreme power'. When the inhabitants of Westminster petitioned in May that it should sit in the parliament-house, the council replied that it knew nothing to prevent this but that it would be for the supreme power to decide the matter for itself. Nevertheless there were reports in June that the banqueting hall in Whitehall was to house it, and that it was being fitted out with seats for the purpose.[1]

Yet it was neither there nor in the Palace of Westminster that it met for the opening ceremony on Monday, 4 July, but in the council chamber at Whitehall. No religious service and no sermons by prominent divines preceded Cromwell's opening speech, which is surely one reason why it contained more of spiritual exhortation than he would offer on similar occasions in 1654 and 1656, when ordained preachers would have their lengthy say before him.

The room was uncomfortably crowded on this hot summer day, with at least 120 members sitting several deep round the

[1] *CSPD 1652–3*, p. 349 (and *passim* for allocations of lodgings); Johnson and Vaisey, pp. 76–7.

council table. They rose and uncovered when Cromwell entered, followed by as many officers as could find standing room around him. He stood bareheaded, leaning slightly on the back of a chair, facing the middle of the table and with his back to the window. He spoke, as his custom was, extempore. He said more than once that he would shorten his address because of the heat and discomfort, which indeed caused him at one stage to throw off his cloak and hand it to one of his colonels. Nevertheless he spoke for something like two hours.[2]

Right at the start he alluded to an 'instrument' which he and his fellow-officers would shortly tender to the members, thus emphasizing the essential nature of his business, which was to commit the whole care of the Commonwealth into their hands. Then, as in so many of his major speeches, he launched into a retrospect, 'to mind you of the series of Providences wherein the Lord hath appeared, dispensing wonderful things to these nations'.[3] That indeed was his purpose: not just to celebrate past triumphs in order to rouse present enthusiasm, but to scrutinize the workings of providence over the years for some indication of the course that God ordained for his people, now and in the future. Rapidly he ran over the dramatic developments that had succeeded each other from the Short Parliament to the 'marvellous salvation wrought at Worcester', ascribing each of them to direct divine intervention; God and providence figure a score of times in two pages of the printed text.[4] The period that he singled out as having been most marked 'by the very signal appearance of God Himself' was the year 1648, 'the most memorable year', he called it, 'that ever this nation saw'; and since he and his listeners reckoned it as running from March to March it had witnessed not only the victories in the second Civil War but the execution of the king and the establishment of the Commonwealth.

Then, in sombre contrast, he turned from that unbroken chain of providences to the repeated disappointments and frustrated

---

[2] *Severall Proceedings*, no. 197, 30 June–7 July, p. 3117; Abbott, iii, 52–3, 61; HMC, *De L'Isle and Dudley MSS*, vi, 617–18; Johnson and Vaisey, p. 77; Abbott, iii, 52–3, 61. Several newspapers reported about 120 present; Mabbott, who wrote that all were there except 6 or 7 (Hull Corp. MS L581), and Paulucci, who gave all but 5 or 6 (*CSP Ven 1653–4*, p. 100), probably exaggerated slightly.

[3] Abbott, iii, 53.

[4] Ibid. 53–5.

hopes which had been the experience of himself and his officers since Worcester. In this, the longest part of his speech, he recounted and vindicated the army's dealings with the Rump from 1651 to the recent dissolution. His laboured narrative, his rhetorical repetitions, and his sometimes tortured syntax bear witness to the difficulty he evidently felt in presenting the army's case persuasively and in justifying what was perhaps the most troubling decision of his life. The many differences between the surviving texts of the speech in these passages suggest that he may often have corrected himself, or left sentences uncompleted.[5] Clearly he took the printed declaration of 22 April as his basis, and though he enlarged upon it in many particulars the main burden of his complaint was again that for the Rump 'the cause of the people of God was a despised thing', and 'that good was never intended to the people of God'.[6]

This vindication took him well past the half-way point in his long discourse, and the rest was mainly a solemn charge and exhortation to those to whom he was transmitting the sovereign power. He did not try to justify his right to dispose of it; he did not even discuss it. He simply assumed, as he explained in the following year,[7] that when the parliament had ceased to be, unlimited power had devolved upon him as the statutorily appointed general of the Commonwealth's forces. But he was genuinely anxious to end his temporary dictatorship, and the authority which he was committing to the new assembly was formally unlimited except in duration. It was an emotional moment, and if the report is true that he wept frequently in the course of the speech[8] he probably did so here. Yet he spoke in modest and indeed almost apologetic terms: 'Although I seem to speak that which may have the face of a charge, it is a very humble one, and if he that means to be a servant to you, do discharge that, which he conceives to be his duty, in his own and his fellows names, to you I hope you will take it in good part.'[9]

[5] For notes on the early texts, and my reasons for quoting them at crucial points rather than Abbott's edition, see Appendix A.

[6] Abbott, iii, 57.

[7] Ibid. 454.

[8] *Calendar of the Clarendon State Papers*, ed. O. Ogle *et al.* (hereafter *Clarendon Calendar*), 5 vols., Oxford, 1869–1970, ii, 228.

[9] *The Lord General Cromwel's Speech*, p. 19. I have inserted 'if' from the text in Nickolls, and altered 'to' to 'do' before 'discharge'.

He could assume such a tone without hypocrisy because he believed that he and his army were the mere instruments of a divine purpose; the power that he was passing to the company before him came to them, he emphasized, 'by the way of necessity, by the way of the wise Providence of God though through weak hands. ... Truly you are called by God, to rule with him, and for him.' [10]

These great affirmations led quite naturally into the most overtly millenarian passages in his address—passages which bear crucially on the question whether or not he had become converted to the Fifth Monarchist creed of Harrison and his kind. He was of course a millenarian, and had been one since before the Fifth Monarchy movement took shape. 'I am one of those', he had said in Putney Church nearly six years earlier, 'whose heart God hath drawn out to wait for some extraordinary dispensations, according to those promises that he hath held forth of things to be accomplished in the later times, and I cannot but think that God is beginning of them.'[11] In just the same spirit he now asked his listeners: 'Why should wee bee afraid to say, or think, that this may bee the door to usher in things that God hath promised and prophesied of, and set the hearts of His people to wait for, and expect? ... Indeed, I do think something is at the door, we are at the threshold.'[12] The whole concluding section certainly conveys a mood of awed expectancy and exaltation. He was still borne on the wave of euphoria and optimism which he commonly experienced after the strain of anxious wrestlings. His long-standing hopes that the spiritual New Jerusalem would find its first abode in England were probably stronger than they had yet been, or would be again. Moreover he responded sensitively, as good speakers do, to the temper of a particular audience, and a spontaneous empathy probably encouraged him to speculate more freely on what these latest dispensations of providence might portend than he would have done before a more sceptical company.

Nevertheless the whole tone of his language *was* speculative, and his tentative, reverent surmise of glory to come was far

[10] Ibid. 18–19.

[11] Woodhouse, *Puritanism and Liberty*, pp. 103–4.

[12] *The Lord General Cromwel's Speech*, p. 24. I have removed the word 'to' from before 'set', following Nickolls, whose text does not differ in substance.

removed from the strident certainties of the Fifth Monarchy men. They *knew* that Antichrist was about to be violently destroyed and the Kingdom established;[13] he acknowledged the uncertainty of man's light on such mysteries. 'But I may be beyond my line', he said, just after the sentences last quoted; 'these things are dark.'[14] While the Fifth Monarchists incited the saints to wreak the Lord's wrath on Babylon, rend the flesh of the Whore, overturn all merely 'carnal' institutions, and launch England upon a course of universal conquest, Cromwell urged her new rulers to be peaceably spirited, gentle, impartial, and above all tolerant. 'Truly this calls us to be very much touched with the common infirmities of the saints, that we may have a respect unto, and be pittyful and tender towards all, though of different judgments.'[15]

The passage which appears to carry the strongest Fifth Monarchist overtones is that in which he is supposed to have told the assembly that by accepting its call it manifested this 'to be the day of the power of Christ'.[16] But that is not what he actually said. This is how the first published version reports him:

Jesus Christ is owned this day by you all, and you own him by your willingnesse in appearing here, and you manifest this (as farre as poor creatures can) to be a day of the power of Christ by your willingnesse, I know you remember that Scripture in *Psalm* 110.3. *The people shall be willing in the day of thy Power*; God doth manifest it to be a day of the Power of Jesus Christ.[17]

[13] For contemporary examples see John Spittlehouse, *The First Addresses to the Lord General with the Assembly of Elders elected by him and his Council* ([5 July] 1653); John Canne, *A Voice from the Temple* and *A Second Voice from the Temple* ([13 June and 15 Aug.] 1653); W. Aspinwall, *A Brief Description of the Fifth Monarchy* ([1 Aug.] 1653).

[14] The first phrase is from *The Lord General Cromwel's Speech*, p. 25; the second appears only in Nickolls, p. 113.

[15] Nickolls, p. 112. The pamphlet's text seems corrupt here; Abbott follows it, making some dubious changes of punctuation and inexplicably altering 'touched' to 'troubled'. The result is seriously misleading.

[16] Abbott, iii, 63.

[17] *The Lord General Cromwel's Speech*, p. 22. Nickolls (p. 112) has 'owned this day by your call' in the first phrase; either version seems plausible. In the next phrase he too has 'a day of the power of Christ', but in the repetition following the scriptural quotation he has 'the day of the power of Christ'. In both cases he has accurately transcribed his manuscript text (Society of Antiquaries MS 138, fo. 294 and 294^{v}). It may be that Cromwell echoed the psalm's words and used the definite article when he repeated the phrase, but there are several places where the scribe who took down the pamphlet's text seems to have caught his words best (see Appendix A), and it seems likelier that he repeated his own first phrase. Abbott has no authority for 'the day' in the first phrase and is the only editor to have printed it so.

Between 'a day' and 'the day' there is a world of difference. In hailing this as 'a day of the power of Christ', Cromwell was saluting what he believed to be a glorious occasion, but one of perhaps many that would precede the full establishment of Christ's kingdom, in a future as yet beyond the calculation of man. If he had said 'the day' he would have implied that the kingdom had already arrived. Such an implication is out of key with the rest of the speech, fervent in hope though it was, and with such other evidence as we have of his millenarianism. He expected the coming of the kingdom at a point in future time, as men reckon time; he hoped it might come soon; he dared to speculate that the calling of Barebone's Parliament might be a vital stage towards it realization. But it would be realized in the hearts of men, not through the trappings of outward power, and he seems never to have believed otherwise.[18]

The crucial question is whether he had become converted to a belief that representatives elected by the people should be permanently superseded by men selected for their spiritual gifts and commitments. He made it quite clear that he had not. At the height of his eulogy of the new dispensation he had this to say: 'And therefore I say also, never a people so formed for such a purpose, so called—if it were a time to compare your standing with those that have been called by the suffrages of the people, who can tel how soon God may fit the People for such a thing, and who would desire any thing more in the world but that it might bee so?'[19] He touched the millenarian note again in his next sentence, in which he wished that 'all the Lord's people were prophets', and that 'all were fit to be called, and fit to call'. but his very eagerness that the people *should* be fit to choose their

[18] The same emphasis on men's hearts is found in his speeches of 4 July 1653 and 4 September 1654 (cf. Abbott, iii, 64–5, 437); the difference between them can be explained by his disillusion with Barebone's Parliament, without having to suppose any change in basic beliefs.

[19] *The Lord General Cromwel's Speech*, pp. 23–4. In the pamphlet 'so called' is in brackets. I have substituted a comma before and a dash after, but have otherwise left the punctuation unaltered. The Nickolls text is that used by Abbott (iii, 64), though with altered punctuation, and its sense is the same. Here it is worth comparing MS Tanner, 52 fo. 22^v: 'If I had tyme I would compare your calling, to the former call by the suffrage of the people, which is the longing of our hearts that it were so, what joy would it be to us to see them owne the Cause of God and his People, and if they see you lay out your strength for God and his People this is the way to put it upon God to fitt them, and bring them to theyr desyred Priviledges.'

own legislators again, and soon, was quite at odds with the typical Fifth Monarchist belief that any legislative power other than Christ's was an encroachment on his royalty, and that the claim of parliaments to derive power from the people was impious because the people had none to bestow.

His conception of the assembly's role in the settlement of the Commonwealth was made clearer in the 'instrument' that he shortly caused to be read out. It bore his own hand and seal, but it had, he said, been 'drawne up by the consent and advice of the principal officers of the army',[20] which indicates that the Council of Officers had shared in determining the assembly's powers as well as its membership. It simply invested the nominees, or any forty of them, with the supreme authority and government, without any restriction save as to time. It enjoined them to sit no longer than 3 November 1654, the ultimate date that the Rump had formerly fixed for its own duration. Three months before their dissolution they were to choose other persons to succeed them, and this second nominated assembly was to sit for no more than a year. During that time it was 'to take care for a succession in Government',[21] and the clear implication is that Cromwell hoped the people would be in a condition before the end of 1655 to resume their right to elect successive parliaments. Nominated bodies were to play a strictly temporary role, and he never suggested that saintship in itself should confer an implicit right to govern. It may be that in pitching his exhortation to Barebone's Parliament so high he was trying, consciously or unconsciously, to will it to compensate with good works for its dubious constitutional standing.

He had only a few more sentences to add after the reading of the 'instrument', and they were mainly about the interim Council of State which had acted under him as a provisional government since April. He urged that there should be no intermission in the council's executive authority, since the affairs of state needed constant attention, but he told the assembly that it was free to alter the membership as it saw fit, 'they having no authority, nor longer to sit, than you shall take order'.[22] Those were his last words, but before he left the room he had a paper read which

[20] Abbott, iii, 52.
[21] Ibid. 67.
[22] Ibid. 66.

defined the present council's powers.[23] This was presumably for information and guidance only, for there is no mistaking the fact that in principle he surrendered all control over its future functions and composition to the assembly. It was a large surrender, especially in view of his insistence in later speeches on the need to separate the executive power from the legislative, but that was one lesson which he would only learn fully as the year 1653 ran its course.

The members took only one decision before they adjourned, and that was that they would meet in future in St. Stephen's Chapel, where the House of Commons had sat for over a century.[24] There on the morrow they kept a day of prayer and humiliation from eight in the morning until six or seven in the evening. The Long Parliament had of course not infrequently spent whole days in seeking the Lord, but whereas it had called in well-known divines to lead its devotions, this House relied on its own members to do so. A number variously reckoned between seven and twelve performed the office that day, and among them were the Fifth Monarchist Arthur Squibb and the radical Congregationalist Samuel Moyer. Thereafter the House's daily prayers were similarly led by its own members.[25] The practice accorded with the sectarian view which rejected clerical claims to a monopoly of spiritual ministrations and held that every 'gifted' man had a right to pray and preach in public.

Even after their ten hours or more of religious exercises on their first full day's sitting, the members stayed for some further important business. First they elected Francis Rous as their chairman for a month; they did not call him Speaker until they decided to call themselves a parliament, and even then they re-elected him only from month to month. This vigorous septuagenarian was an apt choice, since to a unique degree he combined parliamentary experience, Puritan piety, deep learn-

---

[23] The only source for this is the abridged version of the speech in Bodl. MS Tanner 52, but it is quite specific. After mentioning the reading of the 'instrument' and giving the gist of Cromwell's subsequent remarks, it states (fo. 23): 'Then was read the power of the Councell of State and his Excellency left the Roome.' The document cannot have been intended to define the council's powers for the future, or the House would have considered it when it determined those powers on 9 July.

[24] *CSP Ven 1653–4*, p. 100.

[25] *Exact Relation*, pp. 269–70; *Severall Proceedings*, no. 197, 30 June–7 July 1653, p. 3118; *Impartial Intelligencer*, no. 2, 5–12 July, 1653, p. 9; Thurloe, i, 338; *Clarke Papers*, iii, 8–9.

ing, broad sympathies, good social standing, and strong
commitment to the Commonwealth. Born of a knightly Cornish
family and half-brother to Pym, he had sat in every parliament
since 1626. He held degrees from both Oxford and Leyden, and
he had expounded his profound though irenical and quite
unfanatical faith in numerous publications by the time he was
made Provost of Eton in 1644. He was a Presbyterian by
conviction—indeed he had been a lay member of the Westminster
Assembly—but he was a quite untypical one, for as early as 1645
he had contended, in *The Ancient Bounds, or Liberty of Conscience,
Tenderly Stated,* that the state should have no coercive power in
matters of religion. He had been among the more moderate and
conservative Rumpers, completely dissociated from the act of
regicide, yet within three months of the king's execution he had
published an important argument for *The Lawfulnes of Obeying the
Present Government.*[26]

The assembly then forged a further link with its predecessor
by appointing as its clerk Henry Scobell, who had been Clerk of
the Parliament to the Rump since its earliest days.[27] Next it
voted to desire Cromwell to join the House as a co-opted member,
and before it rose it resolved to extend the same invitation to the
four other army officers who had been serving on the interim
Council of State: Lambert, Harrison, Desborough, and Tomlinson.[28] It is interesting that it felt it had the power to co-opt
additional members by a simple vote, though this was the only
time it did so, and the case was a special one. Its initiative was
both sensible and propitious; it was by the same motion
reciprocating Cromwell's confidence and goodwill, admitting
the army to the share in representation that it had almost denied
itself, and strengthening the rapport between legislature and
executive by giving seats in the House to all whom Cromwell
had chosen as councillors. Alas for good intentions. Cromwell is
not known to have attended except on one day of prayer,
Lambert may never have done so, Harrison withdrew entirely
between the earliest and the last few weeks of the assembly's

[26] On Rous see *DNB*; Quentin Skinner, 'Conquest and consent', in Aylmer (ed.), *The
Interregnum*, pp. 83–7, 89–90, 92–3; Worden, *Rump*, pp. 65–6.

[27] On his career see Aylmer, *The State's Servants*, pp. 256–8.

[28] *CJ*, vii, 281. Further references to the *Commons' Journal* will not normally be given
where it is the obvious source and the date is clear from the text.

existence, and only Desborough took a continuous and active part in its proceedings.

Next morning there was a proposal to devote the whole day to prayer again, but it was decided to set aside the following Monday for the purpose instead. The House then had Cromwell's 'instrument' read to it again, no doubt because it had been hard to take it all in at a single hearing in the hot and crowded council chamber. It seems not to have raised any contention, for the only response recorded in the *Journal* is the correction of three members' names. What did arouse debate was the title which the assembly should assume: was it or was it not a parliament? This evidently took up the rest of the day's sitting before it was decided in the affirmative by 65 votes to 46. Here, it might seem, was the first split between conservative and radical members, in view of the extreme millenarians' aversion to the name of parliament as signifying that power derived from the people rather than from Christ.[29] But the matter was not quite so simple. True, both the tellers for the yeas, Sir William Roberts and William Sydenham, were to become prominent moderates, while one of those for the noes was the Fifth Monarchist John Carew. But Carew's partner on this occasion was Sir Gilbert Pickering, who though he is said to have moved all the way from Presbyterian to Anabaptist in his religious convictions was certainly a moderate in his politics— indeed he would be active five months later in bringing about the parliament's resignation.[30] So the zealots who objected to the title of parliament because it belonged to mere 'carnal' government probably voted alongside others who thought it should be reserved for a body that was summoned and elected in a more constitutional manner. Nor were all the religious radicals offended by it; Samuel Highland, the lay preacher of Southwark, wrote that 'the lowness and innocence of the title, having little of earthly glory or boasting in it, induced some to give their vote for that, though others were much against it'.[31]

These early days' proceedings often display an intriguing blend of parliamentary tradition and millennial aspirations. On 8 July, for instance, the House reappointed Edward Birkhead to the office of Sergeant-at-Arms which he had held since 1646 and

[29] e.g. Aspinwall, *A Brief Description of the Fifth Monarchy*, p. 8; *Clarke Papers*, ii, 244.
[30] *D.N.B.*
[31] *Exact Relation*, p. 270.

sent him to Lieutenant-Colonel Worsley to recover the mace—
the 'bauble' which Cromwell had so unceremoniously confiscated
when he expelled the Rump. Soon afterwards it was restored to
all its old symbolic significance and was thenceforth carried
daily before the Speaker. Yet on the same day that the members
gave their chairman back his ancient title and set up a committee
to consider the business of the mace, they resolved without a
division, 'That no person shall be employed or admitted into the
service of this House, but such as this House shall be first satisfied
of his real godliness.'[32] They duly devoted eight hours of
Monday, 11 July, to 'seeking the Lord, in a special manner, for
counsel, and a blessing, on the proceedings of the parliament',
and as on their first day's sitting they were led in prayer by about
a dozen of their own number. Some of the gathered churches
spent the day similarly in seeking a blessing on their
undertakings.[33]

Next day the House published a declaration, announcing itself
to be the parliament of the Commonwealth of England and
entreating 'the fervent prayers of the Lord's people' for its success
in the weighty work before it. It promised to be 'as tender of the
lives, estates, liberties, just rights and properties of all others as
we are of ourselves and our posterities, whom we expect still to
be governed by successive parliaments'.[34] The declaration was
the work of a committee, and at this point it doubtless expressed
the sentiments of such conservative landowners on it as Pickering,
Sydenham, and Wolseley. It is worth remarking, however, that
the House as a whole was willing to endorse so publicly
Cromwell's intention that a return to elected parliaments should
be only a matter of time. Yet the committee also included such
radicals as Praise-God Barebone, Andrew Broughton, and John
Swinton, as well as that unusual millenarian John Sadler, and it
would be interesting to known which of them penned such flights
as these:

Yet we cannot but acknowledge, that we are not yet at rest, nor can we
believe we have yet enjoyed or seen enough to accomplish the ends of

[32] *CJ*, vii, 282, 284.

[33] *CJ*, vii, 283; *Severall Proceedings of State Affairs*, no. 198, 7–14 July 1653, p. 3130;
Weekly Intelligencer, no. 127, 5–12 July 1653, p. 290; *Exact Relation*, p. 270.

[34] *A Declaration of the Parliament of the Commonwealth of England* (12 July 1653), pp. 1–2.
It is reprinted in *Old Parl. Hist.*, xx, 184–9. For the committee which drafted it see *CJ*, vii,
282.

God, or satisfy the thoughts of men for that vast expense of blood and treasure, which could not have been endured in any patience; but in hope, that at length those bitter pangs and throws would make some way for that birth of peace, freedom and happiness, both to the souls and bodies of the Lords people; and although we do not see it fully brought forth, yet we do not dispair but in Gods good time it shall be so; and that the dark black clouds of the night shall flie before the bright morning star, and the shakings of heaven and earth make way for the desire of all nations: nay, there are many things that make us hope the time is near at hand; for we see the clouds begin to scatter, and the dark shadows flie away; streams of light appear, and the day is surely dawned.

Neither are we wholly alone in these hopes, for if we be not very much deceived; many, if not all the people of God in all the world, are in a more than usual expectation of some great and strange changes coming on the world, which we believe can hardly be paralel'd with any times, but those for a while before the birth of our Lord and Saviour Jesus Christ. And we do not yet know, that any records of all the nations in the world (we scarce except the Jews themselves) can afford such a series of divine providence [*sic*], or more clear impressions of the goings forth and Actings of God in any people, then hath been in these nations.[35]

After much more in the same vein, these seven pages of enthusiasm in the official printer's best black letter ended with this injunction: 'that in peace and joy we may all wait, expect and long for his glorious coming, who is King of Kings, and Lord of Lords, our hope and righteousness; who is still to ride on prosperously conquering and to conquer, till He hath subdued all His enemies, and at length come to deliver up the Kingdom to His Father, that God may reign, and be all in all'.[36]

It was altogether a strange document for a parliament to publish to the nation in its own name, and it probably moved many readers to alarm or ridicule. But the more discerning could observe its solid assurances about rights, properties, and future parliaments, and note that so far from calling, with Fifth Monarchists like Christopher Feake and John Spittlehouse,[37] for the violent conquest of all the nations that still lay under

[35] *A Declaration of the Parliament*, p. 3.

[36] Ibid. 7.

[37] For Spittlehouse's programme of universal conquest see his *First Addresses to the Lord General with the Assembly of Elders Elected by him* ([5 July] 1653). See also pp. 284–7.

Antichrist it expressed the hope 'that all wars may cease to the ends of the earth'.

Meanwhile the parliament had already set about the important business of establishing its Council of State. Its first action, on the 7th, was to appoint Cromwell as one of its members; then on the 9th it reappointed the other twelve who had acted with him as a provisional council since April or May. It added to them Richard Salwey, whom Cromwell had consulted in the early days after the April *coup* but who had evidently declined a place as councillor. He did not attend a single meeting before or after his appointment to Barebone's Parliament; his loyalty was still to the broken Rump.[38] It also settled the council's instructions, taking as a basis those which the Rump had given to its own last council in the preceding November. It approved these with minor additions and omissions,[39] and decided that the number of councillors should be thirty-one, ten fewer than under the Rump. After rejecting a proposal to nominate the remaining seventeen then and there, it set up a committee to consider who they should be and to present their names to the House next Tuesday.

The committee consisted mainly of councillors already appointed, and consequently contained a rough balance of moderates, radicals, and soldiers. The House accepted every one of its recommendations without a division. The new councillors were a very mixed body, representing the extremes of opinion in the House and reflecting the diversity of outlook among their nominators. Lieutenant-General Charles Fleetwood, the only non-member, headed the list, but perhaps more in recognition of his large responsibilities in Ireland (which in the event prevented him from ever taking his seat) than through any pressure by his fellow-officers on the committee. It may have been to please Cromwell that those easy-going Hampshire squires Richard Norton and Richard Major were nominated, for there was not much beyond their personal connections with him to recommend them for places on the national executive, though Norton had served briefly on the Rump's last council. The presence on the committeee of Carew, Harrison, and Moyer probably explains the choice of the Fifth Monarchists John Williams and Hugh Courtney and of three other radicals, Andrew Broughton, Dennis

[38] See p. 106.
[39] *CJ*, vii, 282; instructions summarized in *CSPD 1653–4*, pp. 15–16.

Hollister, and Thomas St. Nicholas. These men, with the partial exception of the last, would soon return to the political obscurity from which they were briefly called. But the more conservative interest was to be strengthened by five young men who were at or near the start of interesting careers: Charles Howard (still only twenty-four), Sir Charles Wolseley (even younger), Sir Anthony Ashley Cooper, Viscount Lisle, and Edward Montagu. Henry Lawrence, a Baptist but essentially a moderate, was brought back to the political stage from which he had retired after Pride's Purge, and so began to gain the experience that would equip him to preside over the Protectoral Council of State throughout its existence.[40] Sir James Hope was brought in to speak for Scotland and Colonel Hewson for Ireland, or at least for Ireland's conquerors. Finally there was Alderman Robert Tichborne, that hardy perennial of radical City politics, doubtless included so as to ensure that London's special interests were represented. The House decided that the council thus chosen was to continue only until 3 November next, by which time it would find itself ready to make sweeping changes.

Meanwhile Britain's new rulers certainly set about their business with dedication and energy. Whereas the Rump had usually sat on only four days a week, and rarely for more than three hours, Barebone's Parliament opened its proceedings at eight o'clock on every morning except Sunday. The council also met on six days a week, and during July and August it more often than not held two sessions in a day. One of these would normally be after the House had risen—this happened even after the eight hours of religious exercises on 11 July—and sometimes an early one was fixed for 7 a.m.[41] This council met forty-two times during the first calendar month after it was made up to full strength, compared with twenty-four meetings held by the Rump's Council of State in the course of March 1653. Yet despite the greater frequency of meetings and the heavier calls of committees, both of the House and of the council, attendance was at first considerably better than in the Rump's latter days: an average of 18·7 out of 31 in the first thirty meetings of the new council, starting on 14 July, compared with 16·4 out of 41 in the

[40] *DNB*; Underdown, *Pride's Purge*, pp. 17, 378.
[41] *Severall Proceedings of State Affairs*, no. 198, 7–14 July 1653, p. 3130; *CSPD 1653–4*, pp. 33, 36, 40, etc.; *CJ*, vii, 338.

last thirty meetings of the Rump's Council of State.[42] It is true that attendance fell off markedly during August, but that can be explained not only by the natural pull of the country in high summer but also by widening divisions, which were already alienating many members. These would affect the House too, but before they made their effect the attendance record of Barebone's Parliament was remarkably good by seventeenth-century standards. The eleven divisions during its first month's sitting show an average of very nearly 105 members present out of 144, compared with the Rump's average, throughout its life, of about 55 out of over 200.[43]

Committees were bound to play an exceptionally important part in the transactions of this parliament. This was partly because its members, moderate and radical alike, felt it was their task to promulgate all those desired reforms on which the Rump had stalled, and committees were essential for formulating the necessary bills; partly because they numbered little more than a third of a full House of Commons, and a sensible system of standing committees was needed to share the work out among them. The House started setting up major committees even before it finished establishing the Council of State, but on 14 July it evidently realized that a random proliferation of them was going to produce a great inequality of burdens. Recognizing the special problems created by a small membership, an even smaller fund of parliamentary experience, and large reforming aspirations, it appointed twenty-five members 'to consider of the right ordering and disposing of business of the House by committees' and started again almost from scratch. Apart from adding some new Commissioners for the Admiralty and Navy that same day, if forbore from naming any more committees until this 'committee for committees' made its report—with one very important exception. This arose from the critical debate on tithes which began on the 13th and will be described in its place; here it need only be said that it resulted in the appointment on the 19th of a committee briefed to consider 'the propriety of incumbents in tithes', though its terms of reference would later be greatly widened.

[42] Tables of attendance in *CSPD 1652–3*, pp. xxvii–xl.
[43] To the voting figures in the *Journal* must be added the four tellers and the speaker. The figure for the Rump is Worden's, in *Rump*, p. 91.

The committee for committees carried such an important responsibility that one would like to know how it was chosen. All that can be said, however, is that it fairly represented such limited political experience as the House could command, and that it included men of such diverse views that it could not possibly be accused of factional interest.[44] When it punctually made its report on the 20th it proposed a total of ten standing committees and recommended a set of names for each of them. The House established all ten of them that same day, though it did not endorse all the lists of nominees without alteration or addition. Some were apparently uncontentious and were approved as they were offered; such were the committees for Irish and for Scottish affairs, which superseded earlier committees appointed on the 7th, the Army Committee, and those for trade and corporations, for investigating public debts and charges of bribery or fraud, for receiving petitions (and channelling elsewhere all that did not specifically concern the legislature), and for relieving the poor and regulating commissions of the peace throughout the nation.[45] The House made a few additions to the proposed committee for prisons and prisoners, and to that 'for inspecting the treasuries, and regulating of officers and salaries'.[46] This last one was to be one of the busiest. It superseded an earlier one which had been appointed on the 12th 'to consider of the state of all the treasuries' and among other things 'how the monies coming into the several treasuries of the Commonwealth may be brought into one treasury', a project which in the event had to await the coming of the Protectorate.[47] Radical members evidently felt a strong interest in this committee, for Harrison, James (another Fifth Monarchist), and Colonel Robert Bennett, who had all been on the earlier committee, were added by the House to the new one, which already included the Fifth Monarchists Squibb and Caley. To counter-balance them were

[44] *CJ*, vii, 285.

[45] *CJ*, vii, 286–7. Two members of the Scottish Committee and two of the Army Committee were voted on separately from the rest, but since they are not recorded as to 'be added to this Committee' but simply to 'be of this Committee' I take it that they were among the nominating committee's recommendations.

[46] *CJ*, vii, 287. The printed *Journal* here has 'treasurers', but in all subsequent references the word is 'treasuries'.

[47] *CJ*, vii, 283. The earlier committee disappears without trace from the *Journal,* and the broadsheet cited in n.50 credits it with power to consider the amalgamation of the Commonwealth's several treasuries.

such moderate and experienced men as Sir William Roberts, John Stone, and (added on the 27th) William Sydenham, but later additions tended to add to the radical predominance here.[48]

The committee which gave rise to most debate, however, was the one 'for the business of the law', for ten votes had to be taken before its membership was finally approved. None of them was taken to a division, but several of the nominating committee's recommendations were evidently challenged and one of them— the only one in the whole day's proceedings—was rejected outright. The member against whom the House excepted was Andrew Broughton, the very radical Clerk of the Peace for Kent and chief clerk for criminal causes in the Upper Bench, who in serving the High Court of Justice of January 1649 in a similar capacity had read out the charge against the late king and subsequently his death sentence.[49] It may have been in reaction to this set-back that three other members of radical tendencies, namely Moyer, William Spence, and Colonel West, were promptly added to the committee; a fourth, Thomas St. Nicholas, was added later in the day. The committee's business was presumably to take up all that the Rump had left undone in the sphere of law reform since it had received the Hale Commission's report, and there were few matters on which members' feelings ran deeper or differed more widely. But it was to remain quite distinct from the committee set up on 19 August 'to consider of a new body of the law'. That one was to have a strong radical preponderance; this was weighted the other way, with John Sadler, Sir William Brownlow, Sir William Roberts, Sir Anthony Ashley Cooper, and the soldiers Desborough and Tomlinson to represent relatively moderate views.

At the end of its day's work in appointing these ten committees the House resolved that it desired yet another one, whose business was to be the advancement of learning. It instructed the nominating committee to recommend a further set of names, which it duly approved the next day, adding four more of its own. The result was a body from which the Fifth Monarchists and other extremes sectarians were conspicuously absent. This was not surprising in view of their opinions about the vanity of

[48] *CJ*, vii, 287, 290, 293.
[49] Sir Edgar Stephens, *Clerks of the Counties* (1961), p. 109; F. A. Inderwick (ed.), *Calendar of Inner Temple Records* (1896–1901), ii, 292, 299; *CSPD 1648–9*, p. 350.

human learning and its irrelevance to preachers of the true gospel, but if they expressed such opinions on this occasion they must have been overborne.

The ten committees appointed on 20 July, together with the committee for tithes approved the day before, seem to have had a special status, for the names of all their members (but of no other committees) were published in a broadsheet early in October, together with an accurate list of all the members of the House.[50] Most of them were active and conscientious. According to Highland they 'sate daily, and took great pains morning and evening, almost every day in the week, to dispatch business, and make things ready for the House'.[51] The number of occasions on which the House added further members to them, and referred matters to them that were not obviously included in their initial terms of reference, showed that it did not quickly lose its reforming impetus and that the committees remained its essential agencies.

Their original composition does not, however, provide any reliable evidence of their members' attitudes to the matters with which they dealt, nor always of any special interest or competence in those matters. The nominating committee obviously took pains to furnish each particular committee with a solid core of appropriate expertise, as a glance at the names of those entrusted with Irish and Scottish affairs and with trade and corporations will confirm. The committee for the law included six of the House's fourteen barristers, besides four other former students at the Inns of Court and John Swinton, who was soon to be a judge in Scotland. On the committee for inspecting the treasuries, Sir William Roberts had been much employed in the sale of Church, crown, and royalists' lands, Arthur Squibb the younger was a Commissioner for Compounding, and John Stone was Receiver-General for London's monthly assessment;[52] but Bawden, Birkenhead, Botterell, Caley, and Cunliffe may conceivably appear alongside them for no better reason than that the nominating committee had got to B and C in an alphabetical list of members. It was quite obviously trying to spread the load as widely as possible, 'so as none might be idle, but all employed in

[50] *A New List of All the Members of this Present Parliament* ([6 Oct.] 1653).
[51] *Exact Relation*, p. 270.
[52] Aylmer, *State's Servants*, pp. 216–18, 241, 251–2.

public service'.[53] Faced with a field in which so many were inexperienced and unknown, what could it do but pick at random when it had allocated the minority who were clearly qualified for their tasks? The difficulty must have been to avoid overcommitting the experienced few.

At any rate, by 21 July only nine members had escaped appointment to one or more committees, or to the Council of State, or to the Commission for the Admiralty and Navy. Of these, three (Brodie, Martyn, and Walcott) apparently never took their seats, but five were probably just late in doing so, since they were added to one or more of the key committees subsequently.

It was a natural consequence of the manner of appointing these committees that most of them represented a fair range of political and religious opinions. This was partly because the nominating committee itself did so and partly because the attitudes of many of the members must have been as yet unknown to it. Although it would be a gross distortion to classify them all as either moderates or radicals, since the attitudes of many were ambivalent or are little known, it will be argued in chapter VII that the majority of the members were generally opposed to extreme views and drastic measures, but that the sizeable minority who did take strongly radical lines mostly did so on political and religious issues alike. Using the terms with all due caution, considerably more moderate members than radicals were placed on committees between 19 and 21 July, but the proportion was not far out of line with the balance in the House as a whole. If it favoured the moderates slightly more than their numbers warranted, that is because there were more men with clearly relevant experience among them.

The committees in which moderate men preponderated were those for Irish affairs (strongly), Scottish affairs (less overwhelmingly, but effectively), the army, the law (strongly, despite the House's addition of three fairly radical members), receiving petitions, public debts (strongly), and the advancement of learning (overwhelmingly). The very important committee for tithes differed from the others in being named by the House directly, after five or six days' debates which must have revealed most members' views. With thirty-two members it was much the

[53] *Exact Relation*, p. 270.

largest committee—no other comprised even twenty initially—and the balance in it between men of moderate and radical views seems to have been exactly even. It must have been the withdrawal of some of the hotter spirits which enabled moderate counsels later to prevail in it.

Two committees which consisted for the most part of rather obscure men with little or no national political experience were those for trade and corporations and for the poor. Both were fairly evenly balanced, the former with a slight leaning in the radical direction, the latter tending perhaps slightly the other way, though we do not know enough about many of these men to be sure. It may seem strange that there was no great eagerness to secure control of the committee for the poor, with its very important power to regulate the commission of the peace—in other words to recommend how the bench of justices should be composed in every county. But it is unlikely that at this stage many members of Barebone's Parliament were thinking in terms of a struggle for power at county level. It is interesting that the two committees in which the radical men started with a clear majority were those for prisons and prisoners, which they dominated overwhelmingly, and for the inspection of the treasuries, on which they further increased their hold when eight additional members were put in on 1 August. Perhaps their strength on the former committee can be partly explained by their sympathy with all who had suffered at the hands of authority in whatever form, and on the latter by a concern to make the burden of taxation fall more justly, coupled with the widespread popular suspicion that the officials who handled the various revenues had been feathering their nests. But this is speculation, because we do not know whether members were consulted before being nominated, or were given any opportunity to volunteer their services. It could well be that in choosing names for the committee for prisons and prisoners, for instance, the nominating committee were thinking that this area of responsibility called for less special experience and expertise than most others, so that the bias towards radical members here can be explained by the fact that these included a much higher proportion of political novices. The bias was greatly increased, however, when the House itself added three Fifth Monarchy men and another strong radical. As for the committee for trade,

it naturally included a considerable number of merchants, mostly
from provincial towns, and among these the incidence of religious
radicalism was higher than in the other social groups in the
House.

The polarization of Barebone's Parliament had begun in
earnest just a week before the great day of committee-making,
over the particularly contentious issue of tithes. It is quite likely
that those who took the sectarian position, finding themselves in
a minority, were already perceiving a need to secure greater
representation for themselves on the committees relevant to their
particular interests. Besides the approximate parity they secured
in the committee for tithes, it is remarkable that of the eleven
members who on 20 July were certainly added by the House to
the nominees of the 'committee for committees', all were men of
radical leanings and five were Fifth Monarchy men. Subsequent
additions, however, did not greatly change the political
complexion of these standing committees, and when the radicals
made a real breakthrough over 'a new body of the law' on 19
August, they fought and won a battle for a new committee to
implement it. But before describing the rifts which opened over
the settlement of religion, the reform of the law, and other
matters, it will be well to take a closer look at the social
composition of the House and to see, from selected examples,
what manner of men the Council of Officers had chosen to
compose it.

VI

The Quality of the House

The ridicule of Barebone's Parliament began as soon as it met. The wits of the town tittered over the awkwardness with which some of its members wore swords, cuffs, and other braveries that they were not used to.[1] The French ambassador reported home that they were of all arts and professions but that their chief talent was for preaching; he thought Cromwell had summoned such people in order to ensure that the real authority remained with himself.[2] A newswriter informed the exiled royal court that they were mostly 'Pettifoggers, Innkeepers, Millwrights, Stockingmongers and such a rabble as never had hopes to be of a Grand Jury',[3] and these silly travesties soon became royalist orthodoxy. 'Abject and mean people', James Heath would call them, and so far from being notable in their counties that they were scarcely known in their own towns and villages until their employment in managing sequestrations, excise, and other war-begotten extortions made them infamous.[4] 'A pack of weak, senseless fellows' was Clarendon's verdict; 'much the major part of them consisted of inferior persons, of no quality, or name, artificers of the meanest trades, known only by their gifts in praying and preaching.'[5]

The threefold sneer at their social inferiority, their Puritan canting, and their political ineptitude found expression in the

---

[1] Clarendon MS 46, fo. 70.

[2] PRO, 31.3 (91), fo. 41; cf. fo. 65.

[3] Clarendon MS 45, fo. 482; cf. fo. 498.

[4] James Heath, *Flagellum* (3rd ed., 1665), p. 141; J. Heath, *A Brief Chronicle of the Late Intestine War* (1663), p. 648.

[5] Clarendon, *History of the Rebellion*, v, 282. Sir William Dugdale (quoted in Abbott, iii, 50) was equally contemptuous and wrong.

nickname Barebone's Parliament. What drew attention to Praise (or Praise-God) Barbon (or Barebone) was not just his vulnerable name but his trade as a leather-seller and his notoriety as a lay preacher to a congregation which worshipped in his warehouse, the Lock and Key in Fleet Street. It made no difference that he was a man of some substance, a liveryman of the Leathersellers' Company since 1634 and its third warden since 1648; he carried the double stigma of sectarianism and trade with which the scoffers quite wrongly branded the House as a whole. Did they fasten his name to it while it was still sitting? 'It was afterwards called Praise-God Barebone's Parliament,' wrote Clarendon, and Gardiner too thought that the sobriquet caught on later.[6] But that imperfect manuscript list of members in Thomason's collection mentioned earlier is headed, in the same hand that wrote it, 'These are the members of Barebones Parliament, as they were pleased to call themselves. 4 July.'[7] 'Are' in the first clause rather suggests that the assembly was still sitting at the time of writing; 'were' in the second probably refers to the title of parliament which it assumed on 6 July. Since Thomason acquired a complete and accurate printed list of members on 1 August,[8] he can have had little motive for purchasing or copying the manuscript one after then. The evidence is neither conclusive nor important, but the point is worth making that the early form of the appellation was Barebone's Parliament; 'the' does not precede the two words in any source. The manuscript just cited, and occasionally a printer, followed the widespread contemporary habit of omitting the apostrophe in the genitive, but while Barebone, Barbone, and Barbon are common contemporary variants of the man's name, Barebones is not. Macaulay, Carlyle, and Gardiner avoided the solecism of 'the Barebones Parliament' or 'the Barebones', so perhaps modern historians may be persuaded to do so too.

The religious complexion of the assembly will be discussed in the next chapter; this one is concerned with its social composition and political experience. As a whole it obviously fell below the social level of a typical House of Commons under the monarchy. The following table makes no claim to precision, but it attempts

[6] Clarendon, *History of the Rebellion*, v, 282; Gardiner, *C & P*, ii, 238 n. 2.

[7] BL, E698 (19); cf. p. 137.

[8] BL, 669 f. 17 (37).

an approximate social classification of the assembly in terms of
the categories employed by Professor Underdown in analysing
the membership of the Long Parliament.[9] with the addition of
two further classes, 'professional gentry' and 'professionals'. It
may be compared with the fuller tables in Appendix B, where
the status of each member is given in the same terms.

Table I

Greater gentry	17
County gentry	22
Lesser gentry	66
Professional gentry	7
Merchant gentry	9
Merchants and professionals	23
Total	144

It is immediately obvious, if the classification is roughly
correct, that at least a third of the membership would have been
socially quite at home in a typical elected House before or after
the Great Rebellion, for to the first two categories can be added
men of respectable but less affluent families who had actually sat
in the Long Parliament (e.g. Anlaby, Lascelles, Salwey,
Sydenham) and others whose professional careers had raised
them to distinction (e.g. Blake, Sadler, Jonathan Goddard). No
elected parliament had ever consisted exclusively of the county
élite, or there would have been no political career for Oliver
Cromwell.

The greater gentry here include two members of the titled
nobility, four baronets, and four knights. Lord Eure, the one
peer in his own right, added less lustre to the House than might
be expected, for he had recently succeeded to the title but not to
the estates of the barony, and his political role was to be as
modest as his fortune. Philip Sidney, styled Viscount Lisle, was
heir to the Earl of Leicester, and though he was arrogant,
quarrelsome, and loose in his morals, his experience as Lord
Lieutenant of Ireland in 1646–7 and on three of the Rump's
Councils of State gave him political as well as social weight. The
baronets, knights, and other greater gentry were of course far
fewer proportionally than in a normal parliament, but there
were three future earls among them.

[9] Underdown, *Pride's Purge*, pp. 366–90.

The county gentry have been so classified where their families had traditionally figured on the Commissions of the Peace or in the returns to parliament, though they include a very few parvenus like Colonel Philip Jones, the uncrowned king of South Wales, whose recently acquired wealth would have made any lower classification misleading. Others such as William Sydenham and Cromwell himself might have been promoted on the same grounds, but they are here left among the lesser gentry. That is the category with the largest numbers, the widest social span, and the most ill-defined upper and lower limits. There has been no systematic attempt to quantify their incomes, since in so many cases the evidence is lacking for even an approximate estimate. Nor have they been confined to those whose arms were registered by the College of Heralds, for that would have excluded a considerable number who were clearly accepted as gentlemen, and would have been even in less revolutionary times.

Most of our lesser gentry present no problem; they include comfortable squires like Henry Birkenhead of Backford in Cheshire and William Spence of South Malling in Sussex, representatives of cadet lines of major families such as Fenwick, Erle, and Strickland, and younger sons from such houses as Cust, Erisey, and Lucy. There are eight or so who can be classed as urban gentry, who together with just over a dozen provincial merchants (not of course classed here as gentry) and the remaining Londoners bring the town-based members up to about thirty. The difficult cases are the parochial squireens and the younger sons of minor families, and here it has been necessary to make cautious use of statutes, commissions, wills, writs, and other contemporay documents which specify their status. The successive Acts for the Assessment, for instance, strove to distinguish between esquires and gentlemen and men who were neither. 116 members had been named in the Act of 10 December 1652 or in earlier Acts, and exactly 100 of these had been styled esquire or higher. Ten more would be so described in subsequent Assessment Acts, and there were a few men of quality in the House, like Sir Charles Wolseley, Sir Robert King, and the Scottish members, who never served in this capacity. Yet the social currency had depreciated so much during the revolutionary years, as it became harder to find men of the old standing to fill the county commissions, that it is not always safe to assume that a man who figures as esquire in the sixteen-fifties would have been rated a gentleman in pre-war days. Henry King, member for Norfolk and alderman of Norwich, illustrates the downward shift of the cut-off point. Norfolk and Norwich had separate bodies of assessment commissioners, but from 1647 to 1657 King served on both. He is named below the gentlemen in the Acts of 1647 and 1648, but in the four passed between 1649 and 1652 he regularly appears as 'Gent' in the county list and 'Esq' in the city one, and finally makes the higher status in both in 1657. Our table places him among the merchants, not the merchant gentry, who were all men of greater standing, such as Moyer and Ireton of London or Dickenson of York.

The small group of professional gentry is very diverse. It comprises the physician Jonathan Goddard, Robert Blake the admiral, the lawyers Nathaniel Taylor, Thomas St. Nicholas, and Augustine Wingfield, and the polymath John Sadler, of whom more will be said in the next chapter. Most of the men in the sub-gentry category of merchants and professionals were engaged in trade, but it also includés the soldiers Desborough, Hewson, and Clarke (the member for Ireland, not the Suffolk one), along with Broughton, who was Clerk of the Peace for Kent, and Coates, who was probably a Skipton attorney. There were of course no 'artificers of the meanest trades' among them; the provincial merchants were all in a comfortable way of business and most were aldermen or the equivalent in their towns.

All in all, at least four-fifths of the members were recognized as members of the gentry class by their unbiased contemporaries, and most of the rest were accorded that status in formal documents of the time. More of them were drawn from further down that broad social band than in typical seventeenth-century parliaments, but to set against its shadowy lower fringe there were some whose family fortunes were rising and whose upward climb would not be reversed when the Commonwealth collapsed. Charles Howard and Edward Montagu, representing cadet lines of noble houses, would acquire earldoms at the Restoration; so in time would Sir Anthony Ashley Cooper. George Monck, the son of a knight, was to become a duke. Edward Smith, Robert Jermy, and Richard Cust were to be made baronets by

Charles II, and Edward Cater was to be knighted by him. There were also to be baronetcies in the course of time for the sons of Sir William Roberts, John Clarke (the Suffolk member), Robert Duckenfield, Joachim Matthews, and Samuel Moyer, for George Bellot's elder brother, and for John Chetwood's grandson.[10] Among more transient honours, seven members were to be knighted by Cromwell and twenty summoned to his new upper house in 1657.[11] As for more durable fame, no fewer than 41 of the 144 are enshrined in *The Dictionary of National Biography*, and at least fifteen published tracts or longer works in their lifetime— not counting Cromwell and Monck and Ashley Cooper, whose speeches and letters were printed as matters of public interest.[12]

Education is another social indicator in this age. Forty-four members had been to a university and the same number to one of the Inns of Court, but these are probably slight underestimates since they exclude doubtful identifications. There was as usual a substantial overlap, and the total number who had received one or both forms of higher education was at least fifty-nine and possibly sixty-four. This compares unfavourably with Elizabethan and early Stuart parliaments, though not with those later in the century. The House was not as destitute of legal knowledge as has sometimes been stated, for despite the army officers' hostility towards professional lawyers, fourteen or fifteen of those who had studied at the Inns had been called to the bar.[13]

It is of twofold interest to know how many members had sat in previous parliaments or served on the Commissions of the Peace, since these are pointers to both social standing and political experience. Few indeed had sat before, as one would expect, for by 1653 most former MPs who were not royalists had either been

[10] G. E. C[okayne], *Complete Baronetage*, 6 vols. (Exeter, 1900–9), under the above names; *CSPD 1664–5*, pp. 413; *Visitations of Bedfordshire*, Harleian Soc. xix, p. 90.

[11] Abbott, iv 951–3.

[12] See D. Wing, *Short–Title Catalogue 1641–1700*, for works by Barebone, Robert Bennett, Danvers, Jonathan Goddard, Gookin, Hollister, Lawrence, Francis Rous, Sadler, Thomas St. Nicholas, Swinton, Tichborne, Wingfield, and Wolseley. Highland wrote *An Exact Relation* under the intials L.D. Authors named Thomas Baker, Nathaniel Barton, Anthony Rous, John St. Nicholas, John Stone, and William West also figure in Wing, but they all appear to be distinct from their namesakes in Barebone's Parliament. Ashley Cooper should perhaps be counted as an author in the full sense: K. H. D. Haley, *The First Earl of Shaftesbury* (Oxford, 1968), pp. 390–4.

[13] In a few cases the evidence comes from sources other than the standard printed lists of admissions to the two universities and the four Inns of Court.

secluded, whether by force or choice, since Pride's Purge or had sat in the Rump. Few in any of these categories commended themselves to Cromwell and the Council of Officers, and fewer still answered their call. Ashley Cooper had once been a royalist, and Henry Lawrence and Edward Montagu had ceased to sit in 1648, but of the total of twenty-two members who had been elected to earlier parliaments (not counting Cromwell and Harrison, the only co-opted members with previous experience), all but four had been Rumpers. Fifteen had been Recruiters, elected at various dates between 1645 and 1651. Eleven are reckoned by Dr Worden to have been among the Rump's least active members,[14] and eight of these seem to have been equally inoperative in Barebone's Parliament. Indeed Martyn and perhaps Salwey never took their seats, while Blake was kept from doing so until 10 October, first by service at sea and later by ill health. What with Sir Anthony Ashley Cooper having served only in the Short Parliament and Samuel Dunch only in that of 1621, the amount of useful parliamentary experience at the service of the new assembly was slight indeed. In fact there were only two genuine 'old parliament-men' besides Francis Rous, the Speaker: John Pyne and Anthony Stapley, each with five previous parliaments to his credit. Not that Stapley can have been of much help, for having attended Cromwell's provisional Council of State since April and been re-elected to it on 9 July, he did not come to a single meeting between 12 July and 28 October, and there is no sign that he sat in the House before 10 November.

Stapley was one of eight members besides Cromwell and Harrison who had served on any of the Councils of State under the Commonwealth, but with him and Salwey and Blake largely inactive, and 'idle Dick' Norton living up to Cromwell's description of him, only Pickering, Strickland, Lisle, and Carew really brought their experience to bear. Fortunately there was more continuity at the administrative and judicial level, and this, coupled with a fair measure of competence and zeal in the successive Councils of State from April onwards, kept ordinary domestic government and justice functioning quite smoothly through 1653.[15] In particular spheres, Anlaby, Carew, Harrison,

[14] He places them in the lowest two categories on a six-point scale: *Rump*, pp. 389–91.
[15] Aylmer, *State's Servants*, pp. 42–4, 85–6.

and Strickland had served on the Rump's Army Committee, Blake, Monck, and Langley had been Admiralty and Navy Commissioners, and Danvers a Trustee for Maintenance of Ministers. The experience in fiscal and financial affairs of Sir William Roberts, Moyer, Squibb, and Stone has already been mentioned, and they were reinforced by Ireton, Langley, Kenrick, and Tichborne.

Subsequent parliamentary experience could not of course affect the performance of members in 1653, but it indicates how many of them could succeed in genuine elections, whether under the reformed franchise and redistribution of seats in 1654 and 1656 or under the old system, as restored in 1659 and later. In fact sixty-seven did, and if one adds the seven (excluding Cromwell) who sat in earlier but not in later parliaments, it transpires that more than half the members were returned at one time or another to an elected parliament. Most of the sixty-seven reappeared only in the parliaments of the Protectorate, when the field was greatly narrowed by the disqualification of former royalists. On the other hand they really did have to win votes, for the Instrument of Government drastically reduced the number of seats that could be directly disposed of by patronage. Even in 1660, when Charles II's return was already a certainty, Ashley Cooper, Henley, Hildesley, Howard, Lascelles, Lucy, Mansell, Martyn, Monck, Montagu, Norton, Phillips, Anthony Rous, West, and Wolseley were all elected to the Convention, though Lascelles and Rous were subsequently unseated. One would not expect to find many of Barebone's fellow-members in the Cavalier Parliament, but Henley, Lucy, Norton, Phillips (until unseated in 1662), and Strickland were there, besides Cooper (Baron Ashley), Monck (Duke of Albemarle), Montagu (Earl of Sandwich), Howard (Earl of Carlisle), and Lord Eure in the Lords. Cust, Henley, Mansell, and Norton attended all three Exclusion Parliaments, and the latter two lived to endorse another revolution in the Convention of 1689.[16] Mansell indeed went on sitting for Glamorgan until he died in 1699.

A strikingly high proportion of members were Justices of the Peace: 119 out of the total of 144, or 117 of the 128 who

---

[16] I am much indebted to Professor B. D. Henning for sending me the list of MPs from 1660 to 1690 which was prepared under his direction for the History of Parliament Trust.

represented the English counties and Wales. Some were certainly new to the bench, and at least thirteen joined it only after Barebone's Parliament met. Yet 89 had been on it in 1650 or earlier, and 119 were to remain or to become JPs under the Protectorate—122 if we include Jaffray, Lockhart, and Swinton, who were appointed when the system was extended to Scotland.[17] There had been a considerable purge of the Commissions of the Peace in 1650, though it varied greatly in extent from region to region. It had slowed down in 1651–2, but had risen to a peak during the last months of the Rump and the remainder of 1653.[18] Unfortunately it is impossible to discover which regime was responsible for most of these changes, since the *liber pacis* which was Chancery's primary record of the Commission covers the period from May 1652 to October 1653. It contains very many deletions, additions, and interlineations, but only a minority of them are dated, though in some cases the dates can be established from other sources. What is striking is the variation between counties. For Surrey, 65 names are struck out from the 93 that appear to constitute the original list in May 1652. More than half the JPs were apparently replaced in Devon, Cornwall, Buckinghamshire, Middlesex, and Westminster, and between a third and a half in Kent, Essex, Berkshire, Herefordshire, and Lincolnshire. On the other hand the changes were very slight in Hampshire, Sussex, Hertfordshire, Leicestershire, Cambridgeshire, Cheshire, and the four northern counties. The extent of the purge on a national scale, however, makes it the more remarkable that nearly two-thirds of our MPs were justices of at least three years' standing.

No such drastic weeding-out followed the establishment of the

[17] The relevant *libri pacis* in the PRO and the dates they cover are as follows: C.193/13/4 (May 1652–Oct. 1653), C.193/13/6 (Sept. 1656–March–Apr. 1657), C.193/13/5 (March 1657–March 1658). There is also a full list of JPs in the Cambridge University Library (MS Dd. 8.1 (A)), which on internal evidence can be dated between August 1652 and April 1653. For 1650 we have a printed list: *The Names of the Justices of the Peace in England and Wales . . . this Michaelmas Terme* (1650, acquired by Thomason on 27 Nov.). I received further help from the card index and computer print-out at the History of Parliament Trust, which embody evidence from docquet books and entry books, and (concerning the Lancashire MPs) from Dr B. G. Blackwood. Unfortunately evidence does not survive to show accurately how many of our MPs were JPs before the Civil War.

[18] Underdown, *Pride's Purge*, pp. 307–12, 340–1; Worden, *Rump*, p. 223; and for the continuity in the JPs' activities through all changes of personnel, Aylmer, *State's Servants*, pp. 305–14.

Protectorate, and very few members were removed from the bench for the radical line they had taken in the House's proceedings. Larger purges followed upon the fall of the Protectorate in 1659, and still more upon Monck's decisive readmission of the secluded members in February 1660, but there were still fifty-three of our members on the bench in March of Restoration year.

Seventeen of them had served as sheriffs before 1653 and eleven more did so subsequently. The great majority had been employed on various parliamentary commissions in their counties or cities; for example, only a dozen of the representatives of England and Wales had not acted as assessment commissioners. Many had been committee-men in the heyday of the county committees, and some had played a role on the county stage that has been likened to that of the French Intendants. Such were John Pyne in Somerset, Robert Bennett in Cornwall, Philip Jones in most of South Wales, perhaps Wroth Rogers in Herefordshire, and on a lesser scale Bingham and Sydenham in Dorset and Blount and Kenrick in Kent.[19] Others had been or were still governors of cities or whole districts, carrying varying degrees of resposibility for civil administration as well as for their garrisons: for example Sydenham as Governor of the Isle of Wight, Bingham of Guernsey, Duckenfield first of Chester and then of the Isle of Man, Howard of Carlisle, Danvers of Stafford, Saunders of Exeter, James of Worcester—the list could be extended. Altogether there was a very considerable stock of experience of local administration among the members, though whether it was the kind of experience that would commend them to their gentry neighbours is quite another question.

Barebone's Parliament was predominantly a middle-aged assembly. The median age of the 101 members whose exact or approximate date of birth has been ascertained was forty-one, the average age just a fraction less: much the same as in the original Long Parliament though (as one would expect) significantly below the Rump, whose median age in 1650 had

---

[19] Underdown, *Pride's Purge*, pp. 306 ff., and for Pyne the same author's *Somerset in the Civil War and Interregnum* (1973), *passim*. For Jones see *Dictionary of Welsh Biography* (hereafter *DWB*) and A. H. Dodd, *Studies in Stuart Wales* (Cardiff, 1952), pp. 121–2, 149–71, and for Rogers G. E. Aylmer, 'Who was ruling in Herefordshire from 1645 to 1661?', *Trans. of the Woolhope Naturalists' Field Club*, xl (1972), 382.

been forty-seven.[20] But Barebone's contained a higher proportion of men whose birth-dates are unknown because they do not figure in such sources as family pedigrees, heraldic visitations, admissions registrars of universities and Inns of Court, funerary inscriptions, and the like. Since most of these relatively obscure men had come to the Council of Officers' attention as reliable work-horses in local administration or as pillars of their churches, their bias was probably towards maturity rather than youth. Of the members whose age is more or less known, fifty-six had passed their fortieth birthdays and only eight were under thirty. That leaves at least thirty-six in their thirties, but the unknowns would probably swell the older age group more than the younger. Nevertheless there were very few old men in the House. Francis Rous was much the oldest at seventy-four; Stapley and Frere came next at sixty-three, and of the rest only Dunch is known to have passed threescore years. What is striking is the youth of a group of men who would win prominence for themselves among the moderates in the assembly and go on to an interesting political future under the Protectorate or later. They include Sir Charles Wolseley (22 or 23), Charles Howard (24), Edward Montagu (not quite 28), and Sir Anthony Ashley Cooper (32); and to these may be added, though their role in Barebone's was smaller, Henry Cromwell (25) and Sir William Lockhart (32).

Although the membership was drawn considerably less from the close-knit ranks of the county families and numbered little more than a third that of a normal House of Commons, ties of blood and marriage were quite numerous. Thomas and John St. Nicholas represented different counties, but they were brothers; the same is true of the Brewsters, Francis and John. Anthony Rous was the Speaker's nephew. Sadler, Sydenham, and Bingham had all married daughters of John Trenchard, while Montagu was brother-in-law to Pickering and Salwey to Wroth Rogers. Lawrence was Pickering's cousin and was related by marriage to Jermy and Hewson. Carew and Erisey were also first cousins, as were Birkenhead and Chetwood, who had been at Brasenose College together. Horseman was a cousin of Pickering at a generation's remove; Christopher Erle's uncle, Sir Walter Erle, was Norton's father-in-law, while Norton's neighbour Major was

[20] D. Brunton and D. H. Pennington, *Members of the Long Parliament* (1954), pp. 45, 188; Mary F. Keeler, *The Long Parliament 1640–1641* (Philadelphia, 1954, p. 19.

father-in-law to Richard Cromwell, Henry's elder brother. William Burton was Desborough's son-in-law, and no doubt the catalogue of kinship could be extended. These men would vary widely in their attitudes to the issues raised in Barebone's Parliament and subsequently to the Protectorate, but they include some of the House's most active and influential members, so it is significant that some of them were well known to each other before it met.

The membership as a whole does not bear the stamp of any undue patronage by individual members of the Council of Officers, unless one counts Harrison's promotion of Welsh Fifth Monarchists. Cromwell himself was in a unique position to influence its composition, but he evidently used it very sparingly. His old comradeship with Norton[21] and his family tie with Major may account for their nomination, but it would seem unlike him to have been the proposer of his own son Henry, who had already won his spurs in Ireland. Nor need one suppose that Samuel Dunch, a former MP and a JP since at least 1647, owed his place to his elder brother's marriage to Cromwell's aunt, or John Ireton his to his deceased brother having married Bridget Cromwell. Desborough was the Lord General's brother-in-law, but he was co-opted, not nominated, and Lockhart's marriage to Cromwell's niece still lay well in the future. With these exceptions, the names of the many families that were linked to Cromwell's house by blood or wedlock are conspicuously absent.[22]

The rest of this chapter consists of a brief portrait gallery, designed to illustrate the variety of types to be found among the various categories of members, though the more conspicuous leaders of the moderate and radical factions that soon emerged are reserved for the next chapter. For that reason the top group of greater gentry will not be dwelt on here, since the more interesting of them are either very well known or will find their place later. They do however include four of Scotland's and two of Ireland's representatives, and our sampling will begin with

[21] Abbott, i, 313, 585, 590–2; ii, 328.

[22] I have been unable to trace whether there was any kinship between Henry Barrington and Sir Thomas, who had married Cromwell's aunt, but if Pink MS 297 fo. 115 is trustworthy it is unlikely to have been at all close. Nor have I found evidence to link Thomas French, the Cambridge alderman and MP, with Dr Peter French, the prebend of Christ Church, who was married to Cromwell's sister Robina.

collective sketches of the first representatives of those countries to sit at Westminster.

Scotland, although her formal union with England had been delayed by the Rump's tardiness and the subsequent legislative hiatus, differed from Ireland in having a few native sons of distinction who were prepared to co-operate with her conquerors sufficiently to give her some genuine representation. Alexander Brodie of Brodie proved not to be one of them, however, so her meagre apportionment of five members was reduced to four. Brodie might have been a good choice, for he was a Lord of Session who had sat in both the Scottish parliament and the General Assembly, but he was an unbending Presbyterian. He thought at first that the breaking of the Rump had 'meikle of the righteousness of God in it', but he was chary of collaborating with the perpetrators of the deed. He set aside 1 May as a day of solemn humiliation, in order to seek the Lord's instruction 'either anent complying with English sectaries or Scottish malignants', and on the 23rd he wrote in his diary 'I have resolved and determined, in the Lord's strength, to eschew and avoid employments under Cromwell.' Nevertheless the latter's writ of summons to Barebone's threw him into a further three-day wrestling-bout with his conscience, aided by the prayers of his friends and kinsmen. In the end his scruples over England's religious heterodoxy and the doubtful legality of her new government made him stay at home, but as the opening date approached and passed he still kept agonizing over 'the snare and strength of this temptation'.[23]

Three of the other four Scotsmen were men of equally strong religious convictions, though in varying degrees they had parted company with the strict Presbyterian orthodoxy of the Coven-anters, and would be reckoned among the religious radicals in Barebone's Parliament. Sir James Hope of Hopetoun had been, like Brodie, a Lord of Session, and at first he reacted to Cromwell's call as Brodie did, but in the end he travelled south in the same coach as his fellow-member John Swinton of Swinton, the head of a powerful Berwickshire family. Both had begun to collaborate with the English forces by the beginning of 1651. Alexander Jaffray, the third of the trio, had fought against them at Dunbar

---

[23] *D.NB*; *The Diary of Alexander Brodie*, ed. D. Laing (Spalding Club, Aberdeen, 1863), pp. 30, 41, 57–61, 63, 65, 84.

and been severely wounded, but in the course of many conversations with Cromwell and John Owen after his capture he had been gradually won over to Independency. That proved to be only a staging post, however, for both he and Swinton later became Quakers. All three were men of considerable learning as well as substantial property, and all three were lawyers. Jaffray was Keeper of the Great Seal of Scotland, while Swinton, his fellow-member Sir William Lockhart, and Hope's elder brother Sir John were the only Scotsmen among the Commonwealth's commissioners for administering justice in Scotland.

Lockhart looks the odd man out in this company, except in terms of birth and property, and he was certainly a more versatile careerist. He was in turn a captain in the French army, a Covenanter, an Engager under Hamilton, and a royalist of sorts before he became a Cromwellian, and he would in time find favour and employment under Charles II. Since he owed his first knighthood to Charles I, he was plain James Lockhart at this time, though he later got a second one from Cromwell, whose niece he had by then married. Yet he gave loyal service to each master to whom he pledged himself, and betrayed none of them; he had, for instance, gallantly covered the rear of Hamilton's army in the dreadful retreat from Preston in 1648. Naturally he took a different line from his fellow-Scots in the House and aligned himself with the moderates. Jaffray by contrast was one of the protesting rump which, on that final day when the moderates marched out to tender their resignation, sat on until it was evicted. Despite that, Jaffray remained Director of the Chancery all through the Protectorate, and Swinton the sectary and Lockhart the soldier-courtier were to remain associated, first as judges and later as members of Cromwell's Scottish Council.[24] Only Hope failed to get preferment from him, and that was probably because of strong political differences, for in 1659 he was recommended to the restored Rump for a judgeship

[24] For the Scottish members see, besides *DNB*, Trevor-Roper, *Religion, The Reformation and Social Change*, pp. 415–17, 421, 432–3, 442–3 (though this account does not wholly avoid the *DNB*'s confusion between Sir James and Sir John Hope); F. D. Dow, *Cromwellian Scotland 1651–1660* (Edinburgh, 1979), as indexed under their names; *Diary of Alexander Jaffray*, ed. J. Barclay (Aberdeen, 1856), p. 57; J. Nicoll, *Diary of Public Transactions* (Bannatyne Club, Edinburgh, 1836), pp. 95, 155, 159, 167–8, 174, 218, 239–40; C. H. Firth, *Scotland and the Commonwealth* (Scot. Hist Soc., Edinburgh, 1895), p. 30; C. H. Firth, *Scotland and the Protectorate* (Scot. Hist. Soc., Edinburgh, 1899), pp. 108, 152.

as 'able, honest, and a knowne Commonwealthes man, for which he was putt out of commission by the late Lord Protector'.[25]

Ireland's representatives differed from Scotland's in that none were of Irish ancestry and none sided with the religious radicals. Three were sons of settlers and three were soldiers—rare exceptions to the general rule which had debarred serving officers from nomination. Two of the former, Sir Robert King and Vincent Gookin, were among the richest landowners in the House, and four of the six—King, Clarke, Hewson, and Henry Cromwell—were to play a particularly active part in its proceedings.

Sir Robert was the eldest son of Sir John King, a busy and thriving administrative pluralist in Ireland whom he had succeeded as Muster-Master General and Clerk of the Cheque. James I had knighted him as long ago as 1621, and he had sat in successive Irish parliaments. He had fought hard against the Irish rebels until he came over to England in 1642 and entered the Long Parliament's service, which took him back to Ulster in 1645. He made large acquisitions of land under the Commonwealth, but his services too had been large. He moved in the circle of Samuel Hartlib and John Dury, who married his sister. This same sister became aunt by marriage to Katherine, Lady Ranelagh, with whom she formed a deep friendship, based on shared religious devotion. Through such channels and his own intellectual interests King came into close touch with Lady Ranelagh's brilliant brother Robert Boyle and the Invisible College. In Barebone's Parliament he sat on the committee for the advancement of learning as well as that for the affairs of Ireland, and he was placed high in the elections to the Council of State on 1 November. He was essentially a moderate, and he opposed the setting-up of the committee 'to consider of a new body of the law'. He died in 1657 at Wimbledon House, one of his many purchases, and his will testifies not only to his large wealth but also to a strong vein of Puritan piety.[26]

Vincent Gookin too sat on the Irish committee, but until he

---

[25] Firth, *Scotland and the Protectorate*, p. 385.

[26] *DNB*; T. C. Barnard, *Cromwellian Ireland* (Oxford, 1973), pp. 119, 215, 225; Charles Webster, 'New Light on the Invisible College,' *TRHS*, 5th series, xxiv (1974), pp. 32–3; Charles Webster, *The Great Instauration* (1975), pp. 37, 62, 225–6; *CJ*, vii, 283–4, 287, 304, 344; PRO 11/265 (PCC 222 Ruthen).

was appointed an Admiralty Commissioner on 3 December he left no other trace in the *Journal*. Irish affairs probably occupied most of his attention, for he cared about the country very deeply. His father, Sir Vincent, had been one of the richest settlers and projectors there, but had fled to England when Wentworth sought to arrest him for publishing a bitter attack on the Irish nation. Soon after he died in 1638, Vincent the younger sold his Gloucestershire estates and returned to Ireland, where he developed views about the Irish which were totally opposed to his father's and altogether rare in his time. In *The Great Case of Transplantation in Ireland Discussed*, which he published in January 1655, he attacked the whole policy of transplanting the native population, on the grounds of humanity, justice, and economic sense; 'the Lord would not deal so with Sodome', he said.[27] 'After so sharp an execution, is it not time at length to sound a retreat? Must we still cry justice, justice? God has aveng'd it; let others take heed how they become guilty ... The fair vertue of justice (overdon) degenerates into the stinking weed of Tyranny.'[28] He found it 'sad to observe how Garrisons are placed in every quarter where the Irish inhabite, Ministers in none; as if our business in Ireland was onely to set up our own interests, and not Christs'.[29] He held strong though tolerant religious convictions, and he thought poorly of the sectaries, whom Charles Fleetwood and the hitherto dominant faction in the Commonwealth's Irish administration strongly favoured. 'And for the gifted men, although ... to convert heathens (as they count the Irish) were a fitter work for new Apostles (as they count themselves) then to pervert Christians, yet 'tis probable they may be as unwilling to preach, where there is need of them, as they have been forward to intrude themselves, where there was no need of them.'[30] His condemnation of the whole concept of national guilt and his compassion for the Irish poor were centuries ahead of his time. Naturally he was attacked, and his chief assailant was Colonel Richard Lawrence,[31] whose kinsman Henry would join with

[27] V. Gookin, *The Great Case of Transplantation in Ireland Discussed* ([3 Jan.] 1655), p. 7 and *passim*.

[28] Ibid. 14.

[29] Ibid. 3.

[30] Ibid. 5.

[31] Richard Lawrence, *The Interest of England in the Irish Plantation, Stated* ([9 March] 1655), to which Gookin made a spirited reply in *The Author and Case of Transplanting the*

Fleetwood in opposing his Irish policies on Cromwell's council. He was to find an ally, however, in Henry Cromwell, whom he came to admire greatly.

The third non-military member was Daniel Hutchinson, alderman of Dublin—'honest Alderman Hutchinson, who letts no man that is a friend to the Parliament nor the publique affairs want anything, that he can help them to'.[32] So wrote Colonel John Jones in 1652, after borrowing £500 from him for the expenses of his wife's last illness and funeral, and indeed Hutchinson had been much engaged since 1649 in supplying the Commonwealth's armies and ships. He was an elder in the congregation of that moderate Independent Dr Samuel Winter, who was Provost of Trinity College from 1651 to 1660 and corresponded with Richard Baxter over the Irish Association, which he helped to form. While Barebone's Parliament was sitting, Zachariah Croft, another moderate minister, dedicated to Hutchinson a long tract called *Bethshemeth Clouded*, which he wrote to refute a still longer one by the Fifth Monarchist John Rogers and to uphold the very topical cause of a publicly maintained ministry. Three years later Winter and Hutchinson both signed a declaration which vigorously denied malicious rumours that their church was disaffected towards Henry Cromwell.[33]

Henry himself had spent three years in Ireland as a very young colonel, though he had not yet divided Irish politics as he was to do in the next few years. He made his presence felt in Barebone's, acting nine times as a teller, and he was high among the successful candidates elected to the Council of State on 1 November. But his colleague Colonel John Clarke held the teller's record in this brief parliament by acting sixteen times, and among his important committees were those not only for Irish affairs but also for the army, for the customs, and for the

---

Irish . . . Vindicated ([12 May] 1655), where p. 59 is the source of the *DNB*'s erroneous statement that Gookin was elected to Barebone's Parliament by the English of Kinsale and Bandon; that was in 1654, not 1653. On Gookin see also T. C. Barnard, 'Planters and Policies in Cromwellian Ireland', *Past and Present*, no. 61 (1973), pp. 31–69, and his 'Lord Broghill, Vincent Gookin and the Cork Elections of 1659', *EHR*, lxxxviii (1973), 352–9.

[32] Mayer, 'Inedited Letters', p. 198; cf. p. 189.

[33] *CSPD 1649–54, passim*; Nickolls, pp. 137–8; Nuttall, *Visible Saints*, pp. 16 n., 120, 123; Barnard, *Cromwellian Ireland*, pp. 41, 81, 83–4, 115, 290; Z. Croft, *Bethshemeth Clouded* ([1 Dec.] 1653), Dedication.

revenue generally. His origins are uncertain, but since he was a JP for Essex, and later for Middlesex too, he may well be the John Clarke admitted to Gray's Inn in 1635 as son and heir of Humphrey Clarke of Edmonton, gent. He had commanded the land forces in Blake's expedition which reduced the Scilly Isles in 1651, and from the following year he had been colonel of an enlarged foot regiment in Ireland. He seems to have taken a consistently moderate line in 1653, and he had in store a lucrative career under the Protectorate as Admiralty Commissioner, while still retaining his colonelcy. His wife was Thurloe's sister.[34] As an MP in 1657 he voted for making Oliver king, and in 1659 he loyally upheld Richard's authority and the Humble Petition and Advice against the republicans. In his correspondence he could write the language of the saints with apparent sincerity, and in the 1656 parliament he defended the Quaker James Nayler against the grave charge of blasphemy, though deploring his 'devilish delusion'. Yet it may betoken a reputation for religious moderation that a naval chaplain appealed to him personally after being virtually driven from his ship because the captain, lieutenant, and most of the officers were 'Anabaptists'.[35]

Hewson, who is ranked here like Clarke as 'professional' because he made his way as a soldier, had gone over to Ireland with Cromwell and stayed to become Governor of Dublin. He had the humblest social origins of anyone in the House, having been, as the army's opponents loved to repeat, a shoemaker before the wars. His career needs no recounting, but his religious stance in Barebone's Parliament is interesting. He belonged to the congregation in Dublin which from 1650 to 1652 had had for its pastor John Rogers, who became notorious during 1653 as a Fifth Monarchy man. Hewson, though not a Baptist himself, was later strongly identified with the 'Anabaptist' faction in Ireland which was to be such a thorn in Henry Cromwell's side. One might therefore expect to find him siding with the sectarian radicals in 1653, yet on 17 November he was a teller *against* the

[34] As stated in *A Narrative in the Late Parliament* (*Harleian Misc.*, vi, 465), and clearly implied in Thurloe, vii, 211; the lady was Col. Ewer's widow (Firth and Davies, *Regimental History*, p. 355); but in *CSPD 1658-9*, p. 186, a letter is puzzlingly addressed by Thurloe 'to his nephew Col. J. Clarke'.

[35] Folger Library, Add MS 483, fo. 66. For Clarke's career see *CSPD, passim*; Foster, *Gray's Inn Admissions*, p. 154; Burton, *Diary*, i, 75-6; 528-9; iv, 140, 260, 384; Firth and Davies, *Regimental History*, pp. 435, 449-50, 634-5; Pink MS 299, fos. 499-500.

abolition of lay patronage, and he was listed among the members who supported a godly learned ministry and the universities.[36] He too was a prominent member, serving on a variety of committees and on the Coucil of State from July to November.

Wales provides two interesting examples of county-gentry types. The four Fifth Monarchy men placed by Harrison were all minor squires, and only two of them were Welshmen; they will be briefly noticed in the next chapter. But Harrison's writ did not extend to South Wales, and both Bussy Mansell of Briton Ferry in Glamorgan and James Phillips of Tregibby and Cardigan Priory were men of a very different stamp, in their politics no less than in their social status. Both were royalists during much of the Civil War, Mansell a particularly active one. Indeed Mansell, within the span of the single year 1645, and at the ripe age of twenty-two, served in turn as Colonel-General of the king's forces in South Wales, as commander of the local neutralist force known as the Peaceable Army—he was one of those who took the surrender of the royalists in Cardiff—and as commander-in-chief of the parliamentary forces in Glamorgan under the direct authority of Sir Thomas Fairfax. He was also placed on the committees of three neighbouring counties and was made Sheriff of Glamorgan in 1646. He had already inherited estates reckoned at £1,100 a year, and that made his allegiance worth contending for. The records are curiously silent about his doings in the second Civil War, but if he did show any backwardness in military action he made up for it by the zeal with which he served the Commonwealth in all sorts of ways, including the sequestration of royalist estates. The fact that he and Phillips were both Commissioners for the Propagation of the Gospel in Wales, Mansell a notably busy one, is a reminder that that body did not consist exclusively of sectarian enthusiasts. One would expect him to figure as a moderate in Barebone's Parliament, but in fact he does not figure in its records at all from 20 July, when he was placed on his only committee, until he surfaces surprisingly among the thirty or so who sat on in the House on its very last day, in protest against the walk-out by the moderate leaders. This may be why a broadsheet of 1654 listed him with the religious radicals, for there is little else to associate

---

[36] *DNB*; *CJ*, vii, 352; L. F. Brown *Baptists and Fifth Monarchy Men*, pp. 151–66. For the list referred to see pp. 195–8.

him with them, and he seems not to have used his ecclesiastical
patronage to promote them. He served the Protectorate as a JP,
as an Ejector, and in the commissions for the militia, for the
assessment, and for trying treasons against the Protector's person.
Nevertheless the Rump, when it was restored in 1659, seems to
have regarded him as a frustrated commonwealthsman, judging
by the trusts that it bestowed on him. It was mistaken, for he was
already in contact with royalist agents and he rode the tide of the
Restoration with characteristic adroitness. Yet to his credit he
continued to give protection to local Dissenters, though conforming to the Church of England himself, and he became a
determined Whig and (later) anti-Jacobite. His distaste for the
conservative majority's tactics in December 1653 can be
accounted for without supposing that he shared the millenarian
aspirations of his fellow-members from North Wales.[37]

James Phillips too was the heir of a wealthy and long-
established family, and he made his final switch from the king's
to the parliamentary side even later than Mansell. He first
appears as an assessment commissioner in 1647 and was added to
his county committee only in 1648, but he must have held steady
in the second Civil War since he was shortly afterwards put on
the commissions for the militia and for sequestrations. He was
Sheriff of Cardiganshire in 1649–50 and Custos Rotulorum all
through the next decade. Unwisely, he invested in crown lands.
His wife Katharine, the poetess soon to be renowned as the
Matchless Orinda, published her first verses in 1651, prefixed to
Henry Vaughan's; Crashaw and Jeremy Taylor would later
dedicate works to her. Phillips seems to have tired quickly of
Barebone's Parliament, for though he was placed on the Army
Committee in July he obtained leave of absence on 12 August,
and there is no evidence that he ever returned. He served the
Protectorate in various capacities, including the Army Commit-
tee, sat in all three of its parliaments, and supported the second
one's attempt to make Cromwell king. He was out of favour with
the restored Rump in 1659, and steered his way through the

---

[37] A. M. Johnson, 'Bussy Mansell (1623–1699): Political Survivalist', *Morgannwg*, xx
(1976), pp. 9–36; *DWB*; Dodd, *Studies in Stuart Wales*, pp. 124, 158, 165–6; Richards,
Religious Developments in Wales, pp. 171, 421; *Diary of Richard Symonds* (Camden Soc., 1859),
p. 216; Thurloe, i, 637; Firth and Rait, ii, 343, 967, 1040, 1086, etc., *CSPD 1655*, pp. 79,
94, *1689–9*, p. 235; Ronald E. Hutton, 'The Royalist War Effort in Wales and the West
Midlands 1642–1646' (unpublished Oxford D.Phil. thesis, 1980), pp. 258–9.

Restoration well enough to get himself elected to the Cavalier Parliament. Unfortunately the Commons set up a committee to investigate his membership of the High Court of Justice which had tried royalist conspirators in 1654, and he was eventually unseated.[38]

Moving a step down from the county to the lesser gentry, we find ourselves among a body of men whose character was too diverse to be easily conveyed by a few samples. More will be found in the next chapter, but John Crofts is not untypical of many who were called out of relative obscurity in 1653. Squire of the delectable manor of Nether Swell, he was a recent newcomer to the Commission of the Peace, and was not even an assessment commissioner until Barebone's Parliament made him one. He worshipped in nearby Stow-on-the-Wold, where the rector William Beale was a Congregationalist, and he was one of the three men specially recommended to Cromwell and the Council of Officers by the churches of Christ in Gloucestershire, out of the much longer list that they submitted. The several committees to which he was named and his one appearance as a teller suggest a preoccupation with local issues rather than any religious extremes, but he was listed among the radicals, and he was not made an Ejector in 1654. Nevertheless he served the Protectorate loyally, if not uncritically; after helping actively to suppress Penruddock's rising he signed an address from his church to Cromwell, rejoicing at the common enemy's defeat but mentioning many evils that still awaited reformation. He was often styled captain, and whether or not his service had ever extended beyond the local militia he clearly had some military competence. He commanded the county troop during the regime of the Major-Generals and again during Booth's rising, when it captured Sir Hugh Myddelton. He was elected to the Parliament of 1656, but is not known to have spoken in it.[39]

[38] *DWB*; Dodd, *Studies in Stuart Wales*, pp. 141, 165–6, 194; John Aubrey, *Brief Lives*, ed. A. Clark (Oxford, 1898), pp. 153–4; BL, MS Egerton 2979, fos. 107–27; *CJ*, vii, 299; viii, 438; *Narrative of the Late Parliament*, in *Harleian Misc.*, vi 467, 474; Firth and Rait and *CSPD, passim*.

[39] Nickolls, pp. 125, 145–7; *CJ*, vii, 287, 301, 323, 337, 340, 350; Firth and Rait, ii, 1040, 1069, etc.; *CSPD 1655–6*, p. 102; *1658–9*, pp. 117, 353, 360, 362, 365; *1659–60*, pp. 16, 41; *A Narrative of the Late Parliament*, in *Harleian Misc.*, vi, 467; W. R. Williams, *Parl. History of Gloucestershire* (Hereford, 1898, pp. 54–5; Tai Liu, *Discord in Zion*, p. 137. Williams and Pink (MS 299, fo. 659) state that he was removed from the Common Council of Tewkesbury in Aug. 1662, but I suspect that this was the John Croft of

(continued)

Two contrasted figures, Dr Jonathan Goddard and Augustine Wingfield, can stand here for the interesting group of professional gentry. Goddard was as plainly intended to represent Oxford University as John Sadler, Master of Magdalene, was to represent Cambridge. He was not the only future FRS in Barebone's Parliament, for Thomas Blount was rather surprisingly another, but no other member boasts such a place in the early history of science. The son of a Deptford shipbuilder, he began his career at Oxford but went on to Cambridge to pursue his study of medicine. There he took his MB in 1638 and his MD in 1643, in which year he joined the College of Physicians. Even before he became a Fellow in 1646, and while he was still in his twenties, his London lodging was often the weekly meeting-place of that group of experimental scientists, including John Wilkins and John Wallis, which would later be seen as the original nucleus of the Royal Society. He was in turn physician to Charles I during his captivity and to Cromwell on his Irish and Scottish campaigns, and the Rump made him a trustee in its act for advancing the gospel and learning in Ireland. Cromwell, who was Chancellor of Oxford University, recognizing Goddard's qualities and grateful for his devoted care during his own grave illness in 1651, secured his appointment as Warden of Merton College and as one of five Visitors of the university. He sat on three major committees in Barebone's Parliament and came high in the November elections to the Council of State, when the moderates took it over. He was prominent in the Experimental Philosophy Club which met in Wilkin's rooms in Wadham, at any rate until he was appointed Professor of Physic at Gresham College in 1655. Wilkins, Wallis, and others in the club were deeply religious men, and so probably was Goddard, but his range of sympathies was such that the royalist Seth Ward addressed a eulogistic dedication to him in 1653, and Anthony Wood also dedicated a book to him. Wood describes him as an Independent. He lost Merton College at the Restoration, but he was one of the dozen or so men who constituted the active core of the Royal Society during the two or three years before its formal incorporation, and he was on its original council. 'He loved

---

Gotherington (close to Tewkesbury, whereas Swell is far), whose will was proved in 1675 (PCC 3·Dycer). I do not know why L. F. Brown (op. cit., p. 33 n. 16) names him as a Baptist.

wine', Aubrey tells us, 'and was most curious in his wines, was hospitable, but drank not to excess.' He was still in his fifties when in 1675 he fell dead of apoplexy on his way home from a club that he frequented at the Crown tavern in Bloomsbury.[40]

Augustine Wingfield was a much less distinguished man, but he too belies some of the more facile generalizations about the membership, including its supposed lack of legal competence. He was the son and heir of a gentleman of Rickmansworth, but his father died young and he was adopted by his uncle John Brisco, a bencher of Lincoln's Inn. He entered the Inn by special admission in 1629 and was called to the bar seven years later. He was appointed a militia commissioner for Middlesex in 1644 and again in 1650, by which time he was a JP. In Barebone's Parliament he sat on six committees, including the important one for tithes, the two very different ones concerning the law, and the one for the advancement of learning. He had a hand in drafting a number of measures. He reported one bill for constituting commissioners to hear the causes in equity hitherto judged by Chancery, which got no further than its first reading, and another for regulating exorbitant legal fees, which was read twice and committed. Three of the four divisions in which he acted as teller were concerned with the abolition of Chancery, and in two of them—unfortunately the issues in both are obscure—his partners were radicals. He seems to have been that rarity in those times, a keen reforming lawyer. He cared at least as strongly about tithes, although he is listed, no doubt correctly, among the supporters of a godly ministry and the universities. In April 1652 he had presented a petition from Middlesex to the Rump, pressing for a less objectionable form of maintenance for the clergy, and while Barebone's Parliament was sitting he published a pamphlet which cogently and learnedly refuted some of the more preposterous claims which clerical pamphleteers had made about the antiquity of tithes in England. In this piece he incidentally affirmed that the Rump had been 'dissolv'd upon

[40] Webster, *The Great Instauration*, pp. 55–7, 79, 90 ff., 154–5, 158–9, 166; *DNB*; M. B. Rex, *University Representation in England, 1604–1690* (1954), pp. 184 ff.; Lotte Mulligan, 'Civil War politics, religion and the Royal Society', *Past and Present*, no. 59 (1973), p. 95; Nuttall, *Visible Saints*, p. 151; Firth and Rait, ii, 356; *CJ*, vii, 285, 287, 335, 344, 355; *CSPD 1651*, p. 251; *1660–1*, p. 91; Abbott, ii, 581; *Register of the Visitors of the University of Oxford*, ed. M. Burrows (Camden Soc., 1881), pp. 356–7, 524; Aubrey, *Brief Lives*, i, pp. 268–9.

sure grounds of Piety, Publique freedome, right reason, and honestie: and that not without the Generall consent of the major part, either precedent, or subsequent, of the Supreme Authority, the People'.[41] He supported the Protectorate enthusiastically, partly perhaps because he was an Auditor of the Exchequer under it. In 1656 he published a panegyric to Cromwell in Latin verse which ended with this audacious couplet:

> Aurea tunc aetas; tunc Auri Tempora; Quintae
> Atque Monarchiae Tu prior inde clues.[42]

On Richard Cromwell's accession Wingfield addressed him in equally fulsome Latin verse, adding an epicedium to Oliver in twelve four-line stanzas.[43]

If there was nevertheless a vein of radicalism in Wingfield, it was less strong than that in his fellow-lawyer Thomas St. Nicholas, who was even more active in the business of the parliament, and from July to November in that of the Council of State too. Thomas, the elder of the two St. Nicholas brothers in the House, was Recorder of Canterbury and was recommended to Cromwell by the churches of Kent, but he was nominated to represent Yorkshire, where in the forties he had partnered his two brothers-in-law in managing some ironworks in Rotherham and Sheffield. He was often associated, as teller and in various employments, with such thorough-paced men as Carew, Courtney, Broughton, Moyer, and Blount, and the near-contemporary listing of him among the religious radicals is doubtless correct. He was a curious choice in 1654 as one of Cromwell's commissioners for the approbation of public preachers (Triers), and his opposition to the Protectorate led to his being excluded from the 1656 parliament. When he did take his seat, in 1658

---

[41] Augustine Wingfield, *Vindiciae Medio-Saxonicae, or Tithes Totally Routed* (1653, not in Thomason: BL 701, i. 23), p. 6.

[42] Augustine Wingfield, *Carmen Panegyricum, sive Paraeneticum* (1656, not in Thomason). Wingfield's verses are interspersed with long passages in Latin prose by an anonymous well-wisher who is identified in the Bodleian copy (C.q. 15 Linc.) as Robert Creswell of Trinity College, Cambridge.

[43] Augustine Wingfield, *Serenissimo Principi Richardo . . . Carmen Panegyricum* (1658, not in Thomason). Wingfield thought it a happy augury that Britain had honoured Oliver as he lay in state with the sacred symbols of royalty (pp. 5–6). On his career see *Lincoln's Inn Admissions Register*, i, 208; *Black Book of Lincoln's Inn*, ii, 339; Firth and Rait, i, 556; ii, 665, 1073, 1373; *CSPD 1650*, p. 374; *CJ*, vii, 128, 286–7, 289, 304, 332, 335, 338, 340, 342, 355; BL, MS Egerton 2979, fo. 11.

and again in 1659, he made his hostility to the regime abundantly clear.[44]

Turning lastly to those members who ranked below the gentry, there will be further examples of them in the next chapter, but here it is worth taking a glance at Dennis Hollister, since he was rather surprisingly elected to the Council of State on 14 July and made an Admiralty and Navy Commissioner the same day. What is puzzling is not just that this modestly prosperous grocer from Bristol High Street attained such eminence only ten days after the parliament's opening, but that after attending the council's next three meetings he came to no more until 19 September, and there is no sign that he sat in the House either during that long gap. Thereafter he became quite active, but naturally he lost his councillor's seat in the November elections. Were his sectarian susceptibilities shocked by a conference with the envoys of the United Provinces which he attended on 21 July with Cromwell, Strickland, Montagu, Ashley Cooper, and Wolseley, and in which Cromwell put forward revolutionary proposals for a close union between the two commonwealths? It will be seen later how bitterly opposed the radical millenarians were to a peace with the Dutch. But Hollister was no Fifth Monarchy man; he was an elder and lay preacher of the Broadmead Baptist Church, which usually held its Friday 'meeting for conference' at his house. To its horror, however, he became drawn to Quakerism while he was in London for the parliament, and from the Quakers' first coming to Bristol in July 1654 his orchard in the Friars became their regular meeting-place. He himself published several Quaker tracts. He had been a committee-man for the city since 1654 and a militia commissioner since 1648, but he was not added to the Gloucestershire Commission of the Peace until September 1653. After that year he seems to have taken no further part in public affairs, though he was not removed from the bench, and the restored Rump made him a militia commissioner again in 1659. The lengthy will that he made in 1657 gives some idea of his way

---

[44] Gooder, *Parliamentary Representation of Yorkshire*, ii, 61–3; Aylmer, *State's Servants*, p. 131; Nickolls, p. 96; *CJ*, vii, 283, 286–7, 298, 301, 330, 340, 342, 344, 351, 355, 359, 362; Firth and Rait. i, 544, 705; ii, 469, 865, etc.; Burton, *Diary*, ii, 335, 374, 392, 406; iii, 28, 45, 76, 118–19, 327–8, 579–80; iv, 97, 152, 167; *CSPD 1653–4, passim; 1659–60*, pp. 254, 596.

of life. He still lived over his shop in a largish corner house in the city, and he had bought the house next door to improve its amenities. He had also bought warehouses and shops in the city and had recently built two new houses, one in that Friary orchard where the Friends met and one in the nearby village of Frampton Cotterell. He had a lease of yet another house in Almondsbury and a half share in the White Hart Inn in Broad Street. He left bequests totalling over £2,000 besides this property, including small sums to George Fox and nine other Quaker evangelists, who had all, he recalled affectionately, often lodged in his house and eaten at his table.[45]

For a final sampling of the plebeians in the House, and of the misty borderland between gentry and non-gentry, we turn to Suffolk, the only county in which the gathered churches succeeded in placing their candidates in all the available seats, in this case five. It is striking that a shire long dominated by a set of wealthy well-entrenched Puritan families, which on the whole preserved a strong continuity in local administration through the revolutionary decades,[46] was represented by such relatively obscure men in 1653. But Suffolk's ruling élite was predominantly Presbyterian, and the background of the New Model cavalry probably gave the Independent churches there a special pull upon the Council of Officers—perhaps upon that radical saint Colonel Nathaniel Rich in particular. Be that as it may, their nominees were not all below the rank of gentlemen, nor for the most part fanatical zealots. John Clarke was probably the most substantial of them; he was to be Sheriff of Suffolk in 1670 and his son was to be made a baronet in 1698, but how far his rise in the world had gone by 1653, or whence it proceeded, is unclear. An Essex man by birth, he lived in Bury St. Edmunds, where he had married. He was named a parliamentary elder there in the Act of 5 November 1645, but in the following year he was one of the founder members of a congregation based on strict separatist principles. He was made a militia commissioner in December 1648, an assessment commissioner in the following April, and a

---

[45] Nuttall, *Visible Saints*, pp. 124–5; W. C. Braithwaite, *The Beginnings of Quakerism* (2nd ed., 1955), pp. 170–1, 384; Firth and Rait, i, 798, 974, 1234, etc.; *CJ*, vii, 284, 322, 335; D. Hollister, *The Skirts of the Whore Discovered* (1656), address 'To the Reader'; PRO, PROB 11/35 (PCC 91 Bench).

[46] Alan Everitt (ed.), *Suffolk and the Great Rebellion 1640–1660*, Suffolk Records Society, iii (Ipswich, 1960), Introduction.

JP not later than 1650. He sat in all three parliaments of the Protectorate, apparently making as little impression as he did in Barebone's.[47] He was listed as a supporter of a learned ministry.

So too was his colleague Francis Brewster of Wrentham, about whose local standing and religious background rather more is known. His family had been at Wrentham since 1576, and his elder brother Robert, who was Recorder of Dunwich and sat (very intermittently) in the Long Parliament from 1645 to 1653, had raised its landed income to £1,000 a year. The rectory of Wrentham was in its gift, and ever since 1612 (with one break) the rector had been John Phillip, a staunch Puritan who had married a sister of the famous William Ames. The break had come in 1638 when Bishop Matthew Wren had him deprived and he emigrated to New England, but he returned home late in 1641, resumed the rectory, and sat on the Westminster Assembly. From then on the Wrentham church was run on Congregational principles. Although the Brewster brothers were named as parliamentary elders in November 1645, it was formally constituted as a Congregational church in 1650 with the ageing Phillip as its pastor and William Ames's son (also William, and an early graduate of Harvard) as its teacher. The Brewsters, Robert especially, had been active on the county committee from the early days of the Civil War; the fact that they were Independents in a predominantly Presbyterian county helps to explain their temporary eminence in county affairs, but they were men of some substance and they were never fanatics.[48] The same cannot be said with any certainty of the dim figure of Edward Plumstead, who was never a JP and not even an assessment commissioner until 1657. He came of a cadet branch of the Plumsteads of Plumstead in Norfolk,[49] and he was probably

[47] He is mentioned only once in Burton's Diary (i, 287) when the House was called on 21 Dec. 1656 and he was absent. For his career generally: G.E.C., *Complete Baronetage*, iv, 174; Nuttall, *Visible Saints*, pp. 26–9; John Browne, *History of Congregationalism . . . in Norfolk and Suffolk* (1877), p. 610; Pink MSS 299, fo. 499; Nickolls, pp. 94, 126; Firth and Rait, i, 1243; ii, 43 etc.; *CJ*, vii, 283, 286–7, 326; *CSPD 1650*, p. 143; *1655*, p. 82; *1656–7*, p. 183.

[48] Brunton and Pennington, *Members of the Long Parliament*, pp. 110–11; Browne, *History of Congregationalism . . . in Norfolk and Suffolk*, pp. 421–7, 609; Everitt, *Suffolk and the Great Rebellion*, p. 25 and *passim*; Nuttall, *Visible Saints*, pp. 26, 79; Nickolls, pp. 94, 156–8; Firth and Rait, i, 168, etc.; ii, 975, etc.; *CJ*, vii, 283, 286; PRO, PROB 11/275 (PCC 169 Wootton).

[49] *Visitations of Norfolk 1563–1613*, Harleian Soc., xxxii, 224; *Visitation of Suffolk 1664–8*, Harleian Soc., xli, 173. He could confidently be identified as Edward, second son of
(continued)

the Suffolk man of the same name who matriculated from Queen's College, Cambridge, in 1628. What is certain is that he became a Quaker in about 1655. In company with Robert Dunkon, cousin of his fellow MP of the same name, he established a meeting at Mendlesham and gained a reputation for his preaching of his new faith.[50]

So far, Suffolk has yielded three lesser gentry (if Plumstead can be so accounted), the first two religious moderates and the third inclining to sectarianism. The remaining two members, Robert Dunkon and Jacob Caley, were both merchants and religious radicals, though their radicalism differed in degree. Both were Portmen of Ipswich, and both had been on the committee for the town since 1643, though they were not added to the county committee until 1648 and 1649 respectively. Caley was made a JP in July 1652 but struck off under the Protectorate; Dunkon was added to the Suffolk bench in July 1657. Dunkon at fity-seven was almost certainly the older man. He had suffered persecution in Archbishop Laud's time, so it is no wonder that he was specially active on the East Suffolk Committee for Scandalous Ministers between 1644 and 1646. He and Caley were both named as parliamentary elders in November 1645, but both were Congregationalists by conviction. Dunkon was patron of the rectory of St Helen's in Ipswich, and in 1652 he bestowed it on the well-known Independent Robert Gouge, in whose gathered church he already worshipped. But there were two Independent congregations in Ipswich, and Caley worshipped in the other one, whose pastor Benjamin Stoneham, curate of St. Peter's, was a leader of the Suffolk Fifth Monarchy men. Caley was one of these, which is doubtless why he was out of sympathy with the Protectorate. He and Dunkon were evidently on good terms, however, for the latter's will shows that they went shares in purchasing houses, shops, and gardens in Ipswich. Dunkon also bequeathed lands and tenements in three other Suffolk parishes, and his household goods, including 'my great silver

---

Francis Plumstead of Brightnam, Suffolk, by Clemence, née Skinner, as given in the 1613 Norfolk visitation, were it not that the 1664 Suffolk visitation names their second son Clement, and mentions no Edward. Our man was still living in *c.*1678: W. C. Braithwaite, *The Second Period of Quakerism* (1919), p. 527.

[50] Braithwaite, *Beginnings of Quakerism*, p. 164; Venn, *Alumni Cantab.*, iii, 373 (the identification seems probable); Firth and Rait, i, 556 (identification doubtful); ii, 1080; *CJ*, vii, 286–7.

Beere Boule' and 'my Broad silver dish to put sugar in', suggest solid burgher comfort. Caley, when he died a decade later in 1680, disposed of lands in Badingham and Aldeburgh as well as houses in Ipswich, owned four ships, and could leave £300 apiece to his three unmarried daughters, among other bequests.[51]

Barebone's Parliament differed unquestionably in its social composition from a normal House of Commons, and for nearly half the members this was their sole appearance at Westminster. Nevertheless the great majority of them were drawn from the top 5 per cent of the population, and the traditional governing class was strongly represented. Contrary to popular report, the number of tradesmen was small, and of lay preachers still smaller. The range of experience on which the assembly could draw, especially in local administration, was not contemptible. Neither social inferiority nor ignorance of the tasks of government was a sufficient *a priori* reason why it should fail, given the limited duration and the interim nature of the authority to which Cromwell summoned it. But those were only two of the common accusations levelled against it. The third was that it was dominated by religious fanatics, and that is what the next chapter discusses.

[51] On the two men see Everitt, *Suffolk and the Great Rebellion, passim*; Browne, *History of Congregationalism . . . in Norfolk and Suffolk*, pp. 366, 400–1, 608; Clive Holmes (ed.), *The Suffolk Committees for Scandalous Ministers 1644–1646*, Suffolk Records Soc., xiii (Ipswich, 1970), *passim*. For Dunkon see also Nuttall, *Visible Saints*, pp. 22 n., 150; *CJ*, vii, 282, 287, 323; PRO, PROB 11/335 (PCC 3 Duke). For Caley: Capp, *Fifth Monarchy Men*, pp. 68, 243; *Visitation of Suffolk 1664–8*, Harleian Soc., lxi, p. 150; *CJ*, vii, 283, 287, 348; PRO PROB 11/363 (PCC 105 Bath).

VII

Moderates and Zealots

I. THE NATURE OF THE CLEAVAGE

Barebone's Parliament foundered after five months mainly because its members came to disagree so deeply that they could no longer work together. Acute differences began to emerge among them very early, at least as early as the debates on tithes in mid-July, and before they had sat a month their divisions were being widely reported by newswriters and foreign ambassadors, some of whom were already speculating that the new government would not last long.[1]

It may seem illogical to start analysing the factions in the House before describing the disputes which split it, but there are two reasons for doing so. The first is that so many of its leading actors are otherwise little known to history that some description of the dramatis personae may aid appreciation of the drama that developed. Secondly, a determined minority of militant millenarians and other enthusiasts came to Westminster with strong commitments and with objectives already formed, so it will be useful to identify their leaders and to establish their general characteristics before proceeding further with what they tried to do.

First, however, some cautions. Although the House tended strongly to polarize on certain notoriously contentious issues, it would be quite mistaken to think of it as continually divided between two clear-cut factions, even though some contemporary commentators and pamphleteers convey that impression. There were many matters that it handled without dividing along

[1] e.g. PRO, 31.3/90, fos. 50, 65, 67; Clarendon MS 46, fo. 112; Thurloe, i, 385–7, 393.

anything like party lines, judging by the many divisions in which moderate and radical men were paired as tellers. Even in those which did drive the extremes apart, the line of cleavage varied somewhat according to whether the issue was the Court of Chancery, the reform of the law, lay patronage over church livings, or the proper maintenance of a preaching ministry. It will be found that the correlation between political and religious radicalism was strong, but it was not complete. Although a considerable number of members seem to have assumed consistently moderate or consistently radical attitudes, others behaved more variably, while there is so little evidence about some that their stance remains uncertain.

Labels like 'moderate' and 'radical' are virtually unavoidable, but they can beget misunderstanding. The former does not necessarily imply conservatism, let alone lukewarmness, and the radicals were certainly not all fanatics. Nor should one suppose that most of the members had any desire to fall apart as in time they did. There were perhaps a few solid squires in the House who nursed a low opinion of preaching burghers from the start, and a few Fifth Monarchists who had mentally girded themselves to do battle against Babylon in Westminster itself, but the majority came together with a great deal of shared enthusiasm and a strong sense of common purpose. They did after all enact more than thirty statutes in five months and they had further major ones on the stocks when they broke up. The next parliament in almost the same time passed none. They divided more deeply as the months went by, but the experience of their discord was probably as keenly disappointing to most of them as it was to Cromwell.

The traditional, over-simple two-party analysis derives in large part from a broadsheet which Thomason acquired in June 1654, entitled *A Catalogue of the Names of the Members of the Last Parliament, whereof those marked with a Starre were for the Godly Learned Ministry and Universities*.[2] This is a valuable document so long as it is not taken for more than it is, which is an approximate indication of the members' standpoint on the question of how (or even whether) the Commonwealth should maintain a preaching ministry in the parishes, and so long as it is not treated as

[2] BL, 669 f. 19(3), [22 June] 1654. The asterisks and daggers with which it identifies the members are appended to their names in Appendix B.

infallible. It would be even more valuable if it were simply a division list for that final and fatal vote on 10 December, when the first clause of a comprehensive scheme for settling a godly ministry was defeated. But whereas 56 of the 114 members who voted that day were for the scheme, *A Catalogue* places a star or asterisk against 84 names. Furthermore it marks all the other 60 with a dagger, as if to attribute a positive position, for or against, to every single member. How its anonymous compiler knew the attitudes of three members who never took their seats, or of Henry Dawson who had died on 2 August 1653, or how he gauged opinions about the universities, which were never the subject of a vote, are questions which induce caution in accepting *A Catalogue*'s unsupported testimony. Some of its daggers and asterisks seem dubious, especially the daggers. Was it right, for instance, to suggest that William Burton, the Governor of Yarmouth, was no friend to a learned ministry, or to publicly maintaining one? Burton was a staunch Congregationalist until his death, and his own house was licensed for Independent preaching under the Indulgence of 1672. But in the sixteen-fifties he belonged to the church in Yarmouth whose pastor, the eminent and essentially moderate Independent William Bridge, received £100 a year from public funds, and soon after Barebone's Parliament came to an end he wrote to his friend the secretary of the Admiralty Commission, on which he served, to say he was sorry that Mr Feake and others could not keep their tongues in bounds. He remained busy on Admiralty business at Yarmouth all through the Protectorate, and as a JP he co-operated with the Council of State in dealing with some people who interrupted religious worship in Lowestoft. We catch his voice again in Richard Cromwell's parliament, outspoken, independent, and sometimes choleric, but in no way extreme.[3]

An even more unlikely name to find marked with a dagger is that of William Draper, since he had served as a Visitor of Oxford University from 1647 until at least 1651. It is true that he was not made an Ejector in 1654, but as Sheriff of Oxfordshire in 1657–8 he gaoled three Quakers for (*inter alia*) refusing to pay

---

[3] *CSPD 1652–3*, p. 602; *1653–4*, p. 567; *1654*, p. 3 and *passim* (also many further references throughout 1650s); *1665–6*, p. 342; *1666–7*, p. 36; Burton, *Diary*, iii, 240–1, 500; iv, 219, 232, 286, 391; PRO, PROB 11/342 (PCC 55 Pye); Pink MS 298, fo. 678; Nuttall, *Visible Saints*, pp 140–1, 150 (and *passim* on Bridge).

tithes.[4] One is also suspicious at finding Henry Birkenhead placed on the opposite (and more radical) side from his close friend and associate Robert Duckenfield, though he was to be reckoned somewhat more sympathetic to Quakers. Both men were Ejectors as well as JPs and assessment commissioners throughout the Protectorate.[5] There are others marked with a dagger who may have been religious radicals in other respects, but can hardly have been opposed to the public maintenance of a godly ministry on principle, as the more pronounced sectaries certainly were. Dunkon, as has been seen, had recently used his patronage of a rectory to bestow it on the moderate Robert Gouge, and William Botterell, member for Shropshire, had when Governor of Ludlow Castle petitioned the Rump in 1651 to provide an adequate stipend for a minister to serve the town and garrison, since the benefice was worth only £10 per year.[6]

Nevertheless *A Catalogue* is so much more often right than wrong in the cases where religious attitudes can be checked from other sources that its testimony has sometimes been accepted provisionally where other evidence is lacking, especially when it indicates positive support for a learned ministry.[7] Its compiler, whether or not he was an MP, probably had some knowledge of the way members spoke and voted in the crucial debates in early December, and may have taken pains to ascertain the standpoint of the absent ones. If—and this is merely conjecture—the division on 10 December did form part of the basis for his categorization, that could account for some of his more improbable daggers, for it will be argued later that an appreciable proportion of the fifty-eight who voted against the committee for tithes' scheme did so because they disliked its specific proposals rather than because

[4] Firth and Rait, i, 925; Abbott, iv, 672; PRO, PROB 11/338 (PCC 26 Eure); J. M. Davenport, *Oxfordshire: Lords Lieutenant, High Sheriffs and M.P.s* (Oxford, 1888), pp. 69, 123; Burrows, *Register of the Visitors of the University of Oxford, passim*; N. Penney, *Extracts from State Papers Relating to Friends* (1913), pp. 53, 64–5, 90. He is easily confused with his son of the same name, who died within a year of him in Jan. 1673, when he in turn was serving as sheriff.

[5] Penney, *State Papers Relating to Friends*, p. 110; Birkenhead in his will (made in 1657) particularly asked Duckenfield to assist his wife in executing it: PRO, PROB 11/298 (PCC 99 Nabbs). See Morrill, *Cheshire*, for many references to both men.

[6] H. T. Weyman 'Shropshire Members of Parliament', *Trans. Shropshire Arch. Soc.*, 4th series, xi (1927), 175–6.

[7] I have sone doubts about the asterisk against Bowtell's name and the daggers against those of Cust, Erle, Jermy, Studley, and Taylor.

they opposed a publicly maintained parochial ministry on principle.

It is also worth remembering that men do not always act consistently, and that the clues to apparent inconsistencies may have been lost in the course of three centuries. Samuel Dunch, for instance, Cromwell's kinsman by marriage, a veteran of the parliament of 1621, Visitor of Oxford University from 1647 to 1660 and a 'bitter Justice' to Quakers, is asterisked in *A Catalogue*, as one would expect; but by the will he made in 1668 he left twenty nobles to Vavasor Powell.[8] Edward Cater is placed in the opposite camp, and plausibly enough, one thinks, when one finds him being commended to the Bedfordshire voters in 1654 by William Dell (who along with the Rectory of Yelden and the Mastership of Gonville and Caius held some remarkably radical views) as a man who opposed the paying of tithes and taxes. Yet Cater, having served as an Ejector and a JP throughout the Protectorate, was knighted by Charles II in November 1660 and made Sheriff of Bedfordshire in 1664.[9]

2. THE MODERATE LEADERSHIP

In default of any parliamentary diaries one has to identify the pacemakers in the House by sifting an assortment of evidence: the committees on which they served, especially the major standing committees; the number of times they acted as tellers, as some indication of a positive role in debate; various tasks committed to them by the House, such as preparing bills or chairing grand committees; and service on the Council of State. The councillors, however, varied greatly in their commitment. Those elected or re-elected in July included, besides some of the very busiest of members, radicals like Salwey, Stapley, Harrison, and Robert Bennett who rarely or never attended, and moderates such as Norton, Major, Tomlinson, and Lisle whose role was distinctly lightweight. Most of those elected in November earned their places by their dedication to the House's service, though a few will be found who probably owed their success more to the

[8] Firth and Rait, i, 925; ii, 1027. Penney, *State Papers Relating to Friends*, p. 105; PRO, PROB 11/328 (PCC 137 Hene).

[9] *CSPD 1654*, p. 334; *Bedfordshire Visitations*, Harleian Soc., xix, pp. 90, 205; Firth and Rait, ii, 968 and *passim*. I am indebted to Miss Godber of the Bedfordshire County Record Office for sending me valuable information about Cater.

majority's revulsion against the extremists than to their own zeal or talents.

By these criteria of active involvement, fifteen men stand out from over seventy members who generally took the more moderate line on both political and religious issues—sixteen if Tichborne is included, who though in some respects a radical nevertheless aligned with the moderates on crucial matters of policy. Two things are striking about this group: its relative youth, and the high proportion of it that belonged to established political families, even if the members themselves were in some cases younger sons or represented cadet branches. The youth of Montagu, Howard, Wolseley and Henry Cromwell, all in their twenties, has already been remarked on. Of the very busiest men in these sixteen, Philip Jones was 35, Sydenham and Sadler 38, Ashley Cooper 32, Tichborne probably about the same, Pickering 42, and Strickland many years older than the rest at 55. The only others to have reached middle age were Stone (about 47), Desborough (45), and Sir William Roberts (48). As for the standing of their families, the names of Howard, Montagu, Ashley Cooper, Pickering, Strickland, Sydenham, Sadler, Rous, and Wolseley need no comment. Roberts had like his father been knighted by James I, and Philip Jones, though a more recent parvenu, was such an outstandingly successful one, and also so considerate in his dealings with the royalists in South Wales, that he would live to consolidate his position among the county gentry after the Restoration and serve as Sheriff of Glamorgan in 1671–2. In the whole group only Colonel John Clarke and John Stone were of dubious gentility, for even Tichborne was armigerous.[10] Only Clarke failed to gain election to the Council of State, either in July or November, despite his ten committees and his sixteen tellerships; perhaps he was more pushful than persuasive.

Pickering, Strickland, Sydenham, and Jones had sat together in the Rump and were to be associated much more closely as key figures in the council of the Protectorate. Not much is known about Jones's religious convictions, nor about the means whereby he amassed estates which eventually rose to somewhere between £3,000 and £5,000 in annual value; but he cleared himself of charges that he misappropriated the funds of the Commission for the Propagation of the Gospel in Wales, on which he was named

[10] *Visitation of London 1635–5*, Harleian Soc., xvii, p. 289.

second after Harrison, and Cromwell is unlikely to have chosen a man with no tincture of religion as Comptroller of his Household.[11] The other three were markedly religious men—three examples among many to weigh against any supposition that the moderates in the House were necessarily shallower in their convictions than the zealots. Pickering, 'so finical, spruce and like an old courtier' according to a republican pamphleteer of 1659, was said by Dr John Walker to have run the whole Puritan gamut from Presbyterian through Independent and Brownist to Anabaptist.[12] Whatever he meant by these loose terms, Walker exaggerated. It is true that in the Rump Pickering was twice a teller, in 1649 and 1652, for abolishing tithes forthwith, but when the issue came up in Barebone's he acted as teller for referring the clergy's right of property in their tithes to a committee, against Harrison and Blount who told for the separatist minority that would have denied it then and there.[13] He further showed his commitment to a broad, established preaching ministry by helping to frame the Cromwellian ordinances which set up the Triers and Ejectors. In the mid-fifties he gave valuable practical support to the Polyglot Bible, and he often spoke on religious matters in the parliament of 1656–8. On a bill for discovering recusants, he said that its purpose should be only to secure their obedience to government; he 'would have no man suffer for his bare opinion'. He thought Quakerism 'as infectious as the plague', but he took a notably more humane line than most members towards James Nayler. He supported a bill introduced by Joachim Matthews, another moderate Independent who had sat in Barebone's, for suppressing the celebration of Christmas.[14]

Strickland too was a middle-of-the-road Independent. He favoured such ministers as John Owen and Joseph Caryll, and

[11] *DNB*; *DWB*; Dodd, *Studies in Stuart Wales*, pp. 121–2, 149–51, 171; Burton, *Diary*, i, 331 (gossip that he was worth £7,000 p.a.); *Second Narrative of the Late Parliament*, in *Harleian Misc.*, vi, 493–4; PRO, PROB 11/347 (PCC 26 Dycer); R. Sherwood, *The Court of Oliver Cromwell* (1977), pp. 48–50.

[12] *A Second Narrative of the Late Parliament* and J. Walker, *Sufferings of the Clergy*, both quoted in *DNB*.

[13] *CJ*, vi, 275; vii, 128, 286; Tai Liu *Discord in Zion*, pp. 101–2. The 1652 vote was occasioned by the anti-tithes petition presented by Augustine Wingfield (see p. 187), recollection of which may have prompted the latter's nomination to Barebone's Parliament.

[14] *CSPD 1654*, pp. 1, 27, 76; *1655*, p. 234; Burton, *Diary*, i, 1, 8, 36, 48, 89, 153, 215, 229, 256, 261; ii, 131, 132.

also Patrick Gillespie, the leader of the Scottish Protesters and Principal of Glasgow University. Like Pickering he was relatively lenient towards Nayler, and he made a wise speech against passing a blanket law against Quakers.[15] Sydenham was of like mind. 'I am as much against Quakers as any man', he said, 'but would not bring in a law against Quakers by a general word . . . Let it be plainly explained what the offences shall be.' As for Nayler, 'That which sticks with me most, is the nearness of his opinion to that which is a most glorious truth, that the spirit is personally in us.'[16] Although Sydenham, like Jones, Pickering, and Strickland, became one of Cromwell's very busiest councillors, he was not an uncritical supporter of the regime, and in the spring of 1659 he was a member of that gathered church which Owen formed at Wallingford House, Fleetwood's London residence, and which helped to bring the grandees' discontent with Richard's Protectorate to a head.[17]

Not all the moderate leaders were as much influenced in their politics by their religious convictions as Pickering, Strickland, and Sydenham, and some of their young colleagues might be thought to have had their eye more on the main chance than on the New Jerusalem. Ashley Cooper was obviously such a one, but the other cases are not so clear-cut. Charles Howard would shed his Puritan past pretty thoroughly after Charles II made him Earl of Carlisle, but under the Protectorate he was a member, along with Tichborne, Ireton, and Bulstrode Whitelocke, of the church to which George Cokayne ministered at St. Pancras, Soper Lane.[18] Cokayne had close associations with the leading Fifth Monarchists, and a week after Barebone's Parliament resigned its authority, he followed Feake and Vavasor Powell into the pulpit at Blackfriars to inveigh fiercely against the antichristian clergy[19]—another instance to discourage the

[15] Burton, *Diary*, i, 28, 38, 56–7, 87–8, 162, 164, 173, 215, 360; ii, 97, 144, 146.

[16] Ibid., i, 68–9, 172; cf. pp. 34, 41–2, 51, 86, 216, 274–5; ii, 132.

[17] Ibid., 378; ii, 98, 291–2, 296, 299; *Register of the Consultations of the Ministers of Edinburgh*, ed. W. Stephen (2 vols., Edinburgh, 1921–30), ii, 158; BL, Lansdowne MSS 823, fo. 251.

[18] *Second Narrative of the Late Parliament*, in *Harleian Misc.*, vi, 496. Nathaniel Taylor, member for Bedfordshire, also probably joined his flock: PRO, PROB 11/378 (PCC 155 Hare); Aylmer, *State's Servants*, pp. 40, 371.

[19] *CSPD 1653–4*, p. 307. Cokayne was a co-signatory with Feake and John Simpson of the Preface to *A Faithful Discovery of Mystical Antichrist* ([12 June] 1653), an anti-Quaker tract.

drawing of firm frontiers between moderates and radicals. Edward Montagu would in time strike his secretary Samuel Pepys as 'a perfect Sceptic' and shock him by saying that 'all things would not be well while there was so much preaching', but as the youngest colonel in the New Model Army and for some time after he had the reputation of a strong Independent or even a sectary, and he defended the right of laymen to preach. His continuing interest in religious matters is suggested by his appointment in 1654 to a Council committee briefed to devise a better maintenance for ministers than tithes, and three years later by his acting as a teller (with Philip Jones) in favour of an ordinance continuing the commissions of Ejectors, on which he himself served.[20] But there is a hint that his religious standpoint moderated even before the Restoration, for on 29 March 1659 his former colleague in Barebone's, Colonel Clarke, wrote to him recommending Nathanael Mather (brother of Increase and Samuel) for a minister's place. Clarke mentioned that Mather's views inclined to the Independent way, and though he presumed (so he said) that Montagu would not think him the less qualified for that, there is a faint note of doubt.[21] Clarke's own vein of piety can be sampled from a letter which he wrote to his friend Colonel Robert Bennett on 17 September 1650, enclosing some evidence that the local royalists were plotting a further disturbance,

notwithstanding the signall hand of the Lord of hosts Against them, which of late appeared in so much super-Eminency of mercy to our Brethren in Scotland in particular, and to the Whole Land in generall, as we have just cause with bended knees and boued downe harts to give Glory to our God, who hath bene indeed our strength and deliverer in the day of Distresse.[22]

As for Sir Charles Wolseley, the youngest of all these up-and-coming Cromwellians, he was to remain a devout Independent

[20] *Second Narrative of the Late Parliament*, in *Harleian Misc.*, vi, 493; *CSPD 1654*, p. 76; Burton, *Diary*, ii, 59; *Diary of Samuel Pepys*, ed. R. C. Latham and W. Matthews (1970–6), i, 261, 271. The newswriter who in 1653 described him as 'a great presbyter and pillar of the party' was either mistaken or writing very loosely: *Clarendon Calendar*, ii, 217.
[21] *CSPD 1658–9*, p. 552. Clarke's mention of Barnstaple identifies Mather as Nathanael, who had been admitted as vicar there on 12 Jan. 1657. Clarke's information that Blake, the former vicar, had recently been reinstated by parliament corrects A. G. Matthews' statement in *Calamy Revised* that Mather was ejected from Barnstaple in 1660.
[22] Folger Library, Add. MS 483, fo. 66.

throughout the rest of his long life. He wrote and published more than one defence of liberty of conscience in the sixteen-sixties, when that cause was at its nadir. It was the civil magistrate's duty, he contended, to afford peace and protection to the churches (he still used the plural), to 'remove all Oppression from them', to ensure that the gospel was preached, and to 'endeavour in a Gospel-way, to see all the Laws of Christ put in execution'. But he insisted, in extra large type, 'That no Prince, nor State, ought by force to compel men, to any part of the Doctrine, Worship, or Discipline of the Gospel', and though not apparently a millenarian himself he quoted the German millenarian Alsted in his support.[23] In 1669 he published *The Unreasonableness of Atheism Made Manifest*, which he followed up three years later with *The Reasonableness of Scripture-Belief*, dedicating both works to Arthur Annesley, Earl of Anglesey. In both he attacked the irreligion of the times, for which he mainly blamed Hobbes: 'These and most of the bad Principles of this Age are of no earlier date then one very ill Book, are indeed but the spawn of the Leviathan.'[24]

Of the other prominent moderates, it might be thought that Sir William Roberts and John Stone were chosen primarily for their experience in the Commonwealth's financial administration, and so perhaps they were. But Stone's interest in settling a godly ministry and in evangelizing the Indians has already been mentioned,[25] and Roberts had more to commend him than rank, wealth, and administrative capability. He had not been John Preston's pupil at Emmanuel for nothing, for in the later sixteen-thirties he chose exile in Holland rather than live under episcopal oppression, and he did not return until the Civil War had broken out.[26]

The most singular figure in this whole group was another Emmanuel man. John Sadler not only had a remarkable career

---

[23] Sir Charles Wolseley, *Liberty of Conscience upon its True and Proper Grounds Asserted*, 2nd ed. (1668), pp. 22–3, 26, 50–1. This edition was published together with Wolseley's *Liberty of Conscience, The Magistrates Interest*.

[24] *The Reasonableness of Scripture-Belief* (1672), dedicatory epistle, sig. A4.

[25] See p. 127.

[26] *A Second Narrative of the Late Parliament*, in *Harleian Misc.*, vi, 501. In May 1637 he was made a commissioner to enforce the 1542 Act requiring all men under sixty to practise shooting with the longbow, so he presumably went to Holland later than that. For the rest of his career Aylmer, *State's Servants*, pp. 251–3 is far more informative than the *DNB*.

by any standards, but he exemplifies better than anyone else except perhaps Isaac Newton the way in which an intense preoccupation with millenarianism could go with moderate politics and great intellectual sophistication. Born in a Sussex parsonage in 1615, he gained eminence at Emmanuel for his scholarship in Hebrew and oriental languages and was made a Fellow. He soon turned to the study of the law, however, and with such success that he became a Master in Chancery in 1644 and Town Clerk of London in 1649. Cromwell came to know him as a friend, and valued him for the quality of his piety as well as for his varied talents. He tried to appoint him Chief Justice of Munster late in 1649, and on Sadler's declining he procured for him the Mastership of Magdalene College, Cambridge. By this time Sadler was a well-known virtuoso. He had associated with the natural philosophers who established the Invisible College in 1646 and had helped to promote Samuel Hartlib's scheme for an Office of Address which would foster an international correspondency among scholars. His patronage had helped to secure a Fellowship of Emmanuel for Joseph Mede's pupil and future editor John Worthington, and the Mastership of Caius College for William Dell. His sympathy and influence were helping to strengthen the links between three seminal intellectual circles, which already overlapped: the educational and philanthropic reformers headed by Hartlib and Dury, the group of experimental scientists whose brightest star was Robert Boyle, and the Cambridge Platonists, among whom Sadler himself can be reckoned, along with Benjamin Whichcote, Ralph Cudworth, and Henry More. He was still not quite thirty-eight when Barebone's Parliament met.[27]

When he was in London he worshipped and received the sacrament in a congregation to which Archbishop Ussher ministered, and which also included Oliver St. John and Sir Harbottle Grimston.[28] At the height of the Presbyterian ascendancy, in 1645, he had defended the Congregational way in print, with force and learning, against John Bastwick's intolerant attack. 'It was better with you', he retorted, 'when you

---

[27] *DNB*; Webster, *The Great Instauration*, pp. 66, 72–6, 144–5, 183, 499, 519; G. H. Turnbull, *Hartlib, Dury and Comenius* (Liverpool, 1947), pp. 28, 41, 268, 278.

[28] BL, Add. MS 10, 114, fos. 27–30, 32–3. Ussher, like Sadler, had a keen interest in the date of the Second Coming: Nuttall, *The Welsh Saints*, p. 47.

suffered for Presbyterie in opposition to Prelaticall tyranny, then now, if you would make others suffer by Presbytery, in opposition to the Congregationall government.' But he was no separatist, and like the Dissenting Brethren in the Westminster Assembly he held that the churches of Christ should band together in willing confederation: 'Win us therefore to an association by the beauty of your fellowships, and you shall not need to *compell* us.'[29]

In politics too he was an Independent, and an equally individual one. In May 1646 a body of London citizens, acting in response to an open letter from Charles I, got up a remonstrance to parliament, urging it to stamp out heresy and schism, join in union with the Scots, and open negotiations with the king. Sadler got wind of it and wrote *A Word in Season* in reply. It was published anonymously, and John Lilburne distributed it in Westminster Hall on the day the citizens' remonstrance was presented, but it had little in common with Leveller politics beyond a passionate resistance to any kind of Presbyterian sell-out. Its main theme was that parliament's authority was paramount and must not be impugned, even in the name of 'the glory of God, the setting up of the Kingdome of JESUS CHRIST'. Deeply though Sadler cared for liberty of conscience, to suggest that any power but parliament might 'properly judge of law (or religion so far as concerns the publick)' was in his view the ultimate treason.[30] Three years later he published, again anonymously, one of the more curious defences of the new Commonwealth. *Rights of the Kingdom* ran to over 250 pages and became his best-known work; Milton, who numbered Sadler among his friends, drew on it several times in *Eikonoklastes*, and that radical commonwealthsman John Streater cited it when, as a political prisoner under the regime of Barebone's Parliament, he pleaded for his habeas corpus.[31] But Sadler was not as thoroughgoing a commonwealthsman as Milton or Streater. He frankly deplored the army's violence to parliament in Pride's Purge; he regretted the death sentence on Charles I,

[29] J[ohn] S[adler], *Flagellum Flagelli* ([Sept.] 1645), pp. 3, 15, and *passim*.

[30] *A Word in Season* ([18 May] 1646), pp. 5–6. Thomason's inscriptions on his two copies identify Sadler as author and mention Lilburne's distribution of the tract: see Thomason Catalogue, i, 439, 441.

[31] Milton, *Complete Prose*, iii, 398–9, 403, 592; W. R. Parker, *Milton: A Biography* (2 vols., Oxford, 1968), i, 251, 313; W. Cobbett (ed.), *Complete Collection of State Trials* (1809–28), v, 378, 382.

while acknowledging it to have been unadvoidable; he even cast doubts on the legality of the abolition of the monarchy. Nevertheless, he firmly upheld the ultimate right of parliaments to judge kings and the duty of every subject to obey the government of the Commonwealth.[32]

What is extraordinary in *Rights of the Kingdom* is its mingling of legal antiquarianism, including fantastic excursions into the 'precedents' furnished by mythical ancient British kings, with an ardent millenarianism. This breaks through again and again; here are examples from two consecutive pages:

And yet, I am not an Enemy to Monarchy, but Tyranny. I did, and still doe, believe there may, and shall, be such a Monarchy, ere long, through All the World; that I shall gladly bow, and stoop, and bear the yoak: for it is Easy and the Burthen Light . . . I hope and believe, that God will come, and appear, ere long, to dwell in the World . . . I could desire Him rather (if He pleased) in the still quiet Voyce, then in the rushing Wind, or Fire, or Thunder Claps: yet so, he came before, and shoak the Earth: and So, it seems, again; yet Once again to shake both Heaven and Earth. Overturning, Overturning, Overturning, (for there also, were Three;) till He comes, whose Right it is.[33]

Much discussion follows about the meaning of the destruction of Babylon, the overthrow of Antichrist, Gog and Magog, the four beasts, and the arcane significance of other prophecies in both Testaments. The whole work ends with these words: 'And I am not ashamed both to long and pray for His Coming; who is King of Kings, and Lord of Lords; the Prince of Salem, that is Peace, as well as King of Righteousnesse, Melchizedech; the Lamb upon the White Throne. All the Creation Groaneth, and the Spirit and the Bride saith, Come Lord Jesus, Come quickly.'[34] Yet this fervent chiliast stood poles apart from the Fifth Monarchists and the rest of the zealots who thought it their duty to erect a rule of the saints by their own efforts. Their brash and fierce assurance was not for him: 'I doe not plead an Extraordinary Call; which is a Close Writ, and not a Patent: Those who receive, and Act by such a warrant, should be sure they know the Hand, or Seal, or Dialect of Heaven.'[35] In

[32] *Rights of the Kingdom* ([22 June] 1649), Preface sig. 4; pp. 2 ff., 25 ff., 77 ff. (1st pagination); pp. 30–2, 57–9, 175 ff. (2nd pagination, commencing after p. 93).
[33] Ibid. 32–3 (2nd pagination).
[34] Ibid. 184.
[35] Ibid., Preface, sig. GG2.

Barebone's Parliament Sadler was much in demand for the drafting of bills and for service on committees. He chaired the assembly in Grand Committee on the difficult business of securing greater equality in taxation, and when the House decided to publish a declaration drawing the line between a fitting liberty of conscience and the abuse of it by those who attacked magistracy or uttered blasphemies or heresies, it put Sadler at the head of a small drafting committee. That was one evidence of his reputation for religious moderation; another was his key role on the committee for tithes. It was he who put before the House that committee's proposals for settling and maintaining a godly ministry, thus launching the debate that led to the parliament's end.[36]

His public career further broadened in scope under the Protectorate, for in addition to his former appointments he was made a Master of Requests and a Commissioner for Approbation of Ministers, more popularly known as a Trier. He purchased Vaux Hall and other crown properties; he was largely instrumental in getting permission for the Jews to build a synagogue in London.[37] Yet for all his involvement in political, legal, and academic affairs, his continuing contacts with the leading intellectuals of the time, and his apparent enjoyment of the goods of this world, he was subject to intense experiences of quasi-mystical kind. In 1655 he was reported to have 'had a vision and trance three days together', and six years later he is alleged to have written down, before witnesses, the dictation of an invisible visitant prophesying among other things the Great Plague and Fire of London, Monmouth's rebellion, and the revolution of 1688.[38] Whatever lay behind such stories, Sadler was clearly a man easily credited with revelatory visions, even though he was not given to claiming them. In his later years as Master of Magdalene he was reckoned to be 'not always quite right in the head', and some of his speeches in Richard Cromwell's parliament—the only other parliament he attended—were indeed odd and extravagant as well as prolix, and were apt to provoke irritation or laughter.[39]

[36] *CJ*, vii, 325, 332, 344, 361, and *passim*.
[37] *DNB*.
[38] Alan MacFarlane, *The Family Life of Ralph Josselin* (Cambridge, 1970), p. 191; A. R. Bayley, *The Great Civil War in Dorset* (Taunton, 1910), pp. 441–2.
[39] *DNB*; Burton, *Diary*, iii, 279–81; iv, 75, 110–11, 200–1, 226–8, 231, 279–80, 357.

He must then have been at work on his longest book, *Olbia*, which he published in 1660. It purports to be a translation of an imperfect text left by an anonymous voyager who, when shipwrecked on an uncharted island in the Atlantic in circumstances of great wretchedness, was comforted and instructed by a grave old hermit, 'sent from some higher power'.[40] But the quaint fictitional framework was only a pretext for a vast disquisition on every conceivable scrap of evidence, scriptural or non-scriptural, that could bear on the chronology of the kingdom of Christ on earth and the Second Coming, along with much speculation as to whether the Anglo-Saxons were one of the ten tribes of Israel. Even now that we are aware of the fascination that calculations of the number of the Beast and the date of the world's end held for our fathers of science from Napier to Newton, Sadler's speculations seem to stray far into the reaches of the fantastic, even of the obsessional.[41] But if *Olbia* betrays touches of monomania it also testifies to a profound and compassionate piety, especially in its prolonged meditation on the nature of Christ and its rejection of predestination or indeed any eternal retribution. In utter contrast with the Fifth Monarchists, Sadler suggests that the Beast in Revelation may signify the false image that men make of God in their imaginations—that idolatry worse than the setting-up of physical images, 'our whoorish wanderings from the God of *Love*'.[42] His vision of the kingdom of Christ on earth, whose inauguration he was now inclined to date 1656 years after Christ's resurrection, had none of that bellicose expectation of triumph over Antichrist that characterized the thunderings of Christopher Feake and his kind:

That very Earth, which God so cursed, even *This Cursed Earth*, must become, the *Blessed of the Lord*. Yea so much his Darling; That he resolveth to make it the very Centre of All his Glory: and to fill it so, with his glorious presence, that the very Saints, or Angels in Heaven, rejoyced in the *Revelation*, that they should come (out of Heaven) to *reign upon the Earth*.[43]

This was a very different interpretation of Daniel's prophecy of

[40] *Olbia. The New Iland Lately Discovered... By a Christian Pilgrim* (1660), p. 3 and *passim*.
[41] Ibid., pp. 19, 165 ff., 254 ff., 370–80 (examples only). Sadler pursued his millennial speculations still further in *Christ under the Law* (1664).
[42] *Olbia*, pp. 111–12; cf. pp. 60 ff., 87 ff., 108.
[43] Ibid. 121 (italics in original).

a rule of the saints, but already in 1649 Sadler had condemned the notion that it was to be achieved by force: 'And what ever Force may appear, in pulling down of *Babylon*: I doe not read or know, that the New Temple, or the New Jerusalem shall be built with *Violence*, or by *Violent Men*; that may ruffle much, in *Forcing Babylon*. But they may Perish by the Sword, that use it most.'[44]

3. THE FIFTH MONARCHISTS

The widespread notion that Fifth Monarchy men made most of the running in Barebone's Parliament is largely mistaken. It is entirely understandable, however, for it was sedulously fostered after the assembly's demise by hostile pamphleteers, and so far as the original intentions of Harrison, Carew, and their preacher friends went they were not far wrong. But there were in fact only twelve or thirteen Fifth Monarchists in the House,[45] and half of them, to judge by the silence of the *Commons' Journal* and other records, made very little impact on its proceedings. The tables in Appendix B, which include a rough estimate of each member's degree of involvement on a three-point scale, show fourteen men of radical persuasions in the most active category, but only three of these, John Carew, Hugh Courtney, and Arthur Squibb, were Fifth Monarchists. They indeed did exercise an initiative out of all proportion to their numbers, and John James seems to have been fairly busy too; but of the other Fifth Monarchy men Harrison and Henry Danvers played a far smaller role than might have been expected, given their characters and convictions, while John Browne, Richard Price, John Williams, Jacob Caley, John Bawden, and Francis Langdon apparently made very little mark. It is not even clear how far the Fifth Monarchists acted as a concerted group.

They covered a wide social spectrum, but their geographical distribution was narrow. Five of them—six if we add Baker to Browne, Courtney, James, Price, and Williams—represented Wales or the Welsh borders. With them can be bracketed Harrison, for they had all served with him on the Commission for the Propagation of the Gospel in Wales and they probably all

---

[44] *Rights of the Kingdom*, p. 49 (2nd pagination).
[45] My own identifications are in complete agreement with Dr Capp's in *The Fifth Monarchy Men*, p. 68. The total is thirteen if Bawden and Baker, whose affiliation with the movement is less clear than that of the rest, are both included.

owed their seats, as Browne, Courtney, and Price certainly did, to his consultations with Vavasor Powell. Three more came from Cornwall, and it seems likely that Carew, whose seat was at Antony in that county although he represented Devon, was responsible for proposing those obscure men Bawden and Langdon. He was of course well known to Cromwell and Harrison as a fellow regicide and Rumper, and he was strategically placed on the interim Council of State of April–July 1653. The remaining three were widely scattered, with Danvers representing Leicestershire, Caley Suffolk, and Squibb Middlesex.

There were four Fifth Monarchists in the Council of State which sat from July until November, but only Carew and Courtney took anything like full advantage of this position, and even Carew attended well under half the council meetings after the parliament met. Harrison, who until then had attended the interim council frequently, quickly fell off; he absented himself altogether from 31 July to 10 September and came to only seven meetings thereafter. Williams, who was currently Sheriff of Radnorshire, may have been elected in July as a token Welshman, but after attending on and off during the first three weeks he never appeared again. He was said to be ill during August, but not for long enough to account for such an absence. This raises an interesting question. Did the Fifth Monarchist members split at about the beginning of August, after the initial debates on tithes, between those who washed their hands of both parliament and council when they perceived the strength and temper of the moderate majority and those who continued to fight for their cause at Westminster against the odds? It may be significant that six of them never appear again in the *Journal* after mid-July, but one cannot tell whether this reflects their withdrawal or their political ineffectiveness.

Carew and Courtney, however, were very far from ineffective. Both were Cornishmen, and their fanatical millenarian faith brought them closer and closer together, though their backgrounds differed widely. Carew was a baronet's son, though by a second marriage, and he inherited the title only because his half-brother Sir Alexander, who sat for Cornwall in the Long Parliament, was executed as a traitor for going over to the king's side in the Civil War. Thereafter his wealth and status placed him unquestionably among the greater gentry, and in February 1647, when still only twenty-four, he was elected MP for Tregony. He made little mark, and perhaps appeared only rarely, before Pride's Purge, but thereafter he rose at once to prominence, already identifying himself as Harrison's ally and welcoming the chance to share in condemning the king. He remained a fairly active Rumper, serving on the third Council of State in 1651 and being added to the Committee for the Army and the Admiralty Committee during 1652. His association with Harrison seems to have deepened; they sat together on the Council of State established soon after the Rump's dissolution, and they were the only religious radicals to be re-elected to it in November. Carew was a teller on 6 July against giving the new supreme authority the title of parliament, and subsequently his strongest objection to recognizing the Protectorate was that its constitution included a parliament, thereby implying that power derived from the people instead of from Christ. It was Carew who, when he appeared before the Protector and Council along with Harrison, Courtney, and Rich in 1655, accused Cromwell to his face that 'when the little Parliament was dissolved, he tooke the Crowne off from the heade of Christ, and put it upon his owne'.[46] He has been described as a Baptist, but it was not until early in 1658 that he, again in company with Harrison and Courtney, underwent adult baptism.[47]

Courtney, who came of minor gentry stock, went to North Wales as a soldier and stayed as an administrator. Between 1649 and 1651 he was appointed to every kind of local commission, including that for the propagation of the gospel, and was promoted to Quartermaster-General and to the governorship of Anglesey. His fiery chiliastic faith turned him against the Levellers; he wrote to Morgan Llwyd in April 1649 that

[46] *Clarke Papers*, ii, 243. For the other facts of Carew's career see *DNB*; Worden, *Rump*, pp. 37, 40 n., 46, 55, 249, 270–1, 308, 310, 314, 389; Capp, *Fifth Monarchy Men, passim*; Violet Rowe, *Sir Henry Vane the Younger*, p. 180; Firth and Rait, ii, 500, 562, 689; *CJ*, vii, 282, 344.

[47] *Publick Intelligencer*, no. 120 (1–8 Feb. 1658), p. 286, cited in Capp, *Fifth Monarchy Men*, p. 181. Dr Capp (p. 285) thinks Carew was probably the 'Johannes Cornubiensis' who published *The Grand Catastrophe, or the Change of Government* in January 1654; but since that tract gave a qualified welcome to the Protectorate, described Cromwell's new councillors (mostly Carew's known opponents) as wise and godly, and hoped that with God's blessing a new elected parliament would make all well again, the identification appears improbable.

Lilburne's tactics were 'exploded by all upright men'.[48] He collaborated with Harrison in suppressing the Leveller mutinies of that year, and shortly afterwards the two men were made honorary MAs of Oxford University. He served on several important committees of both the House and the council in 1653, including the former's committee for tithes, and he keenly supported the moves for 'a new body of the law'. He was the most assiduous of the Fifth Monarchists on the Council of State and was much employed by it, but he lost his seat in November. He was greatly dismayed when Barebone's Parliament gave way to the Protectorate, and for his active opposition to Cromwell's rule he, like Harrison and Carew, suffered more than one lengthy term of imprisonment.[49]

John James is remarkable in that he was elected to the Council of State for the first time on 1 November, when the tide was running so strongly against the religious radicals. He seems to have been a moderately effective MP, serving on the committees for the public revenue, for prisons and prisoners, and several more ephemeral ones, and acting as a teller three times, the final occasion being on 10 December when he counted the triumphant majority who defeated the first clause of the committee for tithes' report, and so sparked off the moves which brought Barebone's Parliament to an end. Perhaps his birth and status commended him to one section of the House and his religion to the other. A colonel in the militia, and for two periods Governor of Worcester, he was heir to Astley Hall in Worcestershire, but he generally resided at Trippleton Hall in Herefordshire, which had come to him through his wife (and would one day pass to Stanley Baldwin). He was on the main commissions in both counties, but it was Herefordshire which he served as sheriff in 1650 and as Custos Rotulorum from 1652. His family's position was solid enough to survive his radical connections, for his son was twice sheriff, in 1696 and 1701. Of his radicalism there is no doubt, for he was an elder of Vavasor Powell's congregation and a close associate of Wroth Rogers in running the Herefordshire militia. In December 1655 he signed *A Word for God*, the bitter

---

[48] Worden, *Rump*, p. 197.

[49] Capp, *Fifth Monarchy Men, passim*; Dodd, *Studies in Stuart Wales*, pp. 102–3, 144, 149, 155, 163; W. R. Williams, *Parliamentary History of Wales*, p. 3; *CSPD 1653–4, passim*; Thurloe, i, 639–40; ii, 214–15; iii, 140.

remonstrance in which Powell and his fellow Fifth Monarchists accused Cromwell of betraying the blessed cause which the Long Parliament had championed. Yet he cannot have been so intransigent towards the Protectorate as Harrison, Carew, and Courtney, for he was not only continued in his various commissions, including that of Custos, but was also placed upon new ones to remove scandalous ministers and to try treasons against the Protector's person.[50]

The remaining Fifth Monarchists of the Welsh connection were, like Williams, lesser gentry of some local standing who had all been workers in the vineyard with Powell before 1653. Richard Price's family had held Gunley in Montgomeryshire for over two centuries, and Richard, after serving as sheriff in 1650–1, was Custos Rotulorum of his county. He, like Williams, was an elder of Powell's congregation there, and he not only signed *A Word for God* but also personally delivered it to Cromwell. That did not prevent him, however, from remaining Custos throughout the Protectorate. He bought land and houses in Shropshire and elsewhere during the Interregnum, but his will, made in 1675, shows that part of his estate was mortgaged and that his wealth was modest.[51] John Browne of Little Ness, five miles on the Shropshire side of the Welsh border, was an elder of Morgan Llwyd's church at Wrexham and like Williams a lay preacher and a signatory of *A Word for God*. He had been on his county committee, but alone in this group he was never a JP. Richard Gough, the delightful chronicler of nearby Myddle, was a kinsman of Browne by marriage and remembered him as 'a selfe conceited, confident person'.[52] Thomas Baker of Sweeney Hall in the same county, of which he was sheriff in 1644, was perhaps

---

[50] Nuttall, *Welsh Saints*, pp. 72, 90 n.; W. R. Williams, *Parliamentary History of Worcestershire*, pp. 45–6; Capp, *Fifth Monarchy Men, passim*; Underdown, *Pride's Purge*, p. 314; *Visitation of Worcestershire, 1654*, Harleian Soc., xc, p. 52; *CJ*, vii, 283, 287, 306, 322, 325, 334, 339, 344, 363; Firth and Rait, ii, 971, 1040, etc. *A Word for God* is printed in Thurloe, iv, 380–4.

[51] Dodd, *Studies in Stuart Wales*, pp. 129, 147, 154, 163, 168; Capp, *Fifth Monarchy Men*, p. 259 and *passim*; Williams, *Parl. Hist. Wales*, pp. 3–4; 'J.W.H.', 'The Pryces of Gunley', *Archaeologia Cambrensis*, 4th ser., xiii (1882), 129–34; PRO, PROB/11/352 (PCC 109 Bench).

[52] Richard Gough, *Antiquityes and Memoyres of the Parish of Myddle* (1875, repr. Fontwell, 1968), p. 98; Capp, *Fifth Monarchy Men*, p. 243 and *passim*; Richards, *Puritan Movement in Wales*, pp. 95–6; Pink MS 298, fo. 595. Williams in *Parl. Hist. Wales*, p. 4, partly misidentifies him, and Richards in *Religious Developments in Wales*, p. 232, mistakenly attributes to him a tract written by Capt. John Browne of Orpington.

a less fully professed Fifth Monarchist than the others, for he seems to have taken no part in their agitation against the Protectorate. But he was a great patron of Independent preachers, including Powell, who generally performed every day of the week when he was staying at Sweeney. Gough heard him pray and preach in the dining-room there for four hours on end, and the many who came to hear him were all regaled by Baker with a twopenny bun and a glass of beer.[53] Baker was evidently well-to-do, for he entertained lavishly as sheriff and held lands in Ireland; but he was childless, and he left Sweeney Hall, which he had rebuilt handsomely, to Browne's son Thomas, who had married a cousin of his.[54] One wishes that there was as much to tell about these members' activity in Barebone's Parliament. Williams, Price, Browne, and Baker were all placed on the committee for prisons and prisoners on 20 July, but apart from the subsequent addition of Price to the Committee for the Army and Williams's few appearances on the Council of State, this is the total record of their participation.

Carew's fellow-Cornishmen Bawden and Langdon are even more shadowy figures. Bawden, a Truro man of minor gentry stock, was a major in the garrison of the Scilly Isles, and probably second-in-command; he and the governor were added to the Commission of the Peace at the end of 1652 so that they could exercise civil authority there. His removal under the Protectorate and his reappearance as commander of a troop of Cornish militia in the summer of 1659 suggest that he was a republican who briefly enjoyed a return to favour with the restoration of the Rump.[55] Francis Langdon was the sixth son of Sir Walter Langdon of Keverall, and a recent Baptist convert. He named his residence as Tregalwe in the will he made in 1652, and judging by letters addressed to him it was in the Cornish parish of St. Erme, to whose poor he left £3. He had been a JP since 1650 and remained one throughout the Protectorate.[56] Bawden,

[53] Gough, *Antiquityes of Myddle*, p. 98.

[54] H. T. Weyman, 'Shropshire Members of Parliament', pp. 177-8; *Grantees of Arms*, Harleian Soc., lxvi, p. 12; *CSPD 1649-50*, pp. 372-3; Williams, *Parl. Hist. Wales*, p. 4; PRO, PROB/11/348 (PCC 73 Dycer).

[55] *CSPD 1652-3*, pp. 29, 34; *1659-60*, pp. 16, 50, 564; Capp, *Fifth Monarchy Men*, pp. 68, 102-3, 124, 241-2.

[56] *CSPD 1649-50*, pp. 33, 229, 521; Folger Library, Add. MS 483, fos. 44, 47; PRO, PROB/11/281 (PCC 474 Wootton); *Visitation of Cornwall, 1620*, Harleian Soc., ix, p. 120; Capp, *Fifth Monarchy Men*, pp. 68, 102, 115-16, 254.

after being placed on the committee for the public revenue on 20 July, makes only one more minor appearance in the *Journal*, which at least shows he was still in the House on 1 October, but Langdon makes none at all after his initial appointment to the committee for the poor. Both members gave hospitality to Anna Trapnel, the millenarian prophetess of doom to Cromwell's Protectorate, when she visited Cornwall early in 1654.[57]

Of the remaining Fifth Monarchists, we have already met Jacob Caley, Portman of Ipswich, among the nominees of the churches of Suffolk. The only committee on which he served was that for the public revenue, and he had his one recorded hour of glory on 11 November, when he reported to the House from it concerning the evasion of duty on English-grown tobacco and was ordered to bring in a bill to remedy this.[58] The silence of nearly four months before his second mention in the *Journal* may simply reflect the modesty of his talents and pretensions, but that cannot explain the patchy record of Colonel Henry Danvers, who was too dynamic and passionate a man to fail to leave his mark on such an assembly as Barebone's when he was present. He was Governor of Stafford and a Trustee for Maintenance of Ministers; he already had an estate worth £300 per year in Staffordshire before he inherited his father's Leicestershire estate of Rothley and Swithland. Unlike most of the Fifth Monarchists in the House he was a General Baptist, and he served as an elder in the congregation ministered to by that other military saint, Captain Edmund Chillenden. The main burden of his *Certain Quæries Concerning Liberty of Conscience*, which he had published in March 1649, was to deny the civil magistrate any power whatsoever over belief or worship, and in the sixteen-seventies he would still be writing at great length about adult baptism and the thousand years' rule of the saints.[59] For thirty years he could not for long resist plotting against regimes which his conscience rejected, from Cromwell's to James II's, and after implicating

---

[57] Anna Trapnel, *The Cry of a Stone* ([20 Feb.] 1654), p. 2; *Anna Trapnel's Report and Plea* (1654, not in Thomason), pp. 9, 10, 13, 18–19, 22, 24–5.

[58] *CJ*, vii, 348.

[59] Henry Danvers, *Certain Quæries Concerning Liberty of Conscience* ([27 March] 1649); H. D., *A Treatise of Baptism* (1673); Henry Danvers, *Theopolis, or the City of God* (1672). *Eight Questions in Reference to . . . Laying on of Hands*, by Danvers, Chillenden, and thirteen others, to which John More replied with *A Lost Ordinance Restored* ([24 Jan.] 1654), appears not to survive, but it was probably written while Barebone's Parliament was sitting.

himself in Monmouth's Rebellion he eventually died at Utrecht early in 1688. In Barebone's Parliament he was initially appointed to three important standing committees, including that for tithes, but he disappears from the *Journal* from 20 July to 25 October. Thereafter his name figures again quite prominently, and finally he was John James's fellow-teller in the crucial vote on 10 December against the report of the committee for tithes. It looks as though he withdrew from the House, and subsequently returned, at much the same times as Harrison did.[60]

Arthur Squibb lacked Danvers' social standing, but he was assiduous in his parliamentary duties. He served on a number of important committees, including those for tithes and for a new body of the law; indeed he was a teller in the vote to set up the latter. His house had sheltered a gathered church since 1649, and it would be licensed for Baptist worship in 1672. It became notorious in 1653, as will be seen, as the daily meeting-place of a caucus of radical members, but that was probably more because Squibb was the only one of them with a house in Westminster than because he exercised any particular ascendancy. He was given a number of responsible employments by both the House and the Council of State, but he was never elected a councillor himself. He had an unlikely background for a zealot, for he had originally sought to follow his cousin and namesake Arthur the elder and his brother Lawrence by investing in a reversion to a Tellership of the Exchequer. But whereas Lawrence became a royalist in the Civil War, Arthur junior rose as a zealous sequestrator of delinquents' estates and a man whose financial advice the Rump's Council of State valued. His reward came in April 1650 when he was made a Commissioner for Compounding—as Professor Aylmer has said, 'the only Compounding Commissioner for whom the adjectives extremist or fanatical might seem appropriate'.[61] Barebone's Parliament confirmed the appointment, but Cromwell dropped him when he became Protector, and Squibb sold his reversion to his brother Edmund in February 1654, just before the Exchequer was re-established.

---

[60] *CJ*, vii, 286, 287, 339, 342, 343, 347, 363. On Danvers generally, Capp corrects the frequent confusion, including that by the *DNB*, between Henry and Robert Danvers: *Fifth Monarchy Men*, pp. 211, 248, and *passim*. See also L. F. Brown, *Baptists and Fifth Monarchy Men*, pp. 11, 22, 56, 100–1, 117, 190 n.; J. Nichols, *County of Leicester*, iv, Pt I, 189; Thomas Crosby, *History of the English Baptists* (1740), iii, 90–7.

[61] Aylmer, *State's Servants*, p. 218.

When he made his will in November 1679, shortly before his death, he was living at Chertsey in Surrey and still had lands in Ireland, Essex, and elsewhere, but the scale of his legacies was modest.[62]

4. THE OTHER RADICALS

Turning now to the remaining eleven radicals whose role in Barebone's was particularly active, what strikes one most about them as a group is how few of them, in comparison with the leading moderates, had a political career of any significance before or after 1653. Not that this is surprising, for most of them were chosen in reaction against the kinds of politician who had dominated the stage in the past decade, and they all held convictions that would make them to some degree antipathetic towards the Protectorate. They were not all without reputation, however. Moyer and Ireton had, as has been seen, risen in City politics, and Moyer in the Commonwealth's financial administration too. John Anlaby had been an MP since 1647, though a rather obscure and inactive one. Colonel Robert Bennett had for years wielded great power in Cornwall and had sat in the Rump since 1651, while Thomas Blount had acquired considerable influence and standing in Kent. These five, who will be considered first, were notably free of the fanaticism that characterized the extremer saints.

Moyer was the wealthiest of the group, thanks mainly to the East India trade, and the most markedly radical in his religious and political views. He also carried the most weight, both as an exceptionally busy councillor from April onwards (though he lost his councillor's seat in November) and as a member of a dozen of the House's committees, including those for tithes, for trade, and for a new body of the law. He has often been called a Baptist, but he had long been a member of Thomas Goodwin's church, and when he made his will in 1682 he left £30 to his 'deare Pastor' John Collins, another Independent, with a further

[62] Ibid., pp. 216–18; Capp, *Fifth Monarchy Men*, p. 263 and *passim*; *CSPD 1649–50*, pp. 280, 316; *1653–4*, pp. 86, 152; *1654*, p. 272; *1661–2*, p. 369; *1666–7*, pp. 182–3, 535 (where the reference to 'the late Arthur Squibb' is an error); *CJ*, vii, 283, 285–7, 292, 304, 342; PRO, PROB/11/362 (PCC 50 Bath). I am indebted to Professor Aylmer for the information that Squibb almost certainly never acquired the actual office of Teller, as is suggested in *CSPD 1654*, p. 272.

sum for Collins and John Owen to distribute among poor ministers. He was in fact an Independent of strong though not inflexible separatist principles.[63] He and Robert Bennett were the tellers in favour of bringing in a bill to abolish lay patronage, but when he purchased Pitsea Hall he acquired the advowson with the estate, and on 20 January 1656 he presented John Davis to the rectory of Pitsea.[64] He was temporarily under suspicion soon after Cromwell became Protector and he lost his post in the Customs, but he did not oppose the regime militantly as Harrison and Carew did. Nevertheless he supported the London citizens' petition which alarmed Cromwell into dissolving parliament precipitately in February 1658, and a year later, in company with the Baptists William Kiffin and Josias Berners, he actually presented the same subversive petition to Richard's parliament.[65]

His fellow-alderman John Ireton had experienced life on the fringe of national politics in his brother Henry's time and had been Sheriff of London and Middlesex in 1651. He could not quite match Moyer's number of committees and he was never on the Council of State, but he acted as a teller thirteen times, in the course of which he demonstrated his hostility towards the Court of Chancery and lay patronage as well as his interest in revenue matters. In several of the less contentious divisions he was partnered by moderates, and he was evidently no more of a fanatic than Tichborne, with whom he worshipped in Cokayne's church. He accommodated himself to the Protectorate more easily than Moyer did, for he served on the commissions for the assessment, for the City's militia, for trade, for the excise, and for trying treasons against the Protector's person. Cromwell finally knighted him during his term as Lord Mayor of London.[66]

There were limits too to the radicalism of Anlaby, Blount, and Robert Bennett. The first two were nominated to the High Court of Justice which tried Charles I, but neither was prepared to act,

[63] Tolmie, *The Triumph of the Saints*, pp. 105, 115, 141, 236; PRO, PROB/11/373 (PCC 96 Drax).

[64] *CJ*, vii, 352; Lambeth Palace Library, Presentation deeds, COMM, II/540.

[65] Aylmer, *State's Servants*, pp. 214–16 (an excellent compact account of Moyer's whole career); Robert Brenner, 'The Civil War politics of London's merchant community', *Past and Present*, no. 58 (1973), pp. 93–4, 99; *CJ*, vii, 281–3, 286–8, 296, 298, 300–1, 304, 309, 316–17, 323, 325, 357–9; *CSPD 1653–4, passim*; Burton, *Diary*, iv, 288 f.

[66] *DNB*; Aylmer, *State's Servants*, pp. 419–20; *CJ*, vii, 283, 285, 287, 292, 315, 323, 325, 335, 351–2, 355, 359; *CSPD 1655*, p. 43; *1655–6*, pp. 100, 189; *1658–9*, p. 17; Firth and Rait, ii, 1039, 1073, 1081.

though Anlaby is said to have attended one session—curiously the final one, at which sentence was pronounced. In Barebone's he was a teller with Carew in a division which concerned the liberty of preaching in public meeting-places, but he was partnered with moderates in three other divisions, and the business of the eight committees on which he served was not of the kind that caused the members to polarize. He must have made himself acceptable to the House, for the fifty-two votes which he got on 1 November just gained him a place on the Council of State. He lacked the typical radical's prejudice against lawyers, for in 1657 he sent his son and heir, after a spell at Cambridge, to Gray's Inn, which he himself had entered twenty-six years earlier.[67]

Robert Bennett, like Moyer, lost his seat on the council when Anlaby gained his, though he too had served on numerous committees. In his case it was probably at least in part because he had been away for nearly three months on end, though not (as with Harrison, Salwey, and Stapley, for example) without explanation or permission. On 22 July he obtained six months' leave of absence 'to go into the country upon his necessary occasions', and though he was engaged in public business such as raising Cornishmen for the navy and was back at Westminster by 10 October, he probably lost some ground in the House.[68] He was a Baptist, belonging to a church of strictly separatist principles at Looe; George Fox describes him as a Baptist teacher. His letters express an intense Puritan faith and an austere Puritan morality; he was appalled by 'those grose Evils in opinion and pratis' amongst the Quakers, but that did not prevent him from unconditionally freeing a group of them from gaol.[69] He was neither a bigot nor an extremist. He tendered his services to Cromwell when the latter became Protector,[70] and continued to command St. Michael's Mount and to attend

[67] Gooder, *Parl. Representation of Yorkshire*, ii, 51–3; Pink MS 296, fo. 108; *CJ*, vii, 287, 292, 302, 316, 319, 322, 325, 328, 337, 339, 340; Worden, *Rump Parliament*, pp. 202, 389; Venn, *Alumni Cantab.*, i, 33; Foster, *Gray's Inn Admissions*, pp. 193, 281.

[68] *CJ*, vii, 282–3, 285, 287, 334, 336–7, 339, 342, 348, 351–2, 357; *CSPD 1653–4*, pp. 44, 91. The President of the Council of State (at that time Tichborne) wrote to him on 7 Sept. 1653 that the weighty affairs of the Commonwealth required his attendance at council: Folger Lib., Add. MS 483, fo. 109.

[69] Folger Lib., Add. MS 483, fo. 175; *Journal of George Fox*, ed. J. L. Nickalls (Cambridge, 1952), pp. 254, 266–7; Mary Coate, *Cornwall in the Great Civil War*, p. 347.

[70] Folger Lib., Add. MS 483, fo. 114.

quarter sessions. He gained election to the parliament of 1654, was defeated in 1656 (did Major-General Desborough throw in his weight against him?), but was returned again in 1659. In Richard's parliament he declared frankly that he would have preferred a republic if the people had been more disposed towards one, but that in the circumstances he was for recognizing Richard as Protector and accepting a two-chamber parliament, so long as it did not entail a hereditary peerage. Shortly afterwards he took his seat in the restored Rump, but after the army officers had again interrupted it he ignored their summons to their ill-fated Committee of Safety.[71] He is a clear example of a religious radical who was relatively moderate and pragmatic in his politics.

The same can be said of Blount, who was one of the nominees of the churches of Kent. He had risen to prominence in the county committee, and like most of the Kentish gentry who put national politics before local issues his family were relative newcomers to the shire. His grandfather, an elder Thomas Blount, had come to London from Shropshire and thriven as a collector of the City's customs; his father Edward had married the daughter, appropriately named Fortune, of Sir William Garway of London, and when his elder brother died young our Thomas became heir to a handsome estate at Wricklesmarsh, near Greenwich. In January 1645 he intervened to protect that radical Antinomian minister John Saltmarsh against an armed body of locals who sought to prevent him from preaching at Westerham, and soon afterwards he was busy suppressing the attempted rising by Kentish royalists; but he ingratiated himself with the populace, who missed their May-day games that year, by drawing out two regiments of foot on Blackheath and staging a mock battle between Cavaliers and Roundheads. The dozen committees on which he served in Barebone's included those for tithes, for the public revenue, for the advancement of learning, and for a new body of the law, and among the bills that he introduced were those for civil marriage (on which he also

---

[71] *DNB*; Underdown, *Pride's Purge*, pp. 261, 308–9, 330–1, 360; Coates, *Cornwall in the Great Civil War, passim*; Folger Lib., Add. MS 483, fos. 50, 117, 120–1, 133, 135, etc., *CSPD 1659–60*, pp. 165, 173, and *passim*; Burton, *Diary*, iii, 165–6, 359–61; iv, 29–30, 353–4, 446. Bennett vigorously defended the trial of the king at the Truro quarter sessions in April 1649, and allowed his arguments to be 'published by authority' under the title *King Charles Triall Justified* ([9 May] 1649).

chaired the House in Grand Committee), for abolishing the
· Court of Chancery, and for suppressing highwaymen and
robbers. He was a teller in fifteen divisions, including some which
show him on the radical side regarding tithes and lay patronage.
Despite all this activity he was not elected to the Council of State
and he never sat in another parliament. Yet like Bennett he gave
at least limited co-operation to the Protectorate, and he furnished
both men and arms against Venner's Fifth Monarchist rising in
1657. Three years later he reinstalled the bells in Greenwich
church and hired ringers to toll them for the first time in twenty
years, to greet Charles II's return. That did not save him from a
spell of imprisonment at the Restoration, but he lived to enjoy
the company of the Royal Society and to gain a reputation for
inventions and experiments. Pepys visited him several times at
Wricklesmarsh, 'a very stately sight for situation and brave
plantations', and admired his pioneering invention of a sprung
coach.[72]

Andrew Broughton ranked lower in the social scale than
Anlaby, Bennett, and Blount, but he was even busier in the
House's service than any of them, and more uncompromising in
his politics. A lawyer of Maidstone, he became a common
councilman of the borough in 1638, mayor in 1647–8 and again
in 1659–60, and a member of the county committee of Kent
from 1643. He was never a JP, but that was doubtless because he
was Clerk of the Peace for Kent from 1640 to 1660—the
professional lawyer who kept the amateur justices on the legal
rails. He was clerk to the High Court of Justice which tried
Charles I, and it was he who read out the charge and the
subsequent death sentence. Shortly afterwards he was appointed
chief clerk for criminal causes in the Upper Bench, the office
formerly known as Clerk of the Crown in the King's Bench, and
in 1651 his Inn, the Inner Temple, made him a bencher. He was
not one of the 1653 members recommended by the churches of
Kent, and all but one of the dozen committees on which he sat,
as well as all eight of the divisions in which he was a teller, were

---

[72] *DNB*; *Visitation of Kent, 1619*, Harleian Soc., xlii, 178–9; ibid., *1663*, Harleian Soc.,
liv, 16; Everitt, *Community of Kent*, pp. 95–9, 118, 147–8, 151, 216; D. Lysons, *Environs of
London* (1811), vol. i, Pt II, 544; Leo F. Solt, *Saints in Arms* (Stanford, 1959), p. 113 n.; *CJ*,
vii, 283–90, 292, 297–8, 300, 304, 309, 312, 329–30, 334, 336, 339–40; *CSPD 1655*, pp.
254, 268–9, 299, 363; *1660–1*, p. 486; Pepys, *Diary*, vi, 94, 213; vii, 20.

concerned with legal or political rather than religious affairs. Yet before casting him as that rarest of figures in Barebone's Parliament, a thoroughgoing radical of essentially secular inspiration, one has to reckon with a speech he made in 1659 against compelling ministers to read a parliamentary declaration for a fast-day to their congregations. 'Twenty times I beseech you, be tender', he said, 'and do not impose upon gracious spirits. I know what it is to have peace with God'.[73] It was probably for his legal expertise, however, that he was elected to the Council of State on 14 July, yet when the House set up its original committee 'for the business of law' six days later it voted against including him. He was eventually added to it on 20 October, but it was not until 10 November that he was added to the more radical committee, first established on 19 August, 'to consider of a new body of the law'. He was more employed in the drafting of legislation than any other radical, but he was not re-elected to the council in November. He may have been a contentious figure, judging by his speeches in Richard Cromwell's parliament, the only other one in which he sat. There he spoke very disparagingly of the Humble Petition and Advice, the Other House, and the 'gallantry' of the Protectoral court, and towards Richard himself he was positively insulting. He was given to emotional and extravagant expressions, and was twice taken to task for them. He fled the country before the Restoration, and after surviving twenty-seven years of exile to the age of eighty-four he was buried at Vevay alongside several of the regicides with whom he had sat so long ago.[74]

Broughton was not the only barrister among the leading radicals, for Thomas St. Nicholas, whose background was sketched in the last chapter, was Recorder of Canterbury. He did not serve on as many committees as Broughton or draft so many bills, but from July to the end of October much of his time was taken up by the business of the Council of State, on which he was

---

[73] Burton, *Diary*, iv, 330; cf. p. 144. Broughton was also on the committee which drafted the strongly millenarian declaration of 12 July 1653.

[74] Sir Edgar Stephens, *Clerks of the Counties*, p. 109; J. Cave-Browne, *Knights of the Shire for Kent* (1894), p. 40, and in *Archaeologia Cantiana*, xxi (1895), 235; Pink MSS 298, fo. 575; Inderwick, *Calendar of Inner Temple Records*, pp. 292, 299, 306; Firth and Rait, i, 336, 451, etc.; Ludlow, *Memoirs*, i, 214–15, 228; ii, 276–7, 513; *CJ*, vii, 282, 284, 286, 288–9, 301, 322–3, 325, 334–6, 340, 342, 344, 347–8, 351, 355, 358–9; *CSPD 1653–4, passim*; Burton, *Diary*, iv, 292, 325–6, 330.

quite active except during two spells of absence totalling five weeks. In various conciliar employments and committees he was often associated with Broughton, and with Courtney too, though if his religious stance was anything like as extreme as Courtney's his appointments as a Trier and an Ejector in 1654 would be inexplicable. In fact it was not, though Cromwell and his councillors doubtless misjudged it in so appointing him. Indeed they found his allegiance suspect enough to exclude him from his seat in the 1656 parliament, though he took it in January 1658, and expressed himself thus when a new assembly of divines was proposed: 'I am as much sensible of the growth of errors, and would as fain have a oneness of mind as any man. Yet it has been a great satisfaction to men's spirits that they have not been imposed upon. It will look ill abroad, that you are going again to impose a government upon men's consciences.'[75] All his other recorded speeches, in this session and in Richard's parliament, were concerned with political and constitutional matters and they give the impression of a man much closer to Hesilrige's camp than to Harrison's. This is reinforced by the Rump's appointment of him as Clerk of the Parliament when it was restored in 1659.[76]

Praise-God Barebone and Samuel Highland, lay preachers to their own gathered churches, came much closer to the popular stereotype of the men of 1653 than the seven members so far discussed in this section, but their role was somewhat smaller, though still far above the average. Both sat on a number of important committees, including those for tithes and for a new body of the law, and both (especially Barebone) acted quite often as tellers, but neither was elected to the Council of State, chaired the assembly in Grand Committee, or introduced important bills. Barebone's rise to third warden of the Leather-sellers' Company has been mentioned; it was followed in 1649 by his election to the Common Council of London, though he lost his seat on it in December 1652. He had been a member since at least 1632 of that seminal separatist congregation which Henry Jacob had founded in 1616, and which had survived persecution

---

[75] Burton, *Diary*, ii, 335.
[76] Gooder, *Parl. Representation of Yorks*, ii, 61–3; *CJ*, vii, 283, 285, 287, 298, 301, 319, 322, 330, 340, 342, 344, 346, 351, 355, 359, 362; *CSPD 1653–4, passim; 1655*, p. 1; Burton *Diary*, ii, 374, 392, 406; iii, 28, 45, 76, 118–19, 327–8, 579–80; iv, 97, 152, 167.

under the successive pastorates of John Lathrop and Henry Jessey. In May 1640 it divided by mutual agreement, partly because its growing numbers were making concealment difficult, but also probably so that many of its members could meet for worship nearer home. Jessey went on ministering to one half, with its base in the Liberty of the Tower to the east, while Barebone was chosen as pastor of the other, which met in his own Fleet Street premises, west of the City walls. There on 19 December 1641, at a time when hostile mobs could be drummed up against sectaries almost as readily as against bishops, the sounds of one of Barebone's sermons filtering through his windows attracted a rowdy, derisive crowd, consisting mainly of apprentices. A two-hour riot ensued in which all his windows were smashed and his congregation finally fled over the roofs at the back of the house, though he and a few stauncher disciples stood their ground and were arrested.[77] The crash of Barebone's glass can almost be said to have rung the English Revolution in and rung it out again, for a brave but hopeless anti-monarchical petition of his in February 1660 caused his windows to be again the target of the mob on two nights when it ran wild in celebration of the downfall of the Rump and Monck's readmission of the secluded members, which made the Restoration inevitable.[78]

The pamphleteers who contemptuously reported that 1641 riot depicted him as a ranting fanatic, but that is not how he appears in the three tracts which he himself published in 1642, 1643, and 1645.[79] All three were written to defend the validity of infant baptism, whether or not by the Anglican rite, and to condemn the practice of re-baptizing believers—still more the Baptists' claim that they alone possessed the ordinances of Christ in purity. The first in particular breathes an irenical spirit, urging readers to take less offence over nice points of doctrine and worship and to reckon more the extent to which Protestants

[77] *The Discovery of a Swarme of Separatists* ([Dec.] 1641); *New Preachers, New* ([Dec.] 1641), attributed to John Taylor.

[78] *That Wicked and Blasphemous Petition of Praise-God Barebone ... Anatomized* ([Feb.] 1660); Pepys, *Diary*, i, 53, 62; L. F. Brown, *Baptists and Fifth Monarchy Men*, pp. 190–1, 196.

[79] P[raise-God] B[arebone] *A Discourse Tending to Prove the Baptisme ... to be the Ordinance of Jesus Christ* ([March] 1642). *A Reply to the Frivolous and Impertinent Answer of R. B.* ([14 Apr.] 1643); P[raise-God] B[arebone], *A Defence of the Lawfulnesse of Baptizing Infants* ([22 Feb.] 1645).

of all colours agree over the essentials of the Christian faith. He has often been called a Baptist, but although Jessey was converted to believer's baptism it is far from clear whether Barebone ever was. More interesting in this context is the question whether he was a millenarian. In 1643 he evidently was not; in 1645 he may have been veering that way; by 1675, when he published *Good Things to Come*, he certainly was.[80] In that tract he strongly affirmed that Christ would appear in glory to reign quite literally for a thousand years, and he condemned all attempts to interpret the prophecies allegorically. But he considered the doctrine of the fifth monarchy, in the sense of a kingdom erected through the initiative of the saints, to be doubtful at best; Christ, he believed, was to reign over a new earth, not the present world. Whether these were his views in 1653 there is no knowing, but the probability is that he demurred at the crudity of the Fifth Monarchists' doctrines and the militancy of their politics, while yet feeling more sympathy for their dedication to the New Jerusalem than for the objectives of their moderate opponents. When the first parliament of the Protectorate was about to meet in 1654, members of ten congregations got up *A Declaration of Several of the Churches of Christ*, which violently charged Cromwell with having brought about the dissolution of Barebone's Parliament because it had sought to 'rule as *Saints*, or part of the fifth *Monarchy*, for Christ'. But though a score of his congregation signed, Barebone did not,[81] nor did he engage in any overt resistance to the Protectorate. In January 1660 he boldly raised his voice in the Common Council (to which he had been re-elected) against sending the City's compliments to Monck, and more than a year after the king's return he was reported to be visiting Vavasor Powell (whose views he never fully shared) and Major Bremen in prison, which may have contributed to his own incarceration in the Tower for eight months.[82] It was not the last

[80] Compare *A Reply*, p. 63, with *A Defence*, sig. A2ᵛ, and with P.G.B., *Good Things to Come* (1675), *passim*. The latter tract is discussed in an anonymous article on 'The eschatology of Praise-God Barebone', *Transactions of the Congregational Historical Society*, iv (1909–10), 64–78.

[81] *A Declaration of Several of the Churches of Christ* ([2 Sept.] 1645), p. 4; L. F. Brown, *Baptists and Fifth Monarchy Men*, pp. 54–6.

[82] *Clarendon Calendar*, iv, 526; *CSPD 1661–2*, pp. 82, 197, 447. On Barebone generally see *DNB*; Tolmie, *The Triumph of the Saints, passim*; L. F. Brown, *Baptists and Fifth Monarchy Men, passim*; Underdown, *Pride's Purge*, p. 326; *CJ*, vii, 286–7, 289, 316–17, 325–6, 329, 334, 337, 352; *CSPD 1663–4*, p. 405; Pink MS 297, fo. 79.

harassment he would suffer for his firmly held faith and loyalties before he died at a great age in 1679.

Samuel Highland or Hyland was the lay pastor of a flourishing separatist church in Southwark. He too has been described as a Baptist, though perhaps on no better foundation than the loose contemporary use of 'Anabaptist' to describe separatists of many kinds; nor is there any evidence that he was a millenarian except his involvement in the prayer meetings at Allhallows, Blackfriars, which were certainly not confined to Fifth Monarchy men. Although Southwark was where he lived he was recommended by the churches of Kent, and there is a will made by a Samuel Highland in 1692, possibly his son, which left land in three Kentish parishes as well as in Bodiham and other places in Sussex.[83] Samuel senior was probably of minor gentry stock. He first appears as a militia commissioner for Southwark in 1647; then he became a JP for Surrey in 1649, only to be removed in July 1652 and restored to the bench a year later, this time for Middlesex as well as Surrey. Ties of friendship and sympathy linked him with the Levellers from the heyday of the movement. In November 1648 he acted as a messenger between the committee which was drafting the second Agreement of the People at the Nag's Head and the army's headquarters at St. Alban's.[84] Just a week before the opening of Barebone's Parliament he attended the regular Monday prayer-meeting at Blackfriars, which according to one account met in defiance of an order by Cromwell suspending it. He was the first to rise and offer a prayer; he hinted at the banning order, bade the congregation not to fear what man could do to them, then 'prayed for the imprisoned and persecuted, meaning John Lilburne, as was imagined'.[85] Sympathy for Lilburne and his cause (though not for his more unruly supporters) shows through in his *Exact Relation*, which is of unique value as the only full account of the parliament written by a member and as an eloquent and rational apologia for the radical cause. In it Highland takes a much less extreme standpoint than the Fifth

[83] PRO, PROB/11/415 (PCC 111 Coker). The will contains typical Puritan phraseology, but can hardly be that of our MP because in 1692 all his children were under age and his wife was pregnant.

[84] Firth and Rait, i, 1010, 1123; ii, 44, 195, etc.; Tolmie, *The Triumph of the Saints*, pp. 67, 122, 147, 153, 169, 179–80; Underdown, *Pride's Purge*, p. 317; *Clarke Papers* ii, 258.

[85] Clarendon MS 46, fo. 32.

Monarchists over such crucial issues as the reform of the law and the proper provision for a godly ministry; indeed on the latter he is less uncompromising than Milton, and his whole narrative reinforces the evidence that the radical vote in the House represented not a party but at the most a coalition.[86]

Deeply as he resented the dissolution of Barebone's Parliament, Highland remained a JP and collaborated with the succeeding government in various other ways, even informing the council of seditious talk against the Protector.[87] Like Barebone he refrained from subscribing *A Declaration of Several of the Churches of Christ*, though some of his congregation signed it, and when Venner's violent Fifth Monarchist faction published its manifesto of insurrection in 1657, *A Standard Set Up*, Highland denounced its 'diabolical spirit' and 'wicked designs'. Since, however, its authors were 'but prentices and journeymen' he advised parliament to leave 'their deserved punishment' to the ordinary course of the law.[88] Between these episodes he was returned to the 1654 parliament, but unseated after allegations of electoral malpractice. Elected again in 1656, he was not among the hundred or more members whom the council debarred, and he spoke frequently in the debates on James Nayler, whose offence he considered heinous but not worthy of death. He got into trouble for declaring that 'those that come out of the North are the greatest pests of the nation' (Nayler being a Yorkshireman) and then adding, 'The diggers came from thence.' These rash statements are interesting in showing that Quakers and Diggers were two kinds of radical that Highland could not stomach, and that his tongue could run away with him; he also gave offence with some sharp reflections on the civic government of London. But he was less hostile to the Protectorate than were most of the radicals of 1653, for he defended Cromwell's intervention in Nayler's case, 'he being equally entrusted with the Government', and he described the Protector's escape from Sindercombe's assassination plot as 'an universal mercy'.[89] He vehemently opposed the move to make him king, however, and he sided with the government's opponents on a number of issues. He leaves an

---

[86] *Exact Relation*, pp. 271, 276–82.

[87] *CSPD 1655*, p. 38; *1655–6*, p. 458; *The Trepan* ([20 July] 1656), pp. 9, 13, 15–17, 19.

[88] Burton, *Diary*, ii, 4; L. F. Brown, *Baptists and Fifth Monarchy Men*, pp. 54–6, 130.

[89] Burton, *Diary*, i, 246, 358, and for other points in this paragraph, ibid., i, 39, 67, 155, 178, 256, 264, 269, 364; ii, 90, 160, 174, 215, 239.

impression of courage, independence of mind, and an intense but unfanatical Puritan faith—a preacher rather than a politician, but with a strong sense of the pastoral obligations of both preachers and magistrates. When a new assembly of divines was proposed in January 1658, he opposed it on the grounds that, 'This is but calling them from feeding their flocks. Moral things are as necessary as religious', which he interpreted as meaning, 'To feed and clothe the naked and oppressed'.[90]

The two remaining men in this group of radical pacemakers were lesser gentry who had acquired some authority in their counties through their role during the Civil War and after. William Spence of South Malling in Sussex and Colonel William West of Middleton in north Lancashire both sat on nine or ten committees, including those for tithes and for a new body of the law, and were quite frequent tellers, though neither was elected to the Council of State. Spence's roots in Sussex went back no further than his boyhood, when his father Robert, a radical Puritan, acquired a property at Balcombe. The family, originally a very minor Norfolk one, had migrated to London in the sixteenth century. William's education seems to have been framed for a professional career rather than for life as a country gentleman, for he graduated BA at Sidney Sussex College and then after five or six years at Lincoln's Inn was called to the bar in 1644. He was soon on the county committee, where he showed such zeal for the parliamentary cause that within three more years he was made a JP while still only twenty-six. It was not long before he was found frequently chairing the sessions in Lewes, where the justices of the eastern division of the county regularly met. Lewes was also the main centre of Puritanism in Sussex, and the largest congregation there was that of the Fifth Monarchist Walter Postlethwaite, rector of St. Michael's. Spence was as strong a Puritan as his father; South Malling was close to Lewes, where by the time he made his will he had a 'great house' as well as his country seat. But he is not known to have worshipped under Postlethwaite or to have held millenarian beliefs. At some stage he became a Baptist, but most of the matters with which he can be positively identified in Barebone's

---

[90] Ibid., ii, 333. The odd story told in *The Trepan* (cited in n. 87) suggests that he was deflected by presents from proceeding against an abominable fraud, but so obviously hostile an account must be regarded with scepticism in default of any other evidence.

concerned the law and its reform, as befitted his professional expertise, though he was also on the committees for Irish affairs and for the advancement of learning. In 1655 his father and his brother John, together with many local Baptists, got up a petition to the government asking that tithes and the Court of Chancery be abolished, and the army be disbanded, and that Harrison, Feake, and other imprisoned saints be either brought to trial or set free. Postlethwaite and his congregation refused to sign, however, because it would have implied recognition of the Protectorate, and Spence himself appears not to have been involved[91]—perhaps for the very different reason that he recognized the need for government to be carried on. At any rate he remained a JP and an assessment commissioner until the Restoration, served his turn as sheriff in 1665, and was restored to the Commission of the Peace in 1668. But the strong vein of Puritan piety which presumably commended him to the nominators in 1653 still found expression in the will that he made twenty-three years later, eight months before his death:

Beseeching most Humbly Almighty God the Father of Mercies who remembered us when wee were in our Lowe Estate that he would be pleased still soe to continue his blessing to our ffamily That they may imploy and improue the same to the Advancement of his glory And to the Releife and Comfort of the poore members of Christ who hath promised That the giueing of a Cupp of Cold water to one of his Disciples in the name of a Disciple shall in noe wise lose its Reward.[92]

William West not only served on several key committees but he also quite often reported from them to the House (especially from the one for the public revenues), and he was entrusted with the bringing in of several important bills. He was described as 'of Lancaster, gent' when he was admitted to Gray's Inn in 1637, and it was not until 1650 that he acquired the much subdivided

[91] Major-General Goffe, who reported the leading role taken by John Spence and his father, would surely have mentioned William if he had been implicated: Thurloe, iv, 151, 161. On Postlethwaite see Capp, *Fifth Monarchy Men*, pp. 111, 133, 259.

[92] PRO, PROB/11/354 (PCC 87 Hale). For Spence generally: Anthony Fletcher, *A County Community in Peace and War: Sussex 1600–1660* (1975), *passim*; *Visitations of Sussex*, Harleian Soc., liii, 101; lxxxix, 103; Venn, *Alumni Cantab.*, iv, 363; *Black Book of Lincoln's Inn*, ii, 363; W. T. Whitley (ed.), *Minutes of the General Assembly of the General Baptist Churches in England*, i (1908), xli, 6–9; L. F. Brown, *Baptists and Fifth Monarchy Men*, p. 33 n.; Firth and Rait, i, 624 etc., *CJ*, vii, 283, 286–7, 300, 304, 315, 330, 334–5, 339. Venn and the printed Visitation misdate his death 1671, but his will was made on 26 Oct. 1676 and proved on 7 Aug. 1677.

manor of Middleton and other lands near Lancaster. He was
then a major in the militia; by the next year, when Charles II
and the Scots marched south through the county, he was a
lieutenant-colonel, and the Council of State commended him for
his diligence in countering any moves by the local royalists to
rise in their support. He was a JP by the time George Fox first
visited Lancaster in October 1652, and the Quaker evangelist
made a deep impression on him, as he had already on Thomas
Fell of Swarthmoor Hall, the Chancellor of the Duchy. Fell and
West successfully defended Fox against those who tried to get
him convicted at the quarter sessions. His persecutors included
John Sawrey, who was soon to be West's fellow-member in
Barebone's, and though temporarily thwarted they returned to
the attack at the next Lancaster assizes, at which Sir Hugh
Wyndham was the presiding judge. West was then Clerk of the
Assizes, and Wyndham ordered him to issue a warrant for Fox's
arrest. West flatly refused, maintaining the preacher's innocence
until finally ordered to write the warrant or leave the court; but
still he would not comply, and he offered his person and his
whole estate as surety for Fox. The latter returned to Lancaster
that night intending to give himself up, and went straight to
Fell's and West's chambers. 'What', said West with a smile, 'are
you come into the dragon's mouth?' The upshot was that Fox
walked the town freely until the assizes were over and Wyndham
departed, and that West, though he never became a Quaker,
remained a good friend to Fox throughout his life and spoke up
for him in Barebone's Parliament. West's politics and religion
are hard to glean from the meagre records of that assembly, but
the issues that evidently engaged him were practical and there
is no hint of fanaticism. He was appointed an Ejector in 1654,
and his recorded speeches in Richard Cromwell's parliament,
the only one to which he was elected, convey his guarded but not
wholly hostile attitude towards the Protectorate. He was for
recognizing Richard as Protector, provided that parliament was
first secured against any protectoral veto and was given control
over the militia. He rejected the republican argument that the
Other House contained too many swordsmen—'If anything
makes them capable, it is being soldiers', he said[93]—and he was
in favour of accepting it as part of parliament when it had been

[93] Burton, *Diary*, iv, 12–13; also ibid., iii, 270–1, 278; iv, 139, 155, 211, 443–5.

bounded and approved by the Commons. He disapproved of the Quakers' affronts to the parochial clergy, but he would have had a committee appointed to hear their grievances—the right of the commoners of England, he said. He was a radical but not an extremist, still well enough thought of for Lancaster to elect him to the Convention in 1660. According to Fox he was still a JP in 1664–6. He died childless, and the interest on £50 which he bequeathed to the poor of Heaton (which adjoins Middleton) was still being distributed in the present century.[94]

If our rough-and-ready criteria have more or less correctly identified the men who led the radicals in Barebone's Parliament, they constitute a somewhat surprising group. The prominence achieved by Broughton and Courtney in particular could hardly have been foretold from their previous careers, while more seasoned politicians like Salwey, Stapley, Pyne, and Harrison himself might have been expected to play a much larger role. That they did not was evidently their own choice; for all or most of the duration of the parliament they seem to have opted out. Our fourteen activists varied as much in the degree and type of their radicalism as in their social status and political experience, but in all of them the radical streak seems to have run through both their politics and their religion. There were no parallels among them to those few moderates such as Lisle and Ashley Cooper whose religious convictions, if any, sat lightly upon them, nor any men of the type of Henry Marten, Thomas Chaloner, Henry Neville, or John Wildman whose advanced opinions were purely secular in inspiration and tended towards libertinism. Nevertheless, apart from the three or four Fifth Monarchists who really tried to seize their opportunity and despite our two lay preachers, the radical leadership signally fails to conform to the stereotype of the sectarian fanatic.

5. COMPARISONS

In the following table a further dimension is added to the social analysis set out in Table I in the last chapter, by an attempt to show how moderates and radicals were distributed in each social

[94] Foster, *Gray's Inn Admissions*, p. 213; *VCH, Lancashire*, viii, 33, 74; *CSPD 1650*, p. 509; *1651*, p. 103; *1655*, p. 58; *Journal of George Fox*, pp. 133, 136, 138–41, 148, 309, 461–2, 504; Braithwaite, *Beginnings of Quakerism*, pp. 107–8, 118–19; Firth and Rait, ii, 972.

group. Again it must be emphasized that these are loose terms, each with its spectrum, and that not all the members can be type-cast. Nevertheless for most of the seventy-six MPs classed as moderates there is somewhat more than the evidence of the broadsheet *Catalogue*, while for most of the forty-seven in the third column of figures there are enough indications to identify them as the radical core. The problematical cases are in the second and fourth columns: those where the member's behaviour does not fall in with our simple dichotomy, or where the evidence appears to conflict (especially where *A Catalogue* is crossed by other indications), or where it is just too tenuous. The larger table in Appendix B shows how each individual member has been categorized. The non-participants in the final column are Langley, Martyn, and Walcott, who never appear in the *Journal* or any other records; Brodie, who definitely declined his summons; Dawson, who died before the parliament was a month old; and Oliver Cromwell.

Table II

Social status	Moderate	? Mod.	Radical	? Rad.	Non-partici-pants	Totals
Greater gentry	14	—	3	—	—	17
County gentry	14	—	3	4	1	22
Lesser gentry	32	1	23	7	3	66
Professional gentry	4	—	3	—	—	7
Merchant gentry	4	—	4	1	—	9
Merchants and professionals	8	1	11	1	2	23
Totals	76	2	47	13	6	144

The clearest fact to emerge from this table is the very marked social contrast between the moderate and radical groups. An overwhelming majority of the members who would have been socially eligible for parliament in normal times were on the moderate side. Among the radicals, Carew is the only Englishman who can be counted among the greater gentry; the other two in the top category are the Scotsmen Hope and Swinton. Of the twenty-two members listed as county gentry, only Stapley, Pyne, and James can be unequivocally identified as radicals, and the minimal participation of the first two has been remarked on. The lesser gentry, a category by its nature broad and imprecise, lean slightly to the moderate side, and it is only among the merchants and professional men, with doubtful pretensions to gentility or with none, that radicals appear in a clear majority.

There is no occasion here for surprise. The social centre of gravity of the Baptists, the extreme Independents, and the gathered churches generally lay among the middling sort, though the extent to which they attracted the gentry, especially the lesser gentry, has often been underestimated. Soon, as it will be seen, the radicals' objectives with regard to tithes, lay patronage, the reform of the law, and other matters came to be seen as a threat to property, and this greatly strengthened the tendency of the House to polarize. The members in the upper social brackets had the most to lose, especially if they owned advowsons or impropriate tithes, though material interest was only one factor in the growing cleavage. Class snobbery must have been another, for when the more extreme radicals started to claim a special call from Christ to pursue their unpopular policies, it made it the harder to bear that so many of them were merchants, ex-soldiers, squireens from the backwoods, and other types who would never have been legislators but for the revolutions of the times. And if *A Catalogue* is right that the universities were an issue, far more moderates than radicals had been to Oxford or Cambridge.

The geographical distribution of moderates, radicals, and in-betweens or doubtfuls is shown on the map opposite. It is of limited significance, since the members represented no electorate beyond the Council of Officers and those who may have advised it. The counties in which the churches are known to have recommended candidates are shown by shading, and though this had its effect, especially in Suffolk and Kent, it did not always secure a preponderance of religious radicals. The latter were in any case more to be expected in London and the south-east. The other clusters of them can be explained by the strength of the Harrison–Powell connection in Wales and its borders, and probably by Carew's influence on the nominations for the extreme south-west.

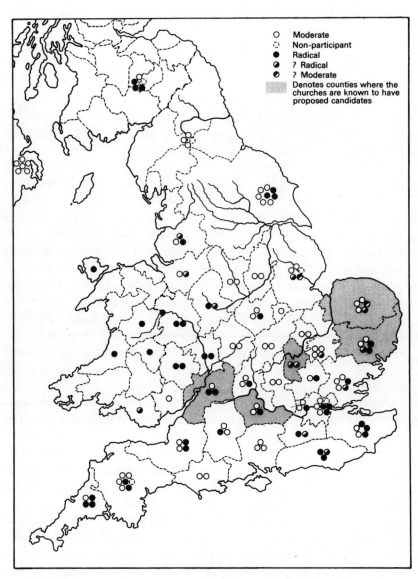

Distribution of moderate and radical members in Barebone's Parliament.

VIII

The Growth of Conflict:
July–September

From the middle of July until the second half of August three
particularly contentious topics explored the potential lines of
fission in the House and its committees. By choice or chance they
arose almost simultaneously. The great debate on tithes opened
on the very day, 13 July, when John Lilburne was arraigned
before the Upper Bench for defying the Rump's Act of
Banishment, and although the parliament was not directly
involved in the proceedings it was troubled and divided by them.
Already, on the 12th, it had first addressed itself to the grievances
of the law and appointed an early date for their debate. The
eventual outcome of that was to be a victory for the radicals on
19 August when they secured a fresh committee 'to consider of a
new body of the law', just one day before a defiant jury gave
victory of a kind to Lilburne—a pyrrhic kind, perhaps, but such
as to cause the new regime grave political embarrassment.

Yet though this chapter will focus mainly on these divisive
issues, they did not yet make Barebone's Parliament as barren of
constructive measures as the Rump had latterly grown or as the
first parliament of the Protectorate was to be. During July and
August it enacted seven statutes, including the important one for
civil marriages, besides spending much time on plans to improve
the Commonwealth's various revenues and to bring them all into
a single treasury. Unfortunately it also made its historian's task
harder by a vote on 6 August which clamped down on the
unlicensed publishing of its proceedings in newspapers and
pamphlets. The weekly prints had been meagre enough in their

reports already, but henceforth even the official ones restricted themselves to a mere digest of the *Commons' Journal*. One editor frankly confessed that 'We would have told you of some proceedings in Parliament if Mr. Henry Scobels hand could have been obtained, without which we dare not speak.'[1]

In taking up the problem of tithes, the House must have known that it was stirring a hornet's nest which had been buzzing ominously since the Civil War. There were at least five grounds for objecting to tithes, variously maintained by different classes of opponent, and ranging from the purely doctrinal to the purely economic. Of the first kind the commonest was that they were popish and superstitious, the argument being that they had lost their divine sanction when the Law gave place to the Gospel and the Levitical priesthood to an apostolic ministry. Strict separatists opposed them even more strongly because tithes maintained a parochial clergy whose doctrines and ordinances they rejected and a national established church whose very existence offended their consciences. As much as a third of the tithes paid in England, however, went not to parish incumbents but to lay impropriators who at some time since the Reformation had acquired the rectorial tithes formerly appropriated by religious houses. This was obviously a grievance in itself, and it was one of several causes of a further one, namely that maintenance by tithes resulted in gross and irrational inequalities in the value of parish livings. Finally, and most basic, tithes were a severe but very unequal economic burden, falling most heavily on smaller landholders, who still generally paid them in kind.

Three main positions were commonly taken on the question of clerical maintenance. The traditionalist one, which was common to Anglicans and Presbyterians, was that tithes retained their scriptural authority despite the supersession of the ceremonial law and that they had been further ordained by the law of the land since time immemorial. To withhold them, therefore, was both to commit sacrilege and to impugn the whole legal basis of property. The scriptural and legal arguments were of course logically separable, but they were more often than not conjoined. Next there was what can be called the reformist position, which acknowledged the economic injustices of tithes to both payers

---

[1] *CJ* vii, 296; *A Perfect Account of the Daily Intelligence*, no. 134, 27 July–3 Aug. 1653, p. 1063. The House's order also covered scurrilous or seditious pamphlets and ballads.

and recipients and sympathized with the scruples that they aroused in tender consciences, but held nevertheless that a Christian commonwealth had a duty to ensure that the Gospel was preached in every corner of the land and that its preachers received a regular and adequate stipend. The reformists' problem was therefore to devise a practical alternative to tithes that would be economically and spiritually less vexatious. The third position—the abolitionist, or in more positive terms the voluntaryist—acknowledged no such problem. It objected to the very institution of a parochial clergy, denied the civil magistrate any authority whatever over matters of religion (except perhaps to punish gross blasphemy or idolatry), and would allow pastors and preachers no other remuneration but the voluntary offerings of their flocks, together with what they might earn by their secular crafts or callings. In 1653-4 Prynne was a notable exponent of the first position, Cromwell of the second, Milton and George Fox of the third. The Rump had been much divided over tithes, but mainly between the first and second positions, whereas in Barebone's the line of cleavage lay more between the second and third.

The correlation between radicalism and voluntaryism was not exact. The Levellers had begun by affirming the third position, compromised with the second in 1647–8, moved back towards the third in their final Agreement of the People in May 1649, and reaffirmed it uncompromisingly in July 1653. The Fifth Monarchists were even less consistent, for though they often denounced tithes at least half a dozen of their preachers held parish livings in 1653. Vavasor Powell was to condemn tithes in the end, but he had earlier accepted an income derived from them, and the Commission for the Propagation of the Gospel in Wales had been to a considerable extent financed by them. At the same time Henry Danvers had been one of the Commonwealth's trustees for the use of sequestered tithes. Fifth Monarchists were by no means alone in managing to reconcile their belief that a true church consisted exclusively of visible saints with acceptance of a stipend based on the enforced contributions of saints and sinners alike, for a fair number of other Congregational pastors held livings while at the same time ministering to gathered churches. To be fair, they generally preferred some other form of remuneration to tithes if they could get it, though those who received stipends from the various government committees which paid lecturers' and augmented incumbents' incomes must have been aware that they were funded partly from impropriate tithes which royalist compounders had surrendered in order to reduce their fines.[2]

It was natural, however, that in Barebone's Parliament the most fervent abolitionists should be those who believed most passionately in the separation of the saints from their fallen brethren. They were not, however, a majority. Contemporary accounts agree that there was a broad consensus about the unsatisfactoriness of tithes as a source of clerical revenue; the contentious questions were what other form of contribution should replace them, and how—or even whether—lay impropriators should be compensated. The first day's debate arrived at no conclusion. During the second, on 15 July, the radicals pressed for a resolution to end the maintenance of ministers by tithes on 3 November, but they were effectually defeated when the House voted against putting the question by 68 to 43. Ashley Cooper and Tichborne were tellers for the majority who would not contemplate abolition until an alternative maintenance had been worked out, Harrison and Blount for the minority who wanted to remove the grievance first and then, as Highland put it, 'make provision as God should direct'.[3] One newspaper reported it as 'the opinion of many' that tithes should be replaced by a parish rate, levied on the same basis as the poor rate, with provision to distribute any yield above £100 per year among poorer parishes in the same county; but these proposals had been advanced in a pamphlet published in April, and the editor may merely have been repeating them from that source. Another current rumour, confidently transmitted by a newswriter to the exiled court, said that the plan was to compensate lay

---

[2] Don M. Wolfe (ed.), *Leveller Manifestoes of the Puritan Revolution* (1944), pp. 140, 193–4, 227, 287, 348, 403; *The Fundamental Lawes and Liberties of England*, p. 4; Capp, *Fifth Monarchy Men*, pp. 176–8 and App. I, *passim*; Richards, *Puritan Movement in Wales*, pp. 162–3, 215–6, 235 ff., 255 ff.; R. Tudur Jones, 'The Life, Work and Thought of Vavasor Powell, 1617–1670' (unpublished D.Phil. thesis, Oxford Univ., 1947), pp. 48 ff., 82 ff., 295–6; Nuttall, *Visible Saints*, pp. 131–41.

[3] *Exact Relation*, p. 270; *CJ* vii, 284–5; Clarke MS XXV, fo. 87; *Perfect Diurnall*, no. 188, 11–18 July 1653, p. 2858; *Impartial Intelligencer*, no. 3, 12–19 July 1653, pp. 22–4; Thurloe, i, 368–9.

impropriators out of the estates of delinquents in England, Scotland, and Ireland.[4]

Whether or not such reports had any foundation, the whole question of tithes bristled with implications for property, and these were what dominated the next two days' debate. The House voted on the 16th to 'take into Debate the Property of Tythes in general', and according to *Mercurius Politicus* a move to confine discussion solely to the clergy's property in them was defeated.[5] Other and less official newspapers reported that the question argued at greatest length was whether property in impropriate tithes belonged by law to individuals or to the state.[6] They are not entirely clear, but they suggest that radical members were fundamentally questioning whether lay impropriators had any right of property at all. The challenge was certainly in the air. During that same day's debate the House favourably received a petition bearing thousands of signatures which called for the outright abolition of tithes and all other forced maintenance, without a word about compensation.[7] A Kentish petition of three or four weeks earlier, presented to Cromwell and Harrison and their fellow-officers (and promptly published), had been much more explicit. Against the claim of lay impropriators that they held their tithes by right of purchase, it asked

Of whom did they buy them? You say of the Kings and Bishops; so that by your ground, and so it is, that they bought them not of the people, from whom they so violently take them. 2. By what Law either of God or Nature, that one man shall sell away the labour of another, and the increase that God giveth him, when there is no forfeiture by transgression committed by him? 3. Kings and Bishops sold them as they were arbitrary and tyrannical by Monarchy, and not by the free consent of the now present people. 4. Monarchy is now conquered, and

---

[4] *Several Proceedings of State Affairs*, no. 198, 7–14 July 1653, pp. 3134–5; *A Supply to a Draught of an Act* ([27 Apr.] 1653), pp. 36–7; Clarendon MS 46, fo. 112.

[5] *CJ*, vii, 285; *Mercurius Politicus*, no. 162, 14–21 July 1653, p. 2595.

[6] *Perfect Diurnall*, no. 188, 11–18 July 1653, p. 2860: ' . . . the businesse concerning propriety of Tithes, whether it was in the State or particular persons'. cf. *Several Proceedings of State Affairs*, no. 199, 14–21 July 1653, p. 3145: 'that about Impropriators was much waved: the chief part of the debate falling upon appropriate tithes, and proprieties set apart for pious uses; whether that was by law in the States [*sic*] or in those particular persons, who claim it'.

[7] *To the Parliament of the Commonwealth of England* ([25 July] 1653, erroneously dated 6 July in Thomason Catalogue), reprinted in *Mercurius Politicus*, no. 163, 21–28 July 1653, pp. 2596–600.

all kingly government proclaimed down, and then in the fall of Monarchy, all tyrannicalness fell with it ... so we the people of England having been under the Prerogative power of Kings oppressed, thereby ought we now* to make good their bargains and sales of Tythes, which we were forced unto by their tyranizing, seeing that we are now come to the time of promised freedom?[8]

The petition went on to denounce impropriators as unfit to bear rule in the Commonwealth, since they grew rich by wronging others and gathered in what they had neither sown nor reaped.

The same theme of property evidently dominated the full day's debate on 18 July, when the House finally voted to 'descend from the general to the particular Consideration of the Propriety of Tythes'. This can be taken to mean that it had determined in principle that property in tithes existed, and that it now intended to consider the cases of clerical incubents and lay impropriators separately. The next day was the last on which the House as a body debated tithes, and as it proceeded a contest developed between moderates and radicals over whether to refer the whole question to a committee. Attendance was still high, with 110 members present at the crucial division compared with 116 on the 15th, for this was a matter on which feelings ran deep. The abolitionists opposed the committee, doubtless because they disapproved of the whole exercise on which it was to be engaged, but Harrison and Blount as tellers could muster only forty-nine Noes, and it would be unwarrantable to suppose that all of these were totally opposed to a publicly maintained ministry. Against them Pickering and Ashley Cooper counted fifty-six Yeas, so the famous committee for tithes was promptly constituted.

Its particular brief was 'to take into Consideration the Propriety of Incumbents in Tythes'. Highland explains that since 'all seemed free and willing that impropriators should be satisfied the value', the committee was directed to concern itself only with providing for ministers. But interesting as his evidence is about the members' general attitude towards impropriators he was wrong about the committee's terms of reference, for it was instructed 'also to consider the Propriety of Rectors, and all Possessors of Donatives, or propriate Tythes', and in due course

---

* The original law has 'not now', but this destroys the sense of the passage and must be an error.

[8] *No Age like unto this Age* ([24 June] 1653), pp. 16–17, 22.

it reported about these too. In view of its contentious business it is striking that the choice of its thirty-two members seems to have been quite smooth, for there is no record in the *Journal* that any of their names were challenged or even separately voted upon. Perhaps this is because they were just about exactly balanced between moderates and radicals—using those terms in the general sense defined in the last chapter, for it is naturally impossible to establish the precise standpoint of each one of the tithes issue. They certainly included many of the most active and influential men in the House, with Sadler, Strickland, Sydenham, Ashley Cooper, Roberts, Tichborne, Desborough, and Colonel Clarke prominent on one side and Harrison, Moyer, Barebone, Highland, Danvers, Courtney, Squibb, Blount, Kenrick, West, Spence, and Swinton on the other. Special care of the committee was committed to Sadler, West, and Taylor (a member of George Cokayne's congregation, like Tichborne and Ireton), and it was to meet every Wednesday and Friday in the Exchequer Chamber. In the terms of appointment the formula 'and all that come to have Voices' gave every member of the House the right to attend and express his views.[9]

This check to the abolitionists' hopes should have given pause to all those hostile members of the public who had assumed that the new supreme assembly was a nest of sectaries, but there is no sign that it did so. The House itself had no doubt strengthened that distorted impression by its first enthusiastic declaration of its objectives and by its practice of dispensing with ordained ministers in its daily prayers. Yet when it appointed a day of thanksgiving on 25 August for the naval victory off the Texel, it voted, as the Long Parliament had done on such occasions, to hold its own devotions in St. Margaret's Church and to invite two famous preachers to lead them. Its choice fell on Walter Cradock and John Owen, and at the same time it asked Cradock to preach to the members in St. Margaret's every Sunday morning.[10] Owen, whose temperate zeal was already justifying

---

[9] *CJ*, vii, 286, 361; *Exact Relation*, p. 270; *Mercurius Politicus*, no. 163, 21–28 July 1653, p. 2600. The other moderates on the committee were Nathaniel Barton, Frere, Gill, Horseman, Anthony Rous, Stone, Wingfield, and Wolmer; the other radicals were Herring, Jaffray, Plumstead, and Taylor. Taylor's radicalism is questionable, but he is balanced by Wingfield, who though a moderate in most respects was a campaigner against tithes: see p. 187.

[10] *CJ*, vii, 297.

Cromwell's choice of him as Vice-Chancellor of Oxford University, calls for no further comment; but Cradock, whose high contemporary reputation was unduly forgotten until Dr Nuttall restored it, was an ideal choice for a body whose religious spectrum was so broad. Although he had founded the first Independent church in Wales, whereby Vavasor Powell and Morgan Llwyd had become his converts and friends, and although he had been an intinerant preacher in South Wales for years before the Propagation, his spirit was essentially tolerant and ecumenical. 'Presbytery and Independency are not two religions', he wrote in 1648, 'but one religion to a godly, honest heart; it is only a little rufling of the fringe.'[11] His sympathies were to remain as broad as ever under the Protectorate, which he was to serve as a Trier and Ejector while many of his former disciples went into militant opposition, and he lived—though only just—to be one of the select group of ministers invited to attend Cromwell's funeral.

Such signs of moderation, however, were offset in the public mind by sundry manifestations of sectarian enthusiasm which the very existence of Barebone's Parliament seemed to encourage, and by the strident millenarian addresses that were made to it. A woman called Mrs Pool, for example, caused scandal by preaching her strange illuminations on several successive Sundays in Somerset House Chapel. On 17 July only a guard of soldiers saved her from being stoned, and a week later it dispersed her congregation and ordered it to meet there no more. That same day another guard had to use force to stop a company of Shakers from taking over St. James's Chapel for their exercises, but the soldiery did not always act the role of peace-keepers, for in Westminster Abbey on the 17th they drowned a sermon that displeased them with their drums and trumpets.[12]

As for petitions and addresses, John Spittlehouse led the way as soon as what he called 'the Assembly of Elders' met by publicly setting forth the extreme Fifth Monarchist case against tithes.

[11] W. Cradock, *Gospel-Libertie* (1648), p. 135, quoted by G. F. Nuttall in *The Welsh Saints*, pp. 16–17, where full justice is done to Cradock's career and beliefs. On Owen see Peter Toon, *God's Statesman: the Life and Work of John Owen* (Exeter, 1971), esp. chs. III and IV.

[12] Clarendon MS 46, fos. 113, 130; Thurloe, i, 368; *The True and Perfect Dutch-Diurnall*, 19–26 July 1653, p. 11; *Weekly Intelligencer*, no. 129, 19–26 July 1653, p. 930; *Several Proceedings of State Affairs*, no. 199, 14–21 July 1653, p. 3149.

Let them consider whether the present priesthood of the nation was *jure divino*, he urged; if it was not, let it be dealt like 'the old Harlot, and her eldest daughter Prelacy'.[13] John Canne followed a few weeks later with *A Second Voice from the Temple to the Higher Powers*, and the message was much the same: that tithes, a national ministry, and the restriction of preaching to ordained clergy were the institutions of popes and popish councils, and that it was this parliament's duty to abolish them all. 'The Lord is now taking vengeance, and doing execution upon Babylon', he warned; he will 'command his sanctified ones, and call his mighty ones, to fulfill all his pleasure upon the great whore ... Whether you be the men whom the Lord will honour in this worke, I know not, but this I know, it is speedily to be done; for Sion is in travail, and ready to bring forth.'[14] Arguments about legal property in tithes were irrelevant for Canne: 'The National Ministry, commonly called the Ministry of the Church of England ... is a plant which the heavenly Father never planted, and therefore to be pluckt up by the roots (howsoever established by Law).'[15]

Between these published addresses by Spittlehouse and Canne, the House received on 4 August an equally millenarian petition from some JPs of Kent. They hailed not just the dawn but the approaching noon of the reign of Christ, and craving relief from 'one Grand Burthen' they begged 'That Tythes of all sorts, Root and Branch, may be abolished, That that Jewish and Antichristian Bondage and Burthen on the Estates and Consciences of the godly may cease, and that we may not be insnared with forced maintenance, or anything like it in the stead thereof.' The Speaker acknowledged their good affections and told them noncommittally 'that the House will do therein as the Lord shall direct'.[16]

---

[13] Spittlehouse, *The First Addresses*, pp. 6 ff.

[14] J. Canne, *A Second Voice from the Temple of the Higher Powers*, Sig. A2–2ᵛ.

[15] Ibid., p. 4; *cf.* pp. 12–14. A further attack on any kind of established clergy, set apart by ordination, was published by John Webster, a former preacher to the army, in *The Saints Guide, or Christ the Rule, and Ruler of Saints* (1653), of which Thomason acquired identical copies on 17 Aug. and 12 Sept.; but since the dedicatory epistles are dated 28 Apr. 1653 this interesting tract was probably written in response to the dissolution of the Rump rather than to the debates of July-August.

[16] *CJ*, vii, 295; *To the Parliament: The Petition of many of the well-affected of the County of Kent* (4 Aug. 1653), reprinted in *Mercurius Politicus* and other newspapers.

This sectarian pressure against any kind of national church quite soon produced a backlash, which came initially not from the conservative Presbyterians but from those Independent congregations which called themselves the churches of Christ. It was encouraged when the House decided on 22 August to broaden its discussions to the larger questions of ecclesiastical settlement which the Rump had failed to determine. On the 26th, which it devoted to a full debate on 'the business of religion', it heard two petitions, one from three churches of Christ in Devonshire and the other from several in Gloucestershire. Both called for the removal of profane and unworthy ministers and their replacement by zealous ones, thus affirming the mainstream Puritan conviction that the state should bear a responsibility for providing godly preachers, though neither mentioned tithes. The Devonshire one was the more explicit, and since it found an immediate and positive response in the House it is worth quoting. It asked:

That the godly, faithfull and conscientious Ministers of the Gospel in all place[s], may be setled, duly countenanced and encouraged; That some course may be taken for their comfortable subsistence out of the publique Treasury, in such places where it cannot be otherwise raised: it being the Law of Christ, who hath ordained, That they which preach the Gospel should live of the Gospel, and that they may not wholly be left to the voluntary contributions of the people; which way of maintenance hath been usually attended with several inconveniences, temptations and snares.[17]

The petition further asked for commissioners to be appointed in every county to remove ignorant and scandalous clergymen, for the power of presentation to be taken from loose and profane men and given to others more fitly qualified, and for 'a select number of Ministers and others' to approve the godliness and abilities of every new incumbent. This was a striking anticipation of the Cromwellian ordinances of 1654, and it also foreshadowed the Protectoral concept of a 'public profession' of the Christian religion by asking, 'That there may be some choice and able men appointed and set apart to maintain the Truths of Christ against

[17] *CJ*, vii, 306, 308. Both petitions are printed in *Several Proceedings of Parliament*, no. 6, 23–30 Aug. 1653, pp. 69–75, and the Devon one (from churches in Exeter, Bideford, and Luppit) in *Mercurius Politicus*, no. 168, 25 Aug.–1 Sept. 1653, where the quoted passage is on pp. 2696–7.

the subverters of the Faith, and also to reconcile the Differences amongst the godly.'[18]

The outcome of the day's debate on 26 August was a vote, very much in the spirit of these petitions, to appoint a committee to bring in proposals for some means of ejecting ignorant, profane, and scandalous ministers and of encouraging godly and able preachers of the Gospel. This was followed by a further vote to refer the matter to the existing committee for tithes, whose responsibility was thus immensely enlarged. In fulfilling it, that committee was to provoke the final and fatal breach.[19]

The case for maintaining a parochial ministry was further made in a petition from the corporation of Sudbury in Suffolk, which was read in the House on 19 September. It was couched in the language of the saints and it was radical in its plea 'that the unGospel-like Power of Patrons be taken away', but it offered the interesting argument that out-and-out voluntaryism might work to the advantage of Anglican priests. It asked 'That a competent and certain maintenance may be setled (as your honors shall think fit) for godly and painful Preachers in all places, that such may not be exposed unto Tempations of Men-pleasing, nor Malignant Service Book men introduced by that device, of leaving Ministerial maintenance to every mans will and lust.'[20] Another petition, presented a fortnight later by 'the godly party' in Shropshire and full of the rhetoric of the saints, likewise called for 'some speedy course' for the ejection of unworthy ministers and for settling fit and faithful ones in their place.[21]

Few petitioners solicited the parliament in favour of retaining tithes, but the Lord Mayor and Corporation of London were a weighty exception. The petition which a delegation headed by Stephen Estwick, the City Sheriff, presented on 2 September paid pointed tribute to the Long Parliament's encouragement of godly ministers, and reprehended the scorn and contempt that had lately been cast upon them. It particularly deplored 'what endeavours are used by Petitioning and otherwise to destroy the Universities, and undermine the preaching of the Gospel, by

[18] Ibid. 2697.
[19] *CJ*, vii, 308.
[20] Printed in *Mercurius Politicus*, no. 171, 15–22 Sept. 1653, pp. 2746–7.
[21] Printed in *Mercurius Politicus*, no. 173, 29 Sept.–6 Oct. 1653, pp. 2774–8.

taking away that ancient setled Maintenance which hath been Owned and Acknowledged as their due, by all Parliaments and Courts of Justice, time out of mind.'[22] With typical Presbyterian extravagance these City counter-petitioners saw in such efforts the hand of the Jesuits, who would come close to achieving their design against England if they could get her clergy disestablished and her civil government debarred from any authority over religion. The only other such plea was more moderate; it came from Hampshire and was presented by the Recorder of Winchester and others on 28 September. It urged the retention of tithes, 'at leastwise until the right of patrons be legally determined', and until a no less productive alternative provision had been established, with due satisfaction for the interests of impropriators. It expressly confuted the recent petition from Kent, but the House returned the same impartial answer, namely that it would do as God should direct it.[23]

The defence of tithes, however, was less often presented directly to the parliament, in which conservatives had little confidence, than in pamphlets and treatises aimed at the reading public. In this genre the abolitionists were outnumbered and outgunned. The only fresh items which Thomason collected from their side during September were a broadsheet entitled *Twelve Queries ... about the two soule-oppressing yokes of a Forced Maintenance and Ministry* and another effusion from John Spittlehouse, addressed to the committee for tithes.[24] Against these slight and unoriginal contributions, the same month saw the publication of at least eight vindications of tithes and an established clergy, some of them substantial.[25] One 'Theophilus Philadelphus', for example, devoted over sixty pages to refuting the anti-tithes petitions which the House had heard on 16 July and 4 August.[26] William Prynne's *A Gospel Plea* laboured the case

[22] *To the Supreme Authority of the Nation ... The Petition of the Lord Mayor* [etc.] (2 Sept. 1653), reprinted in *Mercurius Politicus*, no. 169, 1–8 Sept. 1653, pp. 2712–14.

[23] *Severall Proceedings of State Affairs*, no. 209, 22–9 Sept. 1653, pp. 3311–12; *CJ*, vii, 325–326.

[24] *Twelve Queries* ([12 Sept.] 1653); J. Spittlehouse, *An Explanation of the Commission of Jesus Christ* ([22 Sept.] 1653).

[25] *An Item against Sacriledge* ([1 Sept.] 1653); *A brief Apologie for the pious and painfull Ministers of the Church of England* ([12 Sept.] 1653); *The Right of Tithes asserted: by our old Saxon Lawes* ([6 Sept,] 1653); Bevill Turmiger, *A Briefe Treatise concerning the chiefe dispute of this time about Tithes* ([8 Sept.] 1653); and the pieces cited in notes 26–8 and 36.

[26] Theophilus Philadelphus, *Exceptions many and just against the two Injurious Petitions* ([9 Sept.] 1653).

for the sacred tenth at nearly three times that length, on scriptural, rational, and legal grounds, and it was with this work that Milton mainly joined issue (though without naming it) six years later in the *Considerations Touching the Likeliest Means to Remove Hirelings out of the Church.*[27] Shorter, but to most contemporary readers probably more persuasive, was *The Case of Ministers Maintenance by Tithes* by John Gauden, the compiler of *Eikon Basilike* and future Bishop of Worcester. Its well-sustained argument was a refreshing change from all those tracts of the 1650s which plundered Selden's *Historie of Tithes* to demonstrate that the traditional maintenance had had the sanction of law from Offa's and Æthelwulf's reigns onwards, and concluded that the clergy's right to it rested on the same unquestionable basis as a landlord's to his rent. Since the feeling in favour of tithes remained so strong that they survived all attacks, and since the emphasis so far has been on the abolitionists' and reformists' cases, it is worth pausing to summarize Gauden's arguments for retaining them, not because he was particularly original but because he stated competently what most conservative church-men believed.

He was hardly tactful in telling the parliament-men that it would ill become them, 'being but extraordinary, and temporary Pilots, applyed to the helm of this State, to preferre your counsels or conclusions before those of your wise and godly forefathers',[28] but they were not the audience to which he was primarily appealing. As a priest and scholar he concentrated mainly on arguments from the Scriptures and from the practice of Christian churches. He had to face the contention, endlessly repeated by his opponents, that since tithes were not specifically enjoined any-where in the New Testament, what had been divinely ordained for the Levitical priesthood was not only invalid for a Gospel ministry, being merely judaical and ceremonial, but also superstitious and offensive to Christian consciences. He replied that tithes were older than the Law, since Melchizedeck had received them from Abraham and Jacob had vowed them to God. There were many 'Patternes of Prudence and Policy in Church or State' which had been observed by the Jews and

---

[27] W. Prynne, *A Gospel Plea ... for the Lawfulness and Continuance of the ancient settled Maintenance* ([24 Sept.] 1653).

[28] J. Gauden, *The Case of Ministers Maintenance by Tithes* ([14 Sept.] 1653), p. 5.

remained 'by Gods pattern recommended as best to Christians', such as the practice of prayer and praise, keeping the Sabbath holy, giving to the poor, and reconciling quarrels before coming to the altar. By such analogies, Gauden maintained, tithes 'are Gods still after the Law, as they were his in a Religious light before the Law'.[29]

Where he stood furthest from all radical Puritans was in his contention that Christ did not abolish all priesthood, 'but onely he changed the Aaronical line, order and Ceremony of Succession; himself continuing a King and Priest for ever after the order of Melchisedeck',[30] whence it followed that he never annulled the ancient priestly right to tithes. The reasons for the New Testament's silence about them, Gauden argued, lay in the special circumstances of Christ's own ministry and of the young churches under persecution. When persecution ceased and the spontaneous fervour of the earliest age passed, a settled income for the clergy again became proper, and divine precept again enjoined tithes as its source. So did Origen, Cyprian, Jerome, Augustine, and other early Fathers, and in time tithes were confirmed by imperial edicts, church councils, and the positive laws of particular countries. Summing up, Gauden upheld them on grounds of natural equity, the word of God, the 'Catholick custome anciently observed by beleevers in all times and places of setled Churches',[31] the free donation of many early English benefactors of the Church, and the immemorial laws of the land.

He vehemently opposed the proposals, currently advanced by some reformists, that the government should bring all church revenues into a common purse and dispense equitable stipends from it. He thought this would debase both clergy and people, 'where, besides the brow, coyness, the insolencies and the swellings of the givers, (which the poor Minister must bear, from those, upon whose almes he must depend:) his hungry and flexible soul will soone be warpt to the warmer beames of the liberall hands that drop fatness, and wholly be withdrawn from any care or regard of the poorer sort of people.'[32] This reads more like an argument against dependence on voluntary

---

[29] Ibid. 9–10.
[30] Ibid. 12.
[31] Ibid. 22 *et* 17–25 *passim*.
[32] Ibid. 35.

offerings than against the state as paymaster, and it would have lost what force it had if the agencies which selected the approved candidates for livings were separated from those which fixed and paid their stipends. Clerical servility was much likelier to result from the vast post-Reformation extension of lay patronage, but about that Gauden had nothing to say, for he probably realized that if and when Anglican supremacy was restored it would find in gentry patronage an indispensable mainstay. For similar reasons, perhaps, he did not squarely face the problem of lay impropriators. He may have been condemning them obliquely when he called it a sin 'for any man to challenge to himself this maintenance, who is no minister in the sense of the law',[33] but he was probably thinking more of unordained and itinerant preachers, for whom he had a large contempt. The Gospel of Christ, he said, would never be propagated by 'arbitrary, weak and disorderly teachers; by ambulatory pensioners, by vagrant and inconstant journeymen'.[34] To all the complaints of the economic hardship of tithes he could rejoin only with some rather insensitive rhetoric, and with the threadbare argument that no one parted with his property in paying them, since tithes were not part of any man's estate but 'a publike patrimony, to which God is proprietor, and his Ministers are his pensioners'.[35]

On 14 September, the same day on which Thomason bought Gauden's tract, the committee for tithes heard learned counsel argue the case for the right of patrons to their advowsons and of rectors, both lay and clerical, to their tithes. The argument was highly technical, but it was taken down in shorthand and published.[36] The committee had been under pressure to take legal opinion on the right to tithes, to the indignation of radicals like Canne. No one doubted, he wrote, that there were laws and statutes to compel the payment of tithes, but they were bad laws and it was this parliament's duty to abrogate them.[37] It is significant that the question of lay patronage had become conjoined with that of tithes in the committee's deliberations, as

[33] Ibid. 28.
[34] Ibid. 45.
[35] Ibid. 39.
[36] *An Argument in Defence of the Right of Patrons to Advowsons, as it was delivered to the Committee for Tythes, 14 Sept. And incidently of the Right of Tithes in general* (14 Sept. 1653). Thomason wrote on it 'by Counseller Nortclife'.
[37] J. Canne, *A Second Voyce from the Temple*, p. 12.

it had in more than one of the petitions that have been referred to. This was another issue with powerful implications for rights of property, and though two more months were to elapse before the House pronounced on it, the fact that it was under debate cannot have been lost on those whose distrust of Barebone's Parliament was growing steadily.

If tithes kept the presses tolerably busy, Lilburne's case easily outdid them during these months in the sheer quantity of printed matter than it generated. What calls for attention here is not its merits or its detailed progress, but its impact on Barebone's Parliament and on the prevailing political climate. Tracts and broadsheets are not the only evidence that the Leveller cause enjoyed a brief Indian summer after Lilburne's return, but they played their part in winning him strong popular sympathy. During July and August alone Thomason collected twenty-five pieces bearing on his case, only two of them hostile, and these do not include the countless reports and comments in the weekly newspapers, among which Daniel Border's *Faithful Scout* and Robert Eeles's *Faithful Post* campaigned particularly hard in his favour. Foreign envoys reported his trial to their governments as eagerly as did the newswriters to the exiled court. The London public expressed its interest and compassion in demonstrations which recalled the heyday of the movement, and at Westminster the parliament itself was divided and disturbed.

Lilburne, it will be remembered, had been behaving with extraordinary inconsistency. Since his banishment early in 1652 he had, as the English government well knew, been mixing freely with a group of prominent royalist exiles, and whatever he actually undertook to them, some of them believed that he was ready on the right conditions to lend all his own and his party's support to restoring the king. Shortly before the Rump was expelled he managed to publish in England a violent diatribe against the army, denouncing Cromwell as 'the grandest Tyrant and Traytor, that ever England bredd'.[38] After the dissolution, however, he soon changed his tune. Hoping that those who had broken the Rump would feel for him as its victim, and longing

---

[38] *L. Colonel John Lilburne revived* ([27 March] 1653), quoted in Gregg, *Free-Born John*, p. 320. The sources for the ensuing paragraphs, where not specifically cited here, are given in Miss Gregg's admirable biography.

to see London again, he wrote by his own account 'many humble addresses' to Cromwell, one of which he published in three countries and in four languages. But even if he had not wrecked his chances by his traffic with the royalists, his presence could only have been an embarrassment during the delicate interregnum from April to July, and the Council of State ignored his pleas for a pass. He then decided to return without one. Evidently he reckoned that he had three strings to his bow: Cromwell and the Council of State might not care to proceed against him, or if they did he might get the Rump's dubious judgement reversed in a court of law, or he might prevail on the new supreme authority to repeal its predecessor's Act of Banishment.

His addresses to the interim government continued to vacillate between invective and pleading. From Dunkirk on 23 May he wrote a wildly vituperative letter to Cromwell, accusing him of every kind of baseness from causing the death of three of his children to instructing Thomas Scot to hire assassins to murder him.[39] He followed this up on 4 June, while awaiting a passage to Calais, with an equally truculent address to the Council of State, which he denounced as a mere cheating cover for Cromwell's ambition to make himself in due course perpetual dictator. Since the forthcoming assembly was not to be chosen by the people but by the army officers, he maintained, it could bear no legal authority but only 'the perfect badge of Conquest'.[40] He scornfully dismissed the question, which he said some of the Council of Officers had put to his wife, whether he would live quietly and privately if he returned home; indeed he boasted that 'My interest is none of the meanest in England; but even among the hobnails, clouted shoes, the private souldiers, the leather and woollen Aprons, and the laborious and industrious people in England, is as formidable, as numerous, and as considerable as any one amongst your whole selves, not excepting your very General; (let him but lay down his sword and become disarmed as I am).'[41]

Ten days later, after a last night out with Buckingham and other royalists at the Silver Lion in Calais, he sailed, and reached

[39] J. Lilburne, *The Upright Mans Vindication* (1 Aug. 1653), pp. 25–7.

[40] Ibid. 11 *et passim*. The fact that these addresses survive only in this pamphlet, which Lilburne published from Newgate after the first phase of his trial, raises a slight doubt as to whether he really sent them to Cromwell and the Council just before his return home.

[41] Ibid. 15.

London the same night. At once he sent his old friend William Kiffin, now the lay pastor of a Particular Baptist congregation, to Whitehall with a very different letter to Cromwell, in which he emotionally cast his life and all that was his on the General's mercy. He now promised his perfect submission to the present and future governments, and offered either to serve the Commonwealth in whatever way he best could, or if that was not acceptable to retire to a totally private life.[42] Kiffin was not admitted, but the letter was on the bookstalls the next day. By that time the Council of State had sent orders to the Lord Mayor for Lilburne's arrest, which was promptly effected. The prisoner addressed two more appeals to Cromwell within a week, the first from the City Sheriff's custody and the second from Newgate.[43] They too were immediately published, and in all three the histrionic pathos, playing much on his wife's tears and importunities and on the constant hazard to his own life in exile, suggests as strongly as their timing that they were aimed at public consumption from the start. So obviously were his two letters of 1 and 10 July to the Lord Mayor, protesting against the latter's compliance with the order for his arrest and challenging in detail the justice and legality of the act for his banishment. By this time his own pleas were being strongly seconded by the petitions and remonstrances of his sympathizers.[44]

Nevertheless his first recourse had failed. Neither the Council nor the Lord Mayor had shown any hesitation about committing him, and he now had to fight his case in a court of law. By the provisions of the act he had only to set foot in the Commonwealth's territory to incur the death penalty as a felon, and all that a court had to do was to establish his presence and identity. But whether a jury would find against him, and whether if it did the government would dare to send him to the gallows, remained to

---

[42] J. Lilburne, *The Banished mans suit for Protection to the Lord Generall Cromwell* (14 June 1653). Thomason acquired this broadsheet on the 15th.

[43] *CSPD 1652–3*, pp. 410, 415, 436; J. Lilburne, *A Second Address directed to the Lord Generall Cromwell, and the Councell of State* (16 June, 1653), and *A Third Address* (to the same: 20 June 1653).

[44] J. Lilburne, *The Prisoner's most mournful Cry* (1 July 1653); *The second Letter from John Lilburne ... to the Lord Major* (10 July 1653); *Lieu. Col. John Lilburn's Plea in Law* (2 July 1653); *A Jury-man's Judgement upon the case of Lieut. Col. John Lilburne*, ([22 June] 1653); Samuel Chidley, *An Additional Remonstrance* (22 June 1653), pp. 19–20; *The Petition rejected by the Parliament* (i.e. the Rump: [24 June] 1653); further petitions in *The Faithful Scout, passim.*

be seen. For all his promises of submission he had thrown down a challenge, and Edward Hyde wrote to a fellow-exile that he would judge of Cromwell's power and interest according to whether John Lilburne were hanged or not. Cromwell at least promised him a fair trial. It was first fixed for 21 June, but at Lilburne's request it was postponed until after Barebone's Parliament had met.[45]

He had among its members-designate at least one friend in Samuel Highland, who (it will be recalled) prayed for him publicly, if not by name, at the Monday prayer-meeting at Blackfriars on 27 June.[46] For all his recent damning words against non-elected legislatures, Lilburne and his supporters started by treating the new assembly with great respect and assumed that it had full authority to reverse the Rump's enactments.[47] They soon began a campaign of petitions to it, not all of which are recorded in the *Journal* because not all were heard. The first to be formally received was from Hertfordshire, and it was read on 13 July, the day the trial opened. Its effect was countered, however, by a lengthy statement which Strickland presented from the Council of State, exposing Lilburne's dealings with the royalists in a series of damaging testimonies and examinations. This body of evidence was already on the bookstalls that morning, officially printed; copies were distributed to the members of the court before which Lilburne was about to appear, and were handed out by army officers at the head of their troops.[48]

Lilburne himself addressed a petition to what he now called 'the Supreme Authority for the Commonwealth of England', urging it to stop the proceedings against him. He dated it 12 July, but it was not read until the 14th, towards the end of a long day's business. It was full of professions of injured innocence, dismissing 'any suspicions of his compliance with Charles Stuart, or his party' as 'a poysonous ingredient that his Adversaries have always in readinesse to cast into his Dish, though they know it as

---

[45] Gregg, *Free-Born John*, pp. 325–6; *CSPD 1652–3*, p. 346.

[46] Clarendon MS 46, fo. 32.

[47] Lilburne, *A Third Address* (final paragraph); *The Faithfull Scout*, no. 120, 8–15 July 1653, p. 1081; and further below.

[48] Clarendon MS 46, fo. 82; *CJ*, vii, 284; *Several Informations and Examinations taken concerning Lieutenant-Colonell John Lilburne* ([13 July] 1653); J. Lilburne, *Malice Detected* ([13 July] 1653).

false as Hell'. Whatever company he had kept in exile, he affirmed that 'he never in the least staggered in his fidelity to the cause of liberty and freedome that he first engaged in'. He clearly aimed his peroration at the millenarian wing: 'Oh dear Christians, quench not that good Spirit; and his deliverence cannot be far off; and honour and indear your selves at the first beginning in the eyes of the honest People of England.'[49] His case was not improved, however, by the presentation on the same day of a mass petition from his sympathizers in London. It roused the House's suspicion because the text was clearly freshly penned, whereas the signatures, which were attached on a torn and soiled paper, looked as though they had been written long ago.[50] Nevertheless his own appeal caused quite a long and sharp debate, 'some members of the house earnestly moving to have had his trial suspended, and the act called in question by which he was banished and made a felon, that the merit of the cause might be looked into; which they professed again and again they did not do it so much in the favour of Mr. Lilburne, as in the right of themselves and their posterities, and all Englishmen'. But the majority, especially the 'gentlemen of note', were so strongly against him that the House voted without a division not to suspend his trial.[51]

By that time it had been in progress for nearly two days. It was held before the London Sessions at the Old Bailey, and those taking part included Baron Wilde, Attorney-General Prideaux, Lord Mayor Fowke, and Recorder Steele. Lilburne showed all his old talent for reducing the court to impotent exasperation and for playing to the crowd. A large crowd it was, too, not just packing the courtroom but noisily thronging the neighbouring streets; several regiments of soldiers were employed in keeping a semblance of order. Papers were scattered about it bearing the lines:

---

[49] *To the Supreme Authority, for the Common-wealth of England* (date, 12 July 1653, from Newgate, and inadvertently omitted from Thomason Catalogue), p. 6; reprinted in *The Triall of Mr. John Lilburn* ([28 July 1553), in which see also p. 33.

[50] *CJ*, vii, 285.

[51] *CJ*, vii, 285; *Exact Relation*, p. 271. Highland's account telescopes the two phases of Lilburne's trial (in July and August), and the passage quoted comes after his mention of the apprentices' petition presented on 2 Aug., but it seems clearly to refer to the debate on Lilburne's own petition. He says that the House 'spent very much time, and held many sharp debates' on Lilburne's case and the various petitions on his behalf.

And what, shall then honest John Lilburne die?
Three score thousand will know the reason why.[52]

A past master in the art of protracting proceedings, Lilburne was really warming to his role by Saturday evening, the fourth day of his hearing, and the support of his friends in the courtroom became so vociferous that troopers with drawn swords were called in to restore quiet. Typically, he refused to proceed until they departed, but eventually he secured what he was contending for: the unusual concession of a copy of his indictment. It was signed by that busy MP John Sadler in his capacity as Town Clerk of London, and in this lay a stroke of irony, for Lilburne would shortly be quoting Sadler's *Rights of the Kingdom* at length in his own vindication. Sadler also signed the court's assignment of counsel to the prisoner, who promptly chose eight of the most famous lawyers in England. That done, the court adjourned until 10 August.[53]

Next day, flysheets pleading Lilburne's cause awaited the Sunday worshippers in many a church, and on Monday they were scattered about the streets.[54] The stream of pamphlets continued,[55] and a brief lull in the pressure on the parliament was broken when the formidable Mrs Katherine Chidley and a dozen other ladies appeared on several days in late July with a petition signed by 6,000 of their sex. Barebone was sent out to speak with them, and he found them more than he could handle.[56] Harder to ignore, because of its openly seditious tone and its immediate publication as a broadsheet, was a petition

---

[52] Thurloe, i, 367.

[53] *The Tryall of Mr. John Lilburne*, pp. 4–5, 13, *et passim*; Clarendon MS 46, fos. 82, 109–10; Bordeaux to Brienne, 18/28 July 1653, PRO 31.3/90, fo. 51; *CSP Ven 1653–4*, p. 109. Lilburne's quotations from Sadler are in his *The Afflicted Mans Out-Cry* (19 Aug. 1653).

[54] *The Faithful Post*, no. 121, 15–22 July 1653, p. 1083 (misprinted as 1567).

[55] *A Conference with the Soldiers* (16 July 1653); *Oyes, Oyes, Oyes* (16 July 1653); *A Caveat to those that shall resolve . . . to destroy J.L.* ([16 July] 1653); J. Lilburne, *The Upright Man's Vindication* (1 Aug. 1653).

[56] Clarendon MS 46, fo. 131; *To Parliament. The Petition of divers afflicted Women* (1653). Thomason wrote 'June 25' on this broadsheet (BL, 669.f.17(26)), which has misled some historians into imagining an earlier women's petition, presented before Barebone's Parliament formally opened. But Thomason's date was a slip for July 25, as is shown by the reprinting of the petition in several newspapers late in July, including *The Faithful Post*, no. 122, 19–26 July, pp. 1096–8. A second women's petition, *Unto every individual member of Parliament* ([29 July] 1653), complained that those who brought the first had attended for several days without being received, but it too was ignored by the House.

from Lilburne's apprentice supporters which six of their number presented on. 2 August:

You no sooner sate, but you voted yourselves the Parliament of the Common wealth of England; notwithstanding you all know you wanted the legal, formal election from the people, due to the Trust: What was it then, that induced you so to Vote, and afterwards declare your selves to be? Certainly, if any thing justly moved you thereunto, it was your reall purpose, that the Justice, life and power of a Parliament ... should be visible amongst you, and acted by you; and that you intended to do the proper works of a true Parliament, which without doubt, are to deliver the Captive, and set the Oppressed free.[57]

In failing to do so, did it not 'cease also from being a Parliament', the petition asked? This was too much, and the House called back the six who had delivered it. The speaker demanded their names, but their leader refused, saying that 'he was commanded, by the rest of his Friends and Fellow-Apprentices, Not to answer any Demands; but to demand an Answer to this Petition'. Four of the others declared under subsequent examination that they knew nothing of the petition until this man met them casually and 'persuaded [them] to go in with him to save a Mans life'.[58] The members were again divided, some in favour of subjecting the petitioners to exemplary punishment, others arguing that this would be 'but as the lion trampling on the mouse'. In the end all six were committed to Bridewell, while Lilburne, in Newgate, was ordered to be kept a close prisoner.[59]

The apprentices' petition was a sign that Leveller attitudes to Barebone's Parliament were changing from provisional acceptance to outright rejection and defiance, though a final respectful plea for Lilburne was addressed to it on the day his trial reopened.[60] He can hardly have expected its favour now, however. At the Old Bailey he spun out his last great public performance for ten days before he finally consented to make his

---

[57] *To every individual Member of Parliament, the representation of divers apprentices of London* (2 Aug. 1653). The Thomason Catalogue lists two editions, but only the broadsheet (669 f. 17 (38)) is the original petition; the pamphlet in E710(5) is a quite different piece, protesting against the gaoling of the six who presented the former.

[58] *CJ* vii, 294; *Several Proceedings of Parliament*, no. 3, 2–8 Aug. 1653, p. 26.

[59] *CJ*, vii, 294, 301; *Exact Relation*, p. 271.

[60] *A Voyce from the Heavenly Word of God* (10 Aug. 1653).

plea of Not Guilty on 20 August. Then his tongue really took fire, and it spoke his true feelings towards the regime. Not all his arguments were worthy of him, but his central one had uncomfortable force: either the Rump's rule had been as unjust and tyrannical as those who had interrupted it claimed, in which case its arbitrary proceedings against him should be annulled, or Cromwell had committed a high crime in expelling it and should be the first to be punished.[61] The court, of course, could not entertain such a plea. From its point of view the Act of Banishment was on the statute-book, and all that the jury had to do was to determine whether the prisoner was the John Lilburne named in it. But this jury was not to be directed, and late at night, after a long absence, it returned its famous verdict that he was 'not guilty of any crime worthy of death'.

In presuming to judge of law as well as fact, the verdict was of course irregular, but that did not prevent it from being extremely popular. A huge shout greeted it as the news spread from the courtroom into the streets, and the very soldiers who kept a massive guard on the precincts sounded their trumpets and beat their drums in sympathy.[62] The parliament, greatly disturbed, ordered the Council of State to examine the judges and jurymen immediately, but the result can have brought them no comfort. All the craftsmen and shopkeepers who composed the jury proved staunchly unrepentant, even defiant, though some admitted that they had met together to concert their verdict at Windmill tavern in Coleman Street on the morning of the 20th, and that they had deliberately gone against the ruling of the bench.[63] They were popular heroes, and to have proceeded further against them would have added fuel to the propaganda that Lilburne and his friends were naturally making out of his victory.[64] He had just made a shrewd bid to enlist the support of the Fifth Monarchy men by addressing a published account of his unjust treatment to Christopher Feake, whom he admitted he

[61] Gregg, *Freeborn John*, p. 332.

[62] *CSP Ven 1653–4*, p. 122; Thurloe, i, 429, 435, 441–2; Clarendon MS 46, fos. 173, 208; PRO 31.3/91, fo. 83.

[63] *CJ*, vii, 306, 309; [J. Canne], *Lieut. Colonel John Lilb. tryed and cast* ([22 Nov.] 1653), pp. 157–64.

[64] *The Tryall of L. Col. John Lilburn at the Session House* (1653: dated 19 Aug., but it covers the proceedings on the 20th too); *The Just Defence of John Lilburn* ([25 Aug.] 1653); contemporary numbers of *The Faithful Post*, *The Faithful Scout*, and *The Moderate Publisher*.

had not met, but whose growing discontent with the regime he clearly sensed.[65]

Council and parliament were in a most embarrassing position. When Lilburne had been committed in June, Cromwell had probably hoped that a verdict of Guilty would be duly secured, and that the new supreme authority would have a chance to gain a reputation for clemency by commuting the sentence from death to indefinite imprisonment. He might have been wiser to have advised the Council of State to indict its prisoner solely for his treasonable dealings with the royalists, not taking issue on the Act of Banishment at all, but the evidence may not have been watertight and there was no knowing how juries would behave when Lilburne was concerned. This particular jury had now faced the parliament with a most unwelcome political choice. Many members felt that in rejecting Lilburne's pleas in July they had endorsed an act of tyranny by their predecessors. If the government held him prisoner now, after the verdict, would it not compound that tyranny? Of what did he stand convicted? Yet if it freed him, all its enemies from royalists to Rumpers would interpret it as a confession of weakness, and it would alienate more powerful interests than it would please. There was the army to consider too; there were enough dangers of division in its ranks without risking a revival of Leveller agitation. It was too late now to think of charging him with his offences since his banishment, for he now had such a strong tide of popular feeling running for him that a further trial did not bear thinking about. What the House actually decided on 27 August, after what were evidently long and troubled debates, was that he should continue to be imprisoned 'for the Peace of this Nation', whereupon the Council transferred him to the Tower.[66] Barebone's Parliament thus saddled itself with its first political prisoner.

The Levellers' reply came during the night of 14 September, when a broadsheet was scattered about the streets containing *A Charge of High Treason exhibited against Oliver Cromwell Esq.* Its gravamen was that Cromwell, 'being a hired servant to serve the Lords the people of England',

did Traytorously and Villanously by force of armes dissolve the late

[65] J. Lilburne, *The Afflicted Mans Out-Cry* (20 Aug. 1653). For Feake's sympathetic attitude towards Lilburne in earlier years see Gregg, *Free-Born John*, pp. 154, 164, 311.
[66] *CJ*, vii, 309; *CSPD 1653–4*, pp. 98, 110–2, 105, 107.

Parliament of the Lords the people of England, . . . And further that he . . . did in an unheard of manner, summon and require upon great penalties, divers persons . . . to take upon them the Supreame Authority of this Common-wealth . . . and . . . in so doing did commit the highest of Treasons that could be committed; for that he the said Oliver did not intreat the Lords the people of England, to Elect their Representative, according to their indubitable Rights.[67]

The broadsheet further charged Cromwell, *inter alia*, with forcing this mock parliament 'to take away the body of our Law' in order to subject the nation to his tyranny. In order to bring him to justice, it called on all the people of England—masters, sons and (specifically) servants—to gather in arms on 16 October in every county town, elect as many members as were wont to represent them in parliament, and then, still under arms, escort them to Westminster.

The Council of State promptly appointed a strong committee to track down the perpetrators of this piece and four men were shortly arrested, including a printer and two tailors.[68] Lieutenant-Colonel Joyce, who as a cornet had abducted Charles I from Holmby, was cashiered, allegedly for saying he wished that the pistol pointed at Cromwell on Triploe Heath in 1647 had gone off, but some rumours linking him with the seditious broadside were probably mere speculation.[69] Later in the month an even wilder printed sheet was scattered about London's streets, headed *A Proclamation by the Supreme Lords the free-borne People of England*. It uttered lurid threats against all who abetted Cromwell, who in order to make the people of England his perpetual slaves and vassals

hath and doth daily take into Confederacy with himselfe, a Numerous Company of debauched and desolute Persons being the Rascallion and Scumme of the late Kings Army of the Nature of turkish Janizaries with certain servile Parasites of his one begetting, who terme themselves the Parliament of the Common-Wealth of England, a Councell of State, and a Councell of the Army, which in combination with that

---

[67] *A Charge of High Treason* [etc.] (1653), misdated 14 Aug. by Thomason, who recorded on his copy that it was scattered about the streets.

[68] *CSPD 1653–4*, pp. 151, 180, 187, 200; *CJ*, vii, 333.

[69] Clarendon MS 46, fo. 274; *CSP Ven 1653–4*, pp. 132–3; PRO 31.3/91, fos. 99, 101, 104. Joyce himself, in *A True Narrative of the occasions and causes . . .* which he published in 1659, maintained that the real motive for charging him with treason in Sept. 1653 had lain in a dispute over a purchase of land between himself and Richard Cromwell.

great Traitor, and Tirant Oliver Cromwell had usurped authority over us their Supreame Lord and Master, and hath broken all our fundamentall lawes, usages and Customes, and as wee are credibly informed, doe intend to burne all our Records that thereby they may have all our Estates, Liberties, and Lives at that their tirannicall Wills and Pleasures.[70]

The threatened day of Leveller action passed without incident, but a government-sponsored reply to *A Charge of High Treason* was published under the title *Sedition Scourg'd*. It was not the first or last piece of official anti-Leveller propaganda to appear under Barebone's Parliament,[71] but it is an adroit performance. Similarities of title and style suggest that it is by the same hand as *Confusion Confounded*, published three months later and plausibly attributed to John Hall, whose *Letter written to a Gentleman in the Country* some five months earlier had assured him the continuance of his state pension.[72] The interest of *Sedition Scourg'd* lies in the kind of defence that Cromwell and the Council of State were presumably willing to endorse. It is essentially a homily on *salus populi*, as to which it is 'the physician, that is to say, The wise man in power, that must be the judge, not the patient, that is to say, the multitude, in danger'. The wise man can only have been Cromwell, and those who charged him with denying the people their electoral rights must, Hall argues, want the nation either to

[70] BL, E714(7). This piece survives only in a MS copy in Thomason's collection. He wrote at the end of it 'This Libell was printed and scattered up and downe ye streets about ye latter end of September 1653.' It created no such stir as *A Charge of High Treason*, so perhaps only a small number of copies were broadcast.

[71] Besides *Several Informations and Examinations* (see n. 48), *A Letter to Leiutenant Collonel John Lilburn* ([8 Sept.] 1653: printed by the government's printer Henry Hills) had shrewdly exposed Lilburne's inconsistencies. In November John Canne's *Lieut. Colonel John Lilb. tryed and cast* was 'Published by Authority'.

[72] Thomason acquired *Sedition Scourg'd* on 20 Oct. 1653; on *Confusion Confounded*, which is attributed to Hall in the British Library's *General Catalogue of Printed Books*, see p. 327. Both works were printed by Henry Hills. On Hall and his *Letter Written To a Gentleman in the Country*, see p. 110 and P. S. Havens, 'A tract long attributed to Milton', *Huntington Library Bulletin*, no. 6 (1934), pp. 109–14. Anthony Wood, in *Athenae Oxonienses*, ed. P. Bliss, ii, 460, names among Hall's works an *Answer to the grand Politick Informer*, and *Sedition Scourg'd* (p. 9) refers the reader to *The Grand Politique Informer better Informed* in a manner which suggests that the same author wrote it. This is surely the same piece, though it appears not to survive under either title. I conclude that Hall wrote both it and *Sedition Scourg'd*. He had been given a salary of £100 p.a. in 1649, and the Council of State ordered a quarterly payment to him of £25 on 29 Sept. 1653: *CSPD 1649–50*, p. 139; *1653–4*, p. 173. It is highly likely that he was instructed to reply both to Streater's *Grand Politick Informer* and to *A Charge of High Treason*, and later to justify the dissolution of Barebone's Parliament.

relapse into strife or revert to its former tyranny: 'For certainly, no man would else, considering the different impressions that the late Civil Wars have made upon the minds of the people, permit them to a choice of their own governors, they being so divided and discomposed, as for the present they are, and working and being unquiet as the Sea after a storm.'[73] He is frank about what would have been the probable consequences of holding free elections in 1653: 'And therefore since, if the people had made use of that freedom, there had been little reason to have trusted the elected, without great consideration of their persons and garbling, and that this was a business which could not be done by a third power, it was rather thought fit, to stay, till he that can stop the raging of the Sea, would quiet the people's minds, [and] to select some particular worthy persons, of good life and conscience, out of the several counties, to that high and supreme trust.'[74] This passage supports the hypothesis that one of Cromwell's chief motives for stopping the bill for a new representative from passing had been that he dared not let general elections proceed without a stricter definition of future members' qualifications and an agreed role for the army in enforcing them.

The Leveller campaign proved to be short-winded, for it soon collapsed after the decision to keep Lilburne in prison. Weary and dejected, Lilburne himself wrote no more, and his supporters had neither the leadership nor the organization to sustain it without him. Contemporary observers overrated its strength, but Barebone's Parliament suffered by it, first by the further divisions it caused when the members were already falling apart over the issues of religious settlement and law reform, and secondly because it fostered an impression that radicals of all kinds were growing bolder under this government's wing, whether it contenanced them or not. Cromwell himself testified to this when, speaking to the parliament of 1654 about the state of the nation before he became Protector, he asked rhetorically: 'The magistracy of the nation, was it not almost trampled under foot, under despite and contempt by men of Levelling principles?'[75]

---

[73] *Sedition Scourg'd*, pp. 3, 8.
[74] Ibid. 9.
[75] Abbott, iii, 435.

When *A Charge of High Treason* accused Cromwell of forcing Barebone's Parliament 'to take away the body of our Law' it was at the same time attributing to him an initiative which he profoundly deplored and making a crime of what had once been a principal plank in the Leveller platform, namely the radical reform of the legal system. The agitation for law reform had a history at least as long as the Interregnum and the initiatives of 1653 constitute only one brief chapter in it,[76] but the debates of that year, in and out of parliament, revealed how wide the differences were among the would-be reformers. Some sought mainly practical or technical improvements which would expedite procedures, remove obscurities and ambiguities, resolve conflicts, cut out parasitic fees, and so on; others wanted chiefly to make the law more humane, by reducing the list of capital crimes, for example, and relieving insolvent debtors, while others again put religion first and sought to bring the law of the land into the closest accord with the revealed law of God. By this time the advocates of reform fell into three main schools. The first still venerated the common law as a unique guardian of personal and civic liberties, but wished to prune it of the dead wood of obstructive archaisms, to reduce its costs and delays, and to make it more widely available and intelligible to the lay public. Secondly there were the heirs of the Levellers, who decried the existing legal system as a relic of the Norman Yoke and aimed to establish a drastically simplified body of law which could be administered by popularly elected magistrates in every county or hundred, without the need for professional advocates or interpreters. Thirdly there were the radical millenarians who believed that in the imminent kingdom of Chirst all merely carnal laws must be abrogated in favour of the Mosaic code, or the precepts of the Gospels, or a blend of the two.

Interest in law reform had been intensified by the Hale Commission's activities in 1652, and although the Rump failed to enact any of its proposed measures, it did give a first reading on 20 and 21 January 1653 to the weightiest of them, called in

---

[76] See Donald Veall, *The Popular Movement for Law Reform* (Oxford, 1970); Charles R. Niehaus, 'The Issue of Law Reform in the Puritan Revolution' (unpublished Harvard Ph.D. thesis, 1957); Stuart E. Prall, *The Agitation for Law Reform in the Puritan Revolution* (The Hague, 1966); Mary Cotterell, 'Interregnum Law Reform', *EHR*, lxxxiii (1968), 689–704.

the *Journal* a 'Bill and Book containing the whole system of the Law' It also had three hundred copies printed,[77] and though these were intended for members only they inspired at least two pamphlets, partly welcoming and partly critical, which appeared after the dissolution.[78] Livelier than these, however, as a representative of those who wished to reform the common law without destroying it was the anonymous barrister who, having given up practising his profession 'as Epidemically evil', published *The Laws Discovery* in June. Many of the thirty wrongs that he identified concerned the law of debt, but they also included such medieval survivals as pressing to death for refusal to plead, trial by battle, and benefit of clergy, as well as the denial of counsel to those charged with capital crimes, the liability of copyholders to uncertain fines on entry, and the long incarceration which prisoners too poor to afford bail suffered before their trial.[79]

The more radical approach was exemplified in a petition which thousands of Londoners addressed to Cromwell and the army—ironically within a day of the Rump's violent end—reproaching them for failing to stand up for the people's interests against a parliament which was blatantly failing to fulful its promises to them.[80] Anticipating one of the next legislature's most notorious projects, it called for 'a new little book of only useful statutes, portable, that those that should keep them may know them', in place of the 'Voluminous Idol' of the common law. It also reiterated the demand, familiar since the Levellers' first spring, for the settlement of all civil actions by county courts, sitting regularly and frequently. To this *A Mite to the Treasury* added in June a plea for county registries to record all land transactions and for county courts to grant probate of wills.[81] There were other Leveller echoes in both documents, and the manifesto which the Levellers published just after Barebone's

---

[77] *CJ*, vii, 250. No copy is known to survive, but the two pamphlets cited in the next note attest that a printed edition was duly produced.

[78]. *A Supply to a Draught of an Act or System proposed . . . by the Committee for Regulations concerning the Law* ([27 Apr.] 1653); *Seasonable Observations on a late book intituled A System of the Law* ([7 July] 1653).

[79] *The Laws Discovery* ([27 June] 1653).

[80] *To His Excellency the Lord General Cromwel. The Humble Remonstrance of many thousands in and about the City of London* ([21 Apr.] 1653).

[81] J.W., *A Mite to the Treasury.*

Parliament met called for a whole range of legal reforms: no form of trial but by jury, no parliamentary encroachment on the judicial function, all witnesses to be sworn, bail to be allowed in all cases, punishments to be proportionable to offences, no fees to be taken by gaolers or officers of courts, no imprisonment for debt, and final settlement of all suits in hundred and county courts.[82] The idea of a two-tier system of local courts, in both hundreds and counties, was further developed in an obviously Leveller-inspired petition from Hampshire which survives among the papers of Richard Major, who sat for that county.[83]

In contrast with this secular and democratic radicalism, Fifth Monarchists were contending that only the laws contained in the Scriptures were to be observed in the imminent kingdom of Christ. Here is William Aspinwall, writing very soon after Barebone's Parliament met:

Though the Laws [of God] be few and brief, yet they are perfect and sufficient, and so large, as the wisdome of God judged needful for regulating Judgment in all Ages and Nations. For no action or case doth, or possibly can fall out in this or other Nations, by sea or land, but the like did, or possibly might fall out in the land of *Israel, Eccl.* 1.9. and yet they had not other Laws or Rules of Judgment, but what now remains to all posterity.[84]

When Barebone's Parliament grasped the nettle of legal reform, it took as its starting-point the sixteen draft bills which the Hale Commission had presented to the Rump a year earlier. On 12 July, more than a week before it appointed its first committee 'for the business of the law', it ordered that the whole set should be printed in a limited edition, one copy for each member of the House.[85] Curiously, *A Charge of High Treason* accused Cromwell personally of procuring its publication, but the decision was the parliament's, and it is very unlikely that he was present when it was taken. Seven of the twenty-one Hale Commissioners—Sadler, Moyer, Roberts, Ashley Cooper, Blount, Desborough, and Tomlinson—were members of the

[82] *The Fundamental Lawes and Liberties of England* pp. 3–4.

[83] BL, Add. MS 24,861, fo. 79ᵛ.

[84] Aspinwall, *A Brief Description of the Fifth Monarchy*, p. 11.

[85] *CJ*, vii, 284. The edition was entitled *Several Draughts of Acts heretofore prepared by Persons appointed to consider . . . the Proceedings of the Law*, and it is reprinted in *Somer Tracts*, vi, 177–245. Wing's *STC* lists only one surviving copy of the original, in the National Library of Scotland.

House, and they were ordered to peruse the bills and supervise their printing. The continuity between the Commission and Barebone's was even stronger, for the powerful nominating committee which the Rump had appointed to propose its membership had included Cromwell and six others who subsequently served on the interim Council of State from 30 April 1653 and were still serving.[86] But the Hale Commission had been on balance a moderate body, and its impressive work has lately been vindicated against the charges of impracticality and lack of professional competence which lawyers and historians used to level at it.[87] Eight of its members had been called to the bar, six more had studied at an Inn of Court, and its minutes show that 'the lawyers not the radicals dominated discussion and set the tone'.[88] Hale himself had been very much the steersman, and his guiding principles were first that any changes must be demonstrable improvements, secondly that they must fit within the framework of the existing constitution, and thirdly that they should be gradual.[89]

When Barebone's Parliament appointed its committee 'for the business of the law' on 20 July it took special care over its composition, judging by the exceptional number of names that were individually voted on. All seven of Hale's former fellow-commissioners were appointed, and the remaining twelve were a balanced body. Moderate men however predominated; of all the members only Moyer, Blount, Spence, Taylor, Coates, West, and Swinton can be rated on any grounds as radicals, and none of these were extremists. The ultra-radical Clerk of the Peace for Kent, Andrew Broughton, was proposed but rejected.[90] The committee was not without professional expertise, for Sir William Brownlow, John Brewster, Sadler, Spence, Taylor, and Wingfield had been called to the bar, Desborough and (probably) Coates had been attorneys, Swinton was learned in Scottish law and a commissioner for the adminstration of justice in Scotland, while Sir Anthony Ashley Cooper and Sir William Roberts had been

---

[86] The six were Carew, Harrison, Robert Bennett, Pickering, Strickland, and Philip Jones.

[87] See especially Cotterell, *passim*, but also Veall, pp. 79–83, and Niehaus, pp. 114–15.

[88] Cotterell, p. 694.

[89] Niehaus, pp. 117 ff., summarizing Hale's *Considerations Touching the Amendment or Alteration of Lawes*.

[90] *CJ*, vii, 284, 286. He was added to the committee on 20 October.

members of Lincoln's and Gray's Inns respectively. There was little prospect that these nineteen men would initiate a wholesale subversion of the common law, and nor did they.

Since this committee clearly launched itself upon the Hale Commission's draft bills from the beginning, it is necessary to describe briefly what it had before it. The first fifteen bills were quite short, running from half-a-dozen lines to at most two folio pages, as printed in the *Somers Tracts*. They aimed at relieving specific burdens, improving specific procedures, remedying specific abuses, and punishing specific offences, such as duelling, bribery, the sale of offices, drunkenness, and Sabbath-breaking, which were escaping the arm of the law. The final measure, however, was nearly five times as long as the rest put together and far more ambitious, and though it respected the basic fabric of the common law and equity it proposed a quite drastic restructuring of their administration. It ranged very widely. It provided for a massive decentralization of justice and legal administration, with county registries to record all land transactions and titles, separate county registers to grant probate and administration of wills, and county courts to hear and determine all ordinary cases, both criminal and civil, under the over-all authority of the Courts of Upper Bench and Common Pleas. It devoted nine folio pages to the reform of the Court of Chancery, and proposed to abolish outright the Court of Exchequer and the palatine jurisdictions of Durham, Lancashire, Cheshire, and Ely. It offered large changes in the laws governing debt and inheritance, and it provided for a process of appeal in all civil and criminal causes.[91]

One might ask why the Commission proposed to include so many sweeping and controversial changes in a single huge statute. The probable explanation is that it felt that they all hung together, and there was indeed considerable interlocking between its proposals for county courts and registries, for the linking of these to the central courts at Westminster, for the major overhaul of equity jurisdiction, and for a system of appeals. The fifteen shorter bills concerned particular reforms which could be enacted separately; the great final one was to be taken as a whole. It is significant that the printed version of this bill, as introduced in the Rump in January 1653, was entitled *A System*

[91] *Somers Tracts*, vi, 191–245.

of the Law, the implication being that its various parts were interdependent.[92] Yet it seems to have divided the Commission itself, for Hale spoke and wrote at length about the difficulties and abuses to which county registries and powerful county courts would give rise. His Commission, however, was accountable to the Rump's own committee for regulating the law, and it has been argued that this committee itself had formulated a scheme for devolving ordinary jurisdiction and legal administration to the counties and insisted on its inclusion.[93] The Commission therefore defined the local agencies' powers, and subordinated them to the central courts, in a manner which it calculated would do the least damage.

Even so, the proposals for county land registries proved to be as contentious as had been expected. The Rump gave the first two readings to a bill for their establishment on 26 January 1653, but though this was referred to a strong committee it had made no headway when the end came in April. According to both Cromwell and Ludlow, the senior lawyers in the House brought progress to a halt over the word 'incumbrance', which occurs on the very first page of the Commission's main bill, as printed.[94] The bill was still being criticized in print a month after Barebone's Parliament met.[95] But Barebone's never actually embarked on any bill to set up either county registries or county courts, though such institutions may well have been given an airing in the general debates on the law in mid-July and mid-August. They were certainly in members' minds, but there is a suggestion that they aroused some hostility, or at least that their early establishment was not expected. When a bill concerning idiots, lunatics, and infants was passed on 13 October, the House rejected a clause whereby it would have remained in force only until county judicatures were erected by Act of Parliament, and decided instead that it should continue until 1 September 1654.[96]

[92] See n. 78.

[93] Cotterell, pp. 695–9; [Matthew Hale], *A Treatise showing how useful . . . the enrolling and registering of all conveyances of land may be* (1694), reprinted in *Somers Tracts*, xi, 81–90. Doubts have been expressed about Hale's authorship, but Veall thinks it probable (op. cit., pp. 223–4 and Worden follows him (*Rump*, p. 114).

[94] *CJ*, vii, 250–1, 253; Worden, *Rump*, pp. 113–15; Abbott, iv, 493; Ludlow, i, 334, *Somers Tracts*, vi, 191.

[95] *Reasons against the Bill entituled An Act for County Registers* ([3 Aug.] 1653).

[96] *CJ*, vii, 334.

The committee for the law did not get very far with the Hale Commision's drafts, for only the first two reached the statute-book. The first abolished the payment of fines for bills and writs initiating actions at law, and was speedily passed on 2 August in virtually the same brief terms as the Commission had framed. The second was the famous Act touching Marriages, and it was passed only after long debates and extensive amendments. It will be considered later, along with the parliament's legislative achievement as a whole. Other matters covered by the Commission's main bill did come before the House, but piecemeal, and not at the instance of this committee. The successful Act for the Relief of Creditors and Poor Prisoners, for instance, was introduced by the committee for prisons, and the much more divisive question of Chancery was brought to a head by the House itself. The long-standing grievances against that tribunal were raised on 4 August and debated at length the next day, when it was voted without a division, 'That the High Court of Chancery of England shall be forthwith taken away.'[97] But it was one thing to vote Chancery blithely away and another to fill the gap that it would leave, and the outcome (as will be seen) was only further division and stalemate.

Whether the protracted debates on the act for civil marriages, which took place almost daily from 9 to 17 August, also ranged radicals against moderates is not clear, but they may have helped to bring the pressure for a more drastic approach to law reform to a head. Two other matters certainly did. One was the simultaneous drama of Lilburne's trial; the other was the set of grave charges which the House heard on 17 August against Sir John Lenthall, Marshal of the Upper Bench and Keeper of the Marshalsea. Lenthall was the brother of the Speaker of the Long Parliament, which is probably why the Rump failed to bring him to book, but the Council of State had inherited a dossier on him from its predecessor, and on 25 July it turned it over to the new parliament's committee for prisons and prisoners. On the latter's preliminary report the House had had Lenthall arrested; now it was treated to a shocking story of venality and extortion by both the Keeper and his gaolers, who had allegedly practised the grossest discrimination between the rich and poor debtors in their charge and inflicted atrocious cruelties and frauds upon the

[97] *CJ*, vii, 296.

latter. The committee for prisons—almost the only standing committee so far with a radical bias—may have accepted some accusations that were neither disinterested nor true, but the members spent most of two days discussing them, and voted at the end of the 18th, 'That the Debate now in the House, touching the Law, be adjourned till To-morrow Morning.'[98]

No such debate had been scheduled; evidently the House's consideration of Lenthall's misdeeds had broadened into something much larger. At any rate its main argument on the 19th, the penultimate day of Lilburne's trial, came to be over whether a new committee should be set up, not just to overhaul the administration of the law but to recast its very substance in the shape of a concise but comprehensive code. Radical members were growing dissatisfied with the existing committee for the law, even though it was less than a month old and its last measure, the marriages bill, had still to be finally passed. But its prevailingly moderate temper probably stood revealed, and according to Highland many of its members took off for the country and spent much time 'in fetching up and settling their families before winter'.[99] The proposal for this new committee was a bid to change the whole direction of the parliament's endeavours towards law reform, and in a House not quite two-thirds full it produced some curious cross-voting. After a motion to adjourn the debate till next day had been defeated by just two votes, with moderate men as tellers on both sides, the substantive motion was proposed, 'That there shall be a Committee appointed to consider of a new Body of the Law.' There was another division over whether the question should now be put, and Sir Charles Wolseley, who had just been a teller against an adjournment, was a teller for the Yeas in a strange partnership with the Fifth Monarchist Hugh Courtney, against the very moderate Sir Robert King. They won; but if young Wolseley expected that an immediate vote would put paid to this new committee he misjudged badly, for the Fifth Monarchist Arthur Squibb and the Lincolnshire radical Barnaby Bowtell proceeded

[98] *CJ*, vii, 293, 297, 302–4; *CSPD 1653–4*, p. 47. For testimonials to Lenthall, and his reinstatement as Keeper in Feb. 1654, see ibid. 399–400; and for the best account of his case, Aylmer, *The State's Servants*, pp. 162–4.

[99] *Exact Relation*, p. 276.

to tell forty-six votes in favour of it, whereas Desborough and Ashley Cooper could count only thirty-eight against.[1]

The committee was immediately constituted, and its radical cast doubtless reflects the tenor of the debate. Its thirteen original members consisted of the Fifth Monarchists Squibb and Harrison (his first mention in the *Journal* for many weeks—was he specially present?), the lay preachers Barebone and Highland, the gentry-radicals Blount, Kenrick, Spence, and West, those saints-cum-men-of-business Moyer and Taylor, and only three men, Pickering, Wolseley, and Wingfield, who are broadly identifiable as moderates—though when it came to law reform Wingfield seems to have been a man for sweeping measures. Bowtell was added to it on 20 October, and its radical complexion was further heightened three weeks later by the addition of Broughton, Robert Bennett, and Sir James Hope.[2] Yet it was not without legal expertise, for Spence, Taylor, Wingfield, and Broughton had all been called to the bar, Hope was a Scottish judge, Blount and Moyer had served on the Hale Commission, and four members besides the barristers had been admitted to Inns of Court.

What did its sponsors mean by 'a new body of the law'? To begin with, their proposal had been for a new *model* of the law; the Clerk of the Parliament simply misheard the word when he drew up the question. Some of them tried to get it corrected, both before and after the vote was taken, but their opponents, angry at their defeat, insisted that the word 'body' should stand, thinking that it would serve better to discredit the whole enterprise. Certainly, common report had it that the committee's purpose was to destroy the whole venerable fabric of the known laws of the land. That was the rather disingenuous accusation in *A Charge of High Treason against Oliver Cromwell*; it was echoed, more or less, by Cromwell himself,[3] and by early official apologias for the Protectorate. 'The Law was looked on as a noisome ruinous building, not capable of repair or alteration, but fit to be pulled down to the very ground', wrote the anonymous author of *Confusion Confounded*; '*Propriety* was struck at.'[4] 'The one Party

---

[1] *CJ*, vii, 304.
[2] *CJ*, vii, 304, 336, 348.
[3] Abbott, III, 438.
[4] *Confusion Confounded* ([18 Jan.] 1654), p. 4; cf. Clarendon MS 46, fo. 209.

was for pruning away its exuberances and superfluities',
according to Marchamont Nedham, 'the other, for a hewing
down of the main Body'.[5] But Highland, who served on the
committee, tells another story, though he might have told it
differently if its efforts had not been foiled. He describes its
objective as 'not a destroying of the law, or putting it down, as
some scandalously reported, but a reducing the wholesome, just,
and good laws into a body, from them that are useless and out of
date'. It proceeded

by reducing the several laws to their proper heads to which they did
belong, and so modelizing and embodying of them, taking knowledge
of the nature of them, and what the law of God said in the case, and
how agreeable to right reason they were; likewise how proportionable
the punishment was to the offence or crime, and wherein there seemed
any thing either deficient or excessive, to offer a supply and remedy, in
order to rectifying the whole.[6]

Yet however sincere Highland and his fellows may have been
in their intentions, such drastic alterations were bound to have
serious implications for property, and conservative lawyers had
strong reason to doubt whether the centuries-old growth of
England's common law was susceptible to the kind of codification
that the committee was attempting. Highland himself seriously
hoped that 'the great volumes of law would come to be reduced
into the bigness of a pocket book, as it is proportionable in New-
England and elsewhere'.[7] It is interesting that the committee had
the recent example of Massachusetts in mind. Back in 1635,
when the colony was barely six years old, its General Court had
appointed a committee to draft 'a body of grounds of laws, in
resemblance to a Magna Carta, which, being allowed by some
of the ministers, and the General Court, should be received for
fundamental laws'.[8] Nothing emerged from that committee, but
another was constituted next year which included the new
governor, Sir Henry Vane, and the ministers John Cotton, Hugh
Peter, and Thomas Shepard. Cotton actually produced a draft
code, commonly known as 'Moses his Judicials', for it attempted

---

[5] *A True State*, p. 16.
[6] *Exact Relation*, p. 278.
[7] Ibid.
[8] *Winthrop's Journal*, ed. J. K. Hosmer, 2 vols. (New York, 1908), i, 151, quoted in G. L.
Haskins, *Law and Authority in Early Massachusetts* (New York, 1960, repr. 1968), p. 124.

a synthesis between the Mosaic law and current legal practice in the colony. It was not enacted, but it appealed to radical Puritan fundamentalists everywhere, and it was printed in London.[9] More generally acceptable to the colonists, however, was the 'Body of Liberties' compiled by Nathaniel Ward, who had practised law in London and been rector of an Essex parish for ten years before he emigrated. This, after much consultation and amendment, was accepted by the General Court in 1643 as a statement of the colony's laws.[10] Yet it did not meet the demand for a full codification, for despite its many precise rulings concerning capital crimes, wills, domestic relationships, and much else, it was as a whole more in the nature of a latter-day Magna Carta or a bill of rights. Governor Winthrop and other leaders of the colony were all along opposed to codification, preferring a gradual accretion of case law after the English fashion and jealously guarding the prerogative of the godly magistrate to determine every case according to what he judged to be its merits. But it was precisely to restrict the discretionary judicial powers of their patriarchal magistrates that the general body of freemen pressed again in 1644 for a comprehensive statement of the laws and their penalties. The result, four years later, came in *The Lawes and Liberties of Massachusetts*, the first modern code of the western world. The biblical influence is very evident in the tariff of capital offences, which included idolatry, blasphemy, witchcraft, adultery, rape, sodomy, kidnapping, and cursing or smiting a parent, but well over half the code's regulations were based on the enactments of the General Court, and a full third on a crop of general laws passed in 1646–7. Perhaps its most interesting feature, for radical Puritan observers in the old country, was its joint authorship by men of legal training like Winthrop and Ward and ministers whose learning was only in the Scriptures; the Bible and the Statutes at Large were almost equally consulted in the framing of it. The result gave the civil magistrate an authority over religion which the extremists in Barebone's could never have stomached, but its

[9] [J. Cotton], *An Abstract or* [sic] *the Lawes of New England, as they are now established* (1641). Another edition in 1655 carried an Address to the Reader by the Fifth Monarchist William Aspinwall.

[10] For this and what follows see Haskins, ch. 8, and Edmund S. Morgan, *The Puritan Dilemma: the story of John Winthrop* (Boston, Mass., 1958), ch. 11. I am indebted to my colleague Dr R. M. Bliss for advice on this subject.

manifold breaks with traditional law must still have disconcerted the moderates, if they read it.[11]

The example of Massachusetts nevertheless helped some of the forty-eight members who voted for the committee for a new body of the law to believe that they were not attempting anything intrinsically absurd or wildly utopian. But of course it was one thing to legislate for a young colonial community with common religious commitments and easily determined proprie-torial rights, and quite another to cram into a pocket-book all the complexities of ownership, possession, title, and tenurial relation-ships which an ancient and very hierarchical society had distilled in its common law during nearly half a millennium. The new committee was perhaps a turning-point, but two things should be remembered before ascribing to it an exaggerated role in bringing Barebone's Parliament to eventual failure. One is that whatever it might propose required the assent of a House in which moderate men could command a majority whenever they troubled to appear in sufficient strength, and that it never got as far as presenting any specific bills or proposals whatever. The other is that it did not supplant the earlier committee for the business of the law, henceforth often described as 'for the regulation of the law' or just as 'for the law'. That predominantly moderate body continued to be entrusted with the drafting of important measures, though from now on it was so much occupied with those which the House and its committees thrust upon it that the Hale Commission's programme of draft bills was pushed into the background. But the separation of function between the old committee and the new, even though Blount, Moyer, Spence, Taylor, West, Wingfield, and later Broughton served on both, manifested the tendency of the root-and-branch reformers to draw apart from those who cared for continuity with the past.

[11] Haskins, op. cit., p. 137.

IX

Governing and Legislating

Cromwell's disillusion with the assembly that he had called into being was ceasing to be a secret. Complaining about it to a confidant early in September, he said he was 'more troubled now with the fool than before with the knave'.[1] He wrote about it in gentler vein, though just as dejectedly, to his son-in-law Charles Fleetwood on 22 August, with an apology for 'thus unbowelling myself':

Truly I never more needed all helps from my Christian friends than now! Fain would I have my service accepted of the saints (if the Lord will), but it is not so. Being of different judgments, and of each sort most seeking to propagate their own, that spirit of kindness that is to them all, is hardly accepted of any ... Yet it much falls out as when the two Hebrews were rebuked: you know upon whom they turned their displeasure.[2]

The reference is revealing, for it was Moses who tried to separate the two fighting Hebrews, and the one who had struck the first blow turned on him and asked, 'Who made thee a prince and a judge over us?'[3] Cromwell trusted that the Lord 'will manifest that I am no enemy', but he confessed to a temptation to say with the psalmist, 'Oh that I had wings like a dove! For then I would fly away, and be at rest.'[4]

He seems not to have attended the House at any time after its

---

[1] Clarendon MS 46, fo. 230. The reporter was a newswriter to the exiled court, but he claimed to be on close terms with the recipient of Cromwell's remark. Cf. *CSP Ven 1653–4*, pp. 118–19.

[2] Abbott, iii, 89.

[3] Exodus 2:14.

[4] Abbott, iii, 89; Psalm 55:6.

first day of prayer and fasting. Towards mid-September a delegation of over twenty members waited on him 'to desire his presence among them and the assistance of his counsel in the weighty affairs that lay on them', but he 'gave them a very cool put off', and afterwards allegedly told a friend 'that he would not intermeddle with persons so inconsiderable both for understanding and merit'.[5]

The disillusion was to some extent mutual. Anna Trapnel, the Fifth Monarchist prophetess, had a vision on 3 September of the breaking-up of Barebone's Parliament when she was in the unexpected company of Colonel John Bingham, one of its most moderate and respectable members. Chanting in a trance-like state, she claimed to see revealed 'the deadness of *Gideons* [i.e. Cromwell's] spirit towards the work of the Lord, shewing me that he was laid aside, as to any great matters, the Lord having finished the greatest business that he would employ him in'. According to her, Bingham called it a prophecy and said he was glad of it, for he thought that little good would be done by this assembly.[6]

It has been argued that Cromwell's difficulties with it, as with its successors, were mainly of his own making and stemmed from his failure to instal and instruct an 'essential nucleus of effective parliamentary managers', who could play a similar role to Elizabeth I's privy councillors.[7] He was, one can readily agree, naïve in hoping that so mixed a body would settle harmoniously to the work of godly reformation, not to mention the daily running of the state, without a more positive leadership than he chose to provide. He himself looked back on it as 'a story of my own weakness and folly', and he certainly learnt from it the importance of separating the legislative and executive powers.[8] He seems, however, never to have appreciated how much parliaments needed to be guided along agreed and purposeful lines by men of ministerial calibre. On the whole he deserved Clarendon's tribute to his 'wonderful understanding in the

---

[5] Clarendon MS 46, fo. 274. The source is the same newswriter as in n. 1, and since no such delegation is recorded in *CJ* it must have been unofficial. Cromwell's reported words must be treated with caution, but the incident is unlikely to be a total invention.

[6] Anna Trapnel, *The Cry of a Stone*, pp. 10–11; cf. pp. 29 and 50 for proof of her identification of Gideon with Cromwell.

[7] Trevor-Roper, *Religion, the Reformation and Social Change*, pp. 356 ff.

[8] Abbott, iv, 488–9; cf. iii, 587–8.

natures and humours of men', but whether he also had 'as great a dexterity in the applying them' is questionable.[9] In handling individuals he could show remarkable penetration and empathy, but he was rather short of the politician's flair for scenting and manipulating the collective attitudes of larger bodies—the army generally excepted, though even there his old sureness of touch sometimes slipped a little as memories of shared dangers and triumphs became more distant.

Yet even if he had fully perceived the need for parliamentary management it is difficult to see where he could have found it in the summer of 1653. There was no 'government' as such, and very few experienced parliament-men were available. The interim Council of State might conceivably have provided a nucleus if it had had more talent and more unity, but it lacked both. Lambert and Harrison, the men who had impelled him most strongly towards breaking the Rump, ceased to be of any help to him. Lambert abruptly stopped attending the council from the day the parliament met, and though the House appointed him to some committees during its first week or two there is no other evidence that he ever took the seat to which it co-opted him. Harrison's attendance at the council faltered during late June and July, after which he came to no more meetings except three in late September and four in October. The two men's motives were probably different. In the opinion of Bordeaux, Lambert's grievance was that having been a dominant figure in the interim council, of which he had been the first president, he resented Cromwell's handing over the supreme authority to the parliament,[10] whose calling (it will be remembered) he had opposed. Harrison on the other hand was probably confirmed as the summer wore on in his suspicion that it had never been Cromwell's purpose to commit unbridled power to the millenarian saints. He was also seriously ill in August, though reported on the 19th to be recovering.[11] Lambert meanwhile solaced himself with the rural delights of Wimbledon House and the visits of some of the greater northern gentry. Late in August he is said to have again been designated, as he had been in the early spring, for the command of an enlarged English

---

[9] Clarendon, *History of the Rebellion*, vi, 91.

[10] PRO 3.3/91, fo. 36; *CSPD 1652–3*, p. 301.

[11] Thurloe, i, 429; cf. p. 396.

army which was to suppress the royalist insurrection in the Highlands. Perhaps he saw it as a device to get him out of the way; at any rate he did not go. There was a dubious report on 16 September that he and Cromwell were 'strangely and strictly cemented', but within the next four weeks he retired to his native Yorkshire.[12] Of the remaining eight councillors of April–July, not counting Cromwell himself or Salwey (who had declined to serve), Carew, Bennett, and Moyer rapidly emerged as radicals, opposed on crucial issues to Pickering, Strickland, Jones, Desborough, and Tomlinson.

As for seasoned parliamentary tacticians, there were so few who had not been alienated either by Pride's Purge and the regicide or by the expulsion of the Rump that their presence in Barebone's Parliament was necessarily very thin. Oliver St. John, who was later suspect as 'the dark Lanthorn, and privy Councellour' who advanced Cromwell to the Protectorate, was out of sympathy with the change of regime and in any case fell into a very prolonged illness in October.[13] Other experienced lawyer–politicians like Whitelocke and Widdrington stayed on the sidelines, tut-tutting at the constitutional improprieties but clinging to their posts.[14] Vane, Fairfax, and Gervase Piggot were probably not the only former MPs to rebuff Cromwell's approach or to decline his summons. Among the ex-Rumpers he still had the support of Speaker Rous, Pickering, Sydenham, Strickland, Philip Jones, Viscount Lisle, and a very few others, but none of them ranked as parliamentary statesmen and it is difficult to think of who else he might have employed as managers. The younger men of talent who would serve him as Protector—Wolseley, Howard, Ashley Cooper, Montagu, Lockhart—were too new to the House to take up such a role at the start.

This general lack of experience created particular difficulties in the sphere of foreign relations. This is a subject that can be treated here only to the extent that it impinged on domestic politics, which it did intermittently, though rather more as time went on. There were many threads for Cromwell to pick up when he shouldered the burdens of state in April. Peace with the United Provinces, which he strongly desired, had been brought

[12] Clarendon MS 46, fos. 113, 208–9, 247, 347; PRO 31.3/90, fo. 85; Thurloe, i, 560.
[13] *The Case of Oliver St. John, Esq.*, pp. 3, 6; BL, Add. MS. 10,114, fo. 34ᵛ.
[14] Whitelocke, *Memorials*, pp. 529, 534; Thurloe, i, 249–50.

within closer reach by a letter which the Rump had received four weeks before the dissolution and had answered favourably. France was seeking an end to protracted unofficial hostilities through the mission of Bordeaux, who had presented his monarch's formal recognition of the Commonwealth on 21 December and was still waiting to negotiate a closer accord. He was jealously watched by Alonso de Cardeñas, who as ambassador for Spain had been trying for rather longer to negotiate a commercial treaty, and Cardeñas was watched in turn by the Count of Peneguiaõ, who was seeking a treaty of peace on behalf of insurgent Portugal.[15]

During the interregnum from April to July these diplomats naturally addressed themselves to Cromwell, but he and his temporary councillors had too much on their hands to give them much satisfaction. After Barebone's Parliament met, the question which constantly exercised them was whether he still held the reins or whether he was sincere in declaring that he had handed them over to the Council of State. To Barrière, the resident minister of the Prince of Condé, who led what was left of the Fronde of the princes, the situation late in May seemed simple: Cromwell was master of England, the most powerful man in Europe, and in a position to make himself king whenever he wished.[16] Bordeaux at first agreed that a crown was within his grasp, and he was well aware that Cromwell was partly prevaricating in making difficulties about an audience and in referring him, both before and after the parliament met, to the Council of State.[17] Cromwell and his fellow-councillors were for long attracted, as a party in the Rump had been, to the idea of supporting Condé and the frondeurs, and particularly to leasing military and naval aid to the quasi-republican rebels who were standing siege in Bordeaux. The possibility of an English army fighting once more in Guienne passed away, however, when Bordeaux surrendered to Louis XIV on 20 July.[18]

[15] Gardiner, *C & P*, ii, 182–9; Worden, *Rump*, pp. 301–6, 330–1.
[16] BL, Add. MS. 35,252, fos. 42–4.
[17] PRO 31.3/90, fos. 656, 666, 670, 673; 31.3/91, fos. 8, 15, 19, 44.
[18] BL, Add. MS 35,252, fos. 47, 70 and *passim*; PRO 31.3/90, fos. 662, 664, 666, 670; 31.3/91, fos. 31, 48, 50. Despite the rapid collapse of the Fronde, Cromwell as late as October 1653 sent the German military engineer Joachin Hane to report on the vulnerability of French maritime fortresses: see Gardiner, *C & P*, ii, 354–7, and C. H. Firth (ed.), *The Journal of Joachin Hane* (Oxford, 1896).

The French, Spanish, and Portuguese ambassadors and the envoys of the Fronde remained frustrated men throughout 1653, for it was hardly conceivable that Cromwell would commit the Commonwealth to any major decisions in foreign policy until the new supreme authority had settled in, or indeed until it had been determined whether there was to be peace or continued war with the Dutch. Their hopes and disappointments need concern us here no further; the one external question which vitally affected Cromwell's relations with Barebone's Parliament was that of the Dutch peace. It was also the touchstone of his personal initiative in foreign affairs, and here one can distinguish three broad phases. From April to July, although he might insist to Bordeaux that in such public business he was no more than an individual,[19] his *de facto* power and his international reputation gave him an inevitable dominance. Limited though his expertise was in matters diplomatic, only Strickland and perhaps Pickering among his fellow-councillors had any experience in them worth mentioning. After his formal transference of the supreme authority on 4 July, however, he tried for a while to renounce the personal steersmanship that all the foreign representatives continued to attribute to him, and dealt with them on his own only occasionally and confidentially, and only when he felt his intervention necessary to prevent the Anglo-Dutch negotiation from foundering. But the council was both inept and divided; it kept changing the composition of its committee for foreign affairs, and weeks went by when it was too distracted by domestic pressures to attend to them at all. The experienced Venetian resident was mildly shocked by these men's sheer ignorance and incompetence in diplomacy; Sir Oliver Fleming, the master of ceremonies, felt obliged to apologize for them, and was himself distrusted by them because of his relative expertise. That is one reason why Cromwell is to be found quietly resuming a larger role from the autumn onwards, ably aided by Thurloe, who as secretary to the council brought a much needed touch of professionalism to this side of its affairs.[20]

Three major impediments stood in the way of a successful peace with the United Provinces: an unbroken run of English naval victories, a lack of realism about the terms that the Dutch

[19] PRO 31.3/91, fo. 8.
[20] *CSPD 1653–4*, pp. 53, 90, 201, 206, 237, 254; *CSP Ven 1653–4*, pp. 132, 141.

would accept, and latterly the fanatical lust for universal conquest that consumed the Fifth Monarchist faction. From the battle fought from Portland to Cap Gris Nez on 18–20 February through the action off the Gabbard on 2–3 June to Monck's devastating victory off the Texel on 31 July, in which van Tromp was killed, the Dutch suffered grievous losses in men and ships, and their trade was hit much harder than England's. This naturally encouraged the English hawks to fight on for total victory, especially those who saw the Lord's hand in such 'mercies'. Yet Cromwell did not share the desire, which was for different reasons common to Hesilrige and Harrison, to bring the Dutch Republic to utter defeat and ruin. On the contrary he wanted to embrace it in what contemporaries called a 'coalition' with the English Commonwealth which would confer common citizenship on the inhabitants of both and involve a partial fusion of sovereignties. This was not a new or a personal aberration, for it had been adumbrated in the Rump's instructions to St. John and Strickland when they went on their abortive mission to The Hague in March 1651, long before Cromwell returned from the Worcester campaign. It has been argued that at that time the overriding motive had been to transfer the entrepôt trade from Amsterdam to London,[21] but Cromwell, while not indifferent to commercial interests, was probably drawn to the scheme more by a desire to bind the two republics into a mighty and indissoluble Protestant power block and to commit them to the mutual exclusion of the Houses of Stuart and Orange.

On the very day that the Rump was expelled, Jan de Witt, who was soon to be the Grand Pensionary of Holland, sent over a proposal for a peace negotiation on neutral territory. It was a matter on which the United Provinces were conspicuously disunited, for de Witt had the support of Holland and three other provinces but not of the States General. The interim Council of State debated his letter at its very first meeting on 29 April, but it took a week to agree on its answer. This was that though it could not consent to negotiate on neutral ground, it was as desirous of a peace as the late parliament had declared itself to be and was prepared to treat on the same terms as the Rump had

---

[21] J. E. Farnell, 'The Navigation Act of 1651, the First Dutch War and the London Merchant Community', *Economic History Review*, 2nd series, xvi (1964), 443.

offered in its letter to the States General of 1 April.[22] It was a safe line to take for a government which was still finding its feet, and when it was shortly followed by the victory off the Gabbard the States General decided to send four commissioners in June to discover what the price of peace might be. The four were Beverning and Nieuport from Holland, Van de Perre from Zealand and Jongestal from Friesland, and the council appointed Pickering, Strickland, Harrison, and Sydenham as commissioners to treat with them.[23] At their first meeting, five days before the opening of Barebone's Parliament, the Englishmen demanded the same three chilling preliminary conditions as the Rump had advanced a year earlier: the Dutch must pay reparations for England's losses in the war, they must hand over some cautionary towns, to be chosen by England, and they must make solemn public acknowledgement that Tromp had been the aggressor in the action in the Downs which had started the war.[24] Cromwell, doubtless sensing that such severe demands might kill the treaty there and then, sent a private communication to Nieuport next day, suggesting that it might suffice if Tromp were dismissed temporarily, say for five or six months, and that (presumably as an alternative to cautionary towns) security might be achieved by each republic appointing two or three representatives to sit on the other's chief governing body—the Council of State in England and either the States General or the Council of State in the Netherlands.[25]

This pattern, with the council collectively reiterating the harsh line taken by its predecessor and Cromwell privately suggesting to one or more of the Dutch envoys that the terms might be modified, was to be repeated several times after Barebone's Parliament had met. The commissioners of the two republics met again on 13, 15, 21, and 25 July; the English ones were doubled in number after the enlargement of the council to thirty-one, and Cromwell himself attended at least three of these conferences. It was in these meetings that the Dutchmen became aware, with acute dismay, of the kind of coalition that the

---

[22] *CSPD 1652–3*, pp. 299, 307; Thurloe, i, 239. I do not read the council's response as a summary rejection, as Gardiner does in *C & P*, ii, 330.

[23] *CSPD 1652–3*, pp. 445, 451; Desborough was added on 29 June.

[24] PRO 31.3/91, fo. 55; Thurloe, i, 308–9.

[25] Gardiner, *C & P*, ii, 341–2.

English had in mind. Nieuport told Fleming that he thought the Council of State must have based its terms on the instructions which its predecessor had given to the commissioners who had been sent north the preceding year to negotiate Scotland's union with England.[26] Union is indeed hardly too strong a word to describe what the council was now proposing, which was 'ut duae republicae coalescant atque adunentur'.[27] Each would retain its own laws and institutions, short of the very highest, but at this time the council was not only proposing common citizenship, common trading privileges and facilities, and the equal right of Englishmen and Dutchmen to reside and hold property in each other's countries; it envisaged a single sovereign body to govern both of them.[28]

The Dutch envoys' first reaction was to ask for their passports and return home, but Cromwell kept contact with them privately through an intermediary, and repeated his suggestion that it would suffice if each republic had a few representatives on the other's highest governing body. Face to face with them, he spoke long and passionately of what they might accomplish together in spreading the kingdom of Christ throughout the world, and declared that each nation would care as dearly for the lives, property, and reputation of the other as for its own. We need not suppose him insincere; he probably just did not appreciate the Dutchmen's fears for their hard-won independence, their commercial hegemony, and their fishing industry, nor perceive how unequal the proposed sharing of rights would in practice be.[29] But though the idea of a coalition strongly appealed to him, he was not going to let it wreck the prospects of a peace. In response to his rather indefinite assurances the Dutchmen compromised: Nieuport and Jongestal went home to report while Beverning and Van de Perre stayed in England.[30] They must have been glad that they had kept the door open, for just before the first two departed came the shattering news of the battle of Texel. On 6 August Cromwell talked privately with Beverning for two hours, walking in St. James's Park. Speaking (he insisted) only as an individual and on his own initiative, he

[26] Thurloe, i, 362, 367, 370, 372; *CSPD 1653–4*, pp. 22, 26, 37, 39, 47.
[27] Thurloe, i, 382.
[28] Gardiner, *C & P*, ii, 345.
[29] Ibid. 342–3; Thurloe, i, 382, 386–7, 394–5, 410, 438; PRO 31.3/91, fos. 66, 69.
[30] Thurloe, i, 401–2.

declared that England did not intend any encroachment upon the sovereignty or privileges of the United Provinces. Beverning was understandably perplexed, since the council's proposals invaded them so heavily, but he hesitantly counselled de Witt that the States General should prolong his stay in England a while longer. 'Truly', he wrote, 'I know not almost what to advise.'[31]

Just over a month later one of Thurloe's trusted intelligencers at The Hague predicted confidently (and correctly) that despite the outcry there against the English terms, Nieuport and Jongestal would be sent back to England, since Holland needed peace so badly. But he confessed he could not understand all this enthusiasm for a coalition, since it would not stop the two republics from deceiving each other, while security could be as well achieved by a straightforward alliance and treaty of commerce, backed by a league with Spain and Sweden.[32] Curiously, at just about this time Cromwell told one or both of the remaining Dutch envoys that he was disposed to give up the idea of a coalition, since it was so disliked, provided that a firm peace could be guaranteed by a league of Protestant states, which might include not Spain but France.[33] Then on 23 September Van de Perre received an extraordinary paper from Sir Cornelius Vermuyden, the Dutch engineer who had been much employed in the drainage of the fens and who claimed to be in Cromwell's confidence. Instead of an outright coalition it proposed a perpetual offensive and defensive alliance, with all previous acts of hostility buried in oblivion and with eight commissioners, half English and half Dutch, residing in each country to settle all their future differences. Each was to be free to ally with Denmark, Sweden, the German Protestant princes, and France too if she guaranteed liberty of conscience to the Huguenots, but both were to treat all states which maintained the Inquisition as enemies. Both were to have freedom of trade with all European and African countries, but commerce with the rest of the globe was to be carved up with breath-taking simplicity: Asia and Brazil were assigned to the Dutch, America north and south

[31] Ibid. 416–18.

[32] Ibid. 461–3. The writer's use of a cipher indicates his status as a regular and trusted informant.

[33] Bordeaux to Brienne, 12/22 Sept. 1653, PRO 31.3/91, fo. 96.

(Brazil excepted) to England. These spheres of dominance were to be won and held by force, each partner assisting the other, and the paper set out how much each should contribute in money and ships to the sustaining of such grandiose enterprises. Each, finally, was to send missionaries to preach the gospel 'unto all people and nations' in their respective areas of influences.[34]

How far Cromwell endorsed these extravagant proposals is uncertain, but they are not out of tune with his own higher flights on 'the Protestant interest' and it would not be many months before he was planning his unprovoked attack on Hispaniola. They were not of course a feasible basis for a treaty with such realists as the Dutch, but by early October a less ambitious set of terms was under hopeful discussion. Significantly, Beverning saw a better prospect of peace because by that time the influence of Harrison and the 'Anabaptist' faction seemed to be declining.[35]

Here is an apparent paradox, for Cromwell in his talks with the Dutch commissioners, and Vermuyden too in his paper, were full of millenarian enthusiasm for what the two great Protestant commonwealths could accomplish together in advancing the kingdom of Christ, whereas the extreme chiliasts, especially Harrison and his friends the Blackfriars preachers, were the strongest opponents of a Dutch peace. This, however, is just one more illustration of the difference between Cromwell's millenarianism and that of the Fifth Monarchists. Cromwell looked forward to the kingdom with longing and searched the workings of providence for pointers to ways in which he might bring it closer, but he accepted that it would unfold only in God's good time and that its nature would be internal and spiritual. Harrison, Feake, Rogers, and their kind believed by contrast that the Civil War had merely begun the overturning of Antichrist and that England's duty was to carry the struggle across the lands of Europe until Rome itself had fallen. They were far less moved than Cromwell by the fact that the Dutch were fellow-Protestants, since they reckoned so much of 'establishment' Protestantism to be part of Antichrist's kingdom.

---

[34] Gardiner in *C & P*, ii, 350–2, convincingly identifies Vermuyden's paper in Thurloe, ii, 125–6, with the document which Van de Perre received. He promptly transmitted it to The Hague: see the letter of intelligence in Thurloe, i, 517.

[35] Gardiner, *C & P*, ii, 353–4; Thurloe, i, 519, 521; see also pp. 485, 488–9, 509–10, 528.

Nevertheless, the fierceness of their belligerence towards the Dutch raises the question whether it was in part economically motivated. The difficulty is to generalize about their economic interests, because the Fifth Monarchists within the parliament spanned a wide social spectrum and the preachers and pamphleteers who made most of the noise outside it tended to be socially untypical of the movement as a whole. Its rank and file were not homogeneous, but artisans, journeymen, and apprentices seem to have made up the bulk of it, with a heavy weighting towards the cloth and leather industries. Radical saints of this social level obviously had few direct common interests with the group of sophisticated worldlings—Marten, Chaloner, Neville, Morley, and their allies—who had been hottest for the war in the Rump, or with Hesilrige and Scot (Harrison's strongest parliamentary opponents) who had been deeply committed to it. Sir Henry Vane, of all the leading Rumpers the one with the strongest sectarian and millenarian sympathies, had been deeply opposed to it. Historians differ as to which commercial interests favoured a war policy or whether in pursuing one the Rump was responding to commercial pressures at all, but the Fifth Monarchists can hardly have felt a sense of identity with any of the wealthy chartered companies or the colonial-interloping traders who have been suggested as supporters of the war. Nor is there any evidence to link them with that other area of economic rivalry, the fisheries. It has been argued that clothworkers were benefiting by the cessation of Dutch competition, and this may have been a contributory reason for the popularity of the war among Fifth Monarchists, though Harrison and the fiery preachers had championed it from the very start, before such benefits became apparent.[36]

These men never acknowledged economic motives; on the contrary they expressly repudiated them. They held it wrong that foreign policy should be directed to the advancement of commerce, and they called down God's wrath on the pride of wealth and the materialist values which they saw as dominating Holland. Many of them had been at the receiving end of

[36] Capp, *Fifth Monarchy Men*, pp. 82 ff., 151–4, 230–1; Worden, *Rump*, pp. 299–306; Charles Wilson, *Profit and Power* (Cambridge, 1957), pp. 54–60 and ch. V, *passim*; R. W. K. Hinton, *The Eastland Trade and the Common Weal* (Oxford, 1959), pp. 84–94; Farnell, 'The Navigation Act of 1651', pp. 449–52; Brenner, 'Civil War Politics of London's Merchant Community', pp. 97–107.

capitalist exploitation at home, and they doubtless focused on the Dutch the revulsion they felt against mercantile greed and oppression in general. This is how John Canne read God's lesson for England in the naval victory off the Gabbard:

In this he tels us, what our proper work is, namely not to look after Merchants, as to grow great and rich by the wealth of other Nations, but to break their power and strength in pieces. The Lord gave their men of Warr into our hands, not their Merchant Ships. Speaking here I say as it were from heaven that it is not prizes, or the Enemies Goods, our hearts or hands should desirously be upon: But to destroy Babylon, stain the Glory of Kings and Kingdoms, and lay low the high and great mountains of the earth.[37]

By August Feake's congregation was singing doggerel hymns of his own composing, of which this is a sample:

> You Belgick Provinces breake forth
>   and weepe most bitterly
> A sore distruction is prepared
>   it draweth very nigh:
> Your Citties rich and Populous
>   famous for Marchandise
> The Lord for thier provoking sinns
>   in iudgment will chastise
> And then the high and mighty states
>   poor and distressed againe
> Having humbld bin for thir pride
>   humble they will remain.[38]

Beverning himself went to the Monday exercises at Blackfriars on 22 August and heard the pulpiteers labouring 'to preach down governments, and to stir up the people against the United Netherlands'. 'But good God!', he wrote to De Witt after suffering two sermons and a long extempore prayer to Feake's god of war, 'what cruel, and abominable, and most horrid trumpets of fire, murther and flame!'[39]

Yet the saints never saw the Dutch war as an end in itself. It was the doing of Providence, and it had a cosmic purpose: Holland was to be the landing-place for a march of conquest that was to end in Rome itself, when all the lesser seats of Antichrist

---

[37] J. Canne, *A Voice from the Temple*, p. 39.
[38] Thomason MS, BL E710 (13): 'Mr. Feakes Hymne: August ye 11: 1653'.
[39] Thurloe, i, 442.

had been destroyed. Though not published until many years later, this passage from Feake's Blackfriars sermon on 11 September has an authentic ring: 'Thou gav'st a Cup into the hand of England, and we drank of it. Then thou carried'st it to Scotland and Ireland, and they drank of it. Now thou has carried it to Holland, and they are drinking of it. Lord carry it also to France, to Spain, to Rome, and let it never be out of some or other of their hands, till they drink and be drunk, and spew, and fall, and never rise any more.'[40] The same pulpit rang with the same message early in October. If England granted terms to the Dutch after she had all but conquered them, 'God's vengeance would follow upon such a heathenish peace; for where should they have a landing-place, when they went to do the great work of the Lord, and tear the whore of Babylon out of her chair, if they gave back by making a peace with them, a people and land, which the Lord had as good as given wholly up into their hands?'[41] John Spittlehouse too saw Holland as just the first stage on a march that was to end in Rome, while Morgan Llwyd wrote:

> Fight not the Dutch but on Christs score . . .
> With them wee quarter but one night,
> and so to Ffrance and Spaine.[42]

Whatever fuel a generalized dislike of rich merchants or higher employment for clothworkers may have fed into the Fifth Monarchists' ardour for the war, it was fired chiefly by an apocalyptic vision of the imminent overthrow of Antichrist, with England's martial saints in the van.

Cromwell could have ignored the clamour of these fanatics had it not been for their close liaison with the zealots in the parliament. As it was, their dark obsessions became a serious obstacle to a peace which the true statesmen of both nations knew they needed, and which had a fair chance to go forward when Nieuport and Jongestal returned to England with fresh instructions on 25 October. The rift over foreign policy between Cromwell and a strident section of the House, and the divisions within the council itself, go far to explain why he took an

[40] Roger L'Estrange, *Dissenters Sayings, The Second Part* (1681), p. 61.
[41] Thurloe, i, 534.
[42] *Gweithiau Morgan Llwyd*, i, 77, quoted by Capp, *Fifth Monarchy Men*, p. 153; J. Spittlehouse, *The first Addresses*, dedicatory address.

increasing (though often clandestine) initiative as the autumn advanced, and why Thurloe's role in managing the foreign correspondence and the diplomatic contacts became steadily more important.[43] Nevertheless it was not a healthy situation, and the distorted relationship between government and legislature was one cause of the tension which eventually brought the regime to an end.

That, however, is to anticipate, for it was not until late in the autumn that the polarization within the House became either continuous or crippling. The sensitive issues quickly defined themselves during July and August, as has been seen, but there remained large areas of business which were relatively unaffected by it. Even in the absence of records of the debates, this can be deduced from the names of the tellers in the votes over which the House divided, though allowance must once more be made for the shortcomings of our categorization of members as moderates or radicals. There were forty-six divisions between 1 September and the closing scene in December, and in only seventeen of them were two moderate tellers pitted against two radical ones. In twenty-four a moderate was partnered by a radical on at least one side, and the pairings were sometimes surprising: Harrison with Strickland, Barebone with Pickering, and Broughton twice with Howard, for example. In four divisions all four tellers were moderates; in one all four were radicals.[44] Such occasions doubtless illustrate the simple truth that people may vote on the same side for quite different reasons, but the number of them does suggest that many questions were debated and determined without splitting the House along sectarian or ideological lines. Even among the seventeen apparently polarizing divisions, not all are likely to have ranged conservative men solidly against zealots, for it is difficult to see deep principles at stake over the question whether the export of horses to Ireland should be channelled, like that of sheep, through certain named ports, or whether two obscure townships should be inserted in the bill for the sale of forests.[45] Most of the other fifteen such divisions, however, were on clearly contentious issues, especially the last

---

[43] Thurloe, i, 500–1, 519, 521, 535, 540–3; Gardiner, *C & P*, ii, 363; PRO 31.3/91, fo. 108; 3/92, fos. 2, 18; Abbott, iii, 109, 111–12, 121–5; *CSPD 1653–4*, p. 201.

[44] *CJ*, vii, 325, 335, 344, 352, 355.

[45] *CJ*, vii, 316, 347.

seven, which took place during the last four weeks of the parliament's existence. The moderates won four of the fifteen, the radicals eight, and three were tied, but six of the radical victories occurred during those four final weeks.[46] This supports the case, to be presented in the next chapter, that ideological conflict intensified as religious issues came to the fore again in November and December, and that on the days that mattered to them the radicals mustered their strength more effectively than ever before.

A fact which emerges unmistakably from the *Journal*'s bald record of divisions is that attendance declined quite steeply as summer passed into autumn.[47] There were over a hundred members present at eight of the twelve divisions during July, and never fewer than 94. In August the highest recorded attendance was 91 and the lowest 71. It was not just that the summer's heat was enticing the members home to the country, for the decline continued. The average number present at September's thirteen divisions was 72, and at October's fourteen it dropped to 70, falling particularly low (to only 47 on one occasion) during the first half of the month. Yet when the business of the day really touched members' interests they still turned up in strength. As will be seen, the election of a new Council of State on 1 November and the debates on religious settlement in December were to attract the largest turn-outs since Cromwell first opened the parliament.

There was probably more than one reason for the falling-off. At the extremes it is likely that some conservatives and a few zealots found the temper of the assembly so uncongenial that they pulled out early, except perhaps when they felt they must rally to defeat their opponents. If Cromwell's disillusion was widely known, as it surely must have been, that would have sufficed to absolve the lukewarm from sacrificing dull days to undertakings that might never be concluded. For the business was often boring and this government had little by way of reward, whether in the shape of offices or perquisites or honours, to bestow upon those who gave themselves to it conscientiously.

---

[46] There were six further divisions in the same period wherein a pair of radical tellers opposed a mixed pair, and they had a majority in five of them. Pairs of moderates faced mixed pairs in thirteen divisions, winning seven and losing five, with one tied.

[47] The attendance figures that follow include the four tellers and the Speaker.

Patronage was needed no less than management to grease the wheels of the parliamentary machine.

The Council of State suffered a comparable decline in attendance, though it followed a slightly different curve. At its 21 meetings between 14 and 30 July, following its enlargement to 31 members, the average number present was just under 16. This fell to 10.75 at the 42 meetings in August, but recovered very slightly to 11 in September (33 meetings) and 12.5 in October (32 meetings). Apart from Fleetwood, whose absence was necessitated by his duties in Ireland, and Lambert and Salwey, who totally boycotted the council after the parliament met, the worst attenders were radicals: Robert Bennett, Harrison, Hollister, Stapley, and Williams. On the moderate side only 'idle Dick' Norton had a comparably poor record. Attendance improved very markedly after the elections on 1 November, which removed most of the radical members.

Yet despite its internal tensions and its shrinking numbers, the parliament continued to attempt an ambitious programme of legislation. The pace slackened a little after the early weeks of enthusiasm, but Highland testifies that right to the end the standing committees were bringing forward measures thick and fast, and that precious time was lost in wrangling over which should be read first.[48] Other factors impeded progress which were common to all the parliaments of the Interregnum: the urgent need for financial provision, the time consumed by the reading, deliberating, and answering of petitions, the frequent failure to distinguish what was properly the business of a national legislature and what would have been better referred to more compact executive or judicial organs. Yet its legislative record is not unimpressive, especially if one considers what it had in active preparation as well as what it actually enacted, and this is a suitable point at which to survey it, before taking up the story of the final breakdown.

Of the more than thirty statutes that passed,[49] only a minority are of much intrinsic interest. Little significance attaches to this parliament's small crop of private acts, though two or three of which consumed an inordinate amount of time. Other acts, such as those appointing the Committee for the Army and the

[48] *Exact Relation*, p. 271.
[49] Only the twenty-nine public acts are listed in Firth and Rait, iii, xci-xciii.

Admiralty Commissioners and settling the jurisdiction and personnel of the Court of Admiralty, simply gave statutory authority to the nominees approved by the House and generally copied earlier statutes in defining their powers, though the choice of Admiralty judges proved remarkably contentious.[50] The first point of departure for genuinely reforming legislation lay, as has been seen, in the drafts which the Hale Commission has presented to the Rump.[51] The committee for the business of the law evidently set about these in the order in which they found them, and the first, an act six lines long to abolish the fines which litigants had had to pay for bills, declarations, and original writs, passed without fuss on 2 August.[52]

The second was the famous act instituting civil marriage, and it proved far more contentious. After its first two readings on 8 August the House spent all the 9th in grand committee on it, and debated it further on all but one of the next seven working days. Many amendments were voted on, but they do not seem to have been of a kind to provoke ideological divisions and none was pressed to a division. Just before it finally passed on 24 August, however, a clause was offered, truly radical in its departure from existing law, which would have made divorce available to either spouse upon proof of adultery by the other. It gained a second reading but was then rejected without a division. The act as it passed retained the Hale draft's central provisions for marriage before a Justice of the Peace and for the registration of births, marriages, and burials, but it differed substantially in particulars. Whereas, for instance, the Hale bill provided that banns of marriage should be posted on the church door for three weeks, the act required that they be read after morning service on three successive Sundays, unless the parties opted instead to have them proclaimed in the market-place on three successive market-days. The act took more elaborate care than the draft that brides and grooms under twenty-one should furnish proof of their parents' or guardians' consent, and it was much more severe on anyone who abducted and married a minor: the penalty was forfeiture

---

[50] Firth and Rait, ii, 703–11, 712–13; *Exact Relation* p. 272; *CJ*, vii, 288–9, 292–3. The bill for the Court of Admiralty was debated on six days and revealed many differences between parliament and council before it passed on 30 July.

[51] See pp. 264–9.

[52] Firth and Rait, ii, 713.

of his whole estate and hard labour for life. Yet by a vote taken just before it passed the act reduced the age of consent by a year to sixteen for men and fourteen for women; indeed there was a proposal to lower it by a further year, but the House rejected it. The act made quite different provisions regarding jurisdiction in matrimonial causes. The draft merely left this to such persons as parliament should appoint, but the Hale Commission's comprehensive final bill would have vested it in the new county courts and in their parent body, the Court of Common Pleas. The act by contrast gave it to the Justices of the Peace in their quarter sessions or to such other persons as parliament might appoint.[53] Perhaps this is another indication that Barebone's Parliament was not enamoured of county judicatures. The act reflects something of the radical Puritans' distrust of both the clerical and the legal professions, and it was predictably attacked as part of a design to disparage and by degrees abolish the public ministry.[54]

That was as far as the House got with the Hale bills, though drafts of five more of them survive among the state papers for 1653.[55] The rest of its legislative initiatives were either responses to immediate pressures or were brought in by other committees than the general one 'for the business of the law'. There was an early promise of administrative reform in a short act, originating in the Council of State and passed through all its stages on 28 July, which appointed three members and three non-members to look into the Commonwealth's various sources of revenue and report how they 'may be brought, with all convenient speed, into one Chanel',[56] but no perceptible progress was made in the overdue task of re-establishing a single treasury in place of the rank proliferation of fiscal agencies that the Civil Wars had generated. Predictably, this assembly was more interested in judicial reform, and here it achieved a little more.

It did for instance pass an Act for the Relief of Creditors and Poor Prisoners, whose plight had preoccupied reformers, especially the Levellers, ever since the Civil War. This act owed

[53] Ibid. 715–18; *Somers Tracts*, vi, 179–81, 214; *CJ*, vii, 297–302, 308.
[54] 'C.C.', *Sad and serious thoughts, or the sense and meaning of the late Act concerning Marriages* (17 Sept., 1653).
[55] *CSPD 1653–4*, pp. 338–9; PRO, SP18, vol. 42, fo. 9.
[56] Firth and Rait, ii, 711–12; *CSPD 1653–4*, p. 44.

nothing to the Hale Commission, which had grappled with only part of the problem, but emanated from the only relatively radical standing committee among those appointed in July, the one for prisons and prisoners. From the number and length of the debates and the prominent members of all shades who were added to the committee before the act finally passed on 5 October, it was clearly a matter of great concern. It tackled both the main abuses in current law and practice: on the one hand the ease with which well-to-do debtors defrauded their creditors by remaining in comfortable confinement, which could be merely nominal if the gaoler were well fee'd, and on the other hand the hopeless predicament of the genuinely impoverished, who rotted in squalid prisons without the means of either supporting their families or earning the wherewithal to pay their debts. The Rump had passed several acts of limited scope to permit the release of helpless debtors, but only of those in prison at the time of the enactment. This act aimed a little higher. It appointed seventeen commissioners to adjudge summarily the cases of all who were held for debt in London's various prisons, and smaller bodies to do the same in each county. Where they found just obligations being wrongfully evaded they were to distrain upon the debtor's property as if he were a bankrupt, but they were empowered to discharge poor prisoners who had no means of paying, unless their plight arose from wilful default or vicious living, in which case they were to be removed to a workhouse or house of correction. The commissioners could make gaolers liable for the debts of prisoners whom they allowed to escape, and they were to ensure that beer and provisions were sold in prisons at reasonable prices. At a first reading the act looks like a bold reform of a large area of abuse and extortion, but its authors lacked the nerve to provide for the future. This act, like its predecessors, applied only to current prisoners for debt, and its duration was to be less than a year. Highland reckoned that it freed three hundred starving souls in London alone, but its implementation gave rise to 'many doubts and difficulties', which caused it to be thrice suspended during the early months of the Protectorate and then substantially amended by two Cromwellian ordinances.[57]

[57] Firth and Rait, ii, 753–64, 860, 888, 897, 911–15, 943–5; *CJ*, vii, 316, 319, 322, 325, 329–30; Veall, *Popular Movement for Law Reform*, ch. VI; Worden, *Rump*, pp. 202–5.

A few days later the parliament passed a much briefer act, of even briefer duration, to protect the persons and estates of idiots and lunatics, who had been under the tutelage of the Court of Wards and had evidently suffered since its demise.[58] Another short act in October sought to counter the depredations of thieves and highwaymen by offering £10 reward for information leading to their arrest and conviction.[59] Two more short bills became law on 4 November. One, for preventing delays in the execution of judgements through vexatious recourse to writs of error, merely re-enacted with minor additions a measure of the Rump's which had lapsed in May. The other related to one of the Rump's more tyrannical enactments, which had denied recourse to the law to anyone who declined to take the Engagement to be faithful to the Commonwealth, as it was established without a king or House of Lords. The House had debated the Engagement as early as 9 July and had appointed a rather radical committee to bring forward recommendations concerning it. What emerged was a bill to abolish it altogether, but the House rejected this on its first reading, and voted instead merely to remove the legal disabilities of those who refused the Engagement, which thus still stood as a political test.[60]

Several other measures to improve the administration of justice were still stuck in the pipeline when the end came. A bill to speed up the settlement of cases in the notoriously dilatory Court of Admiralty was read twice on 9 September but never re-emerged from the committee for the law. From that committee came two further bills aiming at judicial reform, both read twice on 29 September, referred back to it, and heard of no more. One tackled the difficult problems of wills and administrations; the other was 'for the better election of jurors',[61] and was probably prompted by the jury's behaviour in Lilburne's case. One reaction to those twelve stalwarts' defiance, it seems, was to call for the abolition of trial by jury altogether. That radical commonwealthsman John Streater, who had been imprisoned since August for publishing seditious pamphlets but managed to publish a continuation of his *Grand Politick Informer* in October

---

[58] Firth and Rait, ii, 767–8.
[59] Ibid. 772–3.
[60] Ibid. 357–8, 773–5; *CJ*, vii, 283, 336, 346.
[61] *CJ*, vii, 316, 326.

from the Gatehouse, declared that this was the parliament's design, and he promised to expose it in his next number. Council and parliament made sure that he published no more.[62] Yet he may have had a clue, for the Fifth Monarchist preacher John Canne, in a long attack on Lilburne in November which he claimed was 'Published by Authority', had this to say by way of conclusion: 'If we may freely here deliver our opinion, thus we think. The way of proceeding by twelve men in the trial of malefactors is near an end, and shortly to be swallowed up by the Supreme Authority of the nation: So as neither the name nor thing shall be any more in the Commonwealth of England.'[63] In view of Streater's charge, Canne may have been flying a kite on behalf of some of his radical friends in the House, but the majority, like the committee for the law, probably preferred an instrument whereby the choice of jurors could be subjected to closer scrutiny. Unfortunately the bill does not survive.

The parliament's most notorious venture in the jurisdictional sphere was its attempt to abolish the Court of Chancery. This, like so much else in 1653, is just a chapter in a longer story, for Chancery's abuses and inadequacies had been notorious since long before the Civil War, and Bacon had admitted them almost as readily as Coke. By this time no one seriously denied that its procedures were intolerably formal, prolix, inefficient, and subject to vexatious obstruction; its personnel swollen with venal office-holders and supernumerary clerks whose fees bore little or no relation to what they contributed to the rendering of justice; its delays enormous, its costs ruinous, and its judgements (when at last they came) uncertain and open to evasion.[64] Yet only the most tentative initiatives towards reform had been taken before the Hale Commission was appointed. That body dealt at length, and quite radically, with Chancery and equity in its large final bill for judicial reform, but Barebone's Parliament quickly showed that it meant to go much further. On 5 August, after a

[62] J. Streater, *A Further Continuance of the Grand Politick Informer* ([31 Oct.] 1653), p. 42; *CSPD 1653–4*, pp. 106, 143, 243, 261, 268, 435; *CJ*, vii, 353; *Clavis ad aperiendum Carceris Ostia* (21 Nov. 1653).

[63] [J. Canne], *Lieut. Colonel John Lilb. Tryed and Cast*, p. 164.

[64] Veall, *Popular Movement for Law Reform*, pp. 32–5; Prall, *Agitation for Law Reform*, pp. 81–8. Prall's article 'Chancery reform and the Puritan Revolution', *American Journal of Legal History*, no. 6 (1962), pp. 28–42, has some background information but is unreliable on the proceedings in Barebone's Parliament.

single day's debate, it voted for the immediate abolition of the court. It instructed the committee for the law to bring in a bill for the purpose, and also a further bill to provide other means for determining all pending and future cases in equity.[65] This evidently proved a tougher task than the House foresaw, and for the committee a more uncongenial one; at any rate no bill was ready by the time the Michaelmas term was about to begin. The radicals then took the initiative on 15 October with a motion that proceedings in Chancery should be suspended for a month. The House was deeply split; it divided on whether the question should be put, and the fact that Harrison and Strickland were the tellers for the Yeas indicates that both sides hoped to win. In the main vote the radicals had a majority of three in favour of suspension, but when a bill was brought in two days later to give it effect the final division was a tie and the Speaker gave his casting vote against it.[66] Passions rose high; the lay preacher Dennis Hollister had to excuse himself for some remarks spoken in heat. The House finally ordered that the bill for determining the cases currently pending in Chancery should be brought in the day after next.

A bill for abolishing the Court of Chancery and appointing commissioners to adjudge all pending and future cases was duly introduced, read twice, and committed back to the committee for the law, with Robert Bennett and Philip Jones added to it for this purpose. On Saturday, 22 October, however, Wingfield reported from the committee what was evidently a new bill 'for constituting Commissioners for hearing and determining Causes of Equity in Chancery'. This the House rejected after a single reading, and it ordered the committee for the law to sit that afternoon upon the bill which it had formerly committed and to bring it in with the desired amendments on the Monday. These were not reported, however, until the 27th, when after two readings they were rejected. A debate followed on whether to commit the bill once more, at the end of which the ultra-radical Broughton and his fellow-lawyer Wingfield (politically moderate

[65] *CJ*, vii, 296; Veall, pp. 87–8, 178–80; *Somers Tracts*, vi, 202–11.

[66] *CJ*, vii, 335. The tellers' names show the polarizing effect of these votes: Highland and Ireton against Pickering and Col. Clark on 15 Oct., Ireton and Spence against Ashley Cooper and Jonathan Goddard on the 17th. Attendances were between 74 and 83.

but radically inclined on law reform) were tellers for the forty-four Noes against the thirty-six Yeas counted by the moderates Tichborne and Henry King. The bill was then rejected without a further division. Broughton (since 20 October) and Wingfield were both on the committee for the law; it must have been in considerable disarray.[67]

Highland is the only commentator who tells us anything significant about the points at issue in these confrontations, and his account is not easy to square with the *Journal*'s sparse record. But it was probably the first abolition bill, introduced on 17 October, which he says 'was looked on by many as the washing of a blackamoor, or pruning or lopping evil branches, where three or four in a little time will come instead of one cut off'. The next bill, brought in shortly afterwards (presumably on the 22nd, by Wingfield) 'to very many seemed to be a setting up of two courts, rather than a casting down one, and an establishment of the Chancery, rather than taking it away; some gentlemen of great note of the long robe had a hand in it, that is likely will never spoil their own trade; the bill by very many, after a long and sharp debate, was judged short of the end aimed at.'[68] What comes through clearly from Highland, despite apparent confusions over details, is that the radicals distrusted the intentions of the committee for the law and felt that the legal profession was fighting a strong rearguard action even in this least sympathetic of arenas.

The last attempt to break through these persistent disagreements came in a comprehensive new bill which Colonel West introduced from the committee for the law on 3 November. It would not only have abolished the Court of Chancery and appointed commissioners and judges to determine present and future cases in equity, but also extended to various abuses in the common law courts as well. Highland describes it as an altogether more radical measure, which would have dispatched all ordinary cases for a mere twenty or forty shillings, and he accounts for it by the return to Westminster of members of the committee who were no such friends to Chancery as those who drafted the former bills. It was given a second reading the same day and committed back to the same committee, with Harrison and St. Nicholas

---

[67] *CJ*, vii, 336, 338, 340.
[68] *Exact Relation*, pp. 275–6.

added—a sign that the radicals were indeed out in strength, since St. Nicholas had lost his seat on the council only two days earlier and Harrison had only just kept his.[69] But nothing came of it; pressure of business kept the bill from coming before the House again, and the abolition of Chancery, like that of tithes and lay patronage and other outworks of Babylon, remained among the unfulfilled intentions of the radical wing.

Yet another reforming bill which never re-emerged from the committee for the law after its first two readings was one which Wingfield introduced on 29 October 'for regulating the great Exorbitances of Fees in the Law, and elsewhere'.[70] Earlier the radicals did score a minor victory when a bill to continue the jurisdiction of the Duchy and County Palatine of Lancaster was rejected after a single reading on 16 September. Instead a bill was passed next day to renew that of the county court only, but only until 1st January next, and only after the word 'palatine' with its regal connotations had been expressly voted out. The Duchy Court therefore lapsed until a Cromwellian ordinance revived it, and its Chancellor John Bradshaw, the arch-regicide, and Vice-Chancellor Thomas Fell, George Fox's protector, were reduced to mere temporary commissioners.[71] There was a more ambitious move, which arose in a debate on revenue matters on 4 November, to abolish the Court of Exchequer. This had been one of the targets of the Hale Commission, which had proposed to transfer the jurisdiction in all fiscal matters to the Upper Bench. Where Barebone's Parliament would have vested it is unknown, for after referring it to the committee for inspecting the treasuries it never returned to the matter.[72]

Its uncompleted or merely projected legislation was indeed potentially weightier and more interesting than that which it actually accomplished, and much of it was cut short by lack of time rather than by the deepening divisions in the House. An Act of Union to incorporate Scotland in the Commonwealth got as far as being engrossed on 23 November, after very full consideration which included four debates in grand committee.

---

[69] *CJ*, vii, 346; *Exact Relation*, p. 276.

[70] *CJ*, vii, 342.

[71] *CJ*, vii, 319–20; Firth and Rait, ii, 722, 916.

[72] *CJ*, vii, 346; Clarke MS XXV, fos. 150, 152; *Weekly Intelligencer*, no. 143, 1–8 Nov. 1653, p. 47; *A Perfect Account*, no. 148, 2–9 Nov. 1653, pp. 1180–1; *The Perfect Diurnall*, no. 204, 31 Oct.–7 Nov. 1653, p. 3116; *Somers Tracts*, vi, 231.

Only the mounting troubles in the Highlands caused its final passage to be deferred.[73] A large bill for the advancement and regulation of trade was brought in on 29 October from the committee for trade, but its second reading was put off four times by the pressure of other business. The only commercial measures to reach the statute book were a short act to permit tobacco-planting in England until the end of the year, despite the Rump's ban, and an act to incorporate the worsted-weavers of Norfolk and Norwich and to regulate their products.[74] It is perhaps surprising that this of all parliaments did not give higher priority to the problems of poverty and unemployment, but Highland tells us that the standing committee for the poor had a bill ready 'for work-houses and providing for the poor' but failed, in the keen competition for parliamentary time, to get a hearing for it.[75] Nor was the House uninterested in the old grievance of depopulating enclosures, for as late as 28 November it instructed the same committee to investigate it and recommend what should be done.[76]

With so much attempted in so short a time, to ask whether there were any widely desired reforms which Barebone's Parliament left unconsidered might seem otiose. Yet there were two or three conspicuous omissions. Its apparent indifference, even perhaps hostility, to the long-canvassed schemes for county judicatures and land registries has already been noticed. It also seems not to have concerned itself with the subjection of copyholders to uncertain fines on entry, which the Hale Commission had proposed to limit to the value of one year's rent. Both the Hale Commission and the Cromwellian ordinances of 1654 sought to suppress duelling and to deal more strictly with drunkenness, swearing, and Sabbath-breaking, but these familiar targets of Puritan zeal—indeed the whole field of what Cromwell called 'a reformation of manners'—figure hardly at all in the formal records of this parliament's proceedings. Their absence, however, is probably deceptive. The members were certainly kept aware, if they needed reminding, of the need to wage sterner war upon the sins of the flesh and other pleasures of the profane,

---

[73] *CJ*, vii, 329, 333, 336, 339–40, 355; *Exact Relation*, p. 274.
[74] *CJ*, vii, 313, 341, 347, 349–50, 356, 362; Firth and Rait, ii, 718–19, 774–80.
[75] *Exact Relation*, p. 272.
[76] *CJ*, vii, 358.

notably by a petition from Shropshire which they heard sympathetically on 3 October,[77] but they probably agreed with the petitioners themselves that the best means towards such ends lay in the propagation of the gospel and in settling able and faithful ministers in the place of ignorant or scandalous ones, and it was to such objectives that they finally gave priority. Meanwhile the radicals probably expected the committee for a new body of the law to deal comprehensively with profanity, immorality, and other breaches of the Commandments. We know from Highland that it tackled the criminal law first, working from treason downward through murder and theft and constantly taking the law of God as its yardstick, so it can be safely assumed that its code would, like its exemplar in Massachusetts, have covered all kinds of offences against the Puritan canon.[78]

Turning back to the acts which were actually passed, some of them inflamed the antagonism between moderates and zealots much more than one would expect from their content. One such was the Act for a High Court of Justice. The initiative for it came from the Council of State, on account of the mounting evidence of royalist conspiracy, and when Moyer recommended it thence on 10 August the House agreed to it without a division and instructed the council to bring in a bill next morning, with the names of the commissioners who should compose the court. The council then promptly deputed Thomas St. Nicholas, Moyer, and Tichborne—two mild radicals and a mild moderate—to draft the bill. Nothing more is heard of it until 13 September, when the council, which had at last agreed on the commissioners' names, ordered Broughton to draft the necessary bill, and also another which the parliament had called for to clarify what constituted treason. Nine days later the council had to tell Broughton to get on with it, but the bill for a High Court of Justice was ready by the 26th, when parliament ordered that it should be brought in on the 28th. That day, however, a lengthy grand committee crowded it out, after which a thin House divided over whether it should be brought in next morning. Surprisingly, two pairs of radical tellers opposed each other, and

[77] Printed in *Several Proceedings of State Affairs*, no. 210, 29 Sept.–6 Oct. 1653, pp. 3322–5.
[78] *Exact Relation*, pp. 277–8.

the thirty-two Noes counted by Squibb and Barebone beat the twenty-eight Yeas who voted with Broughton and Bowtell. Broughton eventually introduced the bill on 13 October, when it was read twice and committed to a committee on which nine radicals, including Broughton, Harrison, Courtney, and Barebone, sat with only four moderates. They were ordered to meet that very afternoon, but for some reason nothing more happened until Monday 21 November, when a new bill was read, debated, and finally passed on the same day. Highland complains that it was rushed through with indecent haste, and that the House would neither give time to a reading of the various Treason Acts which the High Court of Justice was to enforce nor have the bill engrossed, which would have postponed its passing until next day. Its supporters said, 'That they knew not but by that time they might have their throats cut', but according to Highland their real motive was that many religious radicals, whose opposition they feared, were away at the Monday prayer-meeting at Blackfriars. Yet the House spent most of a day's sitting on the bill, voting on each of the court's thirty-three commissioners individually and rejecting only one. There was apparently an attempt next day to reopen the debate on the act, but it was confirmed without a division.[79] It seems extraordinary that the radicals should have regarded its passing as a kind of conspiracy when they themselves had been given so large a part in framing it, but it is a comment on the polarization that took place during its long gestation that a measure which was aimed against the supporters of King Charles should have come to be feared as an engine for crushing the champions of King Jesus.[80]

The remaining bills which notably bred division fall into two groups, the first being variously concerned with the disposing of the property of the losers in the Civil War, the second with the two main regular sources of revenue, the excise and the monthly assessment. One important bill in the former group failed altogether, though not before it had played its part in the polarizing process. It was styled 'A further additional Act for the sale of several lands and estates forfeited to the Commonwealth

[79] *CJ*, vii, 297, 325, 334, 353–4; *CSPD 1653–4*, pp. 82–4, 145, 161, 199; *Exact Relation*, p. 273. The names of the commissioners, who included no MPs, seem to yield no clue to the radicals' opposition.

[80] Gardiner, *C & P*, ii, 269–70, quoting Pauluzzi and Bordeaux.

for treason', a title very like that of the three acts of sale whereby the Rump had sold up the estates of hundreds of royalists in 1651–2. Whether it envisaged fresh confiscations of royalist property on a comparable scale is not known, but the same William Skinner was to be the leading trustee as in the three former acts.[81] Colonel West introduced it on 17 August from a committee appointed to receive propositions for the raising of money. It was given a second reading immediately and committed back to the same committee, with Sadler added. It began to run into trouble on the 20th, however, with a clause which made over to the trustees for sale all the glebe and rectory lands belonging to all the delinquents named in the former three acts. This was at first approved by 42 votes to 28 and ordered to be engrossed, but when it came back ten days later it was thrown out by 59 to 31. On each occasion West was a teller in favour of it and Sadler against it; at the second vote West's partner was Highland and Sadler's Ashley Cooper, so it looks as though party lines were hardening. The more conservative members may have been alarmed because the bill was calling into question the rights of lay owners to land formerly ecclesiastical, or they may have felt like Cromwell that the mulcting of royalist property had gone too far already. At any rate a succession of provisos, including one to annul the sale of any estate that had been assured to its owner by articles granted during the Civil War, were all defeated, and after much of the next day's sitting had been spent in debating it the bill itself was rejected without a division.[82]

The honouring of articles granted on surrender had been one of the requests in the army officers' petition to the Rump of August 1652, and it was a burning issue in the case of a particular royalist, Sir John Stawell. This came to occupy many hours of the parliament's time and was still being hotly controverted when it resigned its authority. Stawell was a wealthy Somerset landlord who had raised large forces for the king and had eventually surrendered to Fairfax in 1646 upon the Articles of Exeter, which entitled him to compound for his estate. But because he repeatedly refused to take the Negative Oath and the Covenant, and then behaved defiantly when in consequence he

[81] *CJ*, vii, 305; Firth and Rait, ii, 552, 593, 639.
[82] *CJ*, vii, 302, 305, 310–11.

was brought before the Commons, he was charged with high treason for levying war against the parliament and committed to Newgate. After long delays in bringing him to trial, the Rump picked him on 28 June 1650 as one of six prisoners who were to be tried for their lives by a High Court of Justice, and he was moved to the Tower. There were allegations of cruelties committed by him as Governor of Taunton, but whether these really caused the House's animus against him or were prompted by it is not clear. According to Stawell it was Hesilrige who pressed hardest for the capital charge and the forfeiture of his large estate. On hearing him in December, however, the High Court proved unwilling to convict him and referred his case back to the parliament, which left it undetermined but named him first in the Act of Sale of 16 July 1651.[83] All his lands were sold off, and by 1653 they were dispersed among a considerable number of purchasers.

By then the army officers were so incensed at the Rump's frequent breach of articles to which they had pledged their faith that soon after the April dissolution they set up a committee to provide redress for any wrongs done by the recent confiscations. Cromwell personally interested himself in Stawell, who was released from the Tower by the interim Council of State on 25 May, subject to his giving security to render himself up if summoned.[84] His case was referred to the Commissioners for Articles, a strong body whose function was to give relief to royalists who had been denied benefits granted in their terms of surrender. The Rump had revived it in September 1652, presumably in response to the army officers' petition. John Bradshaw headed it, and it included seven of the new MPs: Moyer, Sadler, Tichborne, Ireton, Blount, Desborough, and Tomlinson.[85]

Some of the purchasers, understandably alarmed, addressed a petition to Barebone's Parliament. The House heard it on 8 August and resolved to consider the case on the 12th, meanwhile

[83] Firth and Rait, ii, 520. For Stawell's story see *DNB*; Underdown, *Somerset in the Civil War and Interregnum*, pp. 159–60 and *passim*; Gardiner, *C & P*, ii, 257; Aylmer, *State's Servants*, p. 135; *The Humble Petition of Sir John Stawell* (1653, reprinted in *Somers Tracts*, vi, 32–6); *To the Supreme Authority the Parliament . . . The Humble Remonstrance of Sir John Stawell* (1653); and further sources cited in the next few notes.

[84] *CSPD 1652–3*, 351; Clarendon MS 45, fo. 485, and MS 46, fo. 71.

[85] Firth and Rait, ii, 619; cf. pp. 148–51 for the original Commissioners of 1649–50.

instructing the committee for petitions to brief good counsel to represent the Commonwealth before the Commissioners for Articles. But the pressure of other business prevented it from returning to the purchasers' predicament until the 29th—two weeks after the Commissioners had pronounced. They had adjudged that Stawell had good right to compound for his entire estate, and that when he had paid his composition the purchasers should restore it all to him.[86] The parliament reached no conclusion on the 29th but referred it back to the committee for petitions to recommend with all speed what it thought should be done to relieve the purchasers. Next day an attempt to uphold the Commissioners' judgement in Stawell's favour by means of a proviso to be inserted in the general act of sale then under debate was defeated. The eventual and not very speedy outcome from the committee for petitions was a bill to confirm the sales of his estate which was read twice on 17 September, recommitted, and after further debates finally passed on 13 October.[87] The round had gone to the purchasers, and though he fought back again under the Protectorate Stawell spent the rest of the Interregnum as a prisoner and recovered his lands only after the Restoration. It was a case in which it was hard to do justice after the initial injustices committed by the Long Parliament, for the purchasers had laid out good money in good faith, but it begot unhappy divisions, not only between the army and the parliament but also within the latter. Radicals accused those who spoke for Stawell of espousing the Cavaliers' interest; moderates indignantly denied it, maintaining that all they asked for him, in the name of common justice and the army's honour, was the 'reasonable satisfaction' to which the Commissioners' judgement entitled him.[88]

Much the longest act which this parliament passed, and the gravest in its consequences, was that which provided for the disposal of vast areas of Irish land to satisfy the 'Adventurers' who had advanced money on this security and to meet the arrears of pay of the army in Ireland. If it does not receive the

[86] *To the Supreme Authority . . . The Humble Remonstrance of Sir John Stawell*, pp. 65–72, where the report of the Commissioners is printed in full; *CJ*, vii, 296, 309–10.

[87] *CJ*, vii, 310, 320, 328, 334.

[88] *A True Narrative of the Cause and Manner of the Dissolution of the late Parliament* (12 Dec. 1653: hereafter *True Narrative*), pp. 1, 4; *An Answer to a Paper entituled A True Narrative* ([4 Jan.] 1654: hereafter *Answer to a True Narrative*), p. 6; *Confusion Confounded*, pp. 12–13.

prominence here that it intrinsically deserves it is because it merely gave effect to a policy to which the Commonwealth was already committed, and because it owed little to the parliament's initiative. The Rump's Act for the Settling of Ireland (12 August 1652) had set the course, though it was largely determined still earlier, and within a month of the Rump's dissolution the interim Council of State had deputed Lambert, Philip Jones, Robert Bennett, Scobell, and Thurloe to draft an act for the disposing of lands in Ireland. Soon afterwards the council set up a committee which sat at Grocers' Hall in London and allocated available land to the Adventurers by lot, and four commissioners (Charles Fleetwood, Edmund Ludlow, Miles Corbet, and John Jones) to execute the English government's instructions at the Irish end.[89] The act which Barebone's Parliament passed on 26 September confirmed both bodies, together with the council's earlier orders and instructions. It was introduced on 1 September, given its second reading on the 3rd, and debated on six more days before it was finally passed, but though it occasioned five divisions the points at issue seem to have been practical rather than 'party' ones.[90] If Vincent Gookin uttered any such protest at the wholesale dispossession of the native Irish as he published sixteen months later it went unrecorded, and there is no sign that Irish policy aroused any serious dispute in England during the period covered by this book.

Much more division arose over those other age-long losers, the English Roman Catholics, though here it was not simply between moderates and radicals. On 9 September the House heard a petition from some papists who were under sequestration for recusancy. Four days later it voted ominously that the reading of it should be expunged from the record, and then listened to a brief bill, which Colonel West introduced from the committee for raising money, and which instructed the Commissioners for Compounding to dispose of two-thirds of any recusant's estate that was forfeited or sequestered by any act or order of parliament. It spread its net to catch not only those Catholics who had not yet compounded for delinquency but also all who

[89] *CSPD 1652–3*, pp. 332, 369; cf. pp. 322, 341, 350, 371, 445.

[90] *CJ*, vii, 311, 313, 315–16, 322–5, Firth and Rait, ii, 722–53. For the fullest account of the Irish land settlement and of this act's place in it see K. S. Bottigheimer, *English Money and Irish Land* (Oxford, 1971), chs. 5 and 6.

might fall foul of the act of 1587 whereby failure to pay a
recusancy fine of £20 a month could incur forfeiture of two-
thirds of the whole estate. The new bill gave each recusant three
months in which to redeem those two-thirds for his lifetime by
paying four years' annual value in the case of land, or a third of
the total value in the case of personal property. If he did not take
up the option, the Commissioners were to sell the lease of the
forfeited portion for his remaining lifetime to the highest bidder,
though at his death his heir was to be given the same option. To
discourage fellow-Catholics from coming to each others' rescue,
the lands so disposed of were to remain subject to the penal
laws.[91] It was a harsh measure, since the two-thirds penalty was
in practice never exacted, and it was accorded a second reading
only after a division, in which all four tellers were moderate
men. The Yeas won by 54 to 21 and the bill was sent back after
a full debate to the same committee, powerfully reinforced for
the purpose by Sadler, Jones, Brooke, Tichborne, Barebone, and
Moyer, and later by Carew and Strickland. Sundry amendments
and provisos gave rise to further lengthy debates before the
House divided on 21 October over whether it should finally pass.
It did so by 49 votes to 25, Lord Lisle and Tichborne being tellers
in favour of it and Barebone and Henry King against.[92]
Barebone doubtless opposed it for the same reason as Highland,
namely that severe though it was it amounted to a toleration of
papists, but King, who was shortly to be a teller against the
religious radicals' motion to abolish lay patrons' rights of
presentation, probably had a different motive. Perhaps he
disliked exploiting religious persecution for fiscal ends.

Nevertheless fiscal problems were urgent, and the constant
difficulty of making financial ends meet meant that there was no
way of preventing both the largest sources of revenue, the excise
and the monthly assessment, from becoming (especially the
latter) additional bones of contention just when the major
disputes over religious policy were entering their most divisive
phase.

The excise had been bitterly unpopular ever since its first

---

[91] *CJ*, vii, 317; *An Act enabling the Commissioners . . . to dispose of two parts of the Estates of
Recusants* (21 Oct. 1653); not in Firth and Rait, but printed in *Mercurius Politicus*, no. 176,
20–27 Oct. 1653, pp. 2812–14.
[92] *CJ*, vii, 317, 320, 332, 336–7; voting figures as usual include the tellers.

introduction as a war measure, especially among radical reformers who took up the cudgels on behalf of the hard-hit poor, and after ten years the stream of protest showed no signs of drying up.[93] A riot against some excisemen just after the expulsion of the Rump caused the new Council of State to depute Harrison and Carew to look into the whole state of the tax, and shortly afterwards it constituted a high-powered Excise Committee,[94] but nothing positive was done before the Rump's last renewal of the hated impost ran out in August. Barebone's Parliament passed a brief act for its continuance on 6 September, but there was a division over how long it was to remain in force, and the outcome was that it was to run only until 29 December next—little more than three months, compared with three years in the Rump's last act.[95] This was clear notice that the House intended to consider the whole future of the excise, and this it did in a four-day debate beginning on 25 November in which it voted separately on every single excisable commodity and the rate at which it was charged. A few items, notably all home-produced woollen goods sold in the home market, were exempted altogether; a few others, including lead, hops, and soap, had their rates reduced, while cider and spirits had theirs raised, but the great majority were confirmed.[96] On the 30th, at the end of the long exercise, a bill of about eighty sheets for settling the excise was given its first reading.

It never had a second. Most of the next morning was spent in wrangling over which business to proceed with, some members calling for the bill to abolish lay patronage, others for the report of the committee for tithes, others yet for the almost completed union with Scotland. Highland says that the excise bill 'was by

[93] Recent examples included *Barnabies Summons* ([Sept.] 1652); James Ibeson, *To the Supream Authority . . . A second Remonstrance* ([Oct.] 1652); *The Excise-mans Lamentation* ([1 Dec.] 1652); *The Onely Right Rule for Regulating the Lawes* (28 Jan. 1653), p. 10; *The Judiciall Arraignment . . . of the late pernicious endenized Dutch Devil Excize* ([14 June] 1653).

[94] *CSPD 1652–3*, pp. 301, 305, 332, 343.

[95] *CJ*, vii, 307, 315; Firth and Rait, iii, lxxx. The tellers for 29 December were moderates (Tichborne ahd Henry Cromwell), and against it were the relatively radical Ireton and Wroth Rogers. The Noes may have included some who favoured a longer extension and others who opposed any renewal at all.

[96] *CJ*, vii, 352, 356, 358–61. Other goods exempted were Monmouth caps, beaver hats, tobacco pipes, English alum exported, English salt for preserving fish, and lampreys sold to foreigners for cod bait. The *Commons' Journal* does not list the previous rates for imported items, but sample checking shows them unchanged on such key commodities as tobacco, wine, vinegar, and woollen cloth, though raised on imported spirits.

general consent waved and laid aside', because it contained so many snares and difficulties as to trade and so many burdens 'no way fit for a people that expected freedom at the price of their blood and treasure'. In fact, however, the House ended this sterile sitting by voting that a new bill to continue the excise 'for a time', at the rates already voted, should be brought in by the same committee that had drafted the former one.[97] Why it wanted a new bill, or how it was to differ from that on which it had spent so much time, can only be guessed at. The probable explanation is that after low attendances during the boring debates on the details of the excise[98] the radicals turned up in strength on 1 December in the hope of getting their bill against lay patrons read, and took the opportunity to launch a general assault on the excise of the kind that Highland describes. It may be that a new bill of short duration, possibly containing concessions but at least ensuring that the last week's debates on the rates should not be totally wasted, was the best that could be secured by the responsible members who realized how ruinous the total loss of the excise would be. It was never introduced, for the report of the committee for tithes was read next day and the final breach swiftly followed. It required one of Cromwell's earliest ordinances to save the excise from lapsing.[99]

The monthly assessment was even more vital to financial survival, not only for its great yield but also because it was appropriated to the maintenance of the army and the navy. Barebone's Parliament baulked at renewing it in its current form, and this became yet another polarizing issue, both before and after its resignation. The Rump had raised the rate once more from £90,000 to £120,000 a month in December 1652, but that act had expired six months later, and thereafter its continuance rested on the dubious authority of an order by Cromwell and the interim Council of State to extend it until 25 December 1653.[1] The assessment aroused resentment not just by its grievous weight but by its unequal incidence; critics claimed that some towns and counties were having to pay twelve or

[97] Compare *Exact Relation*, pp. 272, 280, with *CJ*, vii, 361.

[98] The only two divisions during the relevant days show 71 present on 25 Nov. and 74 on 26 Nov., including the Speaker.

[99] Firth and Rait, ii, 823.

[1] Ibid. 653–88, *CSPD 1652–3*, p. 305; *A Declaration and Order . . . for the continuance of the Assessment from 24 June to 25 Dec.* (9 June 1653).

thirteen shillings in the pound while others contributed only two or three.[2] The House took up the grievance on 19 September in a full-scale debate 'touching equality in taxes', over which it spent a further three days in grand committee. It ended the last of them, 14 October, with three votes: that the next assessment should (as before) set a fixed sum for each county to raise; that these sums should be based on a pound rate upon estates real and personal; and that the Committee for the Army was 'to consider how these votes may be made practicable, with the greatest equality'.[3]

If the intention was that the pound rate should be the same everywhere, which was the aim of the radicals,[4] these votes were virtually incompatible. Nobody in this least bureaucratized of major European states could have reckoned with the remotest accuracy what x shillings in the pound would yield throughout all the counties and major towns in the land. The existing assessment doubtless involved inequalities, but its overwhelming advantage was that its commissioners knew how much they must collect and the government how much it would receive. The urgency of continuing it was soon brought home on 26 and 27 October when seamen of the navy stormed mutinously into London, armed and determined. Their grievances included impressment and non-payment of prize money as well as their arrears of normal pay, but it was a fact that ships were being kept in commission only because the money was not there to pay off their crews, whose wives and children were meanwhile often destitute. On the 26th there were casualties on both sides when the seamen found their way barred by a body of troops, but some of them got through to Whitehall and had an angry confrontation with Cromwell and Monck. They marched towards Whitehall again next day, but this time they were broken up and dispersed at Charing Cross, not without bloodshed, by a force which included a foot regiment and Cromwell's life guard. Some were captured and interrogated by the council, and a ringleader was publicly hanged.[5]

[2] *True Narrative*, pp. 3–4; cf. *Exact Relation*, p. 274.
[3] *CJ*, vii, 321, 325, 333–4.
[4] *True Narrative*, pp. 3–4.
[5] *Mercurius Politicus*, no. 177, 27 Oct.–3 Nov. 1653, pp. 2828–9, 2831–3; *CSP Ven 1653–4*, p. 145; PRO 31.3/92, fos. 6–7; Clarendon MS 47, fo. 43; *CSPD 1653–4*, p. 218; Gardiner, *C & P*, ii, 360–1.

A bill to renew the assessment was introduced on 4 November, and after its second reading on the 8th the House voted without a division to keep the rate at £120,000 for six more months. It divided, however, over whether this sum should be apportioned among the counties as in the last act. The Yeas had it by 52 votes to 29, including the tellers, who curiously were all prominent moderates and members of the Council of State.[6] This is interesting not only for the council's disarray but also for the slight resistance to the measure offered by the radicals, in view of the subsequent charges that they opposed the assessment outright and threatened to starve the army. At some stage in the debates, however, some of them did propose that the senior army officers should serve for a year without pay, which was most strongly resented.[7] After a further day's debate the bill was committed to the Committee for the Army. Thence it came back with minor amendments, and the House debated it on three more days, making some trifling adjustments in a few quotas before eventually passing it on 24 November.[8] The radicals gave their loud 'Noes' in that final vote, and Highland claims that if they had pressed for a division they would have 'hazarded the passing of it',[9] but in view of their earlier showing one must doubt him. Another radical member claimed that they opposed the bill only in order that a fairer one based on a pound rate could be brought in,[10] but having already lost that battle they had the worst of both worlds by lacking the nerve to force a division while reinforcing their reputation for financial irresponsibility and hostility to the army.

This account of the parliament's legislative efforts has run on ahead of certain other important events and developments during November and early December which made its survival

[6] Howard and Ashley Cooper for the Yeas, Jones and Wolseley for the Noes: *CJ*, vii, 347.

[7] This was admitted by the radical member who wrote *A True Narrative*, p. 3.

[8] *CJ*, vii, 351, 355. The act is not printed by Firth and Rait, but it was published at the time, and the sums charged on each county are also printed in *Mercurius Politicus*, no. 183, 9–13 Dec. 1653, pp. 3130–5. Gardiner in *C & P*, ii, 263, was mistaken in saying that London's quota was raised from £6,000 to £8,000, for that had been its sum in the 1652 act: Firth and Rait, ii, 655. The differences between the two acts were very few and small.

[9] *Exact Relation*, pp. 273–4.

[10] *True Narrative*, pp. 3–4.

increasingly doubtful. The thematic approach has, it is hoped, indicated which issues were already widening its divisions before the major questions of religious settlement came to the fore from mid-November onwards. It has not conveyed, however, how much time was spent more or less patiently on matters which seldom split the membership along ideological lines and which it would be tedious to chronicle: the constant search for untapped sources of revenue, the suits of royalists whom even this assembly could not quite treat as ordinary subjects, such as Viscount Mansfield, the Earl of Clanrickard, the Duchess of Hamilton, and the Countess of Derby (though she, combative even in defeat, did set moderates and radicals against each other[11]), the claims and pleas of many lesser individuals, the embassy to Sweden of Bulstrode Whitelocke, and all those minor contingencies which distracted every parliament of the Interregnum. Before November no one issue had sundered the membership irreparably, though the lines of fission were pretty clearly drawn and the 'new body of the law' might have precipitated the final breach if the religious disputes had not done so first. To demonstrate how in fact that breach occurred, it is necessary to focus on the last six weeks of the House's existence and to treat events inside and outside its walls in counterpoint.

[11] *CJ*, vii, 325–31.

X

The Breakdown of
Barebone's Parliament

Until those final weeks the radical caucus was very rarely in
command of the House. It could find enough support to win
occasional votes, as over the abolition of Chancery and the
committee for a new body of the law, but it remained to be seen
whether it could translate them into legislative action. So far,
when radicals had divided the House against moderates, they
had lost more often than they had won. This would change
during November and early December, but until then they were
still easily outvoted whenever the more conservative members
troubled to turn up in strength.

This was very strikingly demonstrated when elections to the
Council of State, whose original term had expired, were held on
1 November. The parliament had decided to select by ballot
sixteen of the serving councillors and to elect fifteen new ones, all
from its own membership. The occasion attracted the largest
recorded attendance since the opening ceremony, and before
proceeding to the main business this unwontedly full House chose
the preacher for its customary devotions on the anniversary of
Gunpowder Plot. It voted significantly to invite the eminent and
orthodox Stephen Marshall, who had preached at St. Margaret's
since 1642 and been a pillar of the Westminster Assembly.[1] It
then proceeded to elect the councillors who were to continue
serving, each member writing sixteen names on a piece of paper.
Cromwell received the votes of all the 113 present and Sir Gilbert
Pickering ran him remarkably close with 110. Pickering's

[1] *CJ*, vii, 343.

combination of social eminence, proven competence, devotion to business, moderate politics, and radical Puritan sympathies evidently won him almost universal confidence. There was a big gap before the next two, Desborough with 74 votes and Strickland with 71, and then came a bunch in the sixties: Lawrence, Sydenham, Jones, Wolseley, Tichborne, and Ashley Cooper, in that order. Only after them came the first radicals, Carew with 59 votes and Harrison with 58, and they were the only two to be re-elected. Among those discarded were some of the busiest men in the House, including Moyer, Robert Bennett, Broughton, Courtney, Stapley, Thomas St. Nicholas, and Sir James Hope. It is less surprising that Hollister and Williams were dropped, and not surprising at all that Salwey was, for like Lambert (who also lost his place) he had boycotted the council throughout the session. Bennett and Stapley, though active as MPs, had only attended it eight and six times respectively since July, while Harrison, who just scraped in, had registered only seven attendances in the same period.

Moderate men scored just as sweeping a victory in the election of the fifteen new councillors. Colonel Anthony Rous topped the poll with an extraordinary lead over the next candidate— 93 votes to Sir William Roberts's 63. He must have had, like Pickering, a special capacity for pleasing both moderates and radicals, though his own generally moderate stance and his subsequent loyal service under the Protectorate are well attested.[2] After Roberts came a whole string of moderates: Sadler, Sir Robert King, Henry Cromwell, Jonathan Goddard, Sir William Brownlow, Colonel Nathaniel Barton, Lord Eure, John Stone, and George Fleetwood. Then came the first radical, the Fifth Monarchist John James with 53 votes, and after him only one other, Anlaby (who was no extremist), with a minimal 52. That made four radicals in a council of thirty-one.[3]

The bias of the elections ran in favour not only of moderation but also of social rank. It is difficult to see what else won success for Lord Eure and Viscount Lisle, for Eure's participation in parliamentary business seems to have been exiguous, while Lisle had been a lazy councillor and had avoided parliamentary

---

[2] Firth and Rait, ii, 824, 828, 869, 917, 969, 1039, 1064; Burton, *Diary*, i, cxvi; ii, 289–90; *CSPD 1654*, p. 67; Coate, *Cornwall in the Great Civil War*, p. 293.

[3] *CJ*, vii, 343–4.

committees like the plague. Their baronetcies doubtless helped
young Wolseley (who had been to only nine of the last seventy-
two council meetings) and Ashley Cooper to keep their seats, and
Brownlow (with only two committees to his name) to gain his.
Three even of the four radicals were of good gentry stock.
Harrison was the exception, and the only other non-gentry
councillors were the hard-working Desborough and Stone.

The new council held thirty-six meetings before the parliament's resignation terminated its authority. Harrison was the
only member who attended none of them, though Carew and
James came to few. After a week it reconstituted its six main
standing committees, and except on the large ordnance committee the radicals were almost entirely passed over. The most
significant new departure, however, was that Cromwell was
named first on five of them. His period of self-effacement was
over, for he was also put at the head of a four-man committee of
secrecy which was to handle all secret intelligence that came in
and to communicate it to the council as it thought fit. Its other
three members were the trusted Strickland, Sydenham, and
Lawrence.[4] These arrangements, no less than the parliament's
unanimous vote for him, greatly enhanced his standing in the
executive; indeed with Thurloe's role as Secretary expanding
steadily he was already closely surrounded by nearly all the men
whom he would choose as councillors when he became Protector.
Why then, if the House had pronounced against the zealots and
the council had put him in a position to give the government a
strong lead, could not Barebone's Parliament have taken on a
new lease of life?

The answer is twofold. The moderates attended in force only
when they saw a danger of their opponents winning votes on
major issues, whereas the radicals, though their attendance too
was irregular and selective, were more successful both in
mustering their full strength when they needed it and in winning
over the votes of the uncommitted and the uncertain. On the day
after the council elections there were only 65 members in the
House, including the Speaker, and on the 15th only 49, a number
revealed by a division (otherwise unimportant) in which two
moderate members of the Council of State acted as tellers against
two radicals and lost by ten votes. There were other signs that

---

[4] *CSPD 1653–4*, p. 237.

the moderates were leaving the field to their antagonists, as when Harrison and St. Nicholas were added to the committee for the law on the 3rd, a further five strong radicals to the committee for a new body of the law on the 10th, and Courtney and Hollister to the navy committee on the 14th.[5] If Harrison and some of his Welsh contingent had doubted earlier whether this assembly was worth persevering with, they evidently changed their minds now. Perhaps the conservative landslide in the council elections acted as a spur, though there was a still stronger stimulus when vital questions concerning religious settlement came up for decision.

On 17 November, when the House considered the right of lay patrons to present to benefices, well over a hundred members were present, even though the *Commons' Journal* records no prior notice of the debate. From the conservative standpoint it was not enough. Lay patronage was at least as explosive an issue as tithes. As with tithes, rights of property were powerfully involved, and indeed the link was close because lay owners of impropriated rectorial tithes commonly held the advowson too. Out of 9,284 livings in the pre-Civil War Church 3,845 were impropriated, but lay patronage extended much further than impropriation and was much older. It has been calculated that out of 2,323 parish benefices in the dioceses of York, Lincoln, Norwich, and Rochester, 1,494—just over 64 per cent—were controlled by laymen other than the crown.[6] By 1653 the situation had been transformed, for the patronage of the crown and of bishops, deans, and chapters had been transferred to agencies of the Commonwealth, who also controlled that of most of the royalist nobility and gentry, though the latter's loss of rights was not absolute.

Advowsons were regularly bought and sold, sometimes for large sums; that of Bourton-on-the-Water went for £1,200 shortly before the Civil War.[7] Patrons also often sold the

---

[5] *CJ*, vii, 345–6, 348, 350–1.

[6] Figures cited in Christopher Hill, *Economic Problems of the English Church from Archbishop Whitgift to the Long Parliament* (Oxford, 1956), pp. 145–6; that for the total number of impropriated livings is Spelman's. I am heavily indebted to Hill's invaluable account, but see also Rosemary O'Day, 'Ecclesiastical patronage: who controlled the church?' in F. Heal and R. O'Day (eds.), *Church and Society in England: Henry VIII to James I* (1977), pp. 137–55.

[7] Hill, *Economic Problems*, pp. 65–6.

presentation to a particular vacancy without parting with the
future disposal of the living, and made a profit ranging from a
score or two to some hundreds of pounds.[8] Often the purchasers
were clergymen and often they held other benefices already, and
though such deals were commonly channelled through third
parties to avoid falling foul of canon law they frequently
amounted to barely concealed simony. The common law treated
advowsons as freeholds, thereby encouraging their owners to
regard them as pieces of property like any other. It even
protected those who reduced their presentees to tenants at will
by exacting bonds requiring them to surrender the benefice at
three or six months' notice. The universities had produced a glut
of clergy, and patrons were in a position to fleece their parsons
of much of their already shrunken incomes—'leavings, not
livings', one called them.[9] The other common practice was to
bestow the living on a younger son or some other kinsman or
dependant, or to make it a condition that the presentee should
marry an otherwise undowered daughter. It was hardly a system
that set a premium upon religious vocation, unless that was what
the patron chose to put first, and the commonest criticism of it
was that it bred an obsequious dependence in men whose calling
should have made them no respecters of persons, at least in things
of the spirit. It also made it very hard to remove unworthy
ministers, and obstructed the sort of reforms that could be
achieved by amalgamating adjacent poor parishes or subdividing
those that were excessively large.

Yet there was another side to the coin. Puritan peers and
gentry had been finding livings for Puritan clergy since
Elizabeth's reign, and a few—Lord Brooke was an example—
had encouraged congregations to recommend the pastors they
wanted. Patrons were not necessarily individuals; some advowsons belonged to city companies, some to town corporations, and
a few to the parishes themselves. Most Puritan ministers who
held benefices before the Civil War had lay patrons of one kind
or another to thank for them, and for many years the threat to
patrons' rights had been associated with Archbishop Laud. The

---

[8] O'Day, writing of a slightly earlier period (op. cit., p. 152) reckons a profit normally
in the range of £30–£100, but Hill (pp. 64–5) cites exceptional cases where £1,010 and
£650 were paid for single presentations.

[9] Hill, *Economic Problems*, p. 212.

case for retaining lay patronage rested on more than mere rights of property and the convenience of a permanent means of providing for dependents. It rested on more even than ultimate control of the pulpit which it bestowed on a landed class reliant on the deference of the lower orders, strongly though that must have counted with many of its defenders. At a higher level it was buttressed by a sort of idealized Erastianism, widespread from the mid-forties onwards, which exalted the figure of the godly magistrate and believed that the best hope of achieving a truly Christian commonwealth lay in strengthening his paternal hand.[10] It is no accident that lay patronage was most seriously threatened just when the currents of congregationalism and millenarianism were flowing most strongly together, and when the banks of the propertied interest were weakest to contain them.

We know from Highland that the debate on 17 November aroused strong feelings, and that the more conservative members dwelt much on the destruction of property implicit in the abolitionists' proposals. We know too that the vote taken after that debate and the threat to property that it posed were to be cited by the first speaker on the parliament's very last day as a prime reason for bringing it to an end.[11] Highland's own response to the conservatives' arguments probably typifies what the radicals had to say against them, and is worth quoting at some length:

But seeing that to sell this property were no less than the sin of simony, what worldly advantage can he [the patron] make of it? Thus if the church be full (so they blasphemously call it), Christ being the only fulness of the church, and not some ignorant, prophane, and lazy priest, that is a miserable fulness with which some churches (so called) are filled. In such a case of fulness, the lord patron may sell the reversion for a considerable sum of money, to some one or other that hath sent his son to Oxford or Cambridge to learn the art of logic and philosophy, by which craft he may know how to get his living another day; and so the old incumbent dying, this young artist cometh to be presented one, to enter and take possession, and so to enjoy his portion his father provided for him, the glebe, the tithes, the oblations, together with the care and cure of souls, and right of officiating to God and man there; for this his

---

[10] See W. M. Lamont, *Godly Rule* (1969), ch. 5, and the quotation from Prynne in Hill, *Economic Problems*, p. 72.

[11] *Exact Relation*, pp. 278–9; cf. *True Narrative*, p. 2; *Confusion Confounded*, pp. 16–17.

father bought and purchased for him, and who shall take it from him? But if the church be empty, that is of a priest, then all his property amounteth but to a shadow, unless it [he?] be sure to put in one that, being beholden to him, shall be sure to serve him, and to forbear his lusts; or else marry his kinswoman, or his wife's gentlewoman or chambermaid, in consideration of being presented to be settled there: But can this work of darkness and root of iniquity abide the light, or look in the face without blushing, the glorious light of the gospel that now shineth in this our horizon? Is not this property a relic of the great whore, Rev. xviii. 13, that buyeth and selleth amongst other wares the souls of men?[12]

Other speakers in the debate complained that ministers too often dared not preach anything that displeased their patrons, and that many who had been removed for scandalous conduct or for sowing political disaffection or false doctrine had subsequently been given benefices by patrons who were no friends of the Commonwealth.[13]

It is not known what arguments other than the sanctity of property were voiced on the conservative side, but they did not prevail. Nor is it surprising that they failed to convince an assembly that believed so strongly in liberty of preaching and leaned so much to the congregational way. Eventually a motion was framed that a bill be brought in to take away 'the power of patrons to present to benefices'. The retentionists struggled to secure at least a second day's debate on so great a matter, and there was a division on whether the question be put. The Yeas had it by 61 votes to 43, and the substantive motion was then carried by 60 to 43. In each case two generally moderate tellers lost to two radical ones: first Ashley Cooper and Tichborne to Blount and Ireton, and then Hewson and Henry King to Robert Bennett and Moyer.[14] But this was not a straight issue between moderates and radicals. Tichborne and Ireton, adversaries on the first vote, were fellow-members of the same gathered church. If Tichborne really wanted to retain lay patronage it must have been on grounds of principle, and neither Hewson nor King, who was a nominee of the churches of Christ in Norfolk, is likely to have been an interested party in the sense of owning

[12] *Exact Relation*, p. 279.
[13] *A Perfect Account of the Daily Intelligence*, 16–23 Nov. 1653, pp. 1195–6.
[14] *CJ*, vii, 352; the voting figures as usual include the tellers.

advowsons. On the other hand Highland asserts that some members who owned two or three voted for the bill. The number in favour of it exceeded the votes cast for any radical candidate for the Council of State on 1 November when the House had been fuller by ten. There is no occasion for surprise, however, if the abolitionists included some whose stance was normally moderate, for the abuses of patronage were notorious, and there was nothing in this vote to prejudice the continuance of a publicly maintained parochial ministry under the over-all care of the Commonwealth's supreme authority. Nevertheless the debate created bad blood, and the House uncharacteristically broke up after it without determining who was to prepare the bill.

Religious issues usually raised the emotional temperature, and several subsequent accounts by moderates maintain that it was chiefly the zealots' pretensions to divine inspiration that ultimately made the majority find them intolerable to sit with any longer. But it was not only one side which gave offence. According to Highland the more conservative members were over-free in crediting their opponents with evil motives, intemperate in their accusations of destroying magistracy, ministry, and property, and prone to anger when they received a check.[15] One catches hints that the men of birth and rank who led the final walk-out were lacing their strictures on the saints with innuendos about their social inferiority. Such behaviour may have been counter-productive, since before these final weeks no pair of radical tellers had ever, on a religious or other ideological issue, counted more than the forty-nine votes told by Harrison and Blount on 19 July against referring the question of incumbents' property in tithes to a committee—and that division they had lost.[16]

Before describing the religious debate of November and December any further, they need to be set against an accumulation of other contentious issues within the House and a buildup of disturbing developments outside it, for these all helped to heighten the tension. To take parliamentary business first, the House voted on 1 November, before proceeding to the council

---

[15] *Exact Relation*, esp. pp. 281–2.

[16] *CJ*, vii, 286. The division on 29 July in which Blount and West counted 53 votes was not of this kind.

elections, to devote every Friday 'to the business of the law', and although it did not manage to adhere to its resolve many members were still involved with divisive questions of law reform in committee. On the 3rd came the first two readings of the latest bill for the abolition of Chancery and a debate which revived all the old disagreements. Next day the assessment bill was introduced, and the long and troubled passage it had has already been referred to. Before it was finally forced through on the 24th, the Act for a High Court of Justice aroused more bad feeling on the 21st and 22nd, and the wrangling over the excise filled much of the time from the 25th to the 30th. Meanwhile John Lilburne had raised his disputatious head once more. Shortly before the 14th he had sued out a writ of habeas corpus in the Upper Bench, hoping to get that court to adjudge his imprisonment unlawful. Greatly concerned, the Council of State had ordered the Lieutenant of the Tower not to deliver him, and on the 26th the House confirmed the prohibition 'until the parliament shall take further order'.[17] It had little choice, but this overriding of due process in the senior court of common law is unlikely to have passed without some protest by those who had spoken up for Lilburne earlier. On the same day the House voted that the bill to abolish lay patronage should be reported on 1 December. Yet in between such stressful matters it could apparently get on with less divisive business fairly amicably; in one division on the 18th, for instance, in a debate on the bill for the sale of royal forests, Pickering and Barebone were paired as tellers against Wolseley and Tichborne.[18]

Nevertheless from mid-November onwards the newswriters and foreign residents retailed frequent rumours of an impending dissolution, to be followed by a change in the form of government. They drew their inferences not only from the rifts within the parliament but also from the political situation at large, in which they identified three circumstances which pointed the need for a stronger hand at the helm: the escalation of the royalist insurrection in the Scottish Highlands, the reaching of a critical phase in the Anglo-Dutch peace negotiations, and the increasingly strident behaviour of the millenarian enthusiasts—the

[17] *CJ*, vii, 358; *CSPD 1653–4*, pp. 242–3, 253–4, 262, 266.
[18] *CJ*, vii, 352.

'Anabaptists', as the foreign commentators usually called them—
outside as well as inside the House.

Glencairn's Rising, as it came to be called, was the furthest
from Westminster of these three problems, but it was disturbing
enough to strengthen the feeling that the Commonwealth needed
stable government. Each week *Mercurius Politicus* carried news,
generally on its front page, of the movements of the royalist
clansmen, and although it was at pains to rebut exaggerated
reports of their strength it had to admit that their raids during
November alone reached Falkirk and came within a few miles of
Glasgow and even Berwick.[19] The English had always overesti-
mated the degree to which they had subjugated Highland
Scotland and what they now faced was a continuing resistance
movement rather than a fresh insurrection, but its scale was
plainly growing. They had gauged its strength, which was
always fluctuating and uncertain, at about 1,300 in August, but
by December 1653 and January 1654 their estimates ranged
between 4,000 and 8,000, and Scottish claims were higher. As
yet the Highlanders were deployed in small bands and confined
themselves to ambushes, harassing attacks, and horse-stealing
raids, but their leaders hoped to take the field in strength by
March, and the latest historian of the movement judges that it
had already developed into a full-scale military rising by the end
of 1653.[20] Although it was overtly royalist, in the tradition of
Montrose rather than of Hamilton and Engagers, it awoke
plenty of sympathy in the Lowlands. The Earl of Glencairn was
himself a Lowlander. The Resolutioners were praying defiantly
for the king, and even the Protesters were less hostile to
Glencairn's followers than to the occupying English forces,
though the latter had the invaluable support of the Marquis of
Argyle. One danger was that the rising would spur the English
royalists into action. Colonel Edward Wogan sailed from France
to England in November, recruited twenty-one men in London,
and rode off with them to join Glencairn—a minor adventure in
itself, but this same November was probably the crucial month
in which the leaders of royalist conspiracy in England came

---

[19] *Mercurius Politicus*, nos. 180–4, Nov.–Dec. 1653, pp. 2875–6, 2891–2, 3007–8, 3021–
5, 3039–40, 3042–3.
[20] Dow, *Cromwellian Scotland 1651–1660*, p. 77 and Part II, *passim*, to which this
paragraph is much indebted.

together to form the Sealed Knot.[21] The Council of State did not
know this, of course, but Cromwell was aware that the English
commander in Scotland, Colonel Robert Lilburne, was not fully
up to the job of quieting the country, either militarily or
politically. The council therefore sent for Lambert from
Yorkshire, and on 23 November appointed a committee under
Cromwell to confer with him and any other officers it thought fit
concerning the Scottish situation and what should be done about
it.[22]

The difficulties over the Dutch peace were twofold: the
Council of State seemed to lack a realistic conception of what
terms the Dutch might accept, and the millenarian faction both
inside and outside parliament was doing its utmost to prevent
any terms from being agreed at all. Those who like Cromwell
wanted peace took fresh hope when Jongestal and Nieuport
returned to England on 25 October, but progress was delayed by
the major changes in the council's composition a week later, for
the new members took their time to settle in. Cromwell sent a
confidant to the four Dutch deputies on 10 November to urge
patience on them, and Hugh Peter assured them four days later
that the council was working day and night on the terms. If these
should not at first appear acceptable, he urged them (as if already
aware of reefs ahead) not to be discouraged, for he was confident
that agreement would eventually be reached.[23] Meanwhile the
council appointed no new commission to treat with them,
presumably because eight of the nine former commissioners had
retained their seats. When the Dutchmen were at last admitted
to a conference on the 17th, Cromwell acted as spokesman and
opened with a prepared speech. He said that since a coalition of
the two commonwealths was unacceptable to the United
Provinces, England was content to treat for as firm and close a
league[24] as was ever made between two nations. He also made
the strange stipulation that the deputies should swear an oath not
to divulge what passed that day and the next to anyone

---

[21] D. E. Underdown, *Royalist Conspiracy in England 1649–1660* (New Haven, 1960),
pp. 70–5.

[22] *CSPD 1653–4*, p. 267; Thurloe, i, 589, 610.

[23] Thurloe, i, 582–4, 600–1.

[24] The word is 'union' in Thurloe, i, 601, but the sense implies a relationship between
two independent sovereign states, not the partial fusion of sovereignties that had
previously been proposed.

whatsoever for a whole week—not even to their masters, the States General.[25] He was probably seeking to minimize the likely ill effects of the council's terms, for when at the next day's meeting he handed them the written draft of a treaty they were shocked by it. Its demands included huge reparations for the cost of the war, permanent exclusion of the Prince of Orange from civil office or military command, strict limitation of the number of Dutch warships permitted to navigate the Channel, and payment for fishing rights in the 'British seas', in which moreover every Dutch vessel must strike the flag to every English one, whether naval or mercantile. The conference broke up in bitterness, Beverning especially feeling that he had been gulled by Cromwell's personal assurances.[26]

Yet whether such a high opening bid represented Cromwell's way of doing business or whether, as seems likelier, it betrayed some difference of view between him and his fellow-councillors, he certainly wanted the negotiations to go on. On the day of the first conference he sent his son Henry and his cousin Colonel John Cromwell, along with Lieutenant-Colonel Dolman, an Englishman in the Dutch service, to assure them again of his own good inclination to a peace.[27] He explained that the intention of the oath of secrecy was to prevent the resident envoys of other countries from gaining knowledge which they might exploit to their own advantage and to the prejudice of the treaty,[28] which may suggest that he himself was not wholly happy with the terms that he tendered to them on the 18th. To these the Dutchmen returned a stiff written reply, whereupon the council began immediately to moderate some of the more offensive articles. The next round of conferences, three in three days and all lengthy, began on the 29th, though the Dutch deputies were reduced now to three by Van de Perre's mortal illness. By 2

[25] PRO 31. 3/92, fo. 46.

[26] Gardiner, *C & P*, ii, 364–5; Thurloe, i, 616. The latter is a translation of Bordeaux's dispatch in PRO 31. 3/92, fos. 46–7, which suggests that Thurloe was having the French ambassador's correspondence intercepted and copied.

[27] Thurloe, i, 600. Dolman had been employed before in Anglo–Dutch diplomacy; cf. Gardiner, *C & P*, ii, 183; Abbott, iii, 38, 121; *CSPD 1653–4*, p. 448. According to Abbott Col. John Cromwell was also in the Dutch service.

[28] Thurloe, i, 601, 611. The Dutchmen kept their word; the 18th was post-day, and they deferred an account of the terms that they had just received until the next week's post (ibid. 601). Bordeaux was unable to transmit them home until 26 Nov., O.S. (ibid. 616).

December they believed that one more meeting would decide whether they signed a treaty or broke it off and returned home. The meeting went badly; the English concessions went nothing like far enough, and on the 5th the Dutchmen asked for their passports.[29]

Yet they did not depart, and it seems that they were dissuaded from doing so by a tip-off that a change of government was imminent. Rumours of such a change were multiplying; one newswriter sent the exiled royal court a story on 24 November of a petition to parliament to make Cromwell Protector.[30] The main reason that the foreign residents and other reporters gave for their predictions was that the 'Anabaptists' in parliament were making life intolerable for those who were trying to carry on the government, and particularly for those involved in the Anglo-Dutch treaty. Bordeaux met Jongestal on the morning of 8 December and received from him the extraordinary impression that the Dutch deputies had just been to a secret conference at which they had been given a broad hint to stay and wait for the present regime to be changed.[31]

The millenarians had never ceased to condemn the peace negotiations. When a disastrous storm early in November breached the Dutch sea walls in fifteen places, killed two thousand seamen, and destroyed at least a dozen warships, even a newswriter whose job was presumably to supply Thurloe with intelligence could comment thus: 'Now those, that so passionately desire a peace with this country, may see their error in the work of the Lord; and that he is ready to deliver this land into their hands, if they continue their good resolution to extirpate the Whore of Babylon and idolatry.'[32] But it was as usual the Blackfriars preachers who were making the most noise. On 2 November, for the second time in a week or two, Cromwell sent for several of them, and in the presence of Owen, Marshall, Nye,

[29] Thurloe, i, 607, 620, 624; PRO 31. 3/92, fos. 62–4, 69, 74; Gardiner, *C & P*, ii, 365.

[30] Clarendon MS 47, fo. 113; Thurloe, i, 589, 610, 612, 621, 628; *CSP Ven 1653–4*, pp. 152, 155, 157–8; PRO 31. 3/92, fos. 29–30, 48, 74; Barrière to Condé, 2/12 Dec. 1653, BL, Add. MS 35,252, fos. 111–12; Johnson and Vaisey, p. 78; *Nicholas Papers*, ii, 32.

[31] PRO 31. 3/92, fos. 82–5. This is how Bordeaux transmits what he heard from Jongestal on 8 December: 'Il est d'abord convenu de ceste Conférence secrette, et dit qu'il venoit pour réparer la faute qu'avoit faite son Collègue, le matin qu'il n'y avoit point assisté, et n'en sçavoit autre chose sinon qu'on les avoit conviez d'attendre le changement du présent Régime.'

[32] Thurloe, i. 574; cf. pp. 569–71 for particulars of the damage.

Jessey, and others tried gently to reason with them. Everyone, he urged, who professed godliness and owned Christ as head should strive to agree in mutual love and refrain from reviling one another.[33] He pleaded in vain. At the Monday exercises on the 14th the Blackfriars pulpit rang with scurrilous aspersions against the parliament, the army, the Council of State, indeed everyone in power; all were shortly to fall before the approaching triumph of the saints. The reformed churches in general, implying those overseas as well as the parochial establishment in England, all came under the lash as instruments and outworks of Babylon. The anonymous reporter who passed this on to Cromwell offered his opinion that there would be 'no better way for a sure ground work, to obviate the designs of those men as well as those of the common enemies ... than by fixing the nation's interest and your own upon some solid fundamentals in reference to the state both of religion and politie'.[34] When he read of the Instrument of Government a month later he must have felt that he had prophesied.

It was the links between Blackfriars, the parliament, and the army that made it necessary to take these rantings seriously. An unsympathetic reporter of the English scene wrote on 25 November: 'Harrison and his party do rail and preach every day against the General and the peace with Holland, so that it's thought and believed, that they are both embroiled in their cabals or factions ready to make a separation in the House of Parliament. I do hear, Harrison intends to leave this place, and to come no more.'[35] Harrison's movements and his increasing alienation during November were much reported. By one account he had left London by the 26th, but he was back there by the beginning of December, and by the 5th, according to Bordeaux, he had been to see Cromwell three or four times. Bordeaux thought the two men were reconciled, but it is likelier that Cromwell in his typical way was trying what his powers of suasion could do to avert a final breach.[36] Nothing, however, could stop Feake and the Monday thunderers from inveighing

---

[33] *Several Proceedings of State Affairs*, no. 213, 27 Oct.–3 Nov. 1653, p. 3391.

[34] Thurloe, i, 591. The branding of the reformed churches as outworks of Babylon was remembered by Nedham in *A True State of the Case of the Commonwealth*, p. 14.

[35] Thurloe, i, 612; cf. p. 610.

[36] PRO 31. 3/92, fos. 36, 48, 65, 74; Clarendon MS 47, fo. 113; Thurloe, i, 589.

against the government, and by late November they were aiming their bolts chiefly at Cromwell, 'calling him the man of sin, the old dragon, and many other scripture ill names'. Cromwell sent for them again on the 29th, and with Peter Sterry and several other ministers for witnesses warned them that their vituperations were not only encouraging the Commonwealth's enemies, in Scotland and abroad, but were also bringing the parliament into contempt. Feake in reply, calling on heaven to record what was said on both sides, told Cromwell 'that it was his tampering with the king and his assuming an exorbitant power, which made these disorders'. Cromwell angrily retorted that when Feake appealed to the record of heaven he did not expect him to tell such a lie on earth.[37]

The millenarian caucus in the House demonstrated the pull that Blackfriars exerted upon them by their vexation when the Act for a High Court of Justice was pushed through on a Monday when they were away at their devotions.[38] These members met frequently at Arthur Squibb's house to concert their policies and tactics, as Cromwell was to recall resentfully more than three years later.[39] Several near contemporary accounts of the parliament's later proceedings state strongly that their behaviour became insupportable to the moderate majority, but such evidence needs to be considered critically, because they still managed to carry majorities with them in the crucial divisions on 17 November and 10 December. That does not of course imply that they converted large numbers of members to their way of thinking, but merely that their conduct cannot have been quite so outrageous as their accusers made out, or they would not have found so many prepared to vote alongside them. But the issues in both those divisions were complex, and it is quite clear that after the second the majority of members were in favour of terminating the parliament's authority. Since the sources for these final stages, apart from the laconic entries in the *Common's Journal*, are mostly very partisan, they call for some brief description.

Highland's *Exact Relation* remains the fullest narrative written

---

[37] Thurloe, i, 621; PRO 31. 3/92, fo. 65.

[38] See p. 301; and for other allegations of the Blackfriars–Westminster connection see *Answer to a True Narrative*, p. 3; *Confusion Confounded*, p. 7; Nedham, *A True State*, pp. 14–15.

[39] *Confusion Confounded*, p. 6; *Answer to a True Narrative*, p. 3; Abbott, iv, 489.

by a radical; it is first hand and factually trustworthy, but its tone of injured innocence glosses over the fact that some of Highland's associates were much more extreme in their aims than himself. The earliest radical account is *A True Narrative of the Cause and Manner of the Dissolution of the late Parliament*, which was written by an anonymous member the day after the event. Though only six pages long it is unconsciously revealing about some of the matters which gave the moderates and the army such offence. An unknown member who had joined in the final walkout promptly countered with *An Answer to a Paper entituled A True Narrative*, which though no less biased has value as the only version written by a moderate who was actually present. It is drawn on quite heavily in two early anonymous vindications of the Protectorate, both published with official blessing and both seeking at some length to explain why Barebone's Parliament failed: *Confusion Confounded*, probably written by John Hall and printed in mid-January 1654 by the government's printer Henry Hills,[40] and *A True State of the Case of the Commonwealth*, written by Marchamont Nedham and published early in February. Both Hall and Nedham were on the government's pay-roll; Cromwell commended the latter's tract to his next parliament, and as further proof of its official status it is the only source which prints the short instrument of resignation whereby the moderate members signed away their authority.[41] Neither Hall nor Nedham were present in the House, of course, but both had time and opportunity to consult members who were, and both in fact contribute a little independent evidence. There are a few belated radical reminiscences in *A Faithful Searching Home Word*,[42] which in December 1659 urged the ruling Committee of Safety to give the government back to the faithful members of Barebone's Parliament. To supplement the pamphlet material there are a few gleanings to be got from foreign residents, newspapers, newswriters, and intercepted letters, but there is no stage of this story at which the lack of parliamentary diaries is more keenly felt.

The apologists for the moderates level three main accusations

[40] Acquired by Thomason on 18 Jan. 1654 and reprinted in *Somers Tracts*, vi, 297–303; plausibly attributed to Hall in the British Library's *Catalogue of Printed Books*. On Hall's other propagandist activities see ch. viii, n. 72.

[41] Abbott, iii, 587; reprinted in facsimile by The Rota (Exeter, 1978).

[42] Acquired by Thomason on 13 Dec. 1659.

against the actual conduct of the zealots in these later stages, as
well as denouncing those policies of theirs which threatened
property and the law and frustrated religious settlement. The
first is that they claimed an overriding and infallible authority
as Christ's saints; the second, that they threatened to secede from
the House and set up on their own if they did not get their way;
the third, that they schemed to undermine the army and transfer
military power to their fellow-saints. An evaluation of these
charges will help us to judge whether those last debates on the
settling of a godly ministry were really the proximate cause of
the parliament's resignation or just its occasion.

The moderate member who replied to *A True Narrative* gave as
his first reason for deciding to sit with his opponents no longer
that they claimed 'to Rule the Nation only as Saints, to whom the
right of Civil Government did belong, and as having an
extraordinary call from Christ thereto, being the beginning of a
fifth Monarchy, which was never to cease, but to break in pieces
all Powers by making War with them'. By arrogating the sole
right to govern to self-appointed saints, 'excluding all others who
had never so great Interest in the Nation, and other fitness
thereto', they 'put the stamp of infallibility upon all they should
do'. Furthermore

their manifestly rigid Principles of Imposition . . . [were] laying such
foundations as would shortly have introduced the bitterest and sorest
persecution; To this none are so conscious, or can be, as those that sate
daily with them in the House, where they heard men unsainted and
condemn'd unto the fourth Monarchy, and looked upon as obstructors
of Reformation, and no longer fit for the work, if not through paced to
all the Principles of Reformation held forth by Mr. *Feake* and others at
Black-Fryers and other places, and stickled for by som in the House.[43]

When a member could defend his opinion by claiming that, 'He
spake it not, but the Lord in him', it was fairly remarked that he
was putting an end to reasoned debate and demanding implicit
obedience.[44] In case it should be thought that such charges were
maliciously exaggerated, here is a specimen of the advice that
John Rogers had been offering in print just a few weeks earlier:

[43] *Answer to a True Narrative*, pp. 2–3; probably Nedham's main source in *A True State*,
pp. 15, 17–18.
[44] *Answer to a True Narrative*, p. 10; cf. *Confusion Confounded*, p. 8, and Nedham, *A True
State*, p. 15.

Are you a Parliament man? minde your worke then, and the Fifth Monarchy; or else the stone, Dan. 2. and the wheel Eze. 1. may hap to minde you, and grind you too . . . Your worke is about the Lawes and Tithes, to strip the Whore both of her outward Scarlet-array, and to rend the flesh off her bones, by throwing down the standing of Lawyers, and Priests. It is not enough to change some of these Lawes, and so to reforme them (as is intended by most of you), according to the rule of the Fourth Monarchy, which must all to pieces; O no! that wil be to poor purpose and is not your worke now, which is to provide for the Fifth . . . by bringing in the Lawes of God given by Moses for Republique Lawes.[45]

The radical member who wrote *A True Narrative* recalled how he and his brethren had met on several days to seek the Lord in prayer and fasting, and claims that when they afterwards came to the House with their Bibles in their hands, God so bore them witness in the consciences of their fellow-members that none could withstand the Spirit by which they spoke.[46] It was because of this, he maintained, that the moderate leadership had conspired to dissolve the parliament, but one can appreciate that from the other side such pretensions were seen rather differently. The rebukes which the extreme faction drew down from fellow-radicals as various as John Goodwin, William Erbery, William Kiffin, and John Spilsbery confirm that there was substance in the charge that they shortened the parliament's life by striving for an immediate, literal, and exclusive rule of the saints.[47]

The accusation that they threatened to secede from the House and set up as a rival authority rests on slighter evidence. The main witness is the member who replied to *A True Narrative*: 'To this purpose Letters are written to the Churches all the Nation over, to blast that part of the House that agreed not with them; and at a set-meeting at a Members house, of divers Members, Consultation had to leave the House, and Remonstrate against them as hinderers of Reformation, and not fit to Govern the Nation any longer.'[48] This writer goes on to say that these

---

[45] John Rogers, *Sagrir, or Doomes-day drawing nigh* ([7 Nov.] 1653), sigs. A4–4v.

[46] *A True Narrative*, pp. 5–6. The author recommended his readers to ponder Isaiah 66:5, which reads: 'Hear the word of the Lord, ye that tremble at his word; Your brethren that hated you, that cast you out for my name's sake, said, Let the Lord be glorified: but he shall appear to your joy, and they shall be ashamed.'

[47] See pp. 349–51.

[48] *Answer to a True Narrative*, p. 3 (two obvious misprints corrected).

members spent several days in such prayer-meetings, and that latterly they seldom came to the House except when their own particular ends were to be 'driven forward', so that the moderates began to fear that the real purpose of the meetings was 'to make a faction and get Proselytes'.[49] Whether Nedham had more than this evidence to go on or not, he was rather more explicit:

They resolved to divide and separate themselves from the other Members, who followed them not in their excesses, and to constitute themselves into a Power distinct from them. To this end, they led off divers well-meaning Gentlemen of the House along with them, to private Meetings of their own appointment, upon pretence of seeking the Lord by prayer for direction. But . . . the use that was made of those Meetings by the Contrivers of them, was, only for the better carrying on of things that they had beforehand resolved to act. And in order thereto, they took liberty to arraign and condemn the persons and proceedings of their fellow-members, and provoked others to Remonstrate and Protest against them; saying, That if the House then sitting should send for them, they ought not to obey them.[50]

There may be a further hint of secession in the letter of 25 November already quoted, which talked of Harrison and his faction being 'ready to make a separation in the House of Parliament' and 'to come no more',[51] but the evidence for this particular charge is inconclusive. There is nothing from radical sources to support it, and if the extreme sectaries had tried 'to constitute themselves into a Power distinct' from the rest of the members they would soon have discovered how isolated they were. Perhaps some of them talked of withdrawing from the parliament and denying its claim to authority if the major votes on the law and the ministry were to go against them, and hostile commentators then construed this as a threat to constitute themselves some kind of alternative government.

The allegation that they were scheming to alter the command of the army is also rather weakly attested, though they certainly alienated a considerable part of the army and Harrison would no doubt have taken it over if he could. Radical sources admit that they proposed that senior officers should forgo a year's pay, but strongly deny that they were aiming to starve the army as a

[49] Ibid. 9.
[50] Nedham, *A True State*, p. 20.
[51] See p. 325.

whole when they voted against the assessment bill.[52] Naturally no radical would admit to such accusations as these: 'There appeared an evident design to alter the Government of the Army, and have put it into such hands as would perfectly have corresponded with their principles, and given them a safe opportunity to have imposed whatever they had pleased upon the Nation ... This was certainly given in direction to divers Members met together to pull down some in the Army, and set up others.'[53] Nedham repeats the charge, and adds that there was a pulpit campaign to asperse the officers as janissaries and pensioners of Babylon. Some MPs, he says, not only encouraged these preachers by their presence but joined with them in their vilifications.[54] Vavasor Powell 'told the Sword-men in general, That the Spirit of God was departed from them; that heretofore they had been precious and excellent men, but that their Parks, and new houses, and gallant Wives had choaked them up.'[55] He was echoing what William Dell had published to 'the Truely Faithful ... in present Authority' at the beginning of December:

It grieves me much to see so many men as I have known hopeful in the Army, and elsewhere, to be now so full gorged with the flesh of Kings, and Nobles, and Captaines, and mighty men, that is, with their Estates, Mannors, Houses, Parkes, Lands, etc. that they can now be contented to take their ease, and to comply with the world and worldly Church and the teachers thereof, and can perswade themselves, that there is enough done for their time, after it has fared well with them.[56]

But it was one thing to inveigh against the army's grandees, which probably struck a chord among many of the junior officers and the more politically conscious of the soldiery, and quite another to replace them with a set of commanders dedicated to the Fifth Monarchy. There was not a remote possibility that Barebone's Parliament would do anything of the sort, as its unanimous vote for Cromwell on 1 November proved beyond doubt. If Harrison, Carew, Courtney, and their kind really believed that their kingdom of the saints was imminent, the only

[52] *A True Narrative*, pp. 3–4; *Exact Relation*, p. 274; *A Faithful Searching Home Word*, p. 18.
[53] *Answer to a True Narrative*, p. 4.
[54] Nedham, *A True State*, p. 20.
[55] *Strena Vavasoriensis* ([30 Jan.] 1654), pp. 18–19. Whether Powell preached this shortly before or after the dissolution is not clear from this hostile tract, which is attributed to Alexander Griffith in *Vavasoris Examen & Purgamen* ([30 March] 1654), p. 21.
[56] William Dell, *The Tryal of Spirits* ([4 Dec.] 1653), sig. aa2v.

way of erecting it lay in seceding from the parliament and
bidding for military power by other means. It is not inconceivable
that this was in their thoughts, and that some inkling of it made
Cromwell send for Harrison more than once in early December.
Their capacity for believing that the Lord would look after his
own was infinite.

Had then the breakdown of the parliament become inevitable
even before the final debate on settling the ministry began? A
month of divisive issues had deepened the mutual antagonism
between entrenched conservatives and sectarian radicals. Pressures from Scotland and the United Provinces strengthened the
former's sense of need for firmer, more stable government;
frustration made the latter more strident in their chiliasm and
readier to look for solutions beyond the realm of human reason.
If the report of the committee for tithes had not led to the final
breach, the promised bill to abolish lay patronage or the yet
unreported proposals of the committee for a new body of the law
might well have done so. Yet that is not to say that the end was
absolutely inevitable. The final division, after all, was extremely
close, and if it had gone the other way—if, that is, there had been
a majority for a scheme that would balance liberty of conscience
with acceptance of responsibility for maintaining a godly
ministry, and if a similar majority could have held to a reformist
rather than a revolutionary course when the business of the law
came back again—then Barebone's Parliament might have had
a longer lease of life and a fuller harvest of legislation. The final
debates were carried on soberly, in a spirit and at a length that
suggest that the majority were still seeking consensus rather than
confrontation; the division that ended them does not look like
the mere detonator of a mine already primed. What we cannot
know is whether the moderates, if they had won it, would have
been encouraged to improve their attendance and exploit their
majority. Even if they had done so the eventual outcome might
not have been very different, for most of their leaders were to
become mainstays of the Protectorate, and they might have
sought to raise Cromwell to the chief magistracy through the
agency of this parliament. As it was they chose the short circuit
of resignation; they had lost confidence in the regime and lost
patience with their opponents. Some had probably had enough
well before 10 December—hence the growing rumours of a

change of government; but it was probably the vote that day that enabled them to persuade a majority to resign with them.

The House could not have put off for much longer the problems of settling the ministry. No solution could have satisfied everybody, because there was no means of reconciling the mainstream Puritan opinion that the Commonwealth was not doing enough in the matter with the sectarian minority who loudly maintained that the civil magistrate had no business to be doing anything at all. There had been plenty of petitions for more action, as has been seen, and they came not only from conservative and Presbyterian-dominated sources like the corporation of London but also from Congregational churches in widely scattered parts of the country. One which the House specially heeded came from a number of such churches in the northern counties and was read on 10 October. It lamented, 'The swarms of horrid Errors, . . . the heaven provoking prophaneness, the hideous Atheism abounding in the Land, and (in some of these dark parts) running apace to flat Heathenism', and it blamed all this mainly on the lack of godly ministers. It deplored, 'The subtle undermining of that soul-saving Ordinance of the Ministry', and with Quakers and Ranters no doubt in mind it called for effective restraints 'of that bold vending, printing, and preaching whatever the Prince of darkness shall blow into corrupt minds'. It recalled the Commission for the Propagation of the Gospel in the Northern Counties, which had lapsed along with that for Wales, as 'the greatest Blessing that ever the North had', and it asked parliament to appoint new commissioners to take up the same task, with the aid of some able ministers. It further urged parliament to take special care to secure for the ministry an assured and comfortable maintenance, and not to heed the loud clamour of those who called for the abolition of tithes, since their real purpose (which they dared not avow) was the destruction of the ministry itself.[57] The House voted to commit this petition to the committee for tithes and then set up a special committee, headed by Sadler, to draft a declaration which, while assuring a fitting liberty of worship for all who

---

[57] Printed in *Mercurius Politicus*, no. 174, 6–13 Oct. 1653, pp. 2788–91, and in several other newspapers.

feared God, should 'discountenance blasphemies, damnable heresies, and licentious practices'.[58]

The widespread feeling that religious liberty was being abused was strengthened by the continuing excesses of some of the wilder preachers and the disturbances that they caused. On 12 October, for instance, John Webster and William Erbery, both notorious for opposing a university-educated ministry, engaged in public dispute with two London ministers in a church in Lombard Street. Erbery is reported to have denounced the established clergy as 'Monsters, Beasts, Asses, greedy dogs, False Prophets,' and to have said, 'That Babylon is the Church in her Members; That the Beast is the Church in her Ministers; and that the Great Whore is the Church in her Worship.'[59] Accounts differ as to whether it was Erbery's opinions that provoked a riot in the congregation or whether they rose up to drive off Webster's opponent, but it is clear that after much railing on both sides the meeting broke up in violent disorder.[60] On the following Sunday there was a more serious tumult at St Paul's. Captain Edmund Chillenden, the army Fifth Monarchy man, was preaching to his gathered congregation in the Stone Chapel when a body of apprentices arrived and began to throw stones at him through the windows. But Chillenden could call upon his fellow-soldiers and soon they turned up, both horse and foot. An angry mêlée broke the sabbath peace; heads were broken, and the noise so disturbed the Lord Mayor and the City fathers, who were hearing a sermon elsewhere in the cathedral, that one of the sheriffs came over to see what was happening. The soldiers demanded that the apprentices should be disciplined, but the sheriff asked by what authority the chapel was being used for preaching. 'By this authority!' said Chillenden, pointing a pistol at the sheriff's breast, and the soldiers had the audacity to take the City marshal prisoner. The Council of State was clearly troubled by the incident, but prudently left the rioters on both sides to the jurisdiction of the City authorities.[61] The feverish

---

[58] *CJ* vii, 332.

[59] *Mercurius Politicus*, no. 175, 13–20 Oct. 1653, p. 2787.

[60] Ibid.; William Erbery, *A Monstrous Dispute* ([18 Oct.] 1653); John Webster, *The Picture of Mercurius Politicus* ([27 Oct.] 1653). If the church was All Hallows, Lombard Street, its incumbent was the Fifth Monarchist John Cardell, who lost his living in 1655 for attacking a national ministry: Capp, *Fifth Monarchy Men*, p. 244.

[61] Gardiner, *C & P*, ii, 255–6; Thurloe, i, 545; *A Perfect Account*, no. 152, 12–19 Oct. 1653, p. 1159; *Several Proceedings of State Affairs*, no. 212, 13–20 Oct. 1653, p. 3355; PRO

atmosphere persisted, however; later in the month, for instance, two 'false prophets' were sent to Bridewell for railing against ministers and uttering horrible blasphemies.[62] Such occurrences prompted the Council of State to publish on 12 November a declaration forbidding anyone to disturb peaceable assemblies for divine worship, so long as they were not popish or idolatrous.[63]

Clearly, however, the parliament needed to make up its mind, both as regards the maintenance of a parochial ministry and the due bounds of religious liberty. Stephen Marshall used his sermon on 5 November to preach to it of the magistrate's duties, particularly in upholding the clergy's right to their tithes, glebes, and other provisions.[64] About a fortnight later appeared Στερέωμα: *The Establishment*, whose two hundred pages written by an anonymous Congregationalist and dedicated jointly to the parliament and to Cromwell, expounded exhaustively the case for the civil magistrate's power in matters ecclesiastical, for a public profession of the Christian faith, and for an established clergy supported by tithes (though the author confessed he had formerly opposed them) and educated by the universities in the best of human learning.[65] The whole business of the ministry and its maintenance had, it will be remembered, been referred to the committee for tithes back in August,[66] but nothing had emerged. Perhaps the committee was jolted into activity by the vote on 17 November for a bill to abolish patrons' rights of presentation and by another, nine days later, to have that bill read on 1 December. At any rate when the 1st came round it offered its own comprehensive report, and Highland and his fellow-radicals were convinced that this was a shift to stave off the bill. A long wrangle ensued, some members calling for the bill, some for the report, and some for the Bill of Union with Scotland. By one o'clock nothing had been decided, and the House rose after voting that the bill abolishing lay patronage should be the first

31. 3/91, fo. 117; *CSP Ven 1653–4*, p. 142; *CSPD 1653–4*, p. 205; J. Streater, *A Further Continuance of the Grand Politick Informer*, p. 43.

[62] *Weekly Intelligencer*, no. 141, 25 Oct.–1 Nov. 1653, pp. 37–8.

[63] *A Declaration of the Council of State . . . for the protection of all persons peaceably assembled for public worship* (12 Nov. 1653).

[64] Tai Liu, *Discord in Zion*, pp. 128–9.

[65] Στερέωμα: *The Establishment* ([20 Nov.] 1653). The anonymous author's recommendation (p. 180) of *The Heavenly Academy* by Francis Rous, 'now Speaker of the Parliament', confirms Thomason's correction of the date on title-page from 1654 to 1653.

[66] See p. 245.

business on the 6th. It was never read, for the tithes committee's report won a hearing on the 2nd, and apart from interludes for Admiralty business on the 5th and 6th it occupied the House throughout its short remaining life.[67]

Sadler was the spokesman who presented it. There were four clauses in it, of which only the first came to the vote, after six days of intense debate.[68] This dealt with the manner in which unfit ministers were to be removed and fit ones installed. It was closer to the scheme which Owen and other Independents had submitted in February 1652, and which the Rump had provisionally endorsed a year later, than to the system of Triers and Ejectors which Cromwell subsequently instituted. It proposed to divide the English and Welsh counties into six circuits, with a seventh for London and Middlesex, and to appoint a national body of twenty-one commissioners who were to operate on the basis of three to a circuit. Each trio was to work with four to six local commissioners in each county, in company with whom they were empowered to eject all ministers in the county whose conduct or ability or diligence they found wanting and to induct able and godly men into all livings that fell vacant. They were further empowered to unite two or three parishes where they saw fit, provided that this left no one more than three miles from a place of worship.

Although the other three clauses were not voted on, they must have influenced members' opinions of the scheme as a whole. The second named the twenty-one national commissioners. The third grasped the nettle of maintenance: the preachers approved were to enjoy that which was already settled by law, which of course included tithes where they were not wholly impropriated, together with such supplementation as parliament had appointed or might appoint. Anyone who scrupled the payment of tithes, however, was to be heard by the two or three nearest justices, who with the aid of sworn witnesses were to compute the value of the tithes due and to arrange for it to be paid in cash or in land assigned for the purpose. This of course was a concession only to those who strained at tithes as a superstitious *mode* of remunerating preachers, and did nothing to help those whose consciences

[67] *Exact Relation*, p. 280; *CJ*, vii, 361–3; *True Narrative*, p. 4.

[68] *CJ*, vii, 361, where the clauses are not numbered, though they are in *Mercurius Politicus* and other contemporary newspapers.

revolted against supporting a national clergy in any manner. One may also wonder what sort of a deal conscientious objectors were likely to receive from gentry magistrates, who commonly hated sectaries and might well be tithe-owners themselves. The final clause must have been even less acceptable to the radical wing, for it recorded the committee's judgement, after hearing evidence, that, 'Incumbents, Rectors, Possessors of Donatives, or Propriate Tythes ... have a legal Propriety in Tythes.'[69] The interests of property, lay and clerical, could hardly have been more clearly upheld. It is difficult to account for so conservative a conclusion by such an apparently evenly balanced committee except by the hypothesis that some of its radical members had pulled out in disgust.

Taken as a whole, its proposals were open to a variety of objections and one would not expect opposition to them to spring only from the uncompromising separatists and voluntaryists. This is confirmed by our two chief radical witnesses. Highland records that the debates were intensely serious and conducted with little heat or passion, except when one or two of the scheme's supporters became impatient at the length to which they were being drawn out. The Speaker told them, however, that every member had a right to be heard and that the question could not be put while any still wished to speak. Because of his age the sittings could not be prolonged beyond one o'clock. At last, towards noon on Saturday 10 December, the opponents of the scheme suggested that the essential question had come to be 'whether upon the whole this in the report was the best expedient for that end', i.e. for ejecting unworthy ministers and encouraging good ones, and they expressed themselves ready to have the decision put to the House.[70] Evidently the emphasis was on 'best', for the supporters of the report moved to omit the word. Highland conveys no impression that the opponents wanted to reject a publicly maintained ministry in principle, much though he disliked tithes as a means of maintaining it; indeed he indignantly repudiates the charge that 'they would have destroyed all the ministers, good as well as bad', and points out that in other countries a public ministry could and did subsist

[69] *CJ*, vii, 361.
[70] *Exact Relation*, p. 281. Highland's syntax is not clear; the above reading seems the likelier, but it may have been the Speaker who summed up the question.

without tithes. For him, evidently, the difference was over means rather than ends. But the millenarian member who published *A True Narrative* just after the dissolution was totally opposed to a 'national clergy', and he condemned the report much more sweepingly: 'This was a way to establish a National Parochial Ministry, consisting of those Popish names of Parsons, Vicars, and Curats, and also that oppressive (to say no more of it here) burden of Tythes; and it lookt rather like the making up of a breach in the Kingdom of Antichrist, then pulling it down, as it was hoped would have been the present work.'[71]

This gives credibility to the moderate member who replied to him, asserting that 'it was confidently averred, None should be countenanced by the Magistrate but such as disclaimed their Ordination', whether episcopal or Presbyterian. According to this witness many members 'professed fully against the Magistrates Power in any matters of Religion, and particularly in that of placing or sending forth men to Preach the Gospel'.[72] John Rogers had lately told the entire ministry that its ordination was antichristian,[73] and Willam Dell warned those 'in present Authority', probably while the debate was actually proceeding, 'to take heed that you neither drink, nor sip of the Clergies cup, which carries in it, the wine of the wrath of the fornication of Antichrist'.[74] Clearly the opponents of the report represented more than one school of thought, but *Confusion Confounded* elaborated the charge that 'they damned the clergy of all denominations as antichristian,[75] and Nedham typically made the most of it:

Upon this account it was, that they and their followers presumed also, to declare the whole Ministry of the Nation *Antichristian*, and because those in Power did not readily concur with them in the same opinion, they branded both the Governors and Government, as *Babylonish* and Antichristian; upon which supposition only (without reasoning the matter) they would have pulled down the Ministry, both root and branch; and their Party abroad in Pulpits, uttered many peremptory predictions of the remove or downfall, both of the one or the other.[76]

[71] *True Narrative*, p. 5.
[72] *Answer to a True Narrative*, pp. 3, 8.
[73] J. Rogers, *Sagrir, or Doomes-day drawing nigh*, sig. B2–4.
[74] W. Dell, *The Tryal of Spirits*, sig. aa 3.
[75] *Confusion Confounded*, pp. 17–18.
[76] Nedham, *A True State*, p. 15.

If Nedham should be thought to exaggerate, as he was prone to do, Cromwell himself found nothing worse among the 'abominations' that had induced him to assume the Protectorate than that 'The axe was laid to the root of the Ministry; it was Antichristian, it was Babylonish.' At one extreme, he complained, it was asserted that none might preach unless they were ordained, whatever their gifts from Christ; at the other, that ordination should positively debar men from preaching because it rendered their calling antichristian.[77]

The only vote in the six-day debate was that which sealed the parliament's fate, though Highland for one had no inkling that it would have such an effect. It was taken towards one o'clock on the 10th on the question whether the House agreed with the first clause of the report. The atmosphere must have been tense as Sydenham and Jones counted 54 Yeas and James and Danvers— only the second time that two Fifth Monarchists had been paired as tellers—triumphantly reported 56 Noes. There was no move to recommit the report, so it was plainly lost.[78]

This was the largest attendance ever recorded, barring the estimated 120 on the first day of all—larger by one than the 114 (including the Speaker) who had been present on 1 November to elect a new Council of State. On that occasion the radicals had suffered a humiliating defeat; on this they enjoyed a sweeping victory. But the contrast is more apparent than real, for a considerable variety of standpoints must lie behind those 56 Noes (58 including the tellers). There were those who like the author of *A True Narrative* were opposed to a 'national parochial ministry' in principle, but none of our evidence suggests that they numbered anything like 58.[79] The report must also have left unsatisfied those strict Congregationalists who, while acknowledging that the labourer was worthy of his hire and needed a more assured income than the voluntary contributions of his flock, believed in the paramount right of each church to choose its own pastor. To be sure there was nothing in the report's proposal to prevent the commissioners from endorsing the congregation's choice where it was suitable, but there was no

[77] Abbott, iii, 436–7; cf, iv, 418: 'These 140 honest men could not governe; the ministry and propriety were like to be destroyed.'

[78] *CJ*, vii, 363; *Exact Relation*, p. 281.

[79] For reasons why the broadsheet *Catalogue* of 1654 cannot be so interpreted, see pp. 195–7.

positive injunction to do so. Since radicals were convinced that the report had been 'brought in to stifle the former Vote for taking away the power of Patrons to present',[80] they would naturally suspect it to be their opponents' intention that the candidates presented by lawful patrons would normally be approved unless they failed to satisfy the prescribed criteria of godliness and ability. Even if the proposed bill to abolish patrons' rights had been passed, the powers of the commissioners would have remained very large. Half a dozen men—the quorum was five, so long as two of the national commissioners were present—could have controlled both ejections and presentations in whole counties. The Cromwellian ordinances that established the Triers and Ejectors avoided putting both powers into the same hands, and in this they may well have responded to objections raised in Barebones' Parliament. To take a specific example of the concentration of patronage that the report's recommendations could have brought about, one of the twenty-one commissioners that it named was Arthur Barnardiston, the merchant son of that great Puritan patriarch Sir Nathaniel Barnardiston, lately deceased, whose spreading family continued to hold the hegemony among the smallish group of county gentry who ruled Suffolk. Another was Samuel Fairclough the elder, rector of Kedington and Sir Nathaniel's eulogist—not surprisingly, for Kedington was the Barnardiston family seat and Sir Nathaniel had presented Fairclough in 1629. The local commissioners in Suffolk would have needed some determination to stand up to this pair. That is not to question Fairclough's integrity, for he had been nominated to the Westminster Assembly and to the Mastership of Trinity College, Cambridge, and he had declined both honours; but his sympathies were Presbyterian, and that no doubt would have been reason enough for Suffolk saints like Caley and Dunkon to look coldly on the report.[81]

The rest of the proposed national commissioners lacked neither variety nor distinction, but to many their prevailing hue must have looked discouragingly conservative. Fourteen of the twenty-one have found a place in the *Dictionary of National Biography*; the same proportion were to be reappointed as Commissioners for Approbation (Triers) under the Protectorate. Sixteen had been

[80] *A True Narrative*, p. 4.
[81] *DNB*; Everitt, *Suffolk and the Great Rebellion*, pp. 16–20.

episcopally ordained, though not all of them cared to remember it, and only four or five were laymen.[82] Most were university men; John Owen, John Arrowsmith, Thomas Goodwin, and John Worthington were heads of Oxford and Cambridge colleges, and the first two were the Vice-Chancellors of their respective universities. Fairclough was not the only one to have declined a college, for Joseph Caryll, the Independent rector of St Magnus, had turned down the Deanery of Christ Church shortly before Owen accepted it. Martin Holbech, as headmaster of Felsted School until 1649, was said to have 'scarce bred any man whoe was loyall to his prince',[83] and had taught Cromwell's four sons. Perhaps the academic bias of this list sparked off those attacks on the universities of which the radical sector of the parliament was accused but of which its *Journal* bears no trace.[84] Denominationally, most of the sixteen ministers were Independents, including (besides those already named) Walter Cradock, William Benn of Dorchester, William Greenhill, Nicholas Lockyer, and John Stalham. But they were mostly beneficed Independents, and the great Stephen Marshall was there too, as well as Fairclough, to bridge any remaining differences between them and the moderate Presbyterians. The Baptists were represented by Henry Jessey, Daniel Dyke (one of Cromwell's chaplains), and John Tombes, whom Clarendon was to introduce to Charles II. The laymen seem more oddly chosen. Besides Barnardiston, there were Colonel William Goffe and Major Hezekiah Haines, both godly officers and sound Cromwellians, and Colonel Nathaniel Camfield of the London militia, a man of many employments,[85] though why he was nominated to this one is not apparent. Goffe had demonstrated his millenarianism in the Putney Debates but was never of Harrison's following, while

[82] The doubt concerns 'Mr. Turner', whom I have not be able to identify with any certainty. Where not otherwise stated this paragraph is based on *DNB* and Matthews, *Calamy Revised.*

[83] *Autobiography of Sir John Bramston*, ed. Lord Braybooke (1845), p. 124, quoted by Clive Holmes, *The Eastern Association in the Civil War* (Cambridge, 1974), p. 19; *VCH, Essex*, ii, 509–10, 534.

[84] See (e.g.) *CSP Ven 1653–4*, p. 160; Clarendon, *History of the Rebellion*, v, 284–5. The printed *Catalogue* of 1654 claimed to identify the members who 'were for the Godly Learned Ministry and Universities', which suggests that these subjects were linked in debate. Radicals may also have attacked the universities on 20 and 21 July, when a committee for the advancement of learning was decided upon.

[85] For which see the index to Firth and Rait.

Haines in 1655 thought it a point in favour of a militia officer that, 'He doth now frequent publique ordinances, and seemeth fixed against Quakers and the Fifth-Monarchy principle.'[86] The radical millenarians in the House must have found the names as well as the functions of the commissioners unacceptable, for only Cradock and Jessey were attuned to them at all, and neither was a Fifth Monarchist.

Finally, the fact that the report carried the confirmation of tithes in its tail may have been enough in itself to incline some members to vote against every part of it. Although the clause on maintenance never came to a vote, tithes were certainly debated, for according to *A True Narrative* 'many (after the Six days Debate) that were before zealous for Tythes were convinced by the Lord, and now stand as firm against it'.[87]

All in all, the proposals before the House were open to a variety of objections, such as could well have added a score of negative votes to those of the hard-core religious radicals. The report's supporters were prepared to consider any reasonable amendments in order to save it: 'It was offered, and would likely have been agreed unto, to the end satisfaction might have been given, that whatever names or things were either evil, or might have given just ground of offence to any, should have been either altered or removed.'[88] What doomed the report was the combination of those who opposed its very ends with those who thought that the means it proposed were too far wrong to be put right by a process of amendment. But the latter did not want to kill the whole endeavour stone dead. Highland for one was appalled by the unexpected consequences of what he called 'that harmless negative, of not complying with the report of the committee, touching *what they offered as the best way* to eject ignorant, prophane and scandalous ministers, and encouraging them that are good'.[89] He felt indignation and contempt towards those on the other side who made it a pretext for throwing away, by a precipitate resignation, all the time and expense that their fellow-members had devoted to serving their country and all the

---

[86] Firth and Davies, *Regimental History of Cromwell's Army*, p. 214 (see also pp. 95, 98–9, 100 on Haines); Woodhouse, *Puritanism and Liberty*, pp. 39–42.

[87] *A True Narrative*, p. 6.

[88] *Answer to a True Narrative*, p. 8. The reference to names strongly suggests that the proposed commissioners were discussed.

[89] *Exact Relation*, p. 280; my italicization.

effort that had gone into the many reforms left uncompleted. He complained bitterly of the false and scandalous accusations which they spread abroad and which the self-styled orthodox divines broadcast from their pulpits. For him the main work was yet to be done; the committee's report was just a false start, comparable to the abortive first bill concerning the Chancery.

On their side the organizers of the resignation did not cite the rejection of the report as their sole justification but only as the latest and gravest of a series of evidences that the parliament was doing the Commonwealth more harm than good. Some of them, almost certainly, were already awaiting a plausible pretext for ending it, for Lambert had now matured his alternative solution and he must have had his contacts among them. The vote on the 10th opened a fair prospect of carrying a majority with them. That being a Saturday, they had the Sunday in which to hold a series of conferences and to contact as many like-minded members as possible. By Monday morning their plans were ready for execution. They came to the House earlier than usual, and in some strength. Those who are named in various sources as most prominent in the *coup* were Wolseley, Sydenham, Pickering, Montagu, Jones, Roberts, Ashley Cooper, Lawrence, Desborough, Hewson, and Colonel Clarke.[90] All but the last two were members of the current Council of State, and all but three would shortly be on the new council established under the Instrument of Government.

Young Sir Charles Wolseley led off with a speech which set the keynote. Though they had sat a good while, he declared, they had not answered the people's expectations; on the contrary they had threatened to deprive the people of their property by undoing the law and of their pastors by taking away tithes and setting nothing in their place. Other speeches followed in the same vein. Their burden—the charges follow a roughly ascending order of gravity—was that the radicals had threatened the army by seeking to suspend the officers' pay and by opposing the Act of Assessment, that the parliament had in Sir John Stawell's case flouted the spirit of justice, that its votes against Chancery and for a new body of the law threatened the

---

[90] *Clarke Papers*, iii, 9–10; *A Second Narrative of the Late Parliament*, in *Harleian Miscellany*, iii, 489–93, 501; *A Faithful Searching Home Word*, pp. 16, 19; Ludlow, i, 366; Thurloe, i, 630, 637; *Exact Relation*, pp. 282–3; *A True Narrative* and *Answer to a True Narrative, passim*.

destruction of the existing law without putting anything
adequate in place of it, that its votes against patron's rights of
presentation threatened the very institution of property, and
that its final vote on Saturday showed an intent to destroy the
ministry.[91] For all these reasons they proposed that it should
abdicate its powers. They clearly had the Speaker on their side,
for their opponents found it hard to get a hearing. One managed
to make himself heard, however, despite their urging that 'it was
not now a time to debate'. He told the Speaker that he had in his
hand an expedient that he hoped would bridge the differences
revealed in Saturday's vote, and he spoke of important bills for
the relief of the people which the committee for regulating the
law had ready and waiting for the House's attention.[92] Others
who wanted the session to continue were on their feet and
demanding their right to speak, but the resigners were already
on the move, and Rous, without putting any question and
ignoring calls to keep the chair, rose hastily and put himself at
their head. Despite protests, the sergeant picked up the mace and
carried it before the Speaker,[93] and the impromptu procession
then made its way to Whitehall Palace.

Irregular and undignified though the proceedings were, there
is no doubt at all that the members who marched out were a
majority of those present. Estimates of their number vary
between forty and fifty, while the count of those who kept their
seats ranges from twenty-seven to thirty-five.[94] The hour was
still early , and it is quite likely that late-comers swelled the

[91] *A True Narrative*, pp. 1–2. The manner in which *An Answer to a True Narrative* took
these points up, and the emphasis on these issues by Highland and Nedham, vouch for the
authenticity of this account by a member who was present.

[92] *True Narrative*, p. 2; *Exact Relation*, p. 282. I take it that both writers refer to the same
speaker, since Highland states that only one 'got audience'.

[93] Highland is specific about the mace, and the newswriter in *Clarke Papers*, iii, 9, states
that 'the major part of the House came out of the House with the Speaker and Mace to
the Horse Chamber'. Against this an eye-witness who stood just outside the House says he
saw a corporal of the guard carry the mace out to the guardroom after his file of
musketeers had ejected the members who stayed behind: Sir Henry Ellis (ed.), *Original
Letters*, 2nd series (1827), iii, 372–3. This is less likely to be true, however, since if Rous
and the resigners had been so careless as to leave the mace behind they would have
enabled those who stayed behind, had they reached the quorum of forty, to claim that
they constituted the parliament. Paulucci's account in *CSP Ven 1653–4*, p. 160, is too
garbled to bear any reliance.

[94] For the estimates: Thurloe, i, 630 (Bordeaux); ibid. 637 (Bussy Mansell); *Exact
Relation*, pp. 282–3; *True Narrative*, p. 3; *Clarke Papers*, iii, 10.

'rump' by seven or eight during the brief time that it was allowed to remain. Monday was the day for prayer and preaching at Blackfriars, and the planners of the walk-out may have reckoned on this to enable them to carry out their design before the radicals could muster a quorum.

On reaching Whitehall, Rous and his cortège mustered in the Horse Chamber, there to consider a short paper abdicating their power to Cromwell; half a dozen copies were circulated. When they had approved it, the Clerk of the Parliament engrossed it on parchment and the members signed it in turn, starting with the Speaker. There was no pressure, indeed the promoters repeatedly assured the rest that 'none were desired to joyn but such as had a freedom thereto'.[95] The company were then admitted to Cromwell's presence, and the Speaker presented the document to him. It read as follows: 'Upon a Motion this day made in the House, that the sitting of this Parlament any longer as now Constituted, will not be for the good of the Commonwealth; and that therefore it was requisite to deliver up unto the Lord General Cromwell, the Powers which they received from Him, These Members whose names are underwritten, have and doe hereby resigne their said Powers to his Excellencie.'[96] Cromwell seemed surprised at first by their arrival, and he told them that their resignation placed a very heavy burden on him. He nevertheless accepted in.[97] Nearly eighty members signed it, either before its presentation or very soon after, for the original company was joined as the morning went on by late-comers to the House, and those who organized it sent for as many more as they could round up.[98] Radical accounts do not deny that it was subscribed by a clear majority.

Meanwhile those who stayed behind in the House realized unhappily that they did not make up the forty needed for a quorum, but they nevertheless called Moyer to the chair. They

[95] *Answer to a True Narrative*, p. 5.
[96] Nedham, *True State*, p. 22 (the sole source for this text).
[97] PRO 31. 3/92, fo. 94.
[98] *Exact Relation*, p. 283. Gardiner in *C & P*, ii, 281, following Highland, suggests that it took several days to get all these signatures. This may be true of a few late subscribers, but the quasi-official account in *Clarke Papers*, iii, 9–10, is dated 14 Dec. and gives the number as already about eighty, conveying a clear impression that they all signed on the 12th, as does *An Answer to a True Narrative*, which has 'near eighty'. That a majority of members signed the resignation is confirmed by *Several Proceedings in Parliament*, no. 21, 6–13 Dec. 1653, p. 280, which is backed by the imprimatur of Henry Scobell.

would not move, because (as they told each other) they had professed in the presence of the Lord 'that they were called of God to that place, which was the principal motive that drew them thither; and that they apprehended their said call was cheifly for promoting the interest of Jesus Christ'.[99] They decided to seek the Lord in prayer, but they were not given long, for soon Colonel Goffe and Lieutenant-Colonel White entered the House and requested them to leave. Some of them protested that they were there as members of parliament, called by the Lord General, and that they would not depart unless the command came from him. Goffe and White would not say from whom they had their orders, and when at their repeated requests the members still refused to move they called in a file or two of musketeers. The company then went quietly, and according to Highland the House was cleared before the Speaker and his procession had got half-way to Whitehall Palace,[1]

All accounts agree that the radical rump's sojourn in the House was short—far shorter than if its ejection had had to await Cromwell's acceptance of the majority's resignation. Who then did give Goffe and White their orders? If it was Cromwell, as Gardiner rightly remarked, they would have said so; and Cromwell, besides showing surprise when the resigning members came to him at Whitehall, solemnly told his next parliament that he 'did not know one tittle of that resignation, until they all came and brought it'.[2] He had too many witnesses before him then to risk a bare-faced lie. The finger points not at Cromwell but (as Gardiner perceived) irresistibly at Lambert. Although there is no positive evidence of his involvement in the cabals on the 11th, those who were said to be so involved included Desborough, Hewson, Sydenham, Pickering, Montagu, and Jones, and it would be straining credulity to suppose that some at least of them were not in touch with him, and aware of the Instrument of Government that he had prepared against the widely expected change of regime. Lambert, who after Cromwell had the most acute political mind in the army now that Ireton was dead, must

---

[99] *True Narrative*, p. 3.

[1] *Exact Relation*, p. 283; Thurloe, i, 637. According to *True Narrative*, p. 3, and Ellis, *Original Letters*, 2nd series, iii, 372, some of the ejected members joined the resigners at Whitehall, and this is confirmed by *Clarke Papers*, iii, 10, where '*from* the Horse Chamber' must be a slip for 'to'.

[2] Abbott, iii, 454–5.

have appreciated the embarrassment that could have resulted if the protesting members had achieved a quorum, as they had every prospect of doing if Highland is right that they numbered 34 or 35 before they were evicted. His dominant role in framing the Instrument and afterwards in persuading Cromwell to accept it, which will be examined in the next chapter, makes Lambert the obvious man to have organized the military side of the *coup*.

What has still to be explained is why as many as about eighty members were so ready to sign away their authority. Highland suggests a number of unworthy motives, such as thoughtless emulation, fear of losing lucrative employment, and a desire to be rid of the troublesome duty of attending the House,[3] but it is unlikely that many were moved by these. More probably, the disillusioned moderates who agreed with the reasons expressed by the leading resigners were joined by others who would have preferred to go on sitting if they could have done so with any prospect of success, but felt that in the emergency which had now arisen the Commonwealth was safest in the hands of Cromwell. The numbers show that some of the Noes in that final division, as well as all or most of the unsuccessful Yeas, were now convinced that if they were so far apart on so basic a matter as the settlement of the ministry they were unlikely to agree on the equally contentious questions which still lay before them, especially lay patronage and the reform of the law. It must also have weighed with many that Cromwell was increasingly embarrassed by the assembly that he had called into being, and they must have shared his concern that their divisions were weakening the Commonwealth when foreign and domestic pressures required it to strengthen itself.

In addition to a sense that *salus populi* required a government set on more stable foundations, two broad themes dominated the justifications of the resignation that soon appeared, over and above the specific controversies over the law, the ministry, and so on. One was the cumulative threat that the radicals' policies posed to property; the other was the increasing extravagance and intolerance of the claim of the saints to rule simply as saints. The implications for property in the cases of tithes, patrons' rights, the Court of Chancery, and the codification of law have been sufficiently stressed, and they were much aired by the early

[3] *Exact Relation*, p. 283.

apologists for the Protectorate. Property raised its head again in the final debate on the ministry. One of the arguments most strongly urged against those who condemned a parochial clergy as in itself antichristian was 'how unjust and cruel it was to turn out the good and the bad together, and put many godly, painful, faithful Teachers, *out of their Freeholds*, to seek a subsistence for them and their Families'.[4] *Confusion Confounded* deprecated the zealots' aim to remove all but the godly from the Commonwealth's employment with the argument that, 'Certainly a man's *office* or *profession* (provided always it consists with the public welfare, and be not oppressive to the people) is as much propriety as any other whatsoever.'[5] The suggestion that army officers should forgo a year's pay was naturally decried on the same grounds. Cromwell had this to say of the saints' recent pretensions when he opened his next parliament: 'Notions will hurt none but them that have them. But when they come to such practices, as to tell us that liberty and property are not the badges of the kingdom of Christ, . . . this is worthy of every magistrate's consideration, especially where every stone is turned to bring confusion.'[6] Years later, he is reported to have said of Barebone's Parliament: 'and what did they? Fly at liberty and property.'[7]

The charge that the saints arrogated to themselves an exclusive right to rule was commonly linked with suggestions of a gulf between their pretensions and their capacities and with appeals to the injustice of excluding the nation's 'natural' rulers. The latter were well represented among the members named as taking a lead in the resignation; they included three baronets, a knight, and several other representatives of ancient families, as well as a military element which probably constituted Lambert's point of contact. The moderate member who replied to *A True Narrative* wrote thus: 'Tis no hard way to discern what a foundation was laid of exalting men (who should take to themselves the name of Saints, though never so unduly) in Government, and excluding all others who had never so great Interest in the Nation, and other fitness thereto, and have a Civil Right to Rule, when Providence shall give them a lawful call

[4] *Answer to a True Narrative*, p. 8; my italicization.
[5] *Confusion Confounded*, p. 10; italics in original.
[6] Abbott, iii, 438.
[7] Abbott, iv, 417. For another report of this speech see n. 77.

thereto.'[8] Nedham exclaimed contemptuously 'at those mens open and violent avowing this Point of State-heresie; *That godly persons, though of small understanding, and little ability of mind in publick Affairs, are more fit for Government than men of great knowledg and wisdom, if endued only with natural Parts, and moral vertues.*'[9] Cromwell echoed these strictures some months later: 'But for men to entitle themselves, upon this principle, that they are the only men to rule kingdoms, govern nations, and give laws to people; to determine of property and liberty and everything else, upon such a pretence as this is: truly, they had need give clear manifestations of God's presence with them, before wise men will receive or submit to their conclusions.'[10] The charge that the extreme millenarians, inspired by the prophets at Blackfriars, claimed an exclusive right to rule for themselves and their fellow-saints on the grounds that Christ had called them, was not just a partisan invention, put about after the dissolution to justify Cromwell's accession to power. So much is proved by a number of remarkable accusations which other religious radicals levelled against them at the time. On 20 January 1654 those prominent Baptists William Kiffin, John Spilsbery, and Joseph Fansom wrote what appears to be a circular letter to the Baptist churches. Invoking 'that great relation wee stand in to you as brethren in the faith once given to the saints', they urged their co-religionaries not to engage in public protest against the new Protectorate, as some were reported to be intending. They testified with dismay to 'the great disesteem that all power began to be in, by reason of the ill-management of it, in the hands of those where it was', a disesteem which had encouraged men, women, and even children to take it upon themselves to judge and contemn God's great ordinance of magistracy. For this they squarely blamed the preachings of the Fifth Monarchists at Blackfriars 'to which many of these lately in power adheared', and particularly their insistence that the magistrate must own that he received his power immediately from Christ and was accountable to no one else. That, as the writers pointed out, was the very plea of Charles I. Equally they deplored the constant preaching that God was

---

[8] *Answer to a True Narrative*, p. 2.
[9] Nedham, *True State*, p. 25; italics in original.
[10] Abbott, iii, 437.

stirring up his people to throw down potentates and powers.[11]
Kiffin, himself a lay preacher, was no tame conformist; he was
to turn gradually against the Protectorate and eventually to
present a highly subversive petition to Richard Cromwell's
parliament,[12] but his present advice to the churches was to accept
the ruling authority and bless God for their liberty.

William Erbery, hardly a conservative figure and certainly no
time-server, delivered a similar rebuke about ten days earlier to
John Rogers and Vavasor Powell, who had continued their
rantings against Cromwell at Christ Church when the Blackfriars
meetings were put down.

First, ... Are you the Prophets of the Lord as Jeremiah was, or are ye
Ministers of the Gospel, as Paul?
Secondly, Do you speak of the People of God as confined to your own
gathered Churches, or the People of God scattered in the Nation?
Thirdly, Were your thoughts theirs; or were they all taken up with you
in the Parliament lately dissolved?[13]

Erbery reproved them eloquently for interpreting the scriptural
prophecies of the kingdom 'too carnally', and told them that
they, like first the bishops, then the Presbyterians, and next the
Independents who had linked their fortunes with the Rump's,
had fallen through meddling in state affairs.

John Goodwin, the radical Independent who would have his
own differences with the Protectorate, asked the Fifth Monarchists why, since no human endeavours could hasten or retard the
time that God had appointed for the kingdom of Christ, they
should 'abuse the simplicity of inconsiderate people' by claiming
'that if they were but permitted to umpire the sovereign Affairs
of their State and Nation, they would out of hand bring the said
blessedness of the fift Monarchy upon the head of the world, even
before the day thereof?'[14] In April 1654 he published another
eloquent denunciation of false prophets:

May it not yet be further queried, Whether such persons, ... who

---

[11] Nickolls, pp. 159–60. The letter begins 'Deere Brethren'; the copy from which it is
printed, in the library of the Royal Society of Antiquaries, bears all three authors'
signatures but is written in a professional clerk's hand.

[12] *Complete Prose Works of John Milton*, vii, 20–1.

[13] W. Erbery, *An Olive-leaf* (9 Jan. 1654), p. 2 *et passim*.

[14][J. Goodwin], Συγκρητισμός, or *Dissatisfaction Satisfied* ([22 Dec.] 1653), p. 16.
Thomason on his copy identifies Goodwin as author and corrects the year from 1654.

publiquely undertake or pretend to know, and predict unto the people, how long the present Government shall stand, and after how many months, or years, it shall presently be dissolved and fall, do not impose a kind of wretched necessity upon themselves to turn every stone for the raising of Tumults and Insurrections in the Land ... ?[15]

Such rebukes were deserved only by a minority of the members of 1653, but that minority stood condemned by fellow-enthusiasts who spoke their language and shared most of their ideals. Their share of the responsibility for bringing Barebone's Parliament to a premature end was a heavy one, but most of them found nothing to reproach themselves for. The last word may be allowed to a manifesto which the London Fifth Monarchists published in the following September, to coincide with the opening of the first Protectorate parliament. It was signed by the whole churches of Rogers and Peter Chamberlain and by some members of eight others, including those of Feake, Hanserd Knollys, Jessey, Barebone, and Highland. It asked 'Yet for all this, were not the last Parliament dissolved, for that they would rule as *Saints* (or part of the *fifth Monarchy*, for Christ) and for doing that the former Parliament neglected, and therefore were dissolved?'[16]

---

[15] J. Goodwin, *Peace Protected, and Discontent Dis-armed* ([Apr.] 1654), p. 63.

[16] *A Declaration of several of the Churches of Christ* (30 Aug. 1654), p. 4 (italics in original); Capp, *Fifth Monarchy Men*, p. 105. The signatures of a few of Barebone's and Highland's congregations are not of course evidence that those men were themselves Fifth Monarchists.

XI

The Protectorate Established

Barebone's Parliament had no other mourners than the millenarian saints. In London, where the zealots' stock was now very low, Bordeaux and Paulucci both sensed an air of general satisfaction. There were even a few bonfires; the lawyers in particular celebrated merrily with sack at the Temple and elsewhere, while the actual organizers of the resignation held a party in Sydenham's rooms. 'Most men upon this dissolution take occasion to cry Aha, Aha, and to speak their pleasure', wrote the ex-Leveller and Independent lay preacher Samuel Chidley reprovingly. Ralph Josselin on the other hand, the minister of Earls Colne, had been forewarned of the parliament's fall and feared 'the approach of evill dayes', but then he had been equally gloomy over the prospects of its first meeting in July. For the most part, however, the country seems to have taken this dissolution as calmly as the last.[1]

The main difference between the situations in April and December was that this time the chief army officers below Cromwell himself knew just what to do next. The circumstantial evidence that Lambert and his colleagues were in collusion with the MPs who led the walk-out is strong. A written constitution was all prepared for formal adoption by the Council of Officers and presentation to the Lord General, and there is no need to doubt the belief of contemporaries and of generations of historians that it was essentially the work of John Lambert. If the

---

[1] PRO 31.3/92, fo. 94; *CSP Ven 1653–4*, pp. 160–1; *Second Narrative of the Late Parliament*, in *Harleian Misc.*, iii, 485; S. Chidley, *A Remonstrance to the Creditors of the Commonwealth* (19 Dec. 1653); *Diary of Ralph Josselin 1616–1683*, ed. Alan Macfarlane (1976), pp. 305, 315; *The Moderate Publisher*, 16–23 Dec. p. 75.

role that he so confidently assumed between 12 and 16 December does not sufficiently tell its own story, his reaction when Hesilrige and Vane taunted him in 1659 with his responsibility for the Instrument of Government provides the confirmation needed. By that time, having fallen out with the Protectorate and formed a wary alliance with the republicans, Lambert would have been glad to disown it if he could, but for all his resentment when Hesilrige brought it up in Richard Cromwell's parliament, he could not deny his authorship.[2] Even without such evidence, who else among the senior officers could be credited with such a relatively sophisticated piece of constitutional engineering, now that Ireton was dead? The only open questions are when he drafted it, whom he took into consultation, and how much Cromwell knew about it before he was formally confronted with it on 13 December. Fortunately the scattered evidence of its gestation that survives, though none of it is unimpeachable, does agree sufficiently to yield a coherent story.

According to Ludlow, Lambert first introduced the Instrument to the Council of Officers on what must have been the morning of the 13th, when he himself read it to them and sought their concurrence before presenting it to Cromwell. When some of them raised objections to it, he 'informed them that it was not now to be disputed, whether this should be the form of government or not, for that was already resolved, it having been under consideration for two months past'.[3] This presumably meant that he himself had begun work on it around mid-October, when he was in Yorkshire. Whether anyone else shared in its formulation so early is not known, but in the latter part of November he evidently discussed it at length with half a dozen fellow-officers, and when they had put it into almost final shape they brought it as a group before Cromwell. At that stage the title that it proposed for him was king.

Lambert, it will be remembered, had been sent for by the council in mid-November, and though a slight illness delayed

[2] The evidence is usefully marshalled by George D. Heath in 'Making the Instrument of Government', *Journal of British Studies*, vi (1967), 18–21. Cf. Dawson, *Cromwell's Understudy*, pp. 175 ff.

[3] Ludlow, i, 369. Despite the doubts cast on Ludlow's text by Dr Worden's researches, his circumstantial account at this point is unlikely to have been subjected to serious editorial tampering.

him for a couple of days he reached London on the 19th.[4] The council wanted to confer with him about the military situation in Scotland, but newsmongers linked his arrival with the growing rumours of an impending change of government, and they were justified to the extent that he shortly divulged his constitutional scheme first to a few confidants and then to Cromwell. The crop of predictions around this time that Cromwell would shortly become head of state, perhaps even as king,[5] may have sprung from a leak from these colloquies, or merely from the fact that they were known to take place. This is how Cromwell recollected them ten months later:

The gentlemen that undertook to frame this government did consult divers days together, (they being of known integrity and ability,) how to frame somewhat that might give us settlement, and they did so; and that I was not privy to their counsels, they know it. When they had finished their model in some measure, or made a very good preparation of it, [they] became communicative. They told me that except I would undertake the government, they thought things would hardly come to a composure and settlement, but blood and confusion would break in upon us. I denied it again and again, as God and those persons know, not complimentingly as they also know and as God knows.[6]

This must have been the occasion to which he referred in his angry speech to the hundred officers on 27 February 1657, when he said that '7 of them made an Instrument of Government, [and] brought it to him with the name of King in it'.[7] The vital question is whether all this happened before the dissolution, as Gardiner assumed and as is argued here, or immediately after; Cromwell does not make the chronology clear. But apart from the further evidence of negotiations prior to the dissolution which will be set forth in the next paragraph, it will shortly be demonstrated that there was hardly time for protracted disputes over whether Cromwell should or should not 'undertake the government' in the tight sequence of events between 12 and 16 December. On the other hand there is evidence of a very special

[4] Thurloe, i, 589, 610; PRO 31.3/92, fos. 36, 48; Clarendon MS 47, fo. 113; see p. 322.
[5] *CSP Ven 1653-4*, p. 155, and cf. p. 152; Clarendon MS 47, fo. 113; PRO 31.3/92, fos. 83-4; Thurloe, i, 628.
[6] Abbott, iii, 455.
[7] Abbott, iv, 418; cf. p. 417 for another summary of this speech which brings out even more clearly Cromwell's emphasis on the royal title in the original Instrument, and his refusal of it.

interest in the royal title about a fortnight earlier. Among the state papers is a collection of specimens of the warrants and dockets used by Charles I in initiating royal grants, proclamations, pardons, and other prerogative actions, together with descriptions of the ensuing procedures. All are dated 1 December 1653.[8] That, as Gardiner surmised, may well have been the time when Cromwell declined the crown.[9]

Confirmation that these consultations took place well before the dissolution is to be found in a pamphlet published in 1655 'By a late Member of the Army, who was an Eye, and an Ear witnesse to many of those Things', and entitled *The Protector, (so called,) In Part Unvailed*. The author was a millenarian who regarded Cromwell as an apostate 'from the good old Cause of God' and identified his own interests and aspirations with the remnant of Barebone's Parliament who stayed behind to be turned out by Goffe and White.[10] He was sure that the resignation and its rapid consequences sprang from a plot; 'the so suddain coming forth of which Instrument, declares plainly, that it was not a new thing, but that which was thought of, contrived, and appointed some time before those Friends (before mentioned) were turn'd out of the House; and all this done by five, or six, or very few more'.[11] These correspond to the seven mentioned by Cromwell. The author, without suggesting any intervening lapse of time, next goes on to describe how all the officers were sent for

upon a pretence of being taken into the consultation; yet when they came thither, they did little else but walk to and fro in the Rooms without, whilst the business was carried on by a few within; and staying several times very late at Night, still expecting to be sent for in, Major-General *Lambert* comes out to them, and tells them they might go home, for there was no occasion at that time to make use of them.[12]

One is not told why they were dismissed with their opinions unsought and their curiosity unsatisfied, but if we are right in dating these transactions around the end of November and

[8] PRO, SP18, vol. 42, fo. 9.

[9] *C & P*, ii, 270–2.

[10] *The Protector, (So called,) In Part Unvailed* ([24 Oct.] 1655), pp. 3, 9, 11, 16, 54, 57, 74, 76.

[11] Ibid. 12.

[12] Ibid. I cannot agree with Gardiner (*C & P*, ii, 283 n. 2) in relating this passage to the discussions on 14 and 15 Dec., for the text itself implies the earlier context, as well as fitting it much better.

beginning of December, the likely explanation is that Lambert and his confidants hoped to get Cromwell's prompt consent to their plan for a change of government and then to get it endorsed immediately by as full a Council of Officers as possible. But their intentions were thwarted when Cromwell 'denied it again and again', and the pamphlet suggests that his resistance was spread over several days' meetings, lasting well into the night. Hostile commentators like Ludlow believed that he was a party to the plot to bring Barebone's Parliament to an end; so did this pamphleteer, but he himself retails the story of 'an honourable person' who tackled Cromwell while it was still sitting about the current fears and rumours 'that he would set up himself', and got the reply 'that if he thought there were such a Principle in him he would presently run out of the world, or dig his own grave, and lie down and die there'.[13] This to the writer seemed sheer hypocrisy, but though the language looks high-flown the sentiment may well have been sincere. There is no good reason for disbelieving Cromwell's frequent assertions that he did not deliberately seek the chief magistracy and that he shouldered it with reluctance, while there were at least three reasons why he should have rejected Lambert's proposals at that time: he was unwilling to dissolve another parliament by force, especially when he himself had allotted it nearly a year more to run; he would not let himself be raised to power by a military *coup*; and he balked at the title of king.

Faced with such a refusal, Lambert had obvious motives for dismissing the assembled officers without further explanation. To disclose his written constitution after it had been rejected would have pointlessly alerted his republican and millenarian opponents, and the time for it might yet come. Cromwell's attitude might well change if the parliament were persuaded to get rid of itself, and if the title were altered. The allegations of Ludlow, *The Protector . . . Unvailed*, and other hostile sources that Lambert was in league with the MPs who led the final walk-out are entirely plausible, but so too is Cromwell's subsequent assertion that he 'did not know one tittle of that resignation, until they all came and brought it'.[14] The men who plotted it, even though most of them were his fellow-councillors, had every

---

[13] Ibid. 7.
[14] Abbott, iii, 454–5.

motive for concealing their plans from him. Perhaps he suspected what was afoot, but did not want to know; perhaps his reported surprise when the resigners arrived at Whitehall was unfeigned.

At this point the story can be resumed where the end of the last chapter broke it off. In what was left of 12 December, Cromwell seems to have spent a long afternoon closeted with the Council of State, though some newspapers say that he also met the Council of Officers that day.[15] The probability is that he sought counsel from whoever he thought fit, and that he called in some leading officers as well as those whom he trusted of the councillors elected on 1 November. A little more is known about what went on the next day, starting with that critical meeting between Lambert and a large concourse of officers already referred to. They were waiting for him in the council chamber at Whitehall, where Cromwell had first addressed Barebone's over five months earlier. On his arrival, all who were not members of the army were ordered to withdraw. He then produced the brief document of abdication which the majority of members had subscribed. Unless it was a copy supplied by one of the resigners, he could hardly have acquired it without Cromwell's consent. This and his taking over the council chamber represent as striking an assertion of initiative and authority as his orders the day before—assuming they were his—for expelling the remnant of the parliament from the House.

After the assembled officers had listened to the resignation, they heard Lambert himself read out the Instrument of Government. He had a ticklish task, for most of them, if we are right, were taking in the lengthy document for the first time, and not all were prepared to accept it without criticism or discussion. As has been said, he dealt brusquely with objections, maintaining that it was already accepted in principle as the form of government. That raises interesting and unanswerable questions as to how far Cromwell had committed himself in the previous day's discussions. Lambert may have been bluffing, but the

---

[15] PRO 31.3/92, fo. 92. Bordeaux, writing on the evening of the 12th, says merely that the council had sat 'toute ceste après-disnée' at Cromwell's house, but it is inconceivable that he was not present. The newspapers which allege a meeting with the Council of Officers include *Severall Proceedings of State Affairs*, no. 220, 8–15 Dec. 1653, p. 3481; *The Moderate Publisher*, no. 84, 9–16 Dec. 1653, p. 68; *The Perfect Diurnall*, no. 210, 12–19 Dec. 1653, p. 3197.

likelihood is that he already had Cromwell's authority for seeking the officers' broad assent. He faced some awkward proposals, such as that in future the general of the army should be debarred from the Protectorship, but he parried them by saying that they would be put before the General (as Cromwell was still being called) and by promising that any amendments offered would receive consideration. Cromwell's future title may have been as yet unsettled; one well-informed source gives it at this stage as Lord Governor.[16] Eventually Lambert did obtain the officers' general concurrence, and the stage was set for detailed discussions between Cromwell and the Council of Officers.

The first of these was probably held later the same day, if there is anything in a newspaper report that Cromwell then declared that he would 'use his uttermost endeavours to defend all honest peaceable people of this Nation in their just Rights and Liberties, against all the enemies of this Commonwealth'.[17] But this anodyne formula may have been an editor's invention, and for the most part the newspapers were almost comically cautious and uninformative about the dissolution and the ensuing days of interregnum. *Severall Proceedings of Parliament*, which carried Henry Scobell's imprimatur and had to cover the awkward week from 6 to 13 December, printed nothing but the bald record of the resignation in the *Commons' Journal*; other less official weekly prints offered even less. Nedham, whose official *Mercurius Politicus* spanned the week of 9–16 December, filled more than fourteen of his sixteen pages with innocuous reports from Scotland and abroad before giving brief news of the parliament's final debates on religion, the *Journal* entry about its resignation, and thereafter just three vague lines to say that there had been 'earnest deliberations for a settling of the Government of this Nation in time to come'.[18] Cromwell, Lambert, and the rest of the officers kept very close counsel during the three clear days available for

[16] This account is based on an intercepted letter in Thurloe, i, 632, written on 14 Dec. by 'T.M.', and on Ludlow, i, 369–70. Ludlow places the discussion a few days after the resignation, but the intercepted letter is firm that it took place the day after, though its author writes 'Thursday' when he means Tuesday. Ludlow was not present and his text may have been edited, but his very circumstantial account gives a strong impression of being derived from an eye-witness.

[17] *A Perfect Account of the Daily Intelligence*, no. 153, 7–14 Dec. 1653, p. 1224.

[18] *Mercurius Politicus*, no. 183, 9–16 Dec. 1653, pp. 3037–8; *Severall Proceedings of Parliament*, no. 21, 6–13 Dec. 1653, p. 280.

discussion between the dissolution and the inaugural ceremony on the 16th. No hard news leaked out at the time; indeed even a week after the Protectorate was established *Mercurius Politicus* said no more than that after the dissolution Cromwell called a Council of Officers 'and advised with other persons of Interest in the Nation', and that 'after several dayes seeking of God, and advising therein' it was resolved that a council of twenty-one should be named and that Cromwell should be chosen as Lord Protector.[19]

Yet despite the official silence, Bordeaux was able on the 15th to describe the broad shape of the new government with tolerable accuracy, and even a day earlier one 'T.M.'—presumably a royalist, for Thurloe had his letter intercepted—wrote a remarkably well-informed account of it to a friend in Paris. He clearly had inside information, and he makes it quite plain that by Wednesday the 14th the essential provisions of the written constitution were already determined. Indeed he reported that the officers had been closeted with Cromwell at the Cockpit in Whitehall over the choice of members of the council, though the names were not known yet. 'I suppose the choosing of this new councell will take up more tyme then is beleeved', he wrote, 'because they will be sure of such as they will intrust, and to satisfie all parties, who have an hand in the choice.'[20] This was indeed a sensitive and crucial business, and it was obviously politic to get the nominees' consent before announcing them. The fact that all the original councillors were willing to serve suggests that this was done. But if the business had progressed to the selection of the council within two days of the parliament's resignation, there can have been no time for the protracted arguing over the whole question whether he should undertake the government, which Cromwell recounted in his speech on 12 September 1654, or for the several days of cabals between him and the Instrument's half-dozen sponsors which are described in *The Protector ... Unvailed*. These had surely taken place well before the dissolution. Some time may well have been spent on minor modifications of the government, but as T.M. reported on the 14th, 'This which Lambert aymed att he hath effected.' Even without this evidence, the ceremony of Cromwell's installation

---

[19] *Mercurius Politicus*, no. 184, 16–22 Dec. 1653, p. 3052.
[20] Thurloe, i, 632; PRO 31.3/92, fo. 9.

on the 16th was well-enough organized to indicate that it was not improvised at a few hours' notice. There are indications that the consultations on the 14th and 15th took place in a smaller and more select Council of Officers than the large gathering which Lambert addressed on the 13th, but that was to be expected when the business consisted mainly in the selection of councillors, the amendment of details, and the stage-managing of the change of government.[21]

The formal inauguration of the Protectorate went off with the rather drab propriety that tends to characterize ceremonies unwarmed by traditional sentiment and panache.[22] A solemn procession of judges, officers of state, City fathers, and senior army officers escorted Cromwell from Whitehall to Westminster Hall. Despite the inevitably large military presence, with ranks of soldiers lining the route, he chose to appear in a plain black suit and cloak. He took special care to associate the Lord Mayor and aldermen of London with his elevation; the Lord Mayor bore the sword of the City before him all the way to the Palace of Westminster, and in the return after the ceremony rode bareheaded in the boot of his coach, still bearing the sword. The central proceedings took place in the Court of Chancery. Next to Cromwell's chair of state stood the Commissioners of the Great Seal; on either side of them were ranged the judges and the barons of the Exchequer, flanked on their right by the new council and the chief army officers and on their left by the Lord Mayor and aldermen. The Instrument was read out by William Jessop, who had been Assistant Secretary to the council since last October and was soon to be its Clerk;[23] it took him half an hour. Cromwell then stood, holding up his hand in assent, while Lord Commissioner John Lisle read the Protector's oath, which committed him to observe all the provisions of 'the Form of

[21] Ludlow (i, 370) states that at the next meeting of officers after the one on the 13th which approved the Instrument in principle Lambert dismissed them back to their units. But his chronology here is unreliable (cf. n. 16), and he (or his editor) may have become slightly confused between pre-dissolution and post-dissolution discussions, since he was not himself present. Nevertheless it is very possible that the majority of the officers were dismissed and a smaller number reconvened as a select and confidential Council of Officers.

[22] The ensuing account is based on Abbott, iii, 136–8; Gardiner, *Documents*, p. 417; *Severall Proceedings of State Affairs*, no. 221, 15–22 Dec. 1653, pp. 3498–500; Ludlow, i, 373.

[23] Aylmer, *State's Servants*, pp. 234–6. Four years earlier he had had many qualms of conscience over subscribing the Engagement.

Government' and to govern the three nations in all else according to their laws, statutes, and customs. He then signed it. It stated that he had been desired to assume the Protectorship 'as well by several Persons of Interest and Fidelity in this Commonwealth, as [by] the Officers of the Army', but despite this claim that he did not owe his great office to the army alone it was Lambert who now knelt before him and offered him a sword in a scabbard. Cromwell took off his own and buckled it on, thus symbolizing the laying-down of the military sword and the taking-up of the civil; but since he did not cease to be Lord General, nor Lambert to be his chief lieutenant in England, the ceremony can have been of limited comfort to those who could not stomach the army's role in politics, especially if they knew whose work the Instrument was. Cromwell then received the great seal, the supreme emblem of civil authority, at the hands of its commissioners, to whom he immediately returned it. Next the Lord Mayor delivered to him the City's sword and cap of maintenance, and at once received them back. Either just before or after these rituals the newly sworn Protector made a short speech, saying he desired to rule no longer than his government ministered to the great work of the Lord, so that thereby the gospel might shine in its full splendour and the people enjoy their just rights and property. The proceedings completed, the company filed out and took coaches at Westminster Hall Gate for the short drive to the Banqueting Hall, where Nicholas Lockyer preached a sermon.

The processions were greeted by salvos from the ships in the river and from the Tower, and by shouts of acclamation from the attendant troops, though some officers later complained that many who were summoned to Westminster Hall had no idea why until Cromwell emerged as Protector before their eyes; 'it was a meer surprize to thousands which were there'.[24] That is probably an exaggeration, but it is difficult if not impossible to gauge what the popular reaction was. Estimates from London mostly reflect the preconceptions of their sources, and from the country scarcely any evidence survives. The more sycophantic newspapers told of general acclamation and joy, but though Salvetti reported some spontaneous applause, Bordeaux and Paulucci both remarked upon the general silence or indifference

[24] *The Protector . . . Unvailed*, p. 13.

of the populace.[25] But the ceremony on the 16th, a Friday, was so unannounced that many Londoners were probably unaware of its significance, unless their business took them to Westminster that day. The formal proclamation of the Protectorate had to wait until the Monday, when it was performed to the sound of trumpets, with heralds, serjeants-at-arms, members of the council, and the Lord Mayor and aldermen in attendance, at a series of points from Palace Yard to the Old Exchange. A royalist newswriter records one small incident at Temple Bar. An 'ordinary fellow' passing by saw the herald and some cavalry drawn up, so he asked a trooper what it was all about. 'Proclaiming His Highness Lord Protector Cromwell', he was told. 'He protects none but such rogues as thou art', the citizen retorted, and when the soldier made to strike him he pulled him off his horse and dealt him some hearty blows. The onlookers shouted and laughed their encouragement, unabashed by the proximity of some of Cromwell's new councillors.[26]

The proclamation itself was issued by the council and dated 16 December, but it was very brief and said no more about the government than that it was to be 'by a Lord Protector, and successive triennial Parliaments'.[27] There was a curious delay in publishing the actual Instrument of Government. Brief reports of its main provisions soon began to appear in the newspapers, but these could have been based on notes taken during the reading of it in Westminster Hall. The text was not available to the public until 2 January, and the first newspapers to carry it appeared after the 5th. Tempting though it may be to suspect that publication was withheld until its more predictable assailants had been dealt with, the true explanation seems to be that the Instrument was still in rough shape when it was first promulgated, and that Thurloe and the council simply did not have time to prepare it for the printers until the turn of the year.[28]

[25] Gardiner, *C & P*, ii, 297–8; *Weekly Intelligencer*, 13–20 Dec. 1653, p. 95.

[26] Thurloe, i, 641; *Mercurius Politicus*, no. 184, 16–22 Dec. 1653, p. 3054.

[27] Reprinted in Abbott, iii, 137, and *CSPD 1653–4*, pp. 297–8.

[28] The council ordered Thurloe on 20 Dec. 'to perfect with speed the instrument' so as to have it ready for enrolling, and on the 22nd to bring it before them, so prepared, next day; but it evidently needed amendment, since on the 27th he was ordered 'to take speedy course for what is further to be done to fit for the press the Instrument' (*CSPD 1653–4*, pp. 301, 309, 314). *A Perfect Account*, no. 156, for 28 Dec.–4 Jan., printed this announcement under Monday, 2 Jan.: 'This day was extant the Government of this Commonwealth by his Highness especial commandement' (p. 1245). The first newspapers

The champions of the outraged saints were not long in making themselves heard. Feake and Powell publicly denounced Cromwell as 'the dissembleingst perjured villaine in the world' at a Sunday service on 18 December in Christ Church, Newgate, where Feake had the living,[29] but they reserved their heaviest thunderbolts for their Monday exercise at St. Anne's, Blackfriars. Feake expounded the seventh chapter of Daniel at great length, and though he named no names he made it very clear that he identified Cromwell as the little horn that was to make war with the saints. Powell mounted the pulpit next and threw caution to the winds. Having interpreted the king of the north in Daniel 11 to mean Charles I, he applied verse 21 to Cromwell: 'And in his estate shall stand up a vile person, to whom they shall not give the honour of the kingdom: but he shall come in peaceably, and obtain the kingdom by flatteries.' Powell went on to inveigh against the great army men in general, to impugn the authority of the new council, and to denounce its claim that Barebone's Parliament dissolved itself as a lie. 'Let us go home and pray', he said, echoing an inflammatory catch-phrase of the previous spring, 'and say Lord wilt Thou have Oliver Cromwell or Jesus Christ to reign over us?' Next to preach was George Cokayne, whose own congregation at St. Pancras, Soper Lane, included Tichborne and Ireton. He was less openly seditious, aiming his shafts mainly at 'the antichristian clergy, parochial priests, Baal's priests', though he did deplore their association with 'the present power'.[30]

All these diatribes were reported to the council at loving

---

to print its authentic text were *Mercurius Politicus*, no. 186, 29 Dec.-5 Jan., and *Severall Proceedings of State Affaires*, no. 223, covering the same dates. Thomason gives less than his usual help in dating publication, for the copy of *The Government of the Common-wealth of England, Scotland & Ireland* in his collection is not an original but is bound up in *A Collection of all the Proclamations* [etc. from 16 Dec. 1653 to 2 Sept. 1654], published by the official printers Dugard and Hills. This is continuously paginated, and the Instrument appears between two ordinances of 26 and 29 December; it is inscribed at the end, presumably by Thomason, 'Printed the 23 December 1653'. The council's order book shows this to be an error. For confirmation, Thomason acquired a pirated summary of the Instrument, entitled *The Articles signed by His Highness Oliver Cromwel*, on 30 Dec., and a somewhat different summary in manuscript which is headed, probably in his hand, 'The Articles. Jan: 2d 1653' (BL, 669 f.17.75). There could have been no demand for either document if the Instrument had been in print earlier. The council finally ordered its formal enrolment on 5 Jan. (*CSPD 1653–4*, p.349).

[29] Thurloe, i, 641.

[30] *CSPD 1653–4*, pp. 304–8.

length by Marchamont Nedham, and as a result Feake and Powell were arrested next day and brought before it. They were kept a few days in the custody of the serjeant-at-arms and the Blackfriars meetings were banned, but on their release they promptly renewed their attacks, using Christ Church as their base.[31] Their further resistance to the Protectorate need not concern us here. Their fellow-Fifth Monarchist John Rogers, to whom Cromwell had seemed a second Moses in the spring, now warned him in a broadsheet dated 21 December to 'Take heed of Protecting the Plantations of Antichrist, or the Towers of Babylon', to eschew 'the Old-State Principles of Carnal Policie', and to beware of 'Protecting Carnal, National Antichristian Clergy'.[32] But at least he addressed him respectfully as 'his highness'; the bitter attacks that would eventually land Rogers in gaol with Feake did not begin to develop for a month or two. None of these preachers, however, constituted as great a potential threat as Harrison, because of his following in the army. Yet speculations that he might raise part of it against Cromwell proved unduly alarmist. He was sounded as to whether he would recognize and obey the new government, and when he declined he was quietly deprived of his commission. Six weeks later, being still openly disaffected, he was given ten days to leave London and ordered to reside in his native Staffordshire until further notice. There were a few desertions in outlying regiments in the north and in Wales, and two or three Fifth Monarchist officers resigned their commissions, but Cromwell was evidently anxious to avoid confrontation and the army as a whole took the change very quietly.[33]

If one asks what was foremost in Cromwell's mind when he accepted the Protectorship, it was almost certainly a conviction that now only he could save the Commonwealth from impending anarchy. Though his own pronouncements must be read with obvious caution, his main self-vindication, consistent over the years, was that when he took the helm all the landmarks of the

---

[31] Ibid. 308–9; Capp, *Fifth Monarchy Men*, p.101.

[32] *To His Highnesse ... The humble Cautionary Proposals of John Rogers* (21 Dec. 1653); Capp, *Fifth Monarchy Men*, pp. 103–4.

[33] Thurloe, i, 641, 650; *CSPD 1653–4*, pp. 286–7; Capp, *Fifth Monarchy Men*, pp. 99–100.

nation's orderly life—political, ecclesiastical, social, legal—were in danger of being swept away. The burden of his opening speech to his next parliament was 'what a heap of confusions were upon these poor nations' when he took up his office. He had bowed to those who pressed it on him, he said soon afterwards, because 'blood and confusion would break in upon us' if he did not. In 1657 he was still maintaining that he had consented 'not so much out of the hope of doing any good, as out of a desire to prevent mischief and evil, which I did see was imminent upon the nation. I saw we were running headlong into confusion and disorder, and would necessarily run into blood, and I was passive to those that desired me to undertake the place that now I have.'[34]

A second justification, which he several times repeated, was that his acceptance had put an end to a brief and unwanted dictatorship, similar to that which he had been anxious to shed in the previous April. 'My power again by this resignation was as boundless and unlimited as before', he said, and the significance of submitting to a written constitution was 'that I did not receive anything that put me into a higher capacity than I was in before, but that it limited me and bound my hands' by the powers that it accorded to council and parliament.[35] Obviously he needed to defend himself against the imputation of military despotism, for the most vulnerable feature of his position was that he would never have been Lord Protector if he had not been Lord General, but his aversion to dictatorship was deeply felt. He also conceived a real difference between his title and that of king. When the crown was pressed on him again in 1657, he defined his sense of his office in words that have often been quoted: 'I am ready to serve not as a king, but as a constable. For truly I have as before God thought it often, that I could not tell what my business was, nor what I was in the place I stood, save [by] comparing it with a good constable to keep the peace of the parish.'[36] A constable's task was not merely to keep the peace, of course, but to uphold the laws of the land. Correspondingly, Cromwell's case for the Protectorate was not just that it had averted political breakdown but that it was the guarantor of the rule of law; he took pride 'that the laws have had a more free exercise, more uninterrupted

[34] Abbott, iii, 434–40, 455; iv, 470.
[35] Abbott, iii, 455.
[36] Abbott, iv, 470.

by any hand of power' than in all the years of peace from
Elizabeth's reign to Charles I's.[37] More uninterrupted too in his
opinion than under the Rump, which he accused in 1654 of
encroaching heavily on the judicial sphere:

so the liberties, and interests, and lives of people [were] not judged by
any certain known laws and power, but by an arbitrary power, . . . by
an arbitrary power, I say, to make men's estates liable to confiscation,
and their persons to imprisonments, sometimes by laws made after the
fact committed, often by taking the judgment both in capital and
criminal things to themselves.[38]

It was their design, he said later, 'that Committees of Parliament
should take upon them, and be instead of, the Courts of
Westminster'[39]—an exaggeration, but it was an abuse of which
he was acutely aware.

The most positive aspect of the new constitution in his eyes,
however, and doubtless in those of its authors, was that it
attempted to steer the Commonwealth clear of all three types of
arbitrary government that had troubled or threatened it in
recent times. 'Having had experience enough by trial of other
conclusions', he said early in 1655, the need was 'to avoid the
extremes of monarchy on the one hand, and democracy on the
other, and yet not to found *dominium in gratia*. And if so, then
certainly to make it more than a notion, it was requisite that it
should be as it is in the Government, which puts it upon a true
and equal balance.'[40] 'Democracy' may seem an odd way of
referring to the Rump's rule, but that had been extreme in that
it had been unbounded, while *dominium in gratia* plainly alluded
to the saints' claims to rule by a direct call from Christ. The
remedy lay in a separation and balance of powers, which the
Commonwealth had so far sadly lacked, 'the Parliament assuming
to itself the authority of the Three Estates that were before,—it
was so assuming that authority,—and if any man would have
come and said, What are the rules you judge by? the answer

[37] Ibid. 469.
[38] Abbott, iii, 454.
[39] Abbott, iv, 487; cf. Nedham, *True State*, p. 9.
[40] Abbott, iii, 587–8. The extreme of 'democracy' could conceivably refer to the
Levellers, but in the context it more probably means the unrestricted power of an
arbitrary parliament.

would have been, Why! we have none, but we are supreme in Legislative and Judicature!'[41]

That was spoken in 1657, but the concept of a correct balance between the legislative, executive, and judicial powers already permeated his first long vindication of his government on 12 September 1654. Clearly it was not a dominant idea in his mind when he established Barebone's Parliament, though the general notion of a balanced polity was familiar enough to his generation of parliament-men. Whether Lambert educated him in the importance of separating and defining the powers, or whether he learnt the lesson for himself, or whether he took it largely from Marchamont Nedham's clever apologia for the Protectoral constitution in *A True State of the Case of the Commonwealth*, can only be conjectured. Certainly he commended Nedham's tract in the speech with which he dissolved the first Protectorate parliament, and it is likely enough that Nedham consulted with Lambert when he wrote his official defence of the change of government, and specifically of the Instrument, in January 1654. *A True State* wedded the central notions of balance and separation to the ancient virtues of mixed government:

But here we see, our Friends have taken in the good of all the three sorts of Government, and bound them all in one. If War be, here is the Unitive vertue (but nothing else) of *Monarchy* to encounter it; and here is the admirable Counsel of *Aristocracie* to manage it: if Peace be, here is the industry and courage of *Democracie* to improve it. And whereas in the present Constitution, the *Legislative* and *Executive* Powers are separated; . . . we conceive the State of this Commonwealth is thereby reduced to so just a Temper, that the Ills either of successive Parliaments, furnished with power both of executing and making Laws, or of a perpetual Parliament, (which are Division, Faction, and Confusion) being avoided on the one side, and the Inconveniences of absolute Lordly power on the other; the Frame of Government appears so well bounded on both sides . . . that we hope it may now . . . prove a seasonable Mean . . . of Peace and Settlement to this distracted Nation.[42]

Apart from the allusions to the evils of over-mighty parliaments (such a volte-face for Nedham from his own *Case of the Common-Wealth of England stated* of 1650), this argument was largely a throw-back to the mixed-monarchy theories current in 1642-3

[41] Abbott, iv, 487–8.
[42] Nedham, *True State*, pp. 51–2; cf. pp. 9–11.

and particularly associated with Philip Hunton. Before the hot blast of civil war quite blew away the comfortable conviction that England's ancient constitution held a perfect balance between the prerogative of the king, the privileges of parliament, and the rights of the subject, the favourite appeal when their equilibrium was upset had been to the fundamental laws. Unfortunately no one could say just what the fundamental laws were, and in 1642 both sides had invoked them with apparently equal conviction. It is too facile to describe the Protectorate merely as the monarchy writ small, for each of the three elements (the 'monarchical' especially) differed as vitally from its older counterpart as did the intended relationship between them. But the Instrument *can* be seen as an attempt to restore the principle of distinct and limited powers, held in equipoise by fundamental laws, and to give those laws precise definition. Cromwell himself saw it thus. 'In every government there must be somewhat fundamental', he said of it to his first parliament, 'somewhat like a *Magna Charta*, that should be standing and be unalterable.'[43]

To contemporaries the most fundamental feature of the constitution, apart from its dubious military origins, must have seemed to be that it was 'settled in one single person and a parliament'. That was to be written into the indenture of election of every MP; that was the first of the 'fundamentals' enunciated by Cromwell when he defended it on 12 September 1654, and that was the substance of the 'Recognition' which members then had to subscribe before they could resume their seats.[44] But the first and most prominent provisions in the Instrument itself were those which separated the legislative authority, vested in the Protector and parliament, from the executive (the 'chief magistracy'), vested in the Protector and the council. The council, it will be remembered, had been announced in the first reports of the new government before the Protector himself, and Cromwell made much of its authority to his first parliament: 'The council are the trustees of the Commonwealth, in all intervals of parliaments, who have as absolute a negative upon the supreme officer in the said intervals, as the parliament hath

[43] Abbott, iii, 459; cf. p. 460: 'Therefore if you will have a balance at all, and that some fundamental must stand which may be worthy to be delivered over to posterity . . .'

[44] Gardiner, *Documents*, p. 410; Abbott, iii, 458, 463.

whilst it is sitting.'[45] He was indeed required to govern 'in all things' by its advice, and in two great matters, namely decisions of peace and war and the disposal of the armed forces in the intervals between parliaments, he was obliged to obtain the consent of the majority. It was at this stage always called simply 'the council'—not the Council of State, probably because under both the Rump and Barebone's the body so named had been firmly subordinated to parliament and subject to re-election at short intervals, nor the Privy Council, presumably because of its monarchical associations, which doubtless explains why that title was revived by the Humble Petition and Advice in 1657. Its maximum size was to be twenty-one, its minimum thirteen, and the first fifteen councillors were named in the Instrument. Until the first Protectoral parliament met in September, Cromwell was authorized, with the consent of the majority, to add further councillors up to twenty-one, but thereafter vacancies were to be filled by parliament nominating six candidates, the council selecting two of them, and the Protector making the final choice. Moreover vacancies were to occur only through death or removal for misconduct, and the power to dismiss and punish erring councillors was vested in a tribunal consisting of seven MPs chosen by parliament, six councillors chosen by the council, and the three Commissioners of the Great Seal. All this subjected the Protector's power to much closer conciliar control than the monarch's had been. The Nineteen Propositions of 1642 and the Newcastle Propositions of 1646 had sought to give tenure to the chief officers of state (though not the whole council) *quam diu se bene gesserint*, but those were measures designed to shackle Charles I. Ireton's Heads of the Proposals of 1647 had proposed that councillors should sit for a fixed term not exceeding seven years, while the Officers' Agreement of January 1649 had envisaged a Council of State elected anew by each biennial parliament and terminating with the meeting of the next one.[46] The Instrument's provision that councillors should serve *ad vitam aut culpam* and its denial to the Protector of any formal authority to initiate their removal are curious features and they prompt interesting speculations about Lambert's ambitions when he framed them.

Although the legislative power was defined as residing in the

[45] Abbott, iii, 460.
[46] Gardiner, *Documents*, pp. 250-3, 321, 365, 368.

Protector and parliament, it appeared at first sight to be as much weighted in the latter's favour as the executive's was (on paper) in the council's. In both cases appearances were to prove deceptive. The Protector was given a mere suspensive veto of twenty days; if parliament wished to enact any bills thereafter despite his withholding his consent, it had only to publish a declaration to that effect and they were to become laws. But the right was severely limited by the proviso that 'such Bills contain nothing in them contrary to the matters contained in these presents'. Those matters included the frequency and duration of parliaments, the qualifications of MPs, the franchise, some very broad provisions for liberty of conscience, and the guarantee of sufficient revenue for an army of 30,000 and a sufficient fleet, plus a modest £200,000 per year for the civil government. This revenue was to be raised through customs duties and such other ways and means as the Protector and the council should agree; parliament's consent was required only for any additional taxation.

Yet it should not be assumed that the authors of the Instrument intended it to be unalterable, even though they included in it no provisions for its own amendment. The sense of the text is that parliament could not transgress the written constitution unilaterally, but there was nothing to prevent it from being modified by mutual consent.[47] Cromwell himself, though he spoke of the need for 'somewhat unalterable', did not regard it as sacrosanct and made a distinction between what was essential in it and what was negotiable. Speaking to his first parliament after it had shown a strong disposition to challenge the Instrument, he said: 'It is true, there are some things in the Establishment that are fundamental, and some things are not so, but are circumstantial. Of such, no question but I shall easily agree to vary, or leave out, as I shall be convinced by reason.[48]

Parliaments were to be elected every three years and to sit for at least five months, with provision for an earlier summons if war broke out or if the Protector and the majority of the council deemed it necessary. Frequent parliaments of modest duration had been the army's goal since at least the *Representation of the*

[47] Ibid. 413. Further references to this familiar text are given only where it is directly quoted.
[48] Abbott, iii, 458.

Army of 14 June 1647, though the Heads of the Proposals and the Officers' Agreement had favoured biennial rather than triennial intervals.[49] Unlike those last two documents the Instrument did not set a maximum term to parliamentary sessions, but it nevertheless implied the view expressed by Nedham, who was echoing a metaphor of Henry Parker's in 1642, that, 'Parlaments always sitting are no more agreeable to the temper of this People, than it is to a natural Body to take always Physick instead of Food.' To quote an earlier page in his tract, 'it was found at length by experience, that a standing Parliament was it self the greatest Grievance'.[50]

There is no need to speculate on exactly what Lambert and his colleagues had in mind in allocating 400 seats to England and Wales and thirty apiece to Scotland and Ireland, since they took these provisions straight from the Rump's bill for a new representative. They were probably moved partly by haste, but partly also by the expediency of following the decisions of an elected parliament in so disputable a matter. In any case, 400 was the number of seats which the army officers had proposed for England and Wales when they amended the second Agreement of the People, and they and the Rump had agreed in greatly increasing the representation of the counties at the expense of the undersized boroughs. It is true that the 1653 apportionment gave the boroughs about a third of the seats in the House and the 1649 one only about a fifth, but that was a small difference compared with the share of more than four-fifths which they had had in the unreformed parliament. The Rump's allocation of seats had also followed, though with some notable discrepancies, the principle that representation should be based on contribution to taxation, which had been the army officers' policy since 1647.[51]

---

[49] Woodhouse, *Puritanism and Liberty*, p. 407; Gardiner, *Documents*, pp. 317, 363.

[50] Nedham, *True State*, pp. 9, 23; cf. Henry Parker, *Observations upon some of his Majesties late Answers and Expresses* ([2 July] 1642), p. 24.

[51] Worden's authoritative discussion of the various reapportionment schemes in *Rump*, ch. 8, supersedes most previous accounts, but see also John Cannon, *Parliamentary Reform 1640–1832* (Cambridge, 1973), ch. 1, and Trevor-Roper, *Religion, the Reformation and Social Change*, pp. 371–4. Gardiner in *C & P*, ii, 283 n., suggests that a large alteration in the apportionment was made on 14 or 15 Dec., on the evidence of T.M.'s letter of 14 Dec. (see n. 16), which reported 280 members for England and 60 apiece for Scotland and Ireland. But this looks like a simple mistake in verbal transmission: T.M. was probably told that there were to be 400 members, with 60 for Scotland and Ireland, and did not

(*continued*)

The Instrument also followed the Rump's abortive bill in vesting the franchise in all adult males, excepting Roman Catholics and abettors of the Irish rebellion, who possessed real or personal estate to the value of £200. According to at least one source the Rump had adopted this scheme on 30 March 1653 to please the army.[52] It had three evident merits: it removed the by then anomalous discrimination in favour of freeholders at the expense of other sorts of landholders who were often better off, it recognized other kinds of property besides land, and it took account of what had happened to prices since the forty-shilling freehold qualification had been fixed over two centuries earlier, for by conventional reckoning an estate worth £200 yielded £10 per year. It applied only to county constituencies, but these now accounted for twice as many seats as the boroughs, and during the last generation there had been a strong trend towards a broadening of the electorate in the more substantial towns.[53] With the tide running towards more equal representation it was probably thought impolitic to challenge strongly entrenched local customs and patronage interests for the sake of theoretical uniformity. It was a different-looking franchise from that proposed in the 1648-9 Agreement, which would have given the vote in counties and boroughs alike to householders rated for poor relief, though not to servants or wage-earners, but its practical effect must have been similar, namely to give a voice in elections to most men who enjoyed some small measure of economic independence but to deny it to the legions of the poor. The obvious difficulty for sheriffs and other returning officers was to determine who was worth £200 and who was not—an even harder task than to identify those who had been active royalists in the civil wars, and who were in consequence debarred from voting in the next four general elections.

The same disqualifications applied to MPs: Roman Catholics and Irish rebels were debarred permanently, ex-royalists (unless they had since given signal service to the parliament) for the next dozen years. Members must in addition be 'persons of known integrity, fearing God, and of good conversation', which

---

grasp that the 60 were to be additional to the 400 or that they were for the two smaller countries together.

[52] Worden, *Rump*, p. 159.

[53] Derek Hirst, *The Representative of the People?*, chs. 3-5.

was at least a token continuance of the demand for godliness and morality in the public service, so much stressed in the previous spring and summer. To protect the regime from its more obvious enemies, the council was empowered to scrutinize the returns to the next three parliaments and determine whether those elected were 'agreeable to the qualifications'.[54] This power was exercised fairly moderately in 1654,[55] but was grossly abused in 1656, when the council excluded over a hundred members. There is nothing to suggest that it was originally intended to be used for the wholesale exclusion of men who were neither royalists nor papists.

In the difficult matter of religion, the Instrument concerned itself mainly with the state's responsibility in general terms, particularly with regard to liberty of conscience, and avoided the particular questions of ecclesiastical settlement on which Barebone's Parliament had finally come to grief. It laid down, 'That the Christian religion, as contained in the Scriptures, be held forth and recommended as the public profession of these nations', and according to Nedham the intention was 'that the Profession so held forth shall extend both to Doctrine, and Worship or Discipline'.[56] In the event the public profession was never formulated, though the Savoy Declaration of 1658 may have been intended for adoption as such.[57] Although parish worship was to be thus far regulated, no one was to be compelled to attend the public services or to be subject to any church's ecclesiastical discipline. On the contrary, the free exercise of their religion was guaranteed to all who professed faith in God by Jesus Christ, so long as they did not abuse this liberty to the civil injury of others, the disturbance of the peace, or the practice of licentiousness. Nor did toleration extend to 'Popery or Prelacy', though where there was a demand for Anglican worship the ban on it was generally more nominal than real. Tithes were to be replaced 'as soon as may be' by 'a provision less subject to scruple and contention'.

Such ordinances were bound to provoke opposition. On the one hand voluntaryists like Milton, unorthodox Independents

---

[54] Gardiner, *Documents*, pp. 410–12.

[55] Paul D. Shuter, 'The Role of Cromwell's Councillors in the First and Second Protectorate Parliaments' (unpublished M.Litt. thesis, University of Lancaster, 1982) Ch. 1..

[56] Gardiner, *Documents*, p. 416; Nedham, *True State*, p. 41.

[57] *Complete Prose Works of John Milton*, vii, 41–5.

like John Goodwin, and sectaries of many hues would resist any attempt by the civil magistrate to prescribe what might or might not be preached from public pulpits or to settle any enforced maintenance for public preachers. On the other hand, there was the more widespread feeling that religious toleration had gone too far and ecclesiastical discipline grown too slack. One reason why Cromwell broke with his next parliament was that it demanded the right to legislate, even without his consent, on such matters as blasphemy, atheism, prelacy, profaneness, enforced attendance at Sunday worship, clerical conformity to the public profession, and the punishment of all who preached or wrote against its doctrines.[58] One of the prices he had to pay for the Humble Petition and Advice in 1657 was its marked restriction, compared with the Instrument, of liberty of religious practice. The authors of the Instrument set a great precedent by writing religious toleration—or at least a large measure of it—into the constitution, but they were wise not to try to prescribe how the clergy should be appointed or ejected or maintained. Such matters were better tackled by specific legislation, which could be amended in the light of experience without the formalities of constitutional amendment.

Cromwell did tackle them, under the power which the Instrument gave to him and the council to legislate by ordinance until the first parliament met in September. Such ordinances were subject to parliamentary confirmation, but those which erected his famous commissions of Triers and Ejectors remained the basis of his ecclesiastical establishment, even though they were not confirmed until 1657.[59] By one account the original Instrument, as presented to him on 13 December, provided for a parliament to meet in February,[60] so the postponement until September may represent a modification which he insisted on. One can understand why Lambert may have wanted to substitute an elected for a nominated parliament as soon as possible; equally one can appreciate Cromwell's unwillingness, if it was his decision, to risk general elections before his regime had had

[58] Gardiner, *Documents*, p. 443.

[59] See Ivan Roots, 'Cromwell's Ordinances', in Aylmer (ed.), *The Interregnum*, pp. 143–64, and on the ecclesiastical ordinances in particular Claire Cross's chapter in ibid. 103–5. The power to legislate by ordinance did not extend, as has sometimes been stated, to the intervals between future parliaments.

[60] This is in T.M.'s otherwise well-informed letter of 14 Dec. in Thurloe, i, 632.

time to settle. More positively, he was eager to grasp the nettle of some long overdue reforms, including that of Chancery as well as of the ministry, without leaving them open to the dissensions or evasions of yet another parliament.

One way of discovering what else was most contentious in this constitution is to examine how the next two parliaments attempted to change it. The two most sensitive areas, apart from religion, were first the relations between the executive and the legislature, and secondly the size, the financing, and the ultimate control of the armed forces. The 1654–5 parliament tried to alter the former drastically by proposing in its abortive constitution that parliament should approve all conciliar appointments, that councillors should not continue in office without a specific fresh approval by each succeeding parliament, and that they should swear to pursue faithfully all such instructions and directions as parliament should give to the council.[61] The Humble Petition and Advice, being the work of a heavily purged parliament, was less extreme in attempting to subordinate the executive, but nevertheless required parliamentary approval both for the appointment and for the removal of councillors.[62] As for the army, the 1654–5 parliament proposed to make totally unacceptable provisions for its upkeep and continuance at a time when Cromwell knew a royalist insurrection to be brewing, but conflict on this score was almost inevitable. The Instrument's requirement of a minimum of 10,000 horse and 20,000 foot was modest in view of the army's commitments in Scotland and Ireland and of the range of opposition which the Protectorate faced in England. The regular forces stood at about twice that strength when the government was inaugurated,[63] though they were to be reduced considerably after Penruddock's rising had been suppressed. What was really unsatisfactory in the Instrument was that it gave the Protector and council a free hand to raise revenue for the nuclear army of 30,000, for a fleet of undefined strength, and for civil government to the tune of £200,000, but put it in parliament's discretion to finance any further needs of the state. The potential for friction in such an arrangement was obvious, and both the next parliaments

[61] Gardiner, *Documents*, pp. 441–2.
[62] Ibid. 453.
[63] C. H. Firth, *Cromwell's Army* (1902), p. 35.

attempted to quantify the financial requirements of the armed forces, as well as the civil government, and to provide for them specifically.

Neither parliament approved of the £200 franchise, in regard to which both displayed the prevailing conservatism of every House elected after 1653. The first one's draft constitution would have restored the forty-shilling freehold qualification in the counties and the customary franchises in the boroughs. The Humble Petition and Advice was staggeringly silent on the matter, but required that in all particulars concerning the calling of parliaments which it did not specifically prescribe 'the laws and statutes of the land be observed and kept', which caused Richard Cromwell's council to revert to the unreformed franchise and constituencies when it summoned the 1659 parliament.[64]

Oliver's refusal of the crown made the succession a problem. The Instrument provided that future Protectors should be elected by the council, and specified that the office should not be hereditary. The next parliament, after briefly considering a motion to press the crown on him again, rather surprisingly agreed to election by the council if the vacancy should occur during the interval between parliaments, but proposed that parliament should determine the manner of election, if it were sitting at the time. The parliament of 1656–7, being thoroughly purged of republican elements, pressed him hard to become king, but upon his refusal requested him to name the next Protector, leaving the future succession an open question.[65]

Cromwell had his own ideas of what was fundamental in the constitution, and when it came under immediate attack from his first parliament he identified four principles which he regarded as unalterable. The first was that the government was vested in a single person and a parliament, though as has been seen he stressed that his personal authority was bounded as much by the council as by the parliament. That parliaments should not make themselves perpetual was his second fundamental, and liberty of conscience as a natural right was his third. Finally, the control of the armed forces should be shared between Protector and parliament, and in the intervals of parliaments between Protector

---

[64] Gardiner, *Documents*, pp. 436–7, 452.
[65] Ibid. 415, 428, 448–9.

and council.[66] Although a considerable number of members gave up their seats rather than subscribe to the first fundamental, their republicanism awoke less response in the political nation than the remaining members' conservative opposition to liberty of conscience as Cromwell understood it—which in turn fell short of what Milton and other religious radicals desired. As for the fourth, the military origin of the regime and the military presence within it were the greatest obstacles to its acceptance, but the vesting in parliament of a constitutional right to share in the control of the army was more than the monarchy had been prepared to grant before the Civil War, or would countenance after the Restoration.

All in all the Instrument was an eclectic document. Some elements, such as triennial parliaments of guaranteed but modest duration, go back to the Long Parliament's legislation of 1641; others such as the principle of majority decisions by the council (at least in certain defined matters of major import) and tenure *quam diu bene se gesserint* to the Nineteen Propositions. But the contribution of the 1647 Heads of the Proposals was larger, for they had embodied the central concept of a council which, being neither a body of royal servants dismissible at pleasure nor a sort of superior committee subject to parliament's directions, should at the same time control the monarch and ensure for the executive a degree of independence of the legislature. The ghost of Henry Ireton hovers over the constitution of the Protectorate, for both in the Heads of the Proposals and in the army's earlier manifestos he had also formulated the principle that parliamentary representation should be reformed on the basis of contribution to taxation. He had left his mark too on the officers' Agreement of January 1649, which first proposed 400 seats for England and Wales and the broad manner of apportioning them. Their precise distribution, however, was taken like the franchise from the Rump's bill of four years later.

Despite these borrowings, the Instrument was not without its original features, notably in its definition of the single person's relationship with the council and with the parliament. The matters, for instance, on which he had to obtain the consent of the majority of the council were carefully thought out, and the twenty-day suspensive veto was a bold and imaginative idea. As

[66] Abbott, iii, 458–60.

a whole, the scheme's main weaknessses lay in the indefinite and over-secure tenure that it gave to the council, the frictions latent in its financial provisions, its lack of attention to the judicature (including its silence regarding parliament's judicial powers), and its failure to provide a clear procedure for its own amendment. But it was not because of these that its life was brief. The main reason for that was that no parliament was going to see why the people's elected representatives should have the rules of the political game dictated to them by a junta of army officers. Cromwell regarded the constitution as a voluntary limitation of a dictatorship which had been thrust upon him; republicans would contend that the dissolution of a government caused authority to return to the sovereign people, from whom it derived. Cromwell argued strenuously on 12 September 1654 that his government *had* the people's consent, since besides all those who had positively acclaimed it or assisted in it, the election indentures of the MPs whom he was addressing bound both electors and elected to it.[67] It was a specious argument, but one senses a touch of self-deception in it. Parliament-men, on the other hand, thought that if it came to constitution-making they had a better right to engage in it than army officers. Their case was hard to answer, but though the Instrument would have benefited much by judicious amendment it is very questionable whether either of the parliamentary constitutions of 1654–5 or of 1657 was an improvement on it.

The quality of the Protectorate naturally depended as much upon the men who actually exercised the government as upon the rules which framed it. Cromwell, of course, towered over the rest, but not to such an extent that the personalities in his council were unimportant. Nor were they the only ones that counted; his chief lieutenants in Scotland and Ireland, his Commissioners of the Great Seal and Treasury Commissioners, and particular individuals such as Chief Justice St. John and (above all) Secretary Thurloe made their own contributions to the collective character of the regime. The dearth of real statesmanship among them would leave the Protectorate fatally exposed after Cromwell's death, but the talent of the best of them and the industry and sense of public service of the majority did more to

[67] Ibid. 455–7; cf. p. 588.

sustain his rule than has been commonly recognized, and the history of the five years 1653–8 has too often been written in terms of one man.

The council in particular deserves more attention. Its compact size demonstrates a shrewd awareness that the Commonwealth's Council of State—forty-one under the Rump, thirty-one under Barebone's—had been too large. In fact it never reached the permitted maximum of twenty-one, and it functioned throughout the Protectorate at something more like Elizabethan strength. Whether Cromwell's admiration for 'that great queen' had anything to do with this, or whether recollections of the relative efficiency of the Committee of Both Kingdoms influenced them, the makers of the Instrument hit on something like the optimum size for a national executive body. Selecting its members must have been one of the most difficult transactions of those crowded days from 13 to 15 December, especially since councillors were to be irremovable except by death or proven misconduct. One would dearly like to know whether Cromwell was presented with a list along with the draft constitution, but it is safe to assume that he was in no way dictated to. Fourteen men at least had been chosen by 16 December; the fifteenth, Major-General Philip Skippon, took the councillor's oath and was admitted on the 20th, though that is no proof that he was not chosen earlier.[68]

The proportion of military to civilian councillors cannot be stated exactly because the status of three was equivocal, but it has commonly been exaggerated. Lambert, Fleetwood, Desborough, and Skippon were of course primarily soldiers, with important commands in the standing army. Viscount Lisle, Francis Rous, Ashley Cooper, Pickering, Strickland, Lawrence, Wolseley, and Major can equally firmly be categorized as civilians, despite Lisle's wartime service in Ireland and Cooper's in Dorset. Of the remaining three, Sydenham had fought in the Civil War only with the local forces in Dorset, though he had commanded a regular foot regiment for a few months in 1649. Since then he had been Governor of the Isle of Wight, where his duties were at least as much administrative as military.[69] He was shortly to

---

[68] *CSPD 1653–4*, p. 300. The first list of councillors published in *Mercurius Politicus* (no. 184, 16–22 Dec. 1653, p. 3054) included Skippon's name but omitted Fleetwood's, perhaps because the latter, being in Ireland, was unable to attend. All fifteen names are in the first printed versions of the Instrument.

[69] *DNB*; Firth and Davies, *Regimental History of Cromwell's Army*, pp. 433–4.

become a Treasury Commissioner, as was his colleague Edward
Montagu, who also liked to be styled colonel. But Montagu had
resigned his colonelcy of a New Model foot regiment at the end
of the 1645 campaigning season and was not to be appointed
joint General at Sea until 1656, so he had no current military
standing.[70] Colonel Philip Jones was another whose active service
in the wars had been purely local, and even the garrison
regiment that he had commanded in South Wales in the late
1640s was disbanded soon after October 1651. He had made his
career more as the busy intendant of South Wales than as a
fighting man, and was well on the way to becoming the richest
administrative pluralist of the decade.[71] On the major issues
which were to divide the military factions from the civilian
Cromwellians, such as the offer of the crown in 1657 and the
Wallingford House party's challenge to Richard Cromwell two
years later, Sydenham was to align himself with the soldiers,
Montagu and Jones with the conservative civilian interest. The
balance in the council was inclined, as far as numbers went, far
more towards the latter than has been generally acknowledged,
and three further appointments in the first half of 1654 tilted it
further. Colonel Humphrey Mackworth, the first to be added on
7 February, owed his military title wholly to local service; he
was Governor of Shrewsbury, and another exemplar of the
intendant type. He died in December 1654.[72] Nathaniel Fiennes,
who took his councillor's oath and seat on 27 April, was entirely
a civilian, at any rate since his unfortunate two months' service
as Governor of Bristol in 1643, which had led to his being
sentenced to death for surrendering the city to Rupert. Edmund
Sheffield, second Earl of Mulgrave, who was rather surprisingly
added at the end of June, had no military pretensions at all. He
had in fact declined to serve on the first Council of State of the
Commonwealth, after being elected by the Rump, because he
disapproved of the execution of the king and the abolition of the
House of Lords.[73] One can only suppose that he accepted this
later call because he hoped that his conservative values were

[70] *DNB*; Firth and Davies, p 398; Abbott, iii, 393.

[71] *DWB*; Firth and Davies, pp. xxiv, xxvi. He commanded one company in Cardiff
Castle, but it had been reduced in Jan. 1653 to fifty men: *CSPD 1652-3*, p. 95.

[72] *CSPD 1653-4*, pp. 382, 391; *VCH, Shropshire*, iii, 112-13, 251-2; Abbott, iii, 558 n.
He is wrongly identified in *CSPD 1653-4* as Col. Thomas Mackworth.

[73] *DNB*.

about to be reasserted, unless the attraction was his councillor's salary of £1,000 a year. He never did much to earn it.

Of the original fifteen, all but Skippon and the absent Fleetwood had been members of Barebone's Parliament. Fleetwood's duties as Lord Deputy of Ireland kept him from attending until the autumn of 1655, but his rank of lieutenant-general virtually entitled him to membership, and he was Cromwell's son-in-law. Skippon may have been added to give the army a greater presence in this predominantly civilian body. There is nothing to suggest that Cromwell and the Council of Officers felt restricted to the men whom they had nominated in the previous June, but it was natural to think of them again if they had given good service, and a high proportion of the new councillors had earned their political spurs in Barebone's Parliament and its Councils of State. That is certainly true of the younger ones. Wolseley (still only twenty-three), Montagu, and Ashley Cooper all got their first chance to play a significant role in national politics in 1653, and all three seized it. The first two pulled their weight in the Protectoral council, Montagu especially, but Cooper proved to be a bad choice, because after a busy year's service in 1654 he abruptly ceased to attend, and shortly went over to the republican opposition.[74] But it was not only the young who really launched their political careers in 1653. Henry Lawrence, President of the Council from its inauguration, had made little mark during his brief membership of the Long Parliament from January 1646 until Pride's Purge, when he willingly returned to obscurity. Jones, Strickland, Pickering, Sydenham, and Desborough were, along with Lambert, probably the other most heavily employed of the original councillors, and unlike Lambert they had all been among the most active and conspicuous MPs, committee-men, and councillors while Barebone's was sitting. It is true that the first four had sat before, but with the partial exceptions of Strickland (for his diplomatic employments) and Pickering (for his activities in the Rump and on three of its Councils of State) they had been very minor figures in national politics before 1653. Of all the fifteen, Francis

[74] *CSPD 1653–4* and *1654, passim*; Haley, *First Earl of Shaftesbury*, pp. 77–88. The break is the stranger because of Cooper's friendship with Henry Cromwell and his support for a motion on 23 Dec. to make Oliver king. Perhaps as Cromwell's exasperation with his first parliament grew, Cooper sided with the latter, and was finally alienated by its abrupt dissolution.

Rous had much the longest and most considerable reputation, and as Speaker he had probably borne the heaviest burden of all in Barebone's.[75]

Not all the new councillors had exerted themselves in it. Viscount Lisle certainly had not, and since he scarcely rated highly for godliness and 'good conversation' he must have owed his place mainly to Cromwell's desire for some aristocratic blood in his service, in order to win the acquiescence if not the support of the nobility and gentry. The same probably prompted the addition of Fiennes and Mulgrave soon afterwards. But if so, why was not Charles Howard selected, after his assiduous service in the House and the council from July to December? True, he was only twenty-five, but Wolseley was younger. Perhaps the army men distrusted him, or he did not want to stay in London; perhaps Cromwell felt the need of his services in the north, particularly in Scotland, on whose council he sat from 1655. Nevertheless he might seem to have merited a seat more than Richard Major, for though that comfortable Hampshire squire had given reasonable attention to his duties as MP and councillor in 1653 one feels that his main qualification was that he was Richard Cromwell's father-in-law.

Since so many moderates who had played a leading role in Barebone's Parliament became Cromwell's councillors, it is worth glancing at the others who did not. Some found, or retained, useful and lucrative employment at a level a step or two below: Colonel John Clarke, for instance, was a very busy Admiralty and Navy Commissioner, and went on drawing a further income as colonel of a foot regiment. Though very obviously a hostile witness, the prisoner who wrote in 1654 of his examination by 'Col. Clarke, with his pricked ears, and little head, and lesser wit, whom I baffled to his face' does suggest a man whose intellectual ceiling was a shade below the higher mysteries of state.[76] Sadler remained Master of Magdalene, a Trier, a Master in Chancery, and a judge for the probate of wills,

---

[75] The indexing in successive *CSPD* volumes of the Rous in Cromwell's council as Col. Anthony Rous is definitely an error. He is Francis Rous Esq. in the official printers' edition of the Instrument and in several newspapers; *The Weekly Intelligencer* for 20–27 Dec. 1653, p. 99, adds 'the late Speaker' after his name. Orders of the council signed by Francis Rous are in BL, Add. MS 30, 170 fo. 54 (29 March 1654) and 29, 319 fo. 110 (25 April 1654). I owe these last two references to the kindness of Mr Paul Shuter.

[76] *CSPD 1654*, p. 412.

and he probably wanted no further employment. His great activity in Barebone's does not prove that he had the makings of a full-time politician, and he may already have shown signs of the garrulity and eccentricity which marked some of his speeches in Richard Cromwell's parliament. Colonel Anthony Rous probably felt sufficiently recompensed for his lesser but still useful role by being retained as a judge for the probate of wills, an Admiralty Commissioner, and an Excise Commissioner, as well as Vice-Admiral of Cornwall, where he had purchased duchy lands and acquired some lucrative tolls on tin.[77] John Stone also did well under the Protectorate, without regaining the councillor's place which he had briefly held in November and December, for within a year of its establishment he was a Teller of the Exchequer and an Excise Appeals Commissioner, and later he added the Accounts Commission, the Trade Committee, and the job of Wine License Agent to his other lucrative employments.[78]

Such men must have felt well-enough rewarded, but two other leaders of the moderates, Robert Tichborne and Sir William Roberts, might reasonably have expected to receive a call to the new council. Tichborne had been as active in the last two (July and November) as he had in the House, and besides a wealth of administrative experience he had a knowledge of commercial matters and a standing in the City which could have been of great advantage to the Protectoral government. There was no question of his being out of favour or seriously disaffected, since Cromwell knighted him in 1656 and named him to the Other House next year, while Tichborne presented a loyal address to the Protector from the City trained-bands in 1658.[79] His public employments, moreover, were profitable as well as honorific. Perhaps he was offered a place and declined it; if so, it may have been his pastor George Cokayne's hostility to the change of government which swayed him. No such radical Puritan influence is likely to have affected Roberts, if he was ever a candidate. As qualifications he had rank, wealth, financial and administrative experience under the Rump, and membership of the last Council of State; under the Protectorate he added to his

[77] Firth and Rait, ii, 824, 828, 869; *CSPD 1654*, p. 67; Coate, *Cornwall in the Great Civil War*, pp. 272, 293.
[78] Aylmer, *State's Servants*, p. 241.
[79] *DNB*; Aylmer, *State's Servants*, p. 162.

public employments as well as to his standing in the City. Perhaps the lesson that he learnt in 1653 was not to commit himself too heavily to any regime that might prove transitory.[80]

Quite a number of other ex-members of Barebone's set their feet on the administrative ladder at levels below the council. Professor Aylmer has demonstrated that 'within the period 1649–60, the main administrative developments were to arise from the political changes of 1653', and that the most strenuous attempts at reform took place in the early months of the Protectorate—though more often than not the Cromwellian ordinances were implementations of projects adumbrated or at least contemplated by the Rump or Barebone's.[81] There is no need to traverse again ground that has been charted so thoroughly, especially since the process of reform extended well beyond the chronological confines of this book. What is here to be noted is the extent to which the new administration was manned by men who had demonstrated their worth in the course of 1653. All nine of the additional judges for the probate of wills appointed by an ordinance of 24 December had sat in Barebone's, as had seven of the existing judges.[82] So had all ten commissioners for inquiring into the arrears of the excise appointed five days later;[83] so had eight of the nine members of the important Committee for the Army established on 28 January 1654, and among them Gervase Bennett, Cludd, Hildesley, and Lucy were common to all these three ordinances, disparate though the employments were.[84] Nine of the eleven Admiralty and Navy Commissioners established by act of parliament nine days before Barebone's fell were MPs, and there were still six ex-members among the eight Commissioners whom Cromwell appointed on 28 August 1654.[85] Five of the eleven laymen among the

---

[80] Ibid. 251–3.

[81] Ibid. 9, 42–8, 69–71, 85–7, 333–4, *et passim.*

[82] New judges: Lucy, Hildesley, Nathaniel Barton, Gervase Bennett, Anthony Rous, Matthews, Cludd, Wood, Tichborne. Existing judges included Cooper, Sadler, Blount, Desborough, Moyer, Tomlinson, Roberts: Firth and Rait, ii, 702, 824, 869.

[83] Roberts, Stone, Gervase Bennett, Hildesley, Lucy, Cludd, Wood, Anthony Rous, Phillips, Nathaniel Barton: Firth and Rait, ii, 828.

[84] The others on the Army Committee were John Clarke (probably the Suffolk man, not the colonel), Horseman, Phillips, Gill, and Captain Adam Baines: Firth and Rait, ii, 835.

[85] Blake, Monck, Desborough, Jones, Col. Clarke, Stone, Horseman, Burton, Gookin in Dec. 1653 (Firth and Rait, ii, 812), of whom the first five were retained, with the addition of Anthony Rous, after 28 Aug. 1654 (Abbott, iii, 426–7).

Commissioners for Approbation of Ministers, or Triers, were former Barebone's members,[86] as were three of the six commissioners to hear appeals relating to arrears of excise, three (the same three as the last) of the six commissioners to enforce the act against planting tobacco in England,[87] and six members of the High Court of Justice established in June.[88]

In these early Cromwellian ordinances the same names often recur, and their frequency is not always related either to their previous experience or to their conspicuousness in Barebone's. Roberts seems to have had a hand in almost everything short of the council itself, but that is understandable, considering how well versed he was already in the Commonwealth's business. The same is true of Tichborne and to a lesser extent Stone, who were also much employed by the new regime. The rest of the pluralists first arrived on the scene of national politics in 1653. Gervase Bennett had, like Anthony Rous, made enough of a mark in Barebone's to get elected to the Council of State on 1 November, though he only just got in, and he had sat on fewer committees than Rous—only those for the law and for the poor. John Hildesley may have distinguished himself on the committees for receiving petitions, for evasions of the public debts, and for inspecting the treasuries, but his Hampshire associations with Major and Richard Cromwell may also have helped him to his several salaried places.[89] Edward Horseman was on the Barebone's Committee for the Army from July onwards, and the work he did on it may account for his reappointment in January 1654. He was also on the committee for tithes, and was briefly appointed an Admiralty and Navy Commissioner on 3 December 1653. In August 1654 he was made a Teller of the Exchequer, and though he resigned this place two years later in favour of George Downing he had already been compensated by being appointed a Customs Commissioner. He may have made his way by merit, but his kinship with Pickering probably counted too; he named two of his sons Gilbert and Oliver.[90] Thomas Wood

---

[86] Francis Rous, Tichborne, Wood, Sadler, Thomas St. Nicholas: Firth and Rait, ii, 856.

[87] Roberts, Stone, Gervase Bennett in both ordinances: ibid. 851, 870.

[88] Roberts, Stone, Tichborne, Anthony Rous, Lucy, and Phillips: ibid. 917.

[89] *CSPD 1651*, p. 293; *1651-2*, p. 461; *1655*, p. 98; Firth and Rait, ii, 824, 835, 869; *A Narrative of the Late Parliament.*

[90] Firth and Rait, ii, 703, 812, 835; *CSPD 1654*, p. 367, and *1655-6*, pp. 189, 238. Abbott, iv, 256; *Visitation of Rutland 1681*, Harleian Soc., lxxiii, 34-5; PRO, PROB

(*continued*)

did almost as well, for within three weeks in the spring of 1654 he was reappointed as a probate judge and made a Customs Commissioner and a Trier.[91] Nothing survives of his record in Barebone's to explain his preferment except the bare fact that he was named to the committees for trade and for the poor. As for Phillips, Cludd, and Lucy, who were confirmed as members of the Committee for the Army to which they had been appointed in July 1653 and given sundry other employments besides, one supposes that it was their service on that committee which advanced them, since this is almost the sum of their recorded activity in Barebone's.[92]

All these men had been among the moderates of that assembly, and very few on the radical side had previously been employed in the Commonwealth's administration at national level. Harrison, Courtney, Carew, and Danvers were among those who had, but their fierce and public opposition to the Protectorate obviously put an end to their public careers, at least until 1659. Moyer was a less extreme radical and a less militant opponent; one senses that the new council parted reluctantly with his services in the Customs and on the Committee for Compounding, after interviewing him about his attitude.[93] Ireton was less uncompromising; he seems to have occupied a segment of the radical spectrum between Moyer and his fellow-worshipper Tichborne, for he became an Excise Commissioner in February 1656, a commissioner to try treasons in the following November, and he accepted a knighthood from Cromwell in 1658 during his term as Lord Mayor of London.[94] Thomas St. Nicholas is another whose radical stance in 1653 was not held against him, for he was made a Trier next year and retained as an assessment commissioner, though the council debarred him from taking his seat in the parliament of 1656–7.[95]

11/414, PCC Coker 80. For his only recorded speech in parliament, on 12 March 1659, Burton commented, 'He was very short, trembling, and to no great purpose' (*Diary*, iv, 146).

[91] Firth and Rait, ii, 824, 828, 850, 856, 869, 1020. In the *liber pacis* covering 1656–7 he is struck off as 'dead', which doubtless explains why he was replaced as Excise Commissioner in Feb. 1656: *CSPD 1655–6*, p. 189.

[92] Firth and Rait, ii, 704, 824, 828, 835, 869, 917, 1039–40.

[93] *CSPD 1653–4*, pp. 363, 366, 368; Aylmer, *State's Servants*, p. 215.

[94] *DNB*: *CSPD 1655–6*, p. 189; Firth and Rait, ii, 1039.

[95] Firth and Rait, ii, 856, 1071; Gooder, *Parliamentary Representation of Yorkshire*, ii, 61–3.

There was no general attempt to exclude the radicals of 1653 from local administration. The council appointed a committee on 3 January, consisting of Wolseley, Ashley Cooper, Rous, Lambert, and Montagu, to regulate the justices of the peace throughout the country, but the only men among their former opponents in the House to be struck off the commission of the peace were Harrison, Danvers, Bawden, and Carew—and the latter was not removed until March 1657.[96] It is indeed interesting to find not only such outspoken critics of the change of government as Highland, Pyne, Blount, and Moyer retained on the commission, but also professed or fellow-travelling Fifth Monarchy men, including Courtney, Baker, Squibb, Langdon, Price, and James; indeed the last two remained Custodes Rotulorum of their respective Welsh counties. Caley, Dunkon, and Reeve, all religious radicals, appear to have become justices for the first time under the Protectorate. The great majority of radical MPs who had been assessment commissioners in 1653 remained so under the Assessment Act of 1657; the only ones removed for reasons other than death were Harrison, Bawden, Carew, Courtney, Danvers, Hollister, Kenrick, Langdon, Salwey, Sawrey, and Taylor.

Nevertheless it remains broadly true that while the Protectorate brought advancement to a substantial number of the moderates in Barebone's, it spelt a relative eclipse for those on the other side who had reached any degree of prominence, except in respect of routine local responsibilities which may have been more nominal than real. As many as forty members who have been categorized in this book as radicals or 'possible radicals'—a considerable majority of them, in fact—made something of a come-back when the Rump was reinstated in 1659, whether in local commissions (the militia especially) or in national employments.

A curious tailpiece to the story of these members links some of them with the subsequent activities of Anna Trapnel, the female prophetess of the Fifth Monarchy and member of John Simpson's

---

[96] Based on comparison between PRO, C193/13/4, covering May 1652–Oct. 1653, with C193/13/6, covering Sept. 1656–Apr. 1657. The date of Carew's removal I owe to the History of Parliament Trust's print-out of evidence from Crown Office docquet books. Herring, like Carew, is struck off the 1656–7 *liber pacis*, but probably because he had died; his will was proved on 11 June 1657 (PRO, PROB 11/263, PCC Ruthen 155).

flock at Allhallows the Great. We met her last in September, prophesying doom to Barebone's Parliament and announcing the Lord's rejection of Oliver Cromwell.[97] Her visions multiplied as the end of the parliament approached. In one a sinister turret with rooms like the council's apartments at Whitehall faced a gleaming white tower filled with the saints, which many senior army officers were trying to blow up by lighting a train of powder leading to it. In another the earth lay covered in a great darkness, with 'a marvellous dust, like a thick smoak ascending upward', while in the foreground a great herd of cattle with the faces of men raised a shout acclaiming the foremost of them as their chief. He had, of course, the face of Cromwell.[98] After the dissolution, the council ordered the arrest of Vavasor Powell on 10 January because he was continuing to inflame his Christ Church congregation against the government. When he was brought before it, Anna Trapnel waited for him in a little room near the council chamber, where she was 'seized upon by the Lord' and 'carried forth in a spirit of Praying, and Singing, from noon till night'.[99] After she took to her bed that night she lay there in a trance-like state for eleven days, eating nothing for the first five and extremely little after that. Every day, however, she spoke or rather prayed and sang for hours on end, and a devout or inquisitive company came to hear her. The majority of those whom she mentions by name were recent members of Barebone's: Sydenham, West, Chetwood, Colonel Robert Bennett and his wife, Bingham, Langdon, Courtney, and Birkenhead.[1] Was Sydenham keeping an eye on her for the council, or was he open to this kind of revelation? Perhaps Bingham, who was his brother-in-law and had listened to her earlier prophecy in September, brought him along, but the presence of this well-born moderate would itself be a slight surprise, if one were not told that her visitors also included Lady Darcy and Lady Vermuyden—as well as Christopher Feake.

A few weeks later, after visiting Feake and Simpson, who by then were prisoners in Windsor Castle, she journeyed to

[97] See p. 275.

[98] Anna Trapnel, *The Cry of a Stone*, pp. 11–13.

[99] Ibid. 1–2, where she dates the occasion 7 Jan. 1654. But the council did not meet that day (a Saturday), and Powell's arrest was certainly ordered on the 10th: *CSPD 1653–4*, p. 253.

[1] Anna Trapnel, *The Cry of a Stone*, pp. 1–3.

Cornwall, and on the way she was met at Exeter by Bennett and his wife and daughter and servants, as well as by Langdon, the Fifth Monarchist who had lately sat for Cornwall. They rode on together, and in Cornwall she stayed first at Bennett's house at Lawhitton, then at Langdon's sister's house, next at her brother's, and finally at Langdon's own at Tregasow near Truro. There her visitors included his fellow-MP and Fifth Monarchist John Bawden. By then her activities, which aroused the special hostility of the local clergy, caused her to be arrested and indicted, but Langdon and Bawden entered into recognizances of £150 each for her appearance before the assizes. Before she was tried, however, the council sent for her to London.[2]

Her further fortunes are not of relevance here, but her entertainment by Robert Bennett, who had borne such a responsible part in the administration of Cornwall for years past, gives some indication of the complexities of allegiance in the first year of the Protectorate. He was a deeply religious man and an advanced sectary; he had been a teller for the abolition of patrons' rights of presentation, and he believed firmly that a preacher of the gospel should never accept a parish living, nor even a lectureship or chaplaincy, nor any kind of fixed maintenance.[3] The Quakers troubled him; he could not deny that they possessed some truth, and thought it important 'not to preferre and exalte soe highly the meere outward forme of ordinances as to carry in Itt either a neglect or a disrespecte off any persons in whome the true power and Image of Jesus Christ might manifestly appeare'. He had debated with them, and one gross error that he could not condone was that 'they have exspresly affirmed unto mee speaking unto them off the Second Comeing off Christ and daye off Judgment that it is already past'.[4] Yet this unbending fundamentalist millenarian had offered his services to Cromwell before leaving London early in 1654, and in June he addressed to him a remarkable confirmation of his allegiance:

And I recon it not a Common priviledge that I have the liberty thus to

---

[2] *Anna Trapnel's Report and Plea*, pp. 9–33; *A Legacy for Saints, being Several Experiences of the Dealings of God with Anna Trapnel* ([24 July] 1654), pp. 49–57; Capp, *Fifth Monarchy Men*, pp. 102–3 *et passim*.

[3] *CJ*, vii, 352; Folger Library, Add MS 483, fo. 177.

[4] Ibid., fo. 175.

doe, because I am persuaded, that upon the miscariages of former authorityes, our God hath placed your Highnes over us. And now our Lord direct you in the way to answere all the gratious intentions of the Lord to this people, and especially to his peculiar ones amongst them; the Lord hath bourn them a very great Love, and he hath a very great jeolosy for them . . .

Bennett went on to warn him of 'the over Laxnes of some in authority' and the 'Iron Rigor' of others, continuing:

oh that your Highnes may so provide agaynst abuse of liberty, that eare we are aware we fall not all agayne into those severe handes which may in tyme leade us backe to the common enimy which is the greatest fear of many good men, who understand it well; that theire dearest concernments this day are imbarqued with your H. as having sufficiently forfited them to all the world besides, and I thinke I have some cause from the late observacon I have made of mens present bent in the Contry Commissions and otherwise to minde your highness hereof.[5]

Bennett is a reminder that thousands of radical Puritans—many more than followed the path of Harrison and Feake—looked to the Protectorate with hope, and that to associate it wholly with ambitious officers and political reactionaries is a grave distortion.

[5] Ibid., fo. 114.

Conclusion

It used to be commonplace to write of the successive changes of government between the Civil War and the Restoration as a series of constitutional experiments, which having been tried and found wanting left England thankful to return to her traditional monarchy. It would be truer to conceive them as a succession of expedients, each rather hastily cobbled up to fill a hiatus in legitimate government or to avert a threatened breakdown of it. This is admittedly less true of the Humble Petition and Advice than of the changes of regime in 1649, 1653, or 1659, but that was the least experimental of all the constitutions of the Interregnum, and where it extended beyond mere cosmetic patching of the Instrument of Government its conservative intentions were obvious. The only true experiment to be promised by anyone in actual possession of power during the Great Rebellion was never carried out. It was announced by the Rump in its votes on 4 January 1649 that all just power derived from the people, and that the supreme authority was therefore vested in the people's representatives in parliament. But though some members voted thus from conviction, the Rump was really just putting on the best face it could while striving to cope with the constitutional mess left behind by Pride's Purge. Itself too depleted to claim to represent the people with any plausibility, it soon became too painfully aware of its unpopularity to risk the early general elections that it had promised. It suppressed the Levellers, whose democratic and republican convictions were much stronger than its own, and thereafter such plans as it had for the future were dominated by the need it felt to fend off the threats of the monarchy's supporters on the one hand and of the army on the other. Whether the bill for a new representative which the army eventually goaded it into framing would or could have redeemed its promises to entrust the Commonwealth's future to the people's suffrages is still an open question, but Cromwell and the army officers thought not.

If it is an error to regard the Commonwealth as originally begotten by a principled belief in the superiority of republican government, it is equally so to see Barebone's Parliament as primarily an attempt to erect a rule of the saints in preparation for the millennium. Neither error is total, of course, for just as there had been some convinced republicans in both parliament and army in December 1648, so in the spring and summer of 1653 there were, both in the Council of Officers and among its nominees to the supreme authority, millenarians of the kind who believed that they had a divine call to erect Christ's kingdom there and then. But they were nothing like a majority in either body, and Cromwell was not one of them. He could hope that 4 July 1653 would prove to be 'a day of the power of Christ', but not *the* day.[1] His precipitate dissolution of the Rump left him with very little freedom of movement. Since he was in no position, legal or practical, to hold elections to an authentic parliament, his choice lay between some form of military dictatorship or a nominated assembly broad-based enough to attempt the desired reforms on which the Rump had stalled for so long. He chose the latter, not as an ideal form of government or as a permanent solution, but as a stage towards the resumption of elected parliaments, which he evidently hoped to see by about the end of 1655. But given his fervent Puritan faith in providence's watch over the people of God in England, he placed extravagant hopes in the assembly that he had summoned, and in his opening speech he expressed them in unguarded terms which the saints would never let him forget.

Reacting extremely to his disappointment, he later wrote it off as 'a story of my own weakness and folly'; 'these 140 honest men could not governe', he said.[2] It was not, however, a change of heart on his part that triggered the next alteration of government but an action initiated by the nominees themselves and endorsed by the majority of them, in revulsion against the pretensions and

[1] See pp. 148–9.
[2] Abbott, iv, 418, 489.

the policies of the saints in their midst. Yet that is not to say that the majority who resigned, any more than the minority who stayed to be evicted, were turning their backs on the goal of a godly reformation for which they had been summoned; nor that Cromwell was, when he accepted the Protectorship. They had simply discovered how much they differed from the zealots over how such a reformation should be achieved, and over the priorities between the kingdom within and the kingdom without.

So how does this reading of the year 1653 leave that other familiar generalization, that the establishment of the Protectorate instituted and indeed constituted a conservative reaction? Once again, the modicum of truth in it is obvious: this was a return to a balanced polity, with distinct powers corresponding very loosely to those of king, council, and parliament in England's ancient *dominium politicum et regale*, and called by another name than monarchy only because Cromwell had rejected the title. Yet a conservative reaction implies some kind of radical establishment to react against, and this is where questioning voices raise themselves. The Rump had never embodied such an establishment; the Commonwealth had been a republic largely without republicans, or at least with too few of them, and even those few too lacking in political stature, to make it viable. The Levellers had been true radicals, but they had never had anything approaching an effective strategy for attaining the power they needed to translate their principles into practice, and if a conservative reaction was set in motion by their downfall it should be dated from 1649, not 1653. As for the plebeian, heretical 'third culture' of which Christopher Hill has written,[3] compounded of Diggers, Ranters, Quakers, extreme General Baptists, Grindletonians, and other heirs of the Familist tradition, one has to ask whether it ever had either the coherence or the political weight to bring about such a change as he attributes to the erection of the Protectorate, even by way of reaction. There is plenty of evidence that Diggers, Ranters, Quakers, and other ultra-radical groups aroused bitter hatred and sometimes fear, but to suggest that they ever even appeared to pose a threat so severe as to cause the English Revolution to change direction seems unwarranted. It is true that a handful of Fifth Monarchists

[3] In *The World Turned Upside Down, passim,* and in *Milton and the English Revolution,* esp. ch. 6.

found a platform in Barebone's Parliament and on certain limited issues drew a disturbing number of fellow-members to their side, but even in this peculiarly chosen assembly they and their policies were finally disowned by a decisive majority. The leaders of that majority promptly became pillars of the Protectorate, without any apparent idea that they were changing course. In the event this proved as unhappy a turning-point for the Fifth Monarchists as the defeat of the 1649 mutinies had been for the Levellers, but both movements had only to make a serious bid for power to discover just how ill-prepared and unsupported they were.

The moderates who handed their authority back to Cromwell did not have to be very conservative to reject the aims and claims that were being aired at Blackfriars and in Arthur Squibb's parlour. Typically they were committed men, Independents or sectaries for the most part, who would have stood out as rather radical against the prevailing political and religious background of the mid-century. From their ranks Cromwell drew most of his councillors and many of his administrators. It is a distortion to interpret the result, whether in the administration or on a wider front, simply in terms of 'reaction'; as has been well said, 'It can also be thought of as the long-delayed and grossly overdue return to normality after the protracted but essentially temporary expedients of a wartime and then post-war regime.'[4] Whether one considers Cromwell himself or the soldiers and civilians who staffed his government under the Instrument, there is a danger of exaggerating both their revolutionary propensities in the later forties and their alleged conservatism in the mid-fifties. There has lately been a salutary reappraisal of the early political stance of the New Model, which first dared to act outside its prescribed military role not in order to launch a revolution but to avert a counter-revolution.[5] Were Cromwell and the men who now served him in any real sense more 'conservative' than they had been two, four, or six years before? He had dropped one or two pilots, but one doubts whether Colonel Rainsborough, had

[4] Aylmer, *State's Servants*, p. 46.
[5] Mark A. Kishlansky, *The Rise of the New Model Army* (Cambridge, 1979), and 'The Case of the Army Truly Stated: The Creation of the New Model Army', *Past and Present*, 81 (1978), 51-75; Valerie Pearl, 'London's Counter-Revolution', in Aylmer (ed.), *The Interregnum*, pp. 29-56.

he lived, would have been any more competent to steer the Commonwealth into radical seas than Major-General Harrison. In constitutional terms the Instrument of Government was very much the heir to the Heads of the Proposals, and where it parted from them the reasons lay in the change of circumstances between 1647 and 1653 rather than in differences of principle.

The constitutional dimension is of course only one by which the change of government has to be assessed. Cromwell was most certainly asserting conservative principles when he opened the first parliament of the Protectorate and denounced Levellers, Ranters, Fifth Monarchists, and sectaries who sought to abolish the established ministry. Like any good politician he was partly matching his tone to his audience, but his sincerity need not be doubted and he was not being inconsistent. He had never thought of the Levellers or any other radical group as offering a serious alternative government, but merely as threatening anarchy, so that the work of reformation would be frustrated and the common enemy strengthened. Few in the Council of Officers or in the Rump would have disagreed with him. In asserting the 'good interest of the nation' in maintaining 'the ranks and orders of men, . . . a nobleman, a gentleman, a yeoman',[6] he was merely affirming the commonplace belief in social hierarchy which he had always held, and which was more widely held even by radical Puritans than is always realized. But reformation was something in which he still believed. It was for neglecting it that he denounced the Rump, and the essential fraudulence of the ex-Rumpers' appeals for the support of the Protectorate's radical opponents would be exposed when they returned to power in 1659. It was chiefly for advancing the work of reformation that he held forth his own government as worthy of parliament's support.

Cromwell and his colleagues still adhered to the same concept of a 'godly reformation' that they had pressed upon the Rump: the propagation of the gospel by a zealous preaching ministry, liberty of conscience, the reform of the law, a clean-up of the administration (especially of its revenue branches), and greater concern for the poor, the hopelessly indebted, and the unemployed. These were all difficult and contentious matters; a government which set its sights no higher than maintaining

[6] Abbott, iii, 435.

stability and reconciling the conservative nobility and gentry would have left them alone, or compromised on them. But Cromwell and his council pressed ahead with measures over which the last two governments had stumbled, without waiting for parliament to meet in September. They set up the controversial but effective Triers and Ejectors, they attempted a major reform of Chancery, they enacted the terms of the union with Scotland and showed a striking concern to improve social justice there, they amended the last parliament's act for the relief of imprisoned debtors, they sorted out the Commonwealth's crazy tangle of fiscal agencies and reconstituted the Exchequer, they legislated against duelling, they appointed Visitors for the universities; they even empowered the Customs Commissioners and their deputies to punish London's porters and watermen for cursing and swearing in their cups. The question is not whether these measures were brilliantly original or effective; the point is that they were attempted.

If in the end the prevailing tone of the Protectorate was conservative, that was due more to parliament than to the Protector, though in the later stages his failing powers allowed the trend to strengthen. Here one may recall what was identified as a unifying theme at the start of this study, the continuing tension between radical Puritanism and moderate constitutionalism. On the face of it the outcome of the crisis-year 1653 looks like a triumph for the latter at the expense of the former, but such an impression needs to be qualified. The defeat of the Fifth Monarchists certainly proved decisive, despite their repeated attempts to rally between 1654 and 1661—but to speak of defeat is to enter into their world-picture, since 'victory' in the sense of a here-and-now kingdom of the saints built by human will and effort was a goal that could and did exist only in their own imaginations. They had, of course, no exclusive right to speak for the saints; the rebukes administered to them by others who spoke their language, particularly Kiffin, Spilsbery, and Fansom, confirm that eloquently. The consequences of the year's events for radical Puritanism need to be viewed more broadly. They spelt a set-back for those who like Milton and Vane and the strictest separatists were utterly opposed to any public provision for a preaching ministry and to any authority in the civil magistrate over matters of religion, but such people were so outnumbered by others of contrary convictions, even among the Puritan devout, that to have acceded to their desires would itself have been an act of intolerance. The general history of the gathered churches in the sixteen-fifties has yet to be written, but for most of them the Protectorate marked a period of peace, consolidation, and liberty.

The reaffirmation of constitutionalism can be acknowledged with fewer qualifications, despite the inevitable failures of the Protectorate to live up to all its constitutional principles. The Instrument obliged it to hold general elections for the first time in nearly fourteen years, and despite all the limitations on who was allowed to stand and vote the result was to bring the local communities back into the political picture to a greater extent than for a long time past. If this book has been largely a story of Westminster politics, that is because government had by 1653 come to be unhealthily cocooned from the feelings and pressures of the regions. The Rump's unrepresentative character had become one of the main causes of its unpopularity, and the pretence at representation offered by the geographical distribution of seats in Barebone's Parliament deceived no one—not even most of its own members, whose readiness by December to resign can be explained partly by their awareness that the assembly had no real claim to speak for their communities.

But once these communities found their voice again, they reawoke the conflict between radical Puritanism and conservative constitutionalism within the breast of Oliver Cromwell. He did not talk in such abstractions, but he spoke repeatedly of 'the interest of the people of God' on the one hand and 'the interest of this nation' on the other, meaning by the latter the prevailingly traditionalist and secular temper that he found in his parliaments and in his dealings with the gentry in their counties. It was the need to carry them with him that made his favourite goals so hard to achieve, but he made it his highest aim to bring the cause of the people of God and the common desires of the political nation into accord. 'He sings sweetly that sings a song of reconciliation betwixt these two interests', he said, 'and it is a pitiful fancy and wild and ignorant, to think they are inconsistent.'[7] His words were far too optimistic, but he did not

[7] Ibid., iv, 490; cf. iii, 585, 590; iv, 271-3, 389, 481-2.

give up the attempt to gain the willing assent of MPs and magistrates to measures that would make England worthy of her role as an elect nation. Had he bowed to the worldly wisdom of frankly pursuing a course of conservative reaction that would have pleased them better, his path might have been smoother.

Appendix A

The Texts of Cromwell's Speech on
4 July 1653

There are two clearly independent early texts of this speech, and also an abridged version which does not derive from either of them. Of the two 'complete' texts, one was published as a pamphlet in 1654 and the other was first printed in J. Nickolls, *Original Letters and Papers Addressed to Oliver Cromwell . . . Found among the Political Collection of . . . John Milton* (1743). The verbal differences between them are so numerous, and sometimes so extensive, as to establish beyond doubt that neither is the source of the other; each appears to derive from a different scribe's attempt to take down Cromwell's words as he spoke them. Their reproduction of those words is for the most part fairly closely similar, and where they differ they seldom fail to convey the same broad sense. But since there are places where Cromwell spoke obscurely, or where his precise words have to be weighed in his explanation of recent and current events, something needs to be said about the provenance of the texts, especially as it is not in either case clear or straightforward.

To take that printed by Nickolls first, its original is in a collection of manuscripts which has been since 1746 in the possession of the Society of Antiquaries of London. It seems on the whole reasonable to accept as valid the account of the collection given by Nickolls in his preface, and in fuller detail by John Bruce in *Proceedings of the Society of Antiquaries*, iii, (1856), 9–10. The documents, one is told, passed from Cromwell's possession to that of Milton, who late in life gave them to his young Quaker friend Thomas Ellwood. On the latter's death they passed to his

friend Joseph Wyeth, who superintended the publication of
Ellwood's autobiography in 1714, and Wyeth's widow gave them
to Nickolls, who published them, and whose father presented
them to the Society of Antiquaries after his son's early death.
The only mystery here is how a collection of state papers
containing so many items dated 1653 or later passed to Milton,
whose modest duties as Secretary for Foreign Tongues shrank to
even smaller proportions after he lost his remaining sight in
1651. The presence in the collection of nearly all the surviving
letters sent to Cromwell by the gathered churches in the spring
of 1653, and of other papers of advice which came to him before
and during the nomination of Barebone's Parliament, raises the
fascinating question whether Milton was first asked to write his
second defence of the English people while that assembly was
still the supreme authority, and whether (if it had sat longer) its
rule might have received the panegyric that the poet accorded
in the *Defensio Secunda* of 1654 to the Protector's. But the fact that
the other documents in the collection are originals, not copies,
and often of considerable political importance, speaks for the
probable authenticity of this version of the speech, for the man
who could obtain the custody of such letters as these was in a
likely position to acquire it from a source close to the government
itself.

The speech itself is fairly copied in a clerk's hand typical of the
mid-seventeenth century. It bears no title or signature; its only
identification is an inscription in another contemporary hand in
the top right-hand corner of the first folio, reading 'July 4. 1653
in the Council Chamber Whitehall'. Nickolls's printed version
contains only a few positive errors of transcription, all of a minor
character, though it amends spelling, capitalization, and punctuation to accord with eighteenth-century practice. It does not
alter or obscure the sense of the manuscript at any material
point.

The pamphlet version is entitled *The Lord General Cromwel's
Speech delivered in the Council-Chamber* ..., and its origins are
mysterious. Its date was not 1653 but 1654—Thomason acquired
it on 13 October of that year—and it was not published by
authority. The title-page declares, 'This is a true copie: Published
for Information, and to prevent Mistakes', but it does not name
the printer or claim official sanction. The old *Parliamentary or*

Constitutional History of England claimed to derive its text of the speech 'from the original edition, printed by W. Du Gard and H. Hills', but this is evidently a mistake, arising no doubt from the fact that Du Gard and Hills became official printers to the Protectorate from its inception. The pamphlet cited above is the only version known to have been printed in Cromwell's lifetime, and Mrs Lomas was clearly right in supposing it to be the source of the text in the old *Parliamentary History* (T. Carlyle, *Oliver Cromwell's Letters and Speeches*, ed. S. C. Lomas, 3 vols., 1904, ii, 272 n. 1). It does not at all resemble the typographical style of Du Gard and Hills and it is produced with nothing like their care. It is marred by a crazy excess of punctuation, and in places the text is verbally garbled to an extent that clouds its sense.

A clue to its source lies in the headpiece that decorates its first page, for this cut reappears in John Spittlehouse's *An Answer to one part of the Lord Protector's Speech* (1654). This was a Fifth Monarchist's reply to Cromwell's derogatory remarks in his speech of 4 September 1654, and its date of publication was very close to that of our pamphlet. It was printed (by whom is not stated) for Livewell Chapman, who published many tracts hostile to the Protectorate, especially by Fifth Monarchist and other sectarian writers. There is no positive evidence that he commissioned the publication of the speech of 4 July 1653, or that this printer did not also work for other booksellers, but there is a strong presumption that this pamphlet version, so far from being officially sanctioned, was sponsored by men who had become Cromwell's opponents. Their motive in October 1654 seems obvious: to point the contrast between his professions to the saints when he opened Barebone's Parliament and his condemnation of the Fifth Monarchy men when he addressed its successor fourteen months later.

There is no suggestion, however, that the pamphlet editor deliberately tampered with Cromwell's words, and he seems to have worked from a text which is often more convincing than that in Nickolls. Sometimes a word has been heard differently: e.g. 'traitors' in the pamphlet (p. 10) is given as 'haters' in Nickolls (p. 108), and 'hast[e]' in the former as 'height' in the latter. In these and some other instances the pamphlet is the more plausible. Comparing the texts, one has the impression of two writers struggling independently to capture Cromwell's flow of words with their primitive speed-writing, and differing where they have to supply what they have not exactly caught, or where they attempt to tidy up his syntactical loose ends. In most places where they differ appreciably, though not in all, the pamphlet text is slightly fuller, though whether because this reporter took down more of Cromwell's actual words or because he or another editor subsequently filled out the defective sentences and attempted to clarify the more cryptic utterances, one can only conjecture. The pamphlet gives the impression of a good text marred by the quirks and carelessness of the copyist or compositor. Each version contains phrases that the other lacks. There are more of these in the pamphlet, but there are places where Nickolls's text conveys a plainer and more plausible sense, and it alone gives the last few sentences that Cromwell spoke after the reading of the 'Instrument' (cf. Abbott, iii, 66).

The abridged version survives in the Bodleian Library, MS Tanner 52, fos. 20–23, the first two sheets being fairly copied in one clerk's hand and the last two in another's. It is headed 'Notes taken of the speech of his Excellency to the new Representative July 4th 1653', and it has all the appearance of being strictly contemporary. This note-taker was obviously much less able to keep up with Cromwell than the other two, but he so often reproduces almost the same actual words as they that where, occasionally, he has a phrase that they miss it may be authentic. A possible instance comes just before Cromwell's account of the conference on 19 April, where he is reported as saying, 'We found from theire owne mouths that they did intend a perpetuating of themselves, we doe not guesse at this we know it' (p. 21).

Carlyle based his text mainly on Nickolls, though he altered and added to it very freely. Mrs Lomas, in her edition cited above, annotates it with many variant readings. Abbott offers a conflation of the two early texts, with no indication of which he is using at any particular point and with many unnoted emendations of his own. These are mostly small, but neither they nor his punctuation are always convincing, and in some crucial passages he is unreliable. For the sake of readers who want to refer to an accessible text I have cited Abbott where Cromwell's sense is not in question. Where his exact words matter, I have quoted whichever of the early texts seems to me clearer or more credible, and occasionally both.

Appendix B

The Members of Barebone's Parliament

This appendix lists all the MPs in alphabetical order, except that the five co-opted members appear separately at the end. The asterisks and daggers against their names are reproduced from *A Catologue of the Names of the Members of the last Parliament, whereof those marked with a Starre were for the Godly Learned Ministry and Universities* (1654). This is discussed on pp. 195–8.

Constituencies are shown in square brackets, following the member's place of residence. Age, where exactly known, is that attained in the course of 1653. Approximate age, indicated by *c.,* is sometimes based on the date of admission to university, assumed to have been at fifteen, or to an Inn of Court, assumed to have been at eighteen—a rough approximation, obviously, but sufficient for the purpose of estimating the average age of the parliament as a whole.

In the Status column, GG stands for greater gentry (including aristocracy), CG for country gentry, LG for lesser gentry, MG for merchant gentry, PG for professional gentry, and M for merchants and other plebeians. The use of these terms is explained near the start of chapter VI. Position in family is indicated, where known, by 'e' for eldest, or eldest surviving son, whether or not he had inherited, and 'ys' for younger son.

The universities and Inns of Court in the Education columns will be readily recognized: it did not seem worth adding separate symbols for Aberdeen, where Swinton had studied, or Leyden, where Francis Rous took a degree as well as at Oxford. Barristers have (b) added after their Inns.

The columns relating to the commission of the peace are primarily concerned to show which members were already JPs in 1650, which were on the bench at the time of Barebone's Parliament, which remained on it through the Protectorate, and which still kept their places in the spring of 1660. The sources are described in chapter VI, n.17. Further research would doubtless yield more dates of first appointment, but the information is given where it has come to hand. Sheriffdoms are derived from *PRO Lists and Indexes,* no. 9 (1898); to save space, what should strictly be shown as (e.g.) 1648–9 appears here as 1649.

The next column shows which members were commissioners for collecting the monthly assessment in the Assessment Act of 1652 or earlier; it does not include those who were made commissioners only after 1653.

Membership of other parliaments is largely self-explanatory. For Recruiters to the Long Parliament the first column shows the date of their election, and a terminal date of 1648 indicates that the member concerned went out with Pride's Purge, whether by choice or not. 1640(S) signifies the Short Parliament. OH stands for membership of the 'Other House' of 1657–9, and P for a subsequent peerage.

Membership of the Council of State is shown only from the last months of the Rump to the early stages of the Protectorate. R signifies the Commonwealth's fifth Council of State (November 1652–April 1653), A the interim council appointed by Cromwell in late April and early May, J that which Barebone's Parliament elected in July, N the body elected in November and P the original council of the Protectorate. Parliamentary activity is measured on a three-point scale, largely on the evidence of the *Journal,* with 3 indicating exceptional prominence in serving on committees, preparing or reporting bills, acting as teller, etc., and 1 denoting very slight participation. The paucity of evidence and the short life of the parliament preclude a finer scale of measurement. Zero is shown for four members who apparently never took their seats, including Cromwell, and for Henry Dawson, who died on 2 August 1653.

The categorization of members' religious standpoints is as described early in chapter VII, and obviously makes no claim to precision. R denotes very varying degrees of radicalism, from Fifth Monarchists (5M) who believed that the saints had an exclusive call from Christ to possess themselves of the kingdom to men of firm but unfanatical separatist principles like Moyer.

Moderates (M) spanned the wide range from Tichborne, the former lay preacher, to Sir Anthony Ashley Cooper. Some attempt has to be made, however, to indicate how each member probably aligned himself on the major issues of ecclesiastical policy. R? and M? are used where uncertainty is considerable, as when the normally well-informed 1654 broadsheet catalogue seems to conflict with other pointers or where a member's stance appears inconsistent or equivocal. P indicates the rare Presbyterians in the House, B the known Baptists, and with some misgiving I has been used to stand for Independent. This category embraces both strict separatists and non-separating Congregationalists, since the frontier between them is shadowy and the evidence incomplete, and there were certainly more MPs in it than there are shown here. They have been given an 'I' where their church membership is known, or where they were recommended to Cromwell by the churches of Christ in their counties, or where there is other positive evidence that they adhered to the principle of the gathered church, whether separatist or non-separating. The identifications by Michael R. Watts in *The Dissenters* (Oxford, 1978), p. 144, and by Tai Liu in *Discord in Zion* and in the *Journal of Ecclesiastical History*, xxii, 232–4, have proved helpful, but I have not invariably accepted them. Fortunately the next column is straightforward: E denotes that the member was named as a commissioner for his county in the ordinance of August 1654 for the ejecting of scandalous, ignorant, disaffected, and otherwise unworthy ministers.

The final column represents a compromise and makes no pretence to completeness. References to all the sources used in collecting biographical material would have swollen this appendix inordinately; its object is a profile of the House, not an exhaustive biographical dictionary of its members. The wills cited were all proved in the Prerogative Court of Canterbury and are listed in the volumes of the British Record Index Library. The heraldic visitations are, except where otherwise stated, published by the Harleian Society. It has not been thought necessary to cite the published admissions registers of the universities and the Inns of Court, and it is assumed that interested readers will find their own way to the record of the members' activities contained in the *Calendar of State Papers, Domestic* and the *Commons' Journal*, and to their public appointments registered in Firth and Rait's *Acts and Ordinances of the Interregnum.* A list of authorities referred to by short titles (additional to those of pp. ix–x) follows this appendix immediately.

One work is regretfully omitted, though it deserves a belated salutation. It is Henry Alexander Glass's pioneering study *The Barebone Parliament,* published in 1899. Glass not only vindicated the assembly with considerable success against the common prejudices and misrepresentations to which most previous historians had subjected it; he also anticipated many much later historical projects by attempting a biographical list of all the members. Alas, the execution was not equal to the conception, for besides leaving many names with little or no information against them he fell into many errors concerning those whose careers he charted more fully, and some he misidentified completely. Since he cites no authorities whatever, information proffered by him alone has not been accepted unless his source has been traced.

Sources referred to in the final column of Appendix B

Alexander	J. J. Alexander, *Devon County Members of Parliament,* reprinted from *Transactions of the Devonshire Association* (1912–25).
Aylmer (*SS*)	G. E. Aylmer, *The State's Servants: The Civil Service of the English Republic, 1649–1660* (1973).
Barnard	T. C. Barnard, *Cromwellian Ireland* (Oxford, 1973).
Barnes	Thomas G. Barnes, *Somerset 1624–1640* (Oxford, 1961).
Baronetage	G. E. C., *Complete Baronetage* (Exeter, 1900–9).
Bates Harbin	W. W. Bates Harbin, *Members of Parliament for the County of Somerset* (Taunton, 1939).
Bayley	A. R. Bayley, *The Great Civil War in Dorset, 1642–1660* (Taunton, 1910).

Beaven	A. B. Beaven, *The Aldermen of the City of London* (1908–13).
Blackwood	B. G. Blackwood, *The Lancashire Gentry and the Great Rebellion* (Chetham Soc., 1978).
Blomefield	F. Blomefield and C. Parkin, *Topographical History of . . . Norfolk* (1739–75).
Boase & Courtney	G. C. Boase and W. P. Courtney, *Bibliotheca Cornubiensis* (1874–82).
Braithwaite	W. C. Braithwaite, *The Beginnings of Quakerism* (1912) and *The Second Period of Quakerism* (1919).
L. F. Brown	Louise F. Brown, *The Political Activities of the Baptists and Fifth Monarchy Men . . .* (Washington, 1912).
Browne	J. Browne, *History of Congregationalism in Norfolk and Suffolk* (1877).
Capp	B. S. Capp, *The Fifth Monarchy Men* (1972).
Cave-Brown	J. Cave-Brown, 'Knights of the Shire for Kent', *Archaeologia Cantiana*, xxl (1895).
Coate	Mary Coate, *Cornwall in the Great Civil War and Interregnum* (Oxford, 1933).
Dict. Brit. Radicals	*Biographical Dictionary of British Radicals in the Seventeenth Century*, ed. R. L. Greaves and R. Zaller, 3 vols (1982–4).
Dodd	A. H. Dodd, *Studies in Stuart Wales* (Cardiff, 1952).
Dore	R. N. Dore, *The Civil Wars in Cheshire* (Chester, 1966).
Dow	F. D. Dow, *Cromwellian Scotland, 1651–1660* (Edinburgh, 1979).
Everitt, *Kent*	A. M. Everitt, *The Community of Kent in the Great Rebellion* (Leicester, 1966).
Everitt, *Suffolk*	*Suffolk and the Great Rebellion* (Suffolk Record Soc., 1960).
Firth & Davies	C. H. Firth and Godfrey Davies, *The Regimental History of Cromwell's Army* (Oxford, 1935).
Fletcher	A. J. Fletcher, *A County Community in Peace and War: Sussex 1600–60* (1975).
Gooder	A. Gooder, *Parliamentary Representation of*

	the County of York (Yorks Arch. Soc. Record Series, 1935–8).
Gough, *Myddle*	Richard Gough, *Antiquityes and Memoyres of the Parish of Myddle* (1875, repr. 1968).
History of Northumberland	*A History of Northumberland . . . Issued under the Direction of the Northumberland County History Committee* (15 vols., Newcastle, 1893–1940).
Holmes	Clive Holmes, *The Eastern Association* (Cambridge, 1974).
Howell	Roger Howell, *Newcastle-upon-Tyne and the Puritan Revolution* (Oxford, 1967); also 'Puritanism in Newcastle before the summoning of the Long Parliament', *Archaeologia Aeliana*, xll (1963), 133–55.
Ketton-Cremer	R. W. Ketton-Cremer, *Norfolk in the Civil War* (1969).
Morant	P. Morant, *History and Antiquities of the County of Essex* (1768).
Morrill	J. S. Morrill, *Cheshire 1630–60* (Oxford, 1974).
Narrative	*A Narrative of the Late Parliament* (1658; reprinted in *Harleian Miscellany*, 1803–13 ed., vi).
Nicoll	J. Nicoll, *Diary of Public Transactions and Other Occurrences*, ed. D. Laing (Bannatyne Club, Edinburgh, 1836).
Noble	Mark Noble, *Memoirs of the Protectoral-House of Cromwell* (1787).
Nuttall (*VS*)	G. F. Nuttall, *Visible Saints: the Congregational Way, 1640–1660* (Oxford, 1957).
Nuttall (*WS*)	G. F. Nuttall, *The Welsh Saints, 1640–1660* (Cardiff, 1957).
Ormerod	G. Ormerod, *History of the County Palatine and City of Chester* (1819).
Penney	N. Penney, *Extracts from State Papers Relating to Friends, 1654–1672* (1913).
Pennington & Roots	D. H. Pennington and I. Roots, eds., *The Committee at Stafford 1643–45* (Manchester, 1957).

Pink MSS	Biographical notes on MPs by W. D. Pink in the John Rylands Library, University of Manchester.
Pink & Beaven	W. D. Pink and A. B. Beaven, *Parliamentary Representation of Lancashire* (1889).
Rex	M. B. Rex, *University Representation in England, 1604–1690* (1954).
Richards (*PMW*)	T. Richards, *History of the Puritan Movement in Wales from 1639 to 1653* (1920).
Richards (*RDW*)	*Religious Developments in Wales, 1654–62* (1923).
Second Narrative	*A Second Narrative of the Late Parliament* (1659), reprinted in *Harleian Miscellany*, vi.
Tolmie	Murray Tolmie, *The Triumph of the Saints: the Separate Churches of London 1616–1649* (Cambridge, 1977).
Underdown (*PP*)	D. E. Underdown, *Pride's Purge* (Oxford, 1971).
Underdown, Somerset	D. E. Underdown, *Somerset in the Civil War and Interregnum* (Newton Abbot, 1973).
Wedgwood	J. C. Wedgwood, *Staffordshire Parliamentary History* (1919–34).
Weyman	H. T. Weyman, 'Shropshire Members of Parliament', *Shropshire Arch. Soc. Trans.* (1926–8).
Williams, *Glos.*	W. R. Williams, *Parliamentary History of the County of Gloucester* (Hereford, 1898).
Williams, *Herefs.*	W. R. Williams, *Parliamentary History of the County of Hereford* (Brecknock, 1899).
Williams, *Oxon.*	W. R. Williams, *Parliamentary History of the County of Oxford* (Brecknock, 1899).
Williams, *Wales*	W. R. Williams, *Parliamentary History of the Principality of Wales* (Brecknock, 1895).
Williams, *Worcs.*	W. R. Williams, *Parliamentary History of the County of Worcester* (Hereford, 1897).

| Age | Status | Position in Family | Education | | J.P. | | | | | Sheriff | Ass. Comm | Other Parliaments | |
			Univ.	Inn	First appt'd	1650	1653	1656-8	1660			Earlier	Later
† ANLABY, John. Etton [Yorks.]													
c.40	LG	e		G		*	*	*	*		A	1647-53	1659
† BAKER, Thomas. Sweeney [Shropshire]													
47	LG	e				*	*	*		1649	A		
* BALDWIN, George. Amersham [Bucks.]													
	LG					*	*	*			A		
† BAR[E]BONE, Praise-God. Fleet St., London [London]													
57?	M												
† BARRINGTON, Henry. Colchester [Essex]													
	M		C?		1652	*	*				A		
* BARTON, Henry. [London]													
	M												
* BARTON, Nathaniel. [Derbyshire]													
	LG				3.1650	*	*	*			A		1654
†BAWDEN, John. Truro [Cornwall]													
	M				12.1652	*					A		
† BELLOT, George. Crackmarsh, Uttoxeter [Staffs.]													
29	LG	ys	O			*	*	*	*		A		
* BENNETT, Gervase. Snelston [Derbyshire]													
	MG	e				*	*	*	*		A		1654, '56, '59
† BENNETT, Robert. Lawhitton [Cornwall]													
43	LG	e	O	MT		*	*	*			A	1651-3	1654, '59
* BINGHAM, John. Bingham Melcombe [Dorset]													
43	CG	e	O	MT		*	*	*	*		A	1645-53	1654, '56, '59
† BIRKENHEAD, Henry. Backford [Cheshire]													
53	LG	e	O		163?	*	*	*	*		A		
* BLAKE, Robert. Bridgwater [Somerset]													
54	PG	e	O			*	*				A	1640(S) 1645-53	1654, '56
† BLOUNT, Thomas. Writlemarsh, Charlton [Kent]													
48	LG	e	O	G	1636 or earlier	*	*	*	*		A		
† BOTTERELL, William. Ludlow [Shropshire]													
	MG				10.1653	*	*				A		

[1] Pink's identification of him (MS 297, fo. 55) as a George Baldwin baptized in 1582 is clearly erroneous. The MP had served in the Civil War (he is styled lieutenant-colonel in *CSPD 1653-4*: a militia commission), and he had at least six children under twenty-one when he made his will in Feb. 1656.

Council of State	Parliamentary activity	Religious standpoint	Ejector	Year of death	Sources
N	3	R		1661	Gooder; Pink MSS; Worden, *Rump*; *Dict. Brit. Radicals.*
	1	R(I:5M?)		1675	Gough, *Myddle*; Richards (*PMW*, *RDW*); Weyman; will.
	1	M		1656	Will; *VCH, Bucks.*; *CSPD 1644-5*, p. 386, and *1649-50*, p. 521.[1]
	3	R(I)		1679	*DNB*; Tolmie; L. F. Brown.
	1	R(I)	E		J. H. Round in *EHR*, xv (1900); B. L. K. Henderson in *TRHS* (1912).
	2	M	E		
N	2	M	E		Firth & Davies; *Clarke P.*, ii; Fox, *Journal.*
	1	R		1685	Capp.
	1	?R	E		*Staffs Pedigrees* (Harl. Soc. lxiii); *Baronetage.*[2]
N	2	M	E		*Narrative*; Braithwaite; Fox, *Journal*; Pink MSS.
J	3	R(B)	E	1683	*DNB*; Folger Lib., Add. MSS 483 etc.; Coates; Pink MSS.
N	1	M	E	1675	Bayley; B & P; *Narrative*; Pink MSS; will.
	1	?R	E	1660	Ormerod; Morrill, *Cheshire.*
	1	M	E	1657	*DNB.*
	3	R(I)			*DNB*; *Vis. Kent, 1619, 1663*; Everitt, *Kent.*
	1	R	E		Weyman.

[2] Not the second son of Edward Bellot of Moreton, Cheshire, as identified by J. C. Wedgwood in *Staffordshire Parliamentary History*, but the third son of Edward's elder son John; described as 'of Uttoxeter' in three Assessment Acts, and married a widow dwelling in Crackmarsh in the parish of Uttoxeter. See *Staffordshire Pedigrees 1664-1700*, Harleian Soc., lxiii, p. 21, and *Complete Baronetage.*

Age	Status	Position in Family	Univ.	Inn	First apptd.	1650	1653	1656-8	1660	Sheriff	Ass. Comm	Earlier	Later
			Education		J. P.							Other Parliaments	

* BOWTELL, Barnaby. Parham, Suffolk [Lincs.]

Age	Status	Position in Family	Univ.	Inn	First apptd.	1650	1653	1656-8	1660	Sheriff	Ass. Comm	Earlier	Later
	LG					*	*	*			A		

* BREWSTER, Francis. Wrentham [Suffolk]

| 53 | LG | ys | C | | | * | * | * | | | A | | |

* BREWSTER, John. Withfield, Barking [Essex]

| 49 | LG | ys | C | L(b) | 10.1653 | | * | * | * | | A | | |

* BRODIE, Alexander. Brodie, Morayshire [Scotland]

| 36 | CG | e | | | | | | | | | | | |

* BROOKE, Thomas. Great Oakley [Northants.]

| 40 | CG | e | | | 9.1646 | * | * | * | | | A | | 1654 |

† BROUGHTON, Andrew. Maidstone [Kent]

| 50 | P | | | I I (G) | | | | | | | A | | 1659 |

† BROWNE, John. Little Ness, Shropshire [Wales]

| 45? | LG | | | | | | | | | | | | |

* BROWNLOW, Sir William. Humby [Lincs.]

| 57 | GG | ys | O | IT(b) | 1636 or earlier | * | * | * | * | | A | | |

† BURTON, William. Yarmouth [Norfolk]

| | M | | | | 1653 or '54 | | ? | * | | | A | | |

† CALEY, Jacob. Ipswich [Suffolk]

| | M | e | | | 7.1652 | | | * | | | A | | |

† CAREW, John. Antony, Cornwall [Devon]

| 31 | GG | ys | O | IT | 3.1647 | * | * | (*) | | | A | 1647-53 | |

* CASTLE, Robert. East Hatley [Cambs.]

| 49 | CG | e | C | | | * | * | * | * | 1650 | A | | 1654, '56 |

† CATER, Edward. Kempston [Beds.]

| c.39 | CG | e | C | IT | 4.1649 | * | * | * | * | 1665 | A | | |

---

[3] Younger brother of Robert B., MP 1645–53; correctly identified by Brunton and Pennington, incorrectly by Pink and by Foster in *Admissions to Grays Inn.* The other Francis, Robert's son and heir, is regularly referred to in acts and ordinances as 'the younger' until the elder's death in 1657. To confuse matters, Francis the elder also had a son called Francis (will).

[4] Younger brother of Francis the elder; short biography in B. W. Quintrell, 'The Divisional Committee for South Essex' (Manchester MA thesis, 1962), p. 180.

[5] Styled colonel, but his commission was in the Northants militia: *CSPD 1650*, p. 505, and *1655–7*, p. 243.

Council of State	Parliamentary activity	Religious standpoint	Ejector	Year of death	Sources
	2	?M	E	1685	Will.
	1	M(I)	E	1657	B & P; Nuttall (*VS*); Browne; will.[3]
	2	M	E	1677	Morant; Penney; Holmes.[4]
	0	M(P)		1680	*DNB; Diary of Alexander Brodie*, ed. D. Laing (Aberdeen, 1863)
	2	M	E	1658	*Vis. Northants. 1681;* will.[5]
J	3	R		1688	Ludlow; Burton, *Diary;* Cave-Brown; Stephens, *Clerks of the Counties.*
	1	R(I:5M)			Richards (*PMW, RDW*); Nuttall (*WS*); Williams, *Wales.*[6]
N	2	M		1666	*DNB; Baronetage;* will.
	2	?M(I)		1673	Nuttall (*VS*); Burton, *Diary;* will.[7]
	1	R(I:5M)		1680	Capp; Everitt, *Suffolk; Vis. Suffolk 1664-8;* Browne; will.
A, J, N	3	R(I:5M)		1660	*DNB;* L. F. Brown; Worden, *Rump;* Coates; *State Trials.*
	1	M	E		*Vis. Cambs. 1619;* Penney; Pink MSS.
	1	?R(I)	E	1668	*Vis. Beds. 1664;* information kindly supplied by Miss Godber from Beds. C.R.O.

[6] The very common name presents pitfalls of identification, which Williams fails to avoid; Richards is more reliable, but in error about this J. B.'s authorship of a millenarian tract in 1655. Useful information in R. Tudur Jones's Oxford D. Phil. thesis on Vavasor Powell, pp. 140, 160–1.

[7] Though not listed in the *liber pacis* for 1652–3, he was certainly a JP by March 1654: see *CSPD 1654*, p. 3. I strongly doubt the description of him as a 'kingling' in 1657, in *A Narrative of the Late Parliament.*

			Education		J. P.							Other Parliaments	
Age	Status	Position in Family	Univ.	Inn	First apptd.	1650	1653	1656-8	1660	Sheriff	Ass. Comm	Earlier	Later
† CHETWOOD, John. Oakley [Staffs.]													
54	LG	e	O	IT	4.1647	*	*	*			A		
* CLARKE, John. Kensington? [Ireland]													
	M		G?		1655			*					1654, '56, '59
* CLARKE, John. Bury St. Edmunds [Suffolk]													
c.43	LG		C?		3.1650	*	*	*		1671	A		1654, '56, '59
* CLUDD, Edward. [Notts.]													
	LG	ys				*	*	*					1656
† COATES, Roger. Skipton [Yorks.]													
	P				3.1650	*	*	*					
* COOPER, Sir Anthony Ashley. Wimborne St. Giles [Wilts.]													
32	GG	e	O	L	10.1643	*	*	*	*	1647	A	1640(S)	1654, '56, '59, '60, P.
† COURTNEY, Hugh. Beaumaris [Wales]													
51?	LG	e?			7.1651		*	*			A		
† CROFTS, John. Lower Swell [Glos.]													
	LG				3.1653		*	*			A		1656
* CROMWELL, Henry. Dublin [Ireland]													
25	LG	ys			1655			*					
* CULLEN, William. Dover [Kent]													
	M				9.1653		*	*			A		1654
* CUNLIFFE, Robert. Sparth [Lancs.]													
49	LG	e						*			A		
† CUST, Richard. Stamford [Lincs.]													
31	CG	ys	C	IT(b)	7.1649	*	*	*			A		1679, '80, '81

[8] Probably the third son of Thomas C. of Arnold, Notts., who was third son of Thomas Cludd of Orleton; not Edward C. of Orleton, as identified by Pink, since one Edward of this (the senior) line died in 1651 aged twenty-four, and his son and heir, also Edward, was baptized only in 1646: *Trans. Shropshire Arch. and Natural Hist. Soc.*, 4th ser. viii (1920–1), 162 ff.

[9] Styled captain, but not the Capt. Roger Coates described in Firth and Davies, who was killed in the siege of Dunkirk in 1658. This man was living in 1659 (*CSPD 1659–60*, p. 73).

Council of State	Parliamentary activity	Religious standpoint	Ejector	Year of death	Sources
	1	R(I)	E	1667	Pennington & Roots; Wedgwood; *Staffs. Pedigrees* (Harl. Soc. lxiii); *Notes & Queries*, 12th ser. iv, 301; Pink MSS.
	3	M			Firth & Davies; Burton, *Diary; Narrative;* Pink MSS.
	2	M(I)	E		Nickolls; Browne; *Baronetage;* Pink MSS.
	1	M	E		*Vis. Notts. 1614;* Penney.[8]
	2	R			Gooder.[9]
J,N,P	3	M	E	1683	*DNB;* K. H. D. Haley, *First Earl of Shaftesbury.*
J	3	R(I:5M)			Capp; Dodd; L. F. Brown; Richards (*RDW*); Williams, *Wales.*[10]
	2	R(I)			Nickolls, pp. 125, 145-7; Williams, *Glos.; Narrative.*[11]
N	3	M		1674	*DNB;* R. W. Ramsey, *Henry Cromwell* (1933).
	1	M	E		Mainly *CSPD* and F & R; also BL, Add. MS 29, 747, fos. 18, 20, 24.
	1	M(I)		1653 (4 Dec.)	Pink & Beaven; *VCH Lancs.;* vi, viii; *Lancs. Inquisitions* (Record Soc. of Lancs. & Ches. xvi, 1887); *Note Book of . . . Thomas Jolly,* ed. H. Fishwick.
	2	?R		1700	*Baronetage; Lincs. Pedigrees,* iv (Harl. Soc. lv).

[10] Parentage uncertain; of Cornish stock, but the only Hugh C. in *Vis. Cornwall 1620,* the second son of George C. of Penkevell, was probably too old. Possibly the son and heir of Robert C. of Molland, Devon (*Vis. Devon 1620,* p. 77); that Hugh was eighteen in 1620.

[11] Probably distinct from the J.C., common councilman of Tewkesbury, with whom Williams and Pink identify him; the 1653 MP was a member of the Congregational church at Stow-on-the-Wold, which is near Swell but quite far from Tewkesbury.

Age	Status	Position in Family	Education		J.P.						Ass. Comm	Other Parliaments	
			Univ.	Inn	First apptd.	1650	1653	1656-8	1660	Sheriff		Earlier	Later
† DANVERS, Henry. Swithland [Leics.]													
c.31	LG		O			*	*				A		
* DAWSON, Henry. Newcastle-upon-Tyne [4 N. Counties]													
	M				7.1652	*	*				A		
* DICKENSON, Thomas. Kirkby Hall, Gt. Ouseburn [Yorks.]													
	MG				5.1646	*	*	*	*	1641	A		1654, '56, '59
† DRAPER, William. Nether Worton [Oxon.]													
43	LG		O			*	*	*	*	1658	A		
* DUCKENFIELD, Robert. Duckinfield Hall [Cheshire]													
34	CG	e		G		*	*	*	*	1649	A		
* DUNCH, Samuel. Pusey[14] [Berks.]													
61	CG	ys	O	G	1.1647	*	*	*	*	1630	A	1621	
† DUNKON, Robert. Ipswich [Suffolk]													
57	M				7.1657		*				A		
* ERISEY, James. Bickleigh [Devon]													
37	LG	e		L		*	*	*	*		A		
† ERLE, Christopher. Topsfield [Essex]													
29	LG	e	C[15]	MT(b)	7.1649	*	*	*			A		
* EURE, George, Lord. Easby [Yorks.]													
	GG	e			10.1653	*	*	*			A		1654, '56, OH
† EYRE, Thomas. Bromham [Wilts.]													
37	LG	e			9.1653	*	*				A		
* FENWICK, Robert. Bedlington [4 N. Counties]													
	LG				7.1650	*	*	*	*		A		1654, '56

[12] Misidentified by Pink and by Foster in *Alumni Oxonienses,* and confused by *DNB* with Robert Danvers. Capp (p. 248) provides the fullest biographical information and bibliography.

[13] There are two wills of a W. D. of Nether Worton, proved within a year of each other: PRO PROB 11/338, PCC 26 Eure, and PROB 11/341 PCC 18 Pye. The former is that of our MP, the latter that of his son and heir, who died when he had only one son, still a child.

[14] Though described as North Baddesley, Hants (a manor which he acquired by marriage) in the 1664 Visitation of Berkshire and in his will ('Badgley'), he was 'of Pusey' in the 1654 ordinance for Ejectors, and he died there.

Council of State	Parliamentary activity	Religious standpoint	Ejector	Year of death	Sources
	2	R(B:5M)		1687	Capp; *DNB;* L. F. Brown; J. Nichols, *History . . . of Leicester,* iv, Pt. 1, 189.[12]
	0	M(I)		1653 (2 Aug.)	Howell, *Newcastle* and 'Puritanism in Newcastle'; will.
	1	M	E	1669 or 1670	Gooder.
	2	?R		1672	Williams, *Oxon.* ; J. M. Davenport, *Oxfordshire Lord Lieutenants, High Sheriffs* (etc., 1888); Penney; will.[13]
	1	M(I)	E	1689	*DNB;* Morrill, *Cheshire;* Dore; Dodd; Nuttall (*VS*); Penney.
	1	M	E	1668	*Vis. Berks. 1664;* Noble, ii, 442; Penney; will.
	1	?R(I)		1670	Everitt, *Suffolk;* Browne; Nuttall (*VS*); Nickolls; will.
	1	M	E	1692	Alexander; *Vis. Cornwall 1620;* Folger Lib., Add. MS 483 fos. 12, 44, 47 etc.; BL, Add. MS 10, 114, fo. 34^{v}.
	1	?R			Hutchins, *Dorset,* iii, 503; Penney; Pink MSS (and see n. 15).
N	1	M	E	1672	Gooder; *Peerage; Second Narrative;* will.
	1	R(I)			*Wilts Visitation Pedigrees* (Harl. Soc. cv), p. 59.[16]
	1	M	E	1668	Pink MSS; will.[17]

[15] Admitted to Corpus Christi College, Cambridge, in 1640; created DCL (Oxon.), 1651: Venn, *Alumni Cantab.*, ii, 81; Foster, *Alumni Oxon.*, ii, 464. He was a nephew of Sir Walter Erle.

[16] I take him to be the T. E. III of Bromham who was seven in 1623 and is named as of Bromham in two *libri pacis* and several Assessment Acts; not the Mayor of Marlborough of the same name nor the T. E. identified by Pink. Styled colonel; possibly the Governor of Hurst Castle who had custody of Charles I in 1648.

[17] Of the many Fenwicks, he is identified as of Bedlington in the Act of Nov. 1656 appointing commissioners for Scotland to try treasons. He lived in Blackfriars, London, when he made his will in 1666: PRO PROB 11/329, PCC 5 Coke.

		Position in Family	Education		J.P.						Ass. Comm	Other Parliaments	
Age	Status		Univ.	Inn	First apptd	1650	1653	1656-8	1660	Sheriff		Earlier	Later
* FLEETWOOD, George. The Vache, Chalfont St. Giles [Bucks.]													
30	CG	e				*	*	*			A	1645-53	1654, OH
† FRENCH, Thomas. Cambridge [Cambs.]													
c.52	MG		G			*	*	*	*		A		
* FRERE, Tobias. Harleston [Norfolk]													
63	LG	ys	G			*	*				A		1654
* GILL, Edward. ? Norton, Derbyshire[19] [Yorks.]													
43	LG	e				*		*	*		A		1654, '56
* GODDARD, Jonathan. Oxford [Oxon.]													
37	PG		O,C		1653			*	*				
† GODDARD, Vincent. Howbery, Oxon. [Berks.]													
	LG	e?			9.1653	*					A		
* GOOKIN, Vincent. Dublin? [Ireland]													
c.34	GG	e			7.1647	*	*	*					1654, '56, '59
† GREENE, Nicholas. Grittleton [Wilts.]													
	LG				1.1649	*	*	*			A		
* HENLEY, Henry. Colway, Lyme Regis[21] [Somerset]													
c.46	CG	e			before 8.1646	*	*	*	*	1649	A		1654, '59, '60, '79, '80, '81, '90.
†HERRING, John. Holmer [Herefordshire]													
	LG					*	*	*			A		
* HEWSON, John. Dublin [Ireland]													
	M				1656?			*					1654, '56
† HIGHLAND, Samuel. Southwark [Surrey]													
	LG				4.1649	*	*	*	*		A		1654, '56
* HILDESLEY, John. Hinton Admiral [Hants.]													
57	LG				3.1647	*	*	*	*	1657	A		1654, '56, '59, '60

[18] Sometimes confused (e.g. by Glass) with the G. F. who became a general in the Swedish army.

[19] He was on the Derbyshire list of Ejectors and assessment commissioners, though he was added to the latter for the West Riding as well in 1657, the year in which his wife inherited Carr House, near Doncaster. He had been Governor of Sheffield Castle, 1644-7: Gooder, ii, 57-8.

[20] Probably the V. G. who was disclaimed to bear arms in the 1623 Visitation of Berkshire, and the V. G., 'gent' of Howbery, Oxon., whose will was proved in Dec. 1657

Council of State	Parliamentary activity	Religious standpoint	Ejector	Year of death	Sources
N	1	M	E		*DNB; Dict. Brit. Radicals;* Pink MSS; will.[18]
	1	R	E		Abbott, i, 32 n., 108-9; *CSPD;* F & R.
	2	M(I)	E	1656	*Vis. Norfolk 1664;* Burton, *Diary,* i, xxxv-vi; Nickolls; Pink MSS.
	1	M	E	1675	Gooder; *Dugdale's Vis. of Yorkshire,* ed. J. W. Clay.
N	2	M		1675	*DNB;* Rex; Webster, *Great Instauration;* Aubrey, *Brief Lives;* Williams, *Parl. Hist. Oxon.*
	1	R(I)		1657?	Will.[20]
	1	M		1659	*DNB;* own pamphlets; *Narrative;* Pink MSS; also ch. vi, n. 31.
	1	?R		1670	Will; Pink MSS.
	1	M	E	1697	Bates Harbin; Bayley; Underdown, *Somerset;* Burton, *Diary;* Pink MSS.
	2	R(I)		1657	Williams, *Herefs.;* Nuttall (*WS*); Nickolls; Braithwaite; will.
J	3	M(I)		1662	*DNB;* L. F. Brown; Burton, *Diary;* Barnard.
	3	R(I)			*Exact Relation;* L. F. Brown; Tolmie; Burton, *Diary; The Trepan* (1656).
	2	M	E	1680	*Narrative of the Late Parliament;* Penney; Pink MSS.

and who bequeathed land in Woollington, Berkshire, to his nephew, another Vincent G.: PRO PROB 11/271, PCC 538 Ruthen.

[21] He also succeeded to his father's seat, Leigh House in Winsham, Somerset, in 1639, but though he served on various commissions for both Dorset and Somerset he was named for Dorset only in the 1652 Assessment Act, and in 1652-3 he was a JP in both Devon and Dorset (Colway is on the border between them) but not in Somerset. He had been a Somerset JP in 1646-8 (*Western Circuit Assize Orders 1629-48,* ed. J. S. Cockburn, Camden Society, Fourth Series, xvii, 244), yet it was for Dorset that he served as sheriff in 1648-9.

Age	Status	Position in Family	Univ.	Inn	First apptd.	1650	1653	1656-8	1660	Sheriff	Ass. Comm	Earlier	Later
\+ HOLLISTER, Denis. Bristol [Somerset]													
	M				9.1653		*	*			A		
\+ HOLMES, Robert. Chastleton? [Glos.]													
	LG				7.1650	*	*	*					
\+ HOPE, Sir James. Hopetoun [Scotland]													
39	GG	ys											
* HORSEMAN, Edward. Stretton [Rutland]													
37	LG	e			9.1653		*	*	*	1668	A		1654, '59
* HOWARD, Charles. Carlisle Castle [4 N. Counties]													
24	GG	ys			9.1647	*	*	*	*	1650	A		1654, '56, '60; OH, P
* HUTCHINSON, Daniel. Dublin [Ireland]													
	M				1651		*	*					
\+ IRETON, John. London [London]													
38	MG	ys			10.1653		*	*		1651			
\+ JAFFRAY, Alexander. Kingwells and Aberdeen [Scotland]													
39	PG						*						
\+ JAMES, John. Trippleton Hall, Herefordshire[22] [Worcs.]													
43	CG	e				*	*	*	*	1650	A		
\+ JERMY, Robert. Bayfield-in-Saxlingham [Norfolk]													
c.50	CG	e[23]	C	MT(b)		*	*	*			A		
*JONES, Philip. Cardiff Castle[24] [Monmouthshire]													
35	CG	e			3.1650	*	*	*		1672	A	1650-3	1654, '56, OH
\+ KENRICK, William. Boughton-under-Blean [Kent]													
39	LG	ys				*	*	[25]	*		A		1659
* KING, Henry. Norwich [Norfolk]													
	M					*	*	*			A		

[22] He also inherited Astley Hall in Worcestershire from his father; he was made sequestration commissioner for Worcs. in 1648, commander of that county's mounted militia in 1651, and assessment commissioner for Worcs. as well as Herefs. from 1649; but he served as sheriff of Herefs. in 1649–50 and is still described as of Trippleton in the 1656 act which appointed commissioners to try treasons. In addition to the sources cited above, see G. E. Aylmer in *Trans. Woolhope Naturalists' Field Club*, xl (1972), 382.

[23] A third son, according to the Middle Temple admissions register, but he had inherited his father's manor of Bayfield by 1659, when he was unseated on a double

Council of State	Parliamentary activity	Religious standpoint	Ejector	Year of death	Sources
J	2	R(I)		1676	Nuttall (*VS*); Braithwaite; Bates Harbin; will; own pamphlets.
	1	R			Williams, *Glos.*
J	2	R		1661	*DNB;* Dow; C. H. Firth (ed.), *Scotland and the Commonwealth* and *Scotland and the Protectorate.*
	2	M	E	1693	*Vis. Rutland 1681;* Aylmer (*SS*); will.
N	3	M(I)	E	1685	*DNB; Narrative* and *Second Narrative;* Burton, *Diary.*
	2	M(I)		*c.*1676	Nickolls; Barnard.
	3	R(I)		1689	*DNB;* Beaven; Aylmer (*SS*); *Dict. Brit. Radicals;* Noble.
	2	R(I)		1673	*DNB; Diary of Alex. Jaffray* (Aberdeen, 1856); Nicoll, *Diary;* Dow; Firth, *Scotland and the Commonwealth* and *Scotland and the Protectorate.*
N	2	R(I:5M)	E	1681	Williams, *Worcs.;* Nuttall (*WS*); *Vis. Worcs. 1634;* Richards (*PMW*); Capp; Pink MSS.
	1	?R		1677	F. Blomefield, *Norfolk; Vis. Norfolk 1664;* C. H. Hopwood, *Middle Temple Records;* Ketton-Cremer; *Baronetage.*
A, J, N, P	3	M	E	1674	*DNB; DWB;* Dodd; Williams, *Parl. Hist. Wales; Second Narrative;* Burton, *Diary;* will.
	2	R(I)			Everitt, *Kent; Vis. Kent 1663; Vis. Northants. 1681;* Burton, *Diary.*
	2	M(I)	E		Nickolls; little else but *CJ* and F & R.

return (see *Official Returns, CJ sub* 6 Apr. 1659, and Burton, *Diary,* iv, 318). Pink unaccountably identifies the 1653 MP as this R. J.'s son, born in 1629.

[24] Resident as Governor; his family estate was in Llangyfelach. Though briefly removed from the commission of the peace in 1659–60 he was reinstated as Custos Rotulorum of Glamorgan soon after the Restoration.

[25] Removed from the commission in March 1657 but reinstated by the restored Rump in 1659.

Age	Status	Position in Family	Univ.	Inn	First apptd.	1650	1653	1656-8	1660	Sheriff	Ass. Comm	Earlier	Later
* KING, Sir Robert. Boyle Castle, Cecil House etc. [Ireland]													
c.54	GG	e	C		1653			*					1654, '56
† LANGDON, Francis. Tregalwe, St. Erme [Cornwall]													
47	LG	ys			5.1650	*	*	*			A		
* LANGLEY, John. London [London]													
41	M	e			10.1653		*	*	*		A		
* LASCELLES, Francis. Stank Hall [Yorks.]													
c.42	LG	e	G			*	*	*	*		A	1645-53	1654, '56, '60 (unseated)
* LAWRENCE, Henry. Goldingtons [Herts.]													
53	CG	e	C	G	7.1656			*			A	1646-8	1654, '56
* LOCKHART, Sir William. Lee Castle [Scotland]													
32	GG	e						*					1654, '56, OH
* LUCY, Richard. (Charlecote)[27] [Warwickshire]													
34	CG	ys[27]	O	G	6.1649	*	*	*	*	1647	A		1654, '56, '59, '60, 61
* MAJOR, Richard. Hursley [Hants.]													
49	LG	e	O		before 3.1647	*	*	*	*	1640	A		1654, OH
† MANSELL, Bussy. Briton Ferry [Wales]													
30	CG	e				*	*	*	*	1678	A		1660, '79, '80, '81, '89, '90, '95, '98
† MARSH, Lawrence. Dorking [Surrey]													
33	LG					*	*	*	*		A		
* MARTYN, Christopher. Plympton St. Maurice [Devon]													
	LG				1647	*	*	*			A	1647-53	1659, '60
* MATTHEWS, Joachim. Havering atte Bower [Essex]													
c.35	MG	e?		L(b)	9.1644	*	*	*			A		1654, '56, '59
* MONCK, George. Great Potheridge [Devon]													
45	LG	ys			1655			*	*		A		OH, 1660, P

[26] Hard to disentangle from his cousin J. L. of Colchester, but a letter to him from the latter (*CSPD 1625–49, Addenda*, p. 667) confirms their separate identities. Beaven identifies him as Prime Warden of the Fishmongers' Company in 1652 and as impoverished in old age (ii, 73, 183), so the will in PRO PROB 11/411, PCC 155 Fane), though proved as late as Aug. 1692, may well be his. He had lands in Wales, of which a John Williams (the 1653 MP?) was a legatee.

Council of State	Parliamentary activity	Religious standpoint	Ejector	Year of death	Sources
N	2	M		1657	*DNB; Narrative;* Pink MSS; Chas. Webster, *Great Instauration;* will.
	1	R(B:5M)		1658	Capp; *Dict. Brit. Radicals;* will.
	0	M	E		Beaven; V. Rowe, *Sir Henry Vane;* Pink MS 306, fo. 43.[26]
	1	M	E	1667	Gooder.
J, N, P	2	M(B)	E	1664	*DNB; Second Narrative;* L. F. Brown; Tolmie; Burton, *Diary.*
	2	M		1676	*DNB;* Nicoll, *Diary;* Firth, *Scotland and the Commonwealth;* Dow.
	1	M	E	1678	*DNB; Vis. Warwicks. 1682-3;* Aylmer (*SS*); Folger MS W. b. 144, fos. 99-100; will.
J, N, P	2	M	E	1660	Noble; Abbott.
	1	?R	E	1699	A. M. Johnson in *Morgannwg,* xx (1976); *DWB;* Dodd; Richards (*RDW*).
	1	R		1665	Pink MSS.
	0	M	E		Underdown (*PP*); Alexander.
	2	M	E	1659	*Baronetage;* Wood, *Fasti;* Burton, *Diary;* Underdown (*PP*); Worden, *Rump;* Tai Liu, *Discord in Zion;* will.
	1	M		1670	*DNB;* M. Ashley, *General Monck.*

[27] Third son; eldest brother Spencer died in 1645, next brother Robert in 1658, when Richard became master of Charlecote, though he may have resided there earlier. Alice Fairfax-Lucy, in *Charlecote and the Lucys* (Oxford, 1958), is much confused about his career.

Age	Status	Position in Family	Univ.	Inn	First apptd	1650	1653	1656-8	1660	Sheriff	Ass. Comm	Earlier	Later
			Education			J.P.						Other Parliaments	
* MONTAGU, Edward. Hinchingbrooke [Hunts.]													
28	GG	e				*	*	*	*		A	1645-8	1654, '56, OH, '60, P
† MOYER, Samuel. Pitsea Hall, Essex [London]													
c.44	MG				6.1647	*	*	*			A		
* NEAST, William. Twyning [Glos.]													
30	LG	e	O	MT		*	*	*					1656
* NORTON, Richard. Southwick [Hants.]													
38	GG	e	O	G		*	*	*	*		A	1645-53	1654, '56, '59, '60, '61, '79, '80, '81, '89, '90
* ODINGSELLS, John. Epperstone [Notts.]													
49	LG	e	C	G	9.1649	*	*				A		
* OGLE, Henry. Eglingham Hall [4 N. Counties]													
53	LG	e				*	*	*	*		A		1654
* PHEASANT, Stephen. Upwood [Hunts.]													
36	LG	e	C	G(b)	7.1652		*	*			A		1654
* PHILLIPS, James. Tregibby, and Cardigan Priory [Wales]													
59	CG	e	O		3.1650	*	*	*	*	1650	A		1654, '56, '59, '60, '61[28]
* PICKERING, Sir Gilbert. Titchmarsh [Northants.]													
42	GG	e	C	G		*	*	*	*		A	1640-53	1654, '56, OH
† PLUMSTEAD, Edward. [Suffolk]													
c.40	LG	ys	C										
* PRATT, John. Lutterworth [Leics.]													
	LG					*	*	*			A		
† PRICE, Richard. Gunley, Montgom. [Wales]													
	LG						*	*			A		
† PYNE, John. Curry Malet [Somerset]													
c.57	CG	e	O	MT(b)	1642 or earlier	*	*	*	*		A	1625, '26, '28, '40(S), 1640-53	

[28] Unseated in 1662 because of his membership of the High Court of Justice which in 1654 tried John Gerard, Peter Vowell, and Somerset Fox for plotting to assassinate Cromwell; see BL, Egerton MS 2979, fos. 107-27, and *CJ*, viii, 438.

[29] Probably second son of Francis P. of Cockfield or Brettenham, Suffolk, but the son

Council of State	Parliamentary activity	Religious standpoint	Ejector	Year of death	Sources
J, N, P	3	M	E	1672	*DNB; Narrative* and *Second Narrative;* Pepys.
A, J	3	R(I)		1683	Aylmer (*SS*); Beaven; L. F. Brown; Tolmie; *Baronetage;* will.
	1	M(I)		*c.*1670	Williams, *Glos.;* Nickolls.
J	1	M	E	1691	B & P; *Vis. Hants. 1634; VCH, Hants.* (unreliable); Underdown (*PP*); Penney.
	1	M	E	1655	*Vis. Notts, 1614;* will.
	1	M	E	*c.*1669	*History of Northumberland,* xiv; W. P. Hedley, *Northumberland Families;* Abbott, ii, 447.
	1	M	E	1660	*VCH, Hunts.,* ii, 238; will. See *DNB* for his father, Peter P.
	1	M	E		*DWB;* Dodd; Williams, *Wales;* Aubrey, *Brief Lives.*
R, A, J, N, P	3	M(I)	E	1668	*DNB;* Keeler; *Narrative* and *Second Narrative;* Burton, *Diary;* Worden, *Rump;* Tai Liu, *Discord in Zion.*
	1	R(I)			*Vis. Norfolk 1613; Vis. Suffolk 1664-8;* Braithwaite.[29]
	1	M	E	1657	Will.
	1	R(I:5M)	E	1675	*Dict. Brit. Radicals;* Williams, *Wales;* Richards (PMW, RDW), Dodd; Nuttall (*WS*).
	1	R		1678	B & P; Keeler; Bates Harbin; Barnes; Underdown, *Somerset;* Penney; will.

between Thomas (eldest) and William (third) is given as Edward in the 1613 Norfolk Visitation and as Clement in the 1664 Suffolk Visitation. His identification with the E.P. admitted to Queens' College, Cambridge, in 1628 is probable; his conversion to Quakerism *c.*1655 is certain (Braithwaite, *Beginnings,* p. 164; *Second Period,* p. 527).

Age	Status	Position in Family	Univ.	Inn	First apptd.	1650	1653	1656-8	1660	Sheriff	Ass. Comm	Earlier	Later
			Education		J. P.							Other Parliaments	

† REEVE, William. [Herts.]

Age	Status	Position in Family	Univ.	Inn	First apptd.	1650	1653	1656-8	1660	Sheriff	Ass. Comm	Earlier	Later
	M				7.1656			*					

* ROBERTS, Sir William. Willesden [Middlesex]

| 48 | GG | e | C | G | 1643 or earlier | * | * | * | * | | A | | 1654, '56, OH |

† ROGERS, Wroth. Llanvaches, Mon. [Herefordshire]

| | M | | | | 3.1650 | * | * | * | * | 1656 | A | | 1656, '59 |

* ROUS, Anthony. Wotton [Cornwall]

| c.50 | CG | e | | MT | | * | * | * | * | | A | | 1654, '56 |

* ROUS, Francis. Lanrake, Cornwall [Devon]

| 74 | GG | ys | O | MT | | * | * | * | | | A | 1626, '28, '40(S), '40-53 | 1654, '56, OH |

* SADLER, John. Magdalene College [Cambridge]

| 38 | PG | e | C | L(b) | | | | | * | | A | | 1659 |

* ST. NICHOLAS, John. Stretton-under-Fosse [Warwickshire]

| 49 | LG | ys | C | | | * | * | * | | | A | | |

† ST. NICHOLAS, Thomas. Ashe, Kent, and Sheffield [Yorks.]

| 51 | PG | e | C | IT(b) | | * | * | * | * | | A | | 1656, '59 |

* SALWEY, Richard. Richard's Castle, Herefs. [Worcs.]

| 38 | MG | ys | | IT | 9.1653 | | * | * | | 1674 | A | 1645-53 | |

* SAUNDERS, Thomas. Payhembury [Devon]

| | LG | | | | 5.1650 | * | * | * | | | A | | 1654, '56 |

[30] Extremely obscure; styled major, and almost certainly distinct from the Lieut.-Col. Reeves who had fought in Ireland (Firth and Davies chronicle his career) because the latter and William Reeve are *both* listed as commissioners for Herts. in the Assessment Act of 1660. A W. R. of Rempstone is listed in *Minutes of the General Assembly of the General Baptist Churches in England*, ed. W. T. Whitley, i (1908), xxxiii, xl, as a Baptist Messenger in 1676, but Rempstone is in Notts., and Rempstone Hall in Dorset. The will of W. R. the elder, brickmaker, of Wigginton, Herts., made and proved in 1657 (PRO PROB 11/268, PCC 359 Ruthen), left a little land to his son W. R. the younger, who may conceivably have been the 1653 MP. The first appearance of a W. R. among the Herts. assessment commissioners is in the act of 1657.

[31] Elected but attended no meetings; his entry in next column ('parliamentary

Council of State	Parliamentary activity	Religious standpoint	Ejector	Year of death	Sources
	1	R			See n. 30.
N	3	M	E	1662	*DNB;* Aylmer (*SS*); *Narrative* and *Second Narrative.*
	1	R(I)	E	1684?	Williams, *Herefs.*; Richards (*PMW, RDW*); Underdown (*PP*); Aylmer in *Trans. Woolhope Naturalists' Field Club,* xl (1972).
N	3	M	E		Boase & Courtney; *Vis. Cornwall 1620;* Burton, *Diary;* Folger Lib., Add. MS 483; Coate.
P	3	M(P)	E	1659	*DNB;* Keeler; Worden, *Rump;* Chas. Webster, *Great Instauration; Second Narrative;* F. Rous, *Treatises and Meditations* (1657).
N	3	M	E	1674	*DNB;* Rex; Webster, *Great Instauration;* G. H. Turnbull, *Hartlib, Dury and Comenius;* Burton, *Diary.*
	2	M	E	1698	*Vis. Wars. 1682-3;* A. G. Matthews, *Calamy Revised;* J. St. Nicholas, *The History of Baptism* (1678).
J	3	R	E	1668	Gooder; *Vis. Kent 1663-8;* Burton, *Diary;* Nickolls.
J[31]	1	R		1685	*DNB;* Worden, *Rump;* B & P and Keeler on his father Humphrey S.; Williams, *Worcs.*; will.
	2	M	E	1659?	Alexander; will.[32]

activity') should perhaps also be zero, since his appointment to the committee for Scotland (*CJ*, vii, 283, his sole mention in the *Journal*) is not evidence that he was ever present in the House.

[32] Distinct from the Derbyshire T. S. (also MP in 1654 and 1656) who was one of the three colonels who presented a famous hostile petition to Cromwell in Oct. 1654 (on which see Barbara Taft in *Huntington Lib. Quarterly*, xiii (1978), 15–41). The 1653 MP was also styled colonel, on account of his commissions as colonel of foot in the Devon militia and Governor of Exeter Castle (*CSPD 1650*, p. 504; *1651–2*, p. 74). He was therefore also distinct from the Major T. S. who was at Plymouth Fort in 1652 and who styled himself captain in 1654 (*CSPD 1651–2*, pp. 242, 562; *1654*, p. 134), though this man may have been the Governor of Plymouth referred to in 1656, e.g. in *A Narrative of the Late*

(*continued*)

Age	Status	Position in Family	Education Univ.	Inn	J.P. First apptd.	1650	1653	1656–8	1660	Sheriff	Ass. Comm	Other Parliaments Earlier	Later

† SAWREY, John. Plumpton [Lancs.]

| | LG | e | | | | | * | * | * | | A | | |

* SIDNEY, Philip, Vct. Lisle. Penshurst [Kent]

| 34 | GG | e | O | G | | * | * | * | * | | A | 1640(S), '40-53 | OH |

* SMITH, Edward. Edmondthorpe [Leics.]

| c.23 | CG | e | | L | | | | * | * | 1666 | | | |

† SPENCE, William. South Malling [Sussex]

| 32 | LG | e | C | L(b) | 3.1647 | * | * | * | * | 1665 | A | | 1659 |

† SQUIBB, Arthur. Chertsey, Surrey [Middlesex]

| | LG | | | | 2.1650 | * | * | * | | | A | | |

† STAPLEY, Anthony. Patcham [Sussex]

| 63 | CG | e | C? | G | 1633 | * | * | | | | A | 1624, '25, '26, '40(S), '40-53. | 1654 |

* STONE, John. Westminster [London]

| c.47 | M | | C? | G? | | | | * | * | | A | | 1654, '56,[33] '59 |

* STRICKLAND, Walter. Flamborough [Yorks.]

| 55 | CG | ys | C | G | | * | * | * | * | | A | 1646-53 | 1654, '56, OH, '61 |

† STUDLEY, Nathaniel. Mayfield [Sussex]

| c.49 | LG | e | | G | 1649 | * | * | * | | | A | | |

† SWEET, Richard. Exeter [Devon]

| | M | | | | 1653 | | | * | * | 1650 | A | | |

† SWINTON, John. Swinton [Scotland]

| c.32 | GG | e | | | | | | * | | | | | 1654, '56, '59 |

* SYDENHAM, William. Wynford Eagle [Dorset]

| 38 | LG | e | | | | | * | * | * | | A | 1645-53 | 1654, '56, OH |

Parliament, which confuses all three men. The Derbyshire, not the Devon, T. S. was prevented from taking his seat in 1656 (Alexander, p. 334). 'Our' T. S. is probably the 'esquire' of Payhembury near Honiton whose will (PRO, PROB 11/302, PCC 274 Nabbs) was made on 29 July 1658 and proved on 8 Dec. 1660; unlike the Derbyshire T. S. he disappears from the assessment commission after 1657. He left money to the poor

Council of State	Parliamentary activity	Religious standpoint	Ejector	Year of death	Sources
	1	?R	E	1665	*Vis. Lancs. 1664-5* (Chetham Soc., 1873); *VCH, Lancs.*, iii, 299, 359; Penney; Braithwaite; Blackwood.
R, J, N, P	1	M	E	1698	*DNB;* Keeler; HMC, *De L'Isle & Dudley* vi; Underdown (*PP*); Aylmer (*SS*); *Narrative* and *Second Narrative;* will.
	1	M	E	1707	*Baronetage.*
	3	R(B?)		1677	Fletcher, *Sussex; Vis. Sussex 1662;* Whitley, *Minutes of the Gen. Assembly of Gen. Baptist Churches* (same man?); will.
	3	R(B:5M)		1680	Capp; Aylmer (*SS*); will.
A, J	1	R	E	1655	*DNB;* Keeler; Fletcher, *Sussex;* will.
N	3	M(I)	E	1678	Aylmer (*SS*).
R, A, J, N, P	3	M	E	1670	*DNB;* Gooder; Underdown, *Somerset;* Burton, *Diary; Second Narrative.*[34]
	1	?R	E		Fletcher, *Sussex; Vis. Sussex 1619; CSPD 1655*, p. 68.
	1	R			Alexander.
	2	R		1679	*DNB;* Dow; Nicoll, *Diary;* Firth, *Scotland and the Commonwealth* and *Scotland and the Protectorate;* etc.
A, J, N, P	3	M	E	1661	*DNB;* B & P; Bayley; Underdown (*PP*); *Narrative* and *Second Narrative;* Burton, *Diary.*

of Payhembury and Broadhembury and disposed of mills in Cullompton as well as some lands.

[33] 'Sick all the Parliament' (Burton, *Diary*, i, 284). See Aylmer, *State's Servants*, pp. 241, 406–7, for his career and Beaven's misidentification of him.

[34] There is much further information in Roy Carroll, 'The Diplomatic Career of Walter Strickland' (MA thesis, Vanderbilt University, 1959).

Age	Status	Position in Family	Univ.	Inn	First apptd.	1650	1653	1656-8	1660	Sheriff	Ass. Comm	Earlier	Later

Education — J.P. — **Other Parliaments**

† TAYLOR, Nathaniel. Colchester [Beds.]
c.33 PG — C³⁵ G(b) — 7.1651 — * * — — — A — —

* TEMPLER, Dudley. Wethersfield [Essex]
26 LG — C — 1.1651 — * * * — — A — 1656

* THOMPSON, William. Roxholm [Lincs.]
LG e — 9.1648 — * * * * — A — —

* TICHBORNE, Robert. London [London]
MG e — 6.1646 — * * * — 1651 A — OH

* WALCOTT, Humphrey. Lincoln [Lincs.]
57 LG e — C G(b) — 7.1650 — * * * * — A — 1656

* WARNER, Samuel. (Isle of Ely) [Cambs.]
LG — A

† WEST, William. Middleton, nr. Lancaster [Lancs.]
c.34 LG — G — * * — A — 1659, '60

† WILLIAMS, John. Radnor [Wales]
LG — * * * * 1653 A

* WINGFIELD, Augustine. Rickmansworth [Middlesex]
c.42 PG e — L(b) — * * * — A

* WOLMER, Ralph. [Norfolk]
LG — 8.1655 — * — A

* WOLSELEY, Sir Charles. Wolseley, Staffs. [Oxon.]
23 GG e — 9.1653 — * * — 1654, '56. OH, '60

* WOOD, Thomas. Windsor, [Berks.]
LG — 9.1653 — * —

CO-OPTED MEMBERS:
* CROMWELL, Oliver. The Cockpit, Whitehall
54 LG e C — * * * — A — 1628, '40(S), '40-53

³⁵ The identifications in Venn, *Alumni Cantab.*, iv, 207, seem probable but not certain.
³⁶ Referred to as Alderman Warner in *CJ*, vii, 339, so probably identical with the London militia commissioner in March 1642, July and Sept. 1647; a S. W. is assessment commissioner for both Middlesex and the Isle of Ely in the 1650 and 1652 Assessment Acts. Cf. *CSPD 1625–49* (Additional), p. 652.

Council of State	Parliamentary activity	Religious standpoint	Ejector	Year of death	Sources
	2	R(I)			*CSPD 1654*, p. 334, and *1656-7*, p. 79; Penney; Nickolls; Aylmer (*SS*); will.
	1	M	E		Venn, *Alumni Cantab.*; Penney; Burton, *Diary*; *Essex Qr. Sessions Order Book 1652-61* (Chelmsford, 1974).
	1	M	E		*Lincs. Pedigrees*, iii (Harl. Soc. lii).
J, N	3	M(I)	E	1682	*DNB*; *Second Narrative*; Beaven; Nuttall (*VS*); Tolmie; *Dict. Brit. Radicals*.
	0	M(I)	E		*Lincs. Pedigrees*, iii (Harl. Soc. lii); Holmes; Stephens, *Clerks of the Counties*.
	1	M			See n. 36.
	3	R(I)	E	1670	*VCH, Lancs.*, iii; Blackwood; Braithwaite; Penney; Burton, *Diary*.
	1	R(I:5M)	E		Dodd; Capp; Richards (*PMW, RDW*); Williams, *Parl. Hist. Wales*.
	2	M			*Black Book of Lincoln's Inn*, ii, 339; BL, Egerton MS 2979, fo. 11; A. Wingfield, *Vindiciae Medio-Saxonicae* (1653).
	2	M(I)	E		Nickolls; little else but *CSPD* and F & R.
J, N, P	3	M	E	1714	*DNB*; *Baronetage*; Williams, *Oxon.*[37]
	1	M	E	1656-7[38]	Mainly F & R.
R, A, J, N	0	M		1658	*DNB*, etc.

[37] His royalist father's career is admirably traced in Aylmer, *The King's Servants*, pp. 202–5, 418.

[38] Struck off the Sept. 1656–Apr. 1657 *liber pacis* (PRO C193/13/6) as 'dead'.

Age	Status	Position in Family	Education Univ.	Inn	J. P. First apptd.	1650	1653	1656-8	1660	Sheriff	Ass. Comm	Other Parliaments Earlier	Later
* DESBOROUGH, John.													
45	P	ys			6.1647	*	*	*			A		1654, '56, OH
† HARRISON, Thomas. Newcastle-under-Lyme													
36	M	e			11.1649	*	*				A	1646-53	
* LAMBERT, John. Calton and Wimbledon													
34	LG					*	*	*			A		1654, '56, '59
* TOMLINSON, Matthew. Ampthill Park													
36	LG	ys			9.1653		*	*					OH

Council of State	Parliamentary activity	Religious standpoint	Ejector	Year of death	Sources
A, J, N, P	3	M	E	1680	*DNB; Narrative* and *Second Narrative;* Burton, *Diary.*
R, A, J, N	2	R(I:5M)		1660	*DNB;* Capp; biographics by C. H. Firth and C. H. Simpkinson.
A, J, P	1	M	E		*DNB;* W. H. Dawson, *Cromwell's Understudy;* G. D. Heath in *Jnl of British Studies,* vi (1967).
A, J	1	M		1681	*DNB; State Trials.*

Index